SOCIAL SCIENCES DIVISION
CHICAGO PUBLIC LIBRARY
400 SOUTH STATE STREET
CHICAGO, IL 60605

R03063 70189

Praise for Peter Novak's Books:

"Fascinating . . . Peter Novak submits compel  history to support [his hypothesis]. He we trances, and mystical experiences seem uncanny reliability, that at death there is split .... To say that Novak's research is impressive in the way he correlated stories, myths, and legends about death and the afterlife to a symbolic representation of left- and right-brain hemisphere functions would be an understatement. I think he is onto something worthy of further investigation."

—*P. M. H. Atwater, author of* Coming Back to Life, Beyond the Light, *and other books on near-death experiences (in a May 21, 2002 letter to* The Journal of Near-Death Studies)

"Novak's two books stand beside Myers' as classics of research into the most disturbing of human problems."

—*Colin Wilson, celebrated author of numerous books, including* Poltergeist *and* After Life

"Peter Novak proposes that the soul is not a single entity and can even divide at death. The thesis he presents in this pioneering book is compelling and deserves serious consideration and empirical research. This book is quite fascinating!"

—*Gary E. Schwartz, Ph.D. Professor of Psychology, Medicine, Neurology, Surgery, and Psychiatry at the University of Arizona, and author of* The Afterlife Experiments.

"This is a strange, disturbing, and brilliant book [. . .] Novak introduces a whole new theory of the human soul and its journey through the afterlife [and] succeeds in providing answers to a surprisingly large number of questions."

—*Gnosis: A Journal of the Western Inner Traditions*

"Unique, fascinating, and highly credible. Amazingly, Novak has discovered a concept that has eluded all the brilliant minds of the past. I applaud him on his achievement and thank him for his insight."

—*Dr. Donald R. Morse, president of The Academy of Religion and Psychical Research*

"To say that this book is thought-provoking and belief-provoking is an understatement. I not only read every word of the book, but re-read my underlinings several times. I am totally impressed with the amount of research Novak obviously did and how he presented his case. His knowledge of the subject is quite impressive. Just one of the many discussions that I particularly enjoyed was that of the 'time dispute.' *The Lost Secret of Death* has most certainly caused me to seriously re-evaluate my thoughts about my hundreds of interviews with NDErs, as well as the many, many ADC accounts which I have been privy to. Timing is everything! At this time in earth's history, this work is particularly important and is most definitely something of great value!"

—*Barbara Rommer, M.D., author of* Blessings in Disguise: Another Side of the Near-Death Experience, *and founder of the South Florida chapter of the International Association for Near-Death Studies (IANDS)*

"Fascinating. It gives a breath of fresh air to theology and yet remains within the broad scope of Christian theology. Any seeker of truth should read Novak. I think it deserves attention that this 'Division Theory' is able to pull different concepts into a unity. This new concept of the double soul . . . helps to explain, and in some cases even simplifies, traditional Christian theological tenets."

—*Bill Lanning, Ph.D., professor of philosophy and religion, Butler College, Andover, Kansas*

"This is a work of great significance. You realize that the secret of the afterlife is staring us right in the face and we don't realize it—that the supposed conflict between reincarnation and 'heaven and hell' can be resolved. . . . If we apply this divided human consciousness to the afterlife equation, a truly momentous understanding results—reincarnation and the heaven/hell model are both true. This division of the afterlife also explains many of the descriptions that arise of wandering ghosts, spirits, and the like."

—*Bob Jackson, editor,* The Independent Review

"Peter Novak brings an amazing discovery to us in the twenty-first century. Most people today refer to 'soul' and 'spirit' interchangeably. The ancient Egyptians and other spiritual teachings tell us otherwise. Novak's scholarly research of ancient teachings brings this wisdom back and places it alongside current scientific knowledge. He has accomplished the

enormous task of bringing together research in near-death experiences, past-life therapy, afterlife communications, and other paranormal information alongside current scientific knowledge. This book is exciting in its scope, logic, and wisdom. Be prepared to have your mind stretched!"
—*Janet Cunningham, Ph.D., author of several books, and past president of The International Association for Regression Research and Therapies, Inc.*

"*The Division of Consciousness* is, quite frankly, the most important book in its field since Elaine Pagel's *The Gnostic Gospels* in 1978, and takes Pagel's conclusions light years further. Some of the conclusions drawn may make casual Christians uncomfortable, but serious Christian scholars will either feel vindicated, be intrigued, or both. Division Theory is such an ingenious concept I'm amazed nobody had been able to think of it in this way before."
—*Christopher Coolidge, Ph.D., Burlington, Vermont*

"Ingenious [. . .] This is too important of a work to be dismissed. It will definitely be looked back upon as a turning point in the scholar's collection of ideas, as one of those hinges that opens the field of vision to possibilities of thoughts that were not possible before this point."
—*Thomas Ragland, Ph.D., Nashville, Tennessee*

"Truly momentous. [. . .] This interpretation of the afterlife is pregnant with meaning. The traditions of the underworld, heaven, hell and reincarnation all come alive and mean so much more. Swedenborg's descriptions of heaven and hell become surprisingly poignant, as does the gloomy afterlife of the Sumerians and Israelites . . . [and t]he Egyptian initiatory system . . . takes on a new relevance."
—New Dawn Magazine

"Do we, perhaps, have here the lateral thinking that will at last move forward the tired old debate between reincarnationists and non-reincarnationists? [. . .] Novak has offered us a novel insight and we ought to ask whether it can be developed in ways compatible with mainstream Christianity."
—*Editorial in* The Christian Parapsychologist, Journal of the Church's Fellowship for Psychical and Spiritual Studies

Also by Peter Novak

The Division of Consciousness

THE
LOST SECRET
OF
DEATH

Our Divided Souls and the Afterlife

PETER NOVAK

HAMPTON ROADS
PUBLISHING COMPANY, INC.

Copyright © 2003 by Peter Novak
All rights reserved, including the right to reproduce this
work in any form whatsoever, without permission in writing
from the publisher, except for brief passages in connection with a review.

Cover design by Marjoram Productions
Cover background image by Nick Gonzolez-Goad/Stellar Creations
Sillouette figures by Anne L. Louque

Excerpts from *Death's Door* by Jean Richie. Used by permission of Dell Publishing, a division of Random House, Inc.

Excerpts from *Other Lives, Other Selves* by Roger Woolger, copyright © 1987 by Roger Woolger, Ph.D. Used by permission of Doubleday, a division of Random House, Inc.

Excerpts from *The Six Pillars of Self-Esteem* by Nathaniel Branden, copyright © 1994 by Nathaniel Branden. Used by permission of Bantam Books, a division of Random House, Inc.

Excerpts from *Ultimate Journey* by Robert Monroe, copyright © 1994 by Robert Monroe. Used by permission of Doubleday, a division of Random House, Inc.

Excerpts from *Hello from Heaven* by William Guggenheim III and Judith A. Guggenheim, copyright © 1995 by William Guggenheim III and Judith A. Guggenheim. Used by permission of Bantam Books, a division of Random House, Inc.

Excerpts from *The Power of Now* by Eckhart Tolle. © 1999. Reprinted with permission from New World Library, Novato, CA 94949, www.new-worldlibrary.com

Excerpts reprinted with the permission of Simon & Schuster Adult Publishing Group from *Many Lives, Many Masters* by Brian L. Weiss, MD. Copyright © 1988 by Brian L. Weiss, MD.

Excerpts from *A Brief History of Everything* by Ken Wilber, © 1996, 2000 by Ken Wilber. Reprinted by arrangement with Shambhala Publications, Inc., Boston, www.shambhala.com

Jung, C. G.; *The Collected Works of C. G. Jung.* Copyright © 1977 by PUP. Reprinted by permission of Princeton University Press.

Excerpts from *Beyond the Darkness* by Angie Fenimore, copyright © 1995 by Angie Fenimore. Foreword copyright © 1995 by Betty J. Eadie. Used by permission of Bantam Books, a division of Random House, Inc.

Excerpts from *The Truth in the Light* by Peter Fenwick and Elizabeth Fenwick, copyright © 1995 by Peter and Elizabeth Fenwick. Used by permission of Viking Penguin, a division of Penguin Group (USA) Inc.

Excerpts reprinted with the permission of Simon & Schuster from *The Eagle's Gift* by Carlos Castaneda. Copyright © 1981 by Carlos Castaneda.

Hampton Roads Publishing Company, Inc.
1125 Stoney Ridge Road
Charlottesville, VA 22902

434-296-2772; fax: 434-296-5096
e-mail: hrpc@hrpub. com
www. hrpub. com

If you are unable to order this book from your local bookseller, you may order directly from the publisher. Call 1-800-766-8009, toll-free.

Library of Congress Cataloging-in-Publication Data

Novak, Peter, 1958-
    The lost secret of death : our divided souls and the afterlife / Peter Novak.
        p. cm.
Includes bibliographical references and index.
    ISBN 1-57174-324-3 (trade paper w/flaps)
    1. Soul. 2. Future life. 3. Jesus Christ--Miscellanea. I. Title.
    BF1999.N73 2003
    133.9'01'3--dc21
                                    2003007482

10 9 8 7 6 5 4 3 2 1

Printed on acid-free paper in Canada

R03063 70189

SOCIAL SCIENCES DIVISION
CHICAGO PUBLIC LIBRARY
400 SOUTH STATE STREET
CHICAGO, IL 60605

This book is dedicated to my father,
who taught me to believe in myself,
and showed me what love could do.
I hope one day to be as fine a man as he.

Acknowledgments

This book owes its existence to many. First and foremost, my gratitude goes to my wife, Cassie, and my daughter Ayriel for enduring the many sacrifices this book required. I must also thank all the friends and researchers I've met and corresponded with since the publication of *The Division of Consciousness*, without whose counsel and assistance this new book would never have been possible, especially Robert Friend, Dr. Don Morse, Kevin Williams, Stan and Cynthia Tenen, Ken Eagle Feather, Bill Barnes, Dr. Tamar Frankiel, Robert Bruce, P. M. H. Atwater, Ramona Louise Wheeler, Dr. Bill Lanning, Ian Lawton, Anthony Solbach, William Pustarfi, Dr. Janet Cunningham, F. James Shepherd, Charles Knowlton, Dr. Barbara Rommer, Canon Michael Perry, Kari Marchant, William McNaughton, Dr. Michael York, Michael W. Norman, Eugene Poliakov, Colin Wilson, David King, Michael Enevoldsen, Gary Osborn, Scott Yancey, Dr. Fredric Schiffer, Russell Wright, Isabella Riley, Dr. Bruce Greyson, Paul Bramer, Richard Stevenson, Jeff Duntemann, Tom Ragland, Dr. René Turner, and all the members of the "DivisionTheory" and "NDE" discussion groups. These folks have been an amazing and priceless resource for me, bringing an endless flow of relevant data to my attention. I also thank all the authors whose names appear in the bibliography; these people are performing the most important work of this generation. And finally, I thank my publisher Frank DeMarco, whose faith in the importance of this research never wavered.

Table of Contents

Preface

Okay, let's just jump right into the thick of it. As you may have surmised from the title, I believe I have discovered the secret of death. *Re*-discovered it, actually. In itself, of course, this is very common; there are hundreds of different theories about what happens after we die. But this discovery is different than all those others, for three very important reasons:

1. It accounts for virtually all the different kinds of strange reports emerging from modern research into afterlife phenomena.

2. It also accounts for the vast majority of humanity's religious teachings about death and the afterlife. This discovery explains why people would have arrived at all those different conclusions.

3. And it is based on modern science. This discovery was arrived at simply by asking the question "Based on what we know today about how the human mind functions, what would happen to that mind if it were to actually survive the death of the physical body?"

No other theory in existence can make such claims, and this frightens me to no end. If this theory is true, it shoulders me with more responsibility than I can comfortably wrap my mind around, and makes me feel completely inadequate to the task.

How did I come to find myself in this predicament? The story begins with my wife's suicide in 1985. Underneath the shock and horror I felt at my wife's passing, something even more distressing loomed. When my initial grief had finally begun to subside, I found myself becoming overwhelmed by a whole new set of feelings—confusion, wonder, and bewilderment. I felt as if I had been blind sided, not so much by my wife's sudden suicide as by her death itself, by the very fact that she could die at all, by the fact that death *existed* at all. I had been a typical twenty-seven-year-old American at the time, and the reality of death had never truly impacted me before. Despite having had a few years of religious education as a child, and despite having witnessed endless simulated deaths and murders on TV, and even despite having gone to a funeral or two in the past, nothing in my education or cultural involvement had ever prepared me for this awful confrontation with reality.

I realize now that everyone probably experiences their first real face-to-face confrontation with death much the same way I did, but our reactions to this supremely personal encounter are always individual. My reaction eventually resolved itself into a desperate need to understand what had happened. To understand death itself, if such a thing was possible.

Be careful what you wish for.

In the summer of 1988, I began studying everything I could get my hands on that seemed to hold any chance of unraveling this most ancient of all mysteries, exploring all manner of foreign and domestic religious scriptures, psychological research, philosophical treatises, and paranormal and metaphysical reports. Wading through this mountain of humanity's present and past thoughts on the subject of death and the afterlife, I eventually stumbled upon a pattern that showed up again and again in seemingly different source materials, a pattern I have been exploring now for more than fifteen years. In my first report on this research, *The Division of Consciousness: The Secret Afterlife of the Human Psyche,* I called this pattern Division Theory. Since that work was published, however, I have discovered that the academic world was not completely unfamiliar with this pattern, calling it the "binary soul doctrine." And so, I have deferred to their terminology in this present work.

The binary soul doctrine, which emerges directly from modern scientific discoveries about the human mind, simply says that the psyche is *divisible.* It is a composite, comprised of two distinct elements, which can and often do divide from each other at death, each element then going off to have its own unique afterlife experience.

This simple twist elegantly explains why half the world has believed in an eternal heaven and hell awaiting them after death, while the other half of the world has believed just as fervently in reincarnation. It thoroughly explains, and even anticipates, the belief systems of hundreds of religions past and present, as well as the findings emerging from modern afterlife research. This discovery indicates that virtually all forms of apparent afterlife phenomena, including near-death experiences, past-life regression, ghosts, apparitions, poltergeists, channeling, and other after-death communications, are all genuine and authentic portrayals of what lies beyond death's door. However, none of these phenomena show the whole picture; they are all fragmentary images. Similarly, the ancient reports of mankind's religions also present valid but ultimately incomplete descriptions of what occurs during the change called death. However, all these descriptions, as different as they seem, do in fact all fit together to form a single, quite simple, internally consistent picture of life after death. The binary soul doctrine takes all these pieces of the afterlife puzzle and shows how they all intertwine, adroitly solving the greatest riddle known to man.

These two books, this one and *The Division of Consciousness*, are ultimately just two sides of the same coin. Hoping to open doors of communication between mankind's various belief systems, that earlier book was primarily addressed to a Judeo-Christian audience, using scriptural quotations in an attempt to demonstrate that the binary soul doctrine was the underlying foundation of the entire Judeo-Christian tradition. This book, on the other hand, is primarily addressed to those interested in modern afterlife research, paranormal phenomena, and nonbiblical traditions, in hopes of also clarifying the relationship the binary soul doctrine has to what they already know to be true. It is, I believe, only within the context of the binary soul doctrine that the world's traditional belief systems can be fully comprehended, and their relationships to each other fully appreciated.

This discovery speaks to much more than just afterlife phenomena. In fact, because the binary soul doctrine addresses such a fundamental, basic, elementary level of reality, its effect on those who study it is a little like a movie with a huge surprise twist ending, like *The Usual Suspects* or *The Sixth Sense*. Once you know the secret, you look back over everything else you thought you already understood, and see it all in a new light. You see that secret twist being telegraphed to you from all directions, and can't quite understand how it all could have escaped your attention before. Well, at least that's how it's been for me, and for a few thousand others around the world who have already been touched by the binary soul doctrine. This discovery, more and more of us are coming to recognize, holds the potential to heal a great many of the divisions afflicting the world today. It is a road uniting science and faith, uniting Eastern and Western religions, and even re-uniting Judaism, Christianity, and Islam.

Unfortunately, it is an answer that few realize even exists.

Foreword

by Colin Wilson

When I read Peter Novak's first book, *The Division of Consciousness*, I found it deeply disturbing and—as he himself said—"scary." This is hardly surprising, for the book itself sprang from a deeply disturbing experience. When his wife committed suicide, soon after the birth of their daughter, Novak was a psychological counselor, having studied psychology at Purdue University. He had been deeply impressed by the Freudian/Jungian doctrine of our division into conscious and unconscious selves.

In Freud, this division is, so to speak, incurable, and his view of human existence is fundamentally tragic. But Jung differed from Freud in being less of a rigid materialist. He was interested in psychical research and in spiritualism. So as his views developed, he came to believe increasingly that this gap between man's two "selves" can he healed, in a process called individuation, of which the mandala was a symbol—the symbol of wholeness.

After his wife's death, Peter Novak had three vivid dreams. In the first, his wife was asleep in a high, rocky place, in the process of healing. In the second dream, she was no longer there, but he was told that she had been healed and flown away. In the third dream, he met his wife again and they embraced; he now felt the healing process was complete. It was after this that he began his quest for the meaning of death, becoming a librarian to facilitate his search of world literature.

His quest soon led him to a disturbing discovery: that the modern

Christian belief that when the soul separates from the body it goes to "heaven" is not accepted by the majority of religions, or even by the early Christians themselves. They seem to have believed that man has two souls, and that at death these two souls may become separated. These souls seem to correspond roughly to the Freudian/Jungian conscious and unconscious minds. So the first thing Novak discovered was that in most ancient religions, there is no comforting doctrine of the survival of the soul.

When P. D. Ouspensky asked Gurdjieff about life after death, Gurdjieff replied that most people possess no "hard core" that might survive death, and that only hard work upon oneself can make one capable of developing that core.

This, of course, is consistent with Gurdjieff's distinction between "personality" and "essence." Personality is that part of us that develops through contact with other people, but essence is the "hard core" of being that is developed by difficulties and problems—in short, suffering. The best way of developing essence is to deliberately subject yourself to problems that develop the will. That is why monks wore hair shirts and flogged themselves; they might be symbolically regarded as workmen filing at a lump of metal to try and shape it. Gurdjieff once said—perhaps with his tongue in his cheek—that the person he had met who possessed the most essence was a Corsican brigand who spent hours peering down the sights of his rifle in the hot sun, waiting for people to rob.

Yet Gurdjieff also told Ouspensky that people who possess an "astral body" can communicate with someone else at a distance, and that in order to do so they must establish some "connection" between them—perhaps some object belonging to the other, which is permeated with "his emanations." He went on to remark that some kind of "thread" runs from some objects, and can even re-establish contact with the dead. This, and other similar passages, seem to demonstrate that Gurdjieff accepted life after death without qualification.

For me, one of the most exciting revelations about the human mind came in the 1970s when I read *The Origins of Consciousness in the Breakdown of the Bicameral Mind* (1976), by Julian Jaynes, and learned from that book about the discoveries of Roger Sperry and Michael Gazzaniga concerning the split brain. It came as a shock to learn that when the *corpus callosum*, the knot of nerves connecting the left and right halves of the brain, is severed (as it sometimes is to prevent epilepsy) such patients turn into two people. One split-brain patient was trying to hit his wife with one hand while the other held it back. What astonished me was the discovery that we ALL have two people inside our heads, in the left and right cerebral hemispheres, and that the person you know as "you" lives in the left, while a complete stranger lives in the right. In effect, the left-brain self is a scientist and the right-brain self an artist. And the "you" lives in the left brain.

Were these, I wondered, Freud's conscious and unconscious minds? The more I learned about split-brain physiology, the more likely this seemed.

It struck me that, in a sense, I had always known about these two selves. All writers do. Because when you are trying to learn to write, you get certain moods where the writing flows easily, and you feel "inspired." But when you look at it later, it seems painfully bad. At which point you realize that your sense of language—which is a left-brain faculty—is still undeveloped. That "other self" that does the creating is being held back by this incompetent "everyday you," with his stupid clumsiness. But when, finally, you learn to write well, these two selves are like two lumberjacks at either end of a cross-cut saw working in perfect harmony. *That* is why all writers and artists know they have two souls.

That piece of information was of enormous practical importance, for it made me aware that I was not alone inside my head: that there was another being, to whom Maeterlinck refers as "the unknown guest," a being inside us who seems to possess paranormal powers—so-called "psychic powers." He can also provide bursts of energy or inspiration. On one occasion, I was in a hotel room in London writing the outline of a film script for Dino de Laurentis. For days it moved on with agonizing slowness. Finally, when I had only one day left, I suspected I was going to have to tell Dino that it had me beaten. Then I recollected the "unknown guest," and as I was lying in bed, addressed a kind of mental prayer to him to send me some inspiration. Suddenly I felt oddly relaxed and cheerful, and fell into a peaceful sleep. The next morning I began work slowly, and induced a relaxed frame of mind. Then the ideas began to flow, and within two hours, I knew I had solved the problem. I wrote steadily all day, and when Dino's secretary came up to my room in the afternoon to collect what I had written, I was able to hand her the finished outline. And as I was driven to Paddington to catch my train, I remembered to breathe a prayer of thanks to the "unknown guest."

All sportsmen know about the "unknown guest"—about those moments when, as William James says, they begin to play with a curious sense of ease and relaxation, and suddenly realize that they are no longer playing the game: the game is playing them.

It was in 1980 that I stumbled on my next important clue in this matter of "the divided soul." I had been looking into a case of poltergeist haunting in Pontefract, in the north of England. Up to that point, I had accepted the theory that poltergeists are a manifestation of the unconscious minds of disturbed adolescents, a form of unconscious psychokinesis (or mind over matter). But when the teenage girl at the center of the disturbances told me how the poltergeist had dragged her upstairs by her throat, leaving black bruises, I suddenly knew that this was not her unconscious mind, but some independent entity—a "spirit." And it was at this point that a paranormal investigator named Guy Playfair advised me to read a book called *The Secret Science Behind Miracles* by Max Freedom Long. I had often seen this volume in "occult" bookshops, but been put off by its title. Long (who is briefly discussed in this present book) was a schoolteacher who lived in Hawaii, and became fascinated by the teachings of Hawaiian Indians called Hunas, whose priests were called Kahunas. Long's interest was excited by the claim that the Kahunas could kill people by something known as "the death prayer." There was much convincing evidence that this was really so.

What Long finally learned was that the Hunas believe that man has two souls, known as the *unihipili* and the *uhane*. The *unihipili* corresponds roughly to what Freud called the unconscious mind, while the *uhane* is the conscious self. The Kahunas also call them the low self and the middle self. When someone dies, the two may go their separate ways; the middle self becomes a ghost, reliving past memories, while the low self becomes a poltergeist, a spirit that possesses no memory, only energy. And it is these latter who can be prevailed upon to cause trouble, from smashing crockery to killing someone by stealing all his vital energy. They may be regarded as stupid, but not particularly malevolent.

And, according to the Kahuna, there is another self that stands above the other two, the "high self" or *aumakua*, which might—on the analogy of the unconscious mind—be called the superconscious mind. You might think of it as our guardian angel. It can foresee the future, and also influence it.

Aldous Huxley, in an introduction to F. W. H. Myers' great book *Human Personality and Its Survival of Bodily Death*, asks: "Is the house of the soul a mere bungalow with a cellar? Or does it have an upstairs, above the ground floor of consciousness as well as a garbage-littered basement beneath?" This latter model, he says, is Freud's. The house with an upstairs is Myers'. Myers calls this higher being "the subliminal self," and Huxley declares he much prefers it to Jung's account of the mind, "being more richly documented with concrete facts and less encumbered with those psycho-anthropologico-pseudo-genetic speculations which becloud the writings of the sage of Zurich."

Myers' account, it seems to me, is basically that of the Huna. Peter Novak says here: "the Hawaiians also named a third, higher sort of soul, the *aumakua*, which was also created out of the two binary souls when united into a single unit." In answer to a question of mine about this higher self, Peter replied: "Furthermore, Long maintained that the two souls which united together to form that high-self pair were themselves nothing more than advanced versions of the *unihipili* and *uhane* souls. Long also taught that the high-self pair is related to the *unihipili*, and the other is related to the *uhane* (see, for example, p. 166 of *The Secret Science Behind Miracles*, where he writes: 'man has two High Selves, one for the low self and its guidance, and one for the middle self')."

Now Peter may be correct; but it seems to me that we would do better to stick to the simpler Huxley-Myers model of a house with basement *and* upstairs. And this notion, it seems to me, also dispels some of the "scary" element of "division theory." I half-suspect that the high self is that "unknown guest" I appealed to when I was having such problems with Dino's script outline, and which brought both relief and insight.

Long tells an interesting story about how in 1932 he made practical use of the high self to solve an important problem. His camera shop was running into financial difficulties due to the depression, and was likely to go bankrupt. He asked help from a Huna healer on how to persuade a competitor to take over his shop for $8,000. This, the healer said, demanded making a prayer to the high self, to ask its help. But in order to make such a prayer, Long had to be entirely free of doubts and uncertainties. And in order to free himself of floating fragments of guilt that were probably causing self-division, and so obstructing the prayer, he was advised to fast until one o'clock for three days and refrain from smoking. After that he must give a substantial gift to charity, "almost more than you can afford." This would finally clear away his guilt feelings.

Having done this, he was instructed to type out his proposal, and call on his competitor at a quarter to two the following Tuesday. He followed these instructions exactly, and as a result, his competitor (who had already turned him down several times) bought his business for $8,000.

I agree that the example has an element of triviality—although it was serious enough for Long—but it illustrates for me the notion of how the "third soul" or subliminal self can not only provide a solution to everyday problems, but to the central question explored by Peter Novak: that of some fundamental division in our psychic being. It involves, of course, an assumption that our world is not the meaningless chaos that it often seems, but is somehow purposeful and benevolent. Only our own inner chaos and fear cause the problems.

The Lost Secret of Death

When Peter Novak's wife committed suicide, he was plunged into the worst kind of doubt and misery. He attempted to establish control over this inner chaos by searching for meaning—for an answer to the problem of death. It is apparent from his two books that his search has been successful in that it has restored his sense that our lives possess underlying meaning. That is why, for me, they stand beside Myers as classics of research into the most disturbing of human problems.

Introduction

A Threatening Babble

I hate to be the one to bring this up, but we have a problem. For many people, it is getting harder and harder to believe in life after death. Why? Because the stories being circulated by all the different so-called authorities on the subject, all our different religions and all our different branches of afterlife phenomena research, do not seem to paint the same picture.

We live in a time of unprecedented upheavals in our thoughts and beliefs about the afterlife. For one thing, a great deal of seemingly relevant new scientific and paranormal data on afterlife phenomena has been thrown at the human race over the last thirty years, and it will take a good stretch of time to see how society ultimately processes this data and integrates it all together. But in addition to this, other upheavals have also undermined the comfort we once found in traditional answers, and the timing for this couldn't be more challenging. The recent explosion of international terrorism has increased people's need to wrap themselves up in the comfort of a secure belief system at the very time that scandals in the single largest denomination on earth are causing record numbers to abandon their religious roots and go off looking for a whole new faith to put their trust in. Even some of the most battle-hardened ranks of the religious are now beginning to seriously question their inherited belief systems; the recent debacle within the Catholic Church is bringing many to leave in disgust, hoping to find enlightenment elsewhere.

When they go looking, what will they find? If they look at mankind's many different contemporary religions with a truly impartial eye, the average person will probably end up concluding that he or she is completely unprepared to accurately determine which of them might actually be the "true" religion. If they then abandon traditional religion altogether and instead seek to find the truth about life after death by exploring man's investigations into the paranormal, will they have any more chance of emerging from this quest with any greater certainty that the truth has finally been found? Perhaps not, because the many different branches of afterlife research are still painting very different pictures of life after death. They all say, "oh yes, our research data leaves no doubt—life after death is certainly real," but then they each go on to describe radically different stories about what actually happens after one dies. One group of reports describes a delightful realm of light and love, but another describes a very different picture, a barren, dreary, gray realm of despair, anxiety, and bewilderment, while yet another describes a perfectly empty, perfectly black, perfectly still limbo devoid of all feeling and emotion, another describes mindless ghosts eternally sleepwalking through their own memories, and still another describes an endless series of memory-robbing reincarnations. It would be easier if we could just ignore, discount, or disqualify one or more of these report categories, but each of these pictures of the afterlife has been substantiated by a continuous stream of similar reports, which suggests that none of them is any more trustworthy than the next. Yet in many respects these reports seem mutually exclusive.

If there is no way to reconcile these different models of the afterlife, to show how they all fit together into a single seamless picture, then there is no reason to believe any of them. No matter how convincing any one model might be, its credibility is terminally undermined by all the other models, unless they can all be shown to be part of the same picture, all effects of the same cause.

The binary soul doctrine does this.

And that is an entirely unique claim.

To many, this will be a frightening book, because it discusses the most important questions a human being can ask—What happens to us after death? What is the meaning of life? How can we find true happiness? and on and on—and demonstrates that the true answers simply cannot be what we've been led to believe. This is distressing indeed, because the answers to these questions hold everything we value in their balance.

Death is the biggest, darkest, scariest thing in life. Much of the reason for this is because most people are under the impression that the mystery of death cannot *be* answered, that the true nature of death always has been and always will be outside the ability of the human mind to discover. Death is the oldest question, the first question, the most important question, but despite having been contemplated for thousands of years by billions of people, it still remains, in the minds of many, a question without an answer. However, death is such a huge issue that most people cannot tolerate leaving the matter up in the air and unsettled, and so, the custom of the human race has been to adopt one theory or another on what death is, and to live our lives as if that chosen theory *had* been proven true. In short, we have always lived on faith. Knowing that we do not really know at all, we have mutually agreed to pretend to be sure anyway.

However, a change has come into the world in our lifetimes which will no longer allow us to do this: the information revolution. The world got quite a bit smaller when we started talking with each other around the world, and because of this, none of our traditional answers to the mystery of death seem to work anymore. They no longer do what they were designed to do; they are no longer able to provide us with a satisfactory level of security.

This book is likely to be shelved in the "New Age" section of libraries and bookstores, which is unfortunate, because anyone who has explored much new age literature is probably convinced that every shmoe with a typewriter is offering another "entirely new and previously unheard-of" revelation that, they claim, is at long last the final absolute and definitive version of truth.

This is *not* one of those books. This book has not been channeled from another planet or dimension, nor is it the result of its author having had any supernatural experience or revelation. I beg everyone I can to be slow to believe such claims. I plead, "Please, let's give those thousands of billions who lived and died before us a little credit." Many in our past have earnestly strived to find answers to the same questions we are trying to find answers to today, and I can think of no reason to assume that all the answers our species has previously come up with should be unceremoniously thrown out the window. If there *is* an answer to the mystery of death, and if people are capable of finding it, then it's a safe bet that it has been found before, and that the legacy of humanity's past will reflect that discovery, to at least some degree.

The information revolution virtually ensures that none of our conventional theories on death will survive much longer. I think this is a far bigger problem than most people realize, one that could end up seriously undermining the stability of our civilization. Indeed, I believe that process has already begun. Because the question of life after death is such a deeply personal and important issue to so many individuals, it is also a pivotal issue to human culture. Since trust, confidence, and a sense of security are the foundations of all stable civilizations, a people that lose their faith in life after death risk falling just as surely as a man who has a rug pulled out from under him.

The more confidence we have in our security, the more we prosper. The more stable we feel our situations are, the more we feel the courage to hold down jobs, get married, assume productive places in society, and generally try our hands at some long-term investing in this thing called life. So long as we have faith that our efforts have at least a reasonable chance of bearing fruit, and won't be destroyed or derailed by forces beyond our control, we can always be counted on to optimistically and enthusiastically put forth that effort.

But the more convinced we become that our efforts do not matter, that forces beyond our control will ultimately prevent our efforts from bearing fruit, the more hopeless we become, and the more we question the value of life, love, law, and morality. This is no great secret; we see evidence of it in the news every day. When societies feel a little insecure, their stock markets plunge. When societies feel more insecure, crime goes up. When societies are extremely insecure, riots, wars, and genocide occur.

The tired cliché had it right all along: everything ultimately comes down to a matter of faith. No one knows the future; indeed, no one even knows the present. All any of us is ever aware of at any one time is just a little micro-snapshot of the entire reality of the present moment. And not knowing, knowing we *don't* know, we find we must guess, forced in each moment of our lives to behave as if we *did* know what was coming next, and what will come in the long run. Will our efforts bear fruit or will they not? We never know. Our every act is an act of faith—faith either that our efforts (and therefore our lives) are of value, or faith that our efforts (and lives) are not of value.

The greatest of all uncertainties, and the greatest of all acts of faith, revolves around the issue of death. What we believe about the nature of death determines our value assessment of life. If death is the great eraser, if it deletes us entirely, if nothing of who we are or what we did remains when we are gone, then death eliminates all possibility that we were *ever* of value, or that life itself is of any genuine value. To leave no effect is to be no cause. To have no possibility of leaving any effect is to be nothing already.

The more we come to question whether or not we survive death, the more insecure we feel, and the more that life, love, law, and morality seem empty, worthless, and meaningless. If death erases everything, if all we are and all we know are but fleeting shadows on the wall of time, then no reason remains not to steal, rape, or kill at will.

Societies absolutely depend on their citizens believing in life after death. No civilization, great or small, has ever existed that did not believe in life after death in one form or another. Without this belief, social structures refuse to be built. Without it, no one feels he can depend on the person next to him, for all human efforts, social structures, and societal values ultimately rest on the mutual assumption that life is real, that life has meaning and substance and lasting relevance.

Our civilization today has come to a great crossroads. Our technological accomplishments have become astounding even to us. Our scientific mastery of the physical world has surpassed the wildest dreams of all past generations, and promises only to keep accelerating at an ever greater rate. But this colossal victory has blind sided us. It has introduced an unexpected wildcard into the game which threatens to undermine everything we have achieved. When the technological revolution began, a mere few hundred years ago, the average person on the planet never traveled more than thirty miles away from his place of birth, and rarely encountered anyone else who had traveled more than a few hundred miles at most. But now, thanks to the Internet, the average individual routinely communicates with others half way across the planet on a daily basis. Although most assume this to be a good thing, it threatens to undermine the bottom-most building-block of civilization itself—faith.

When the average person could go his entire life from birth to death without ever meeting anyone who subscribed to a different belief system from his own, it was relatively easy to believe the faith of one's parents and culture, because everyone in a person's life reinforced that same perspective. Uniformity of belief on the local level helped isolated civilizations thrive and grow. But now, thanks to the information revolution, that isolation is a thing of the past, and all the different belief systems of the world are lined up side by side on an equal playing field, shuffled together regardless of locality. Suddenly, for the first time in human history, no one belief system seems to have an edge over any other.

And the questions are starting. Recently, while waiting to board a plane in Chicago, I encountered eleven different people with completely different ideas about what happens after death. One man, who identified himself as a Christian, maintained that all human beings have eternal souls which immediately and permanently enter either heaven or hell after death, depending on whether or not the person had accepted Christ during his lifetime. But the young lady sitting next to him, who identified herself as a Buddhist, said that the human soul is not immortal at all, but all the various constituent components of self and personality detach from each other at death, dissolving back into the universe, never to exist again. At that, another man emerged from behind his newspaper to smilingly inform us that at death, we die and that's it—nothing survives at all.

A doctoral student told us that his family in India taught him as a child that a deep, hidden part of a person does survive, going on to reincarnate, but all the rest of the person, including all the person's memories and personality, completely disintegrate and permanently cease to exist when we die. One sharply dressed businesswoman begged to differ, insisting that at death we all simply become mindless, sleepwalking ghosts who have nothing *but* memories, and endlessly re-enact them. A young mother carrying a child on her lap then asserted that the dead turn invisible like ghosts, but otherwise are completely unchanged and remain right here with us.[1]

A man from the Middle East spoke authoritatively of the soul entering a dreamlike realm after death where it would wait until Judgment Day. But the Jehovah's Witness sitting next to him thought that at death our souls don't go anywhere, but just cease to exist altogether, having no further experience at all until they are finally re-created again by God at Judgment Day. At that, a casually dressed man insisted that the soul does survive, speaking quietly but compellingly of his own near-death experience (NDE), in which he rose up out of his body, traveled through a dark tunnel to a faraway realm of light where he met God, then watched a panoramic review of all his life's memories pass before him in a flash, and finally visited with his dead relatives among beautiful gardens before returning to his body.

But a middle-aged woman countered this with an afterlife experience of her own, describing a past-life regression (PLR) she had undertaken on a dare some years ago, in which she had been hypnotically regressed to memories of previous lives. In between one lifetime and the next, she said, entire decades seemed to have been spent just floating quietly and comfortably alone in an empty, velvety blackness, never seeing any God, devil, heaven, hell, life review, dead relatives, gardens, or anything at all in the afterlife.

The thing that impressed me most about these people was that they all seemed equally convinced that their own versions were correct. The more they listened to the differing reports, the more anxious and excited and animated each seemed to get, and the more each defended his or her own version and tried to attack or explain away the others.

Watching this spontaneous display of competing beliefs, a chilling thought gripped me: ours may be the last generation in history that finds it possible to arrive at *any* personal conviction about what happens after death.

Every young man and woman seeking answers today is confronted by a end-less array of seemingly inconsistent and mutually exclusive reports about what follows this life. When it comes to reports about the afterlife, nearly every statement from every self-appointed spiritual teacher seems to conflict with at least half of the statements from all the other leaders, and there seems to be no compelling reason to assume any one of them is more author-itative than the rest.

The moral integrity and intellectual honesty of all the different groups who subscribe to all the various afterlife perspectives—the Christians, Muslims, Hindus, Buddhists, NDE-ers, regressionists, and ghost-researchers—all seem equally sincere and honorable. Yet, as the decades go by, the babble of all the conflicting models of the afterlife just seems to keep increasing. How can we expect future generations to be truly confident with *any* choice when all the candidates seem equally viable and equally contradictory?

There's no question about it—humanity's conception of, and confi-dence in, the afterlife is changing. In the last few decades, our culture has begun to embrace new teachings and new mythologies, some of which have declared that everything is fine and there's nothing to worry about. Many don't realize that this is a radically new message, one that does not find any support in the teachings of mankind's honored traditions, which always taught the opposite—that one's situation after death could prove to be quite unfortunate indeed.

But people's afterlife beliefs no longer revolve exclusively around retranslated and reinterpreted teachings of legendary figures who have been dead and gone for fifty generations. Today, people's personal afterlife experiences, such as NDEs, PLRs, encounters with ghosts, poltergeists, apparitions, death-bed visions, after-death communications, and the pro-nouncements of psychics and seers like Edgar Cayce, Robert Monroe, Sylvia Brown, John Edwards, and James Van Praagh, are increasingly being given equal credence alongside humanity's most esteemed cultural traditions. Unfortunately, these new information sources *also* seem to paint very differ-ent pictures about what happens after death.

For example, many past-life regression subjects insist that reincarnation is true; but near-death experiencers often insist that reincarnation is false. Some PLR researchers insist that no such thing as heaven or hell exists, while others insist that both do, while still others maintain that heaven exists but hell does not. Those PLR researchers who support the existence of heaven or hell believe the soul only stays there temporarily, but many NDE-ers main-tain that the soul stays permanently in heaven after death. The majority of

NDE researchers maintain that only heaven exists but hell does not, but a sizable minority are certain that hell is just as real as heaven. Some NDE-ers maintain that souls in hell stay there forever, while others declare that the stay in hell is just temporary. While many NDE-ers insist that everyone goes straight to heaven regardless of his earthly religion, some who have encountered apparitions of Jesus and Mary insist that heaven is reserved only for those who follow Christ.

Curiously, people's personal afterlife experiences often make them feel as if they've lost part of their normal mental faculties, but, even more curiously, *which* functions are affected seems to depend on what category of afterlife experience they happened to have. In large part, this book is a study of these sort of baffling situations, and the implications they lead to. PLR subjects, for example, often report feeling as if they have lost their feelings, emotions, memory, sense of identity, and feeling of personal connection while they are in between lives, while NDE subjects (especially those in the "realm of bewildered spirits") often report a loss of autonomous free will, linear reasoning and logic, objective awareness, and initiative. Those who have witnessed haunting ghosts tend to describe them as being trapped in repetitive cycles of memory-review.

While the race is open to all candidates, the real excitement revolves, as always, around the biggest players. The majority of the world's population are non-reincarnationists—Christians and Muslims—who entered the twenty-first century under attack on two fronts. Unfortunately for them, not only is carefully controlled reincarnation research ongoing in universities around the world, but a far more momentous sociological development is occurring outside the halls of academia. More and more private individuals are experimenting with past-life regression, a hypnotic technique that theoretically makes it possible for anyone to access and review her own past-life memories. The public acceptance of reincarnation would doom Christianity and Islam as they currently stand; for example, if people routinely come back to life again and again, all the air seems to go out of the sails of the Christian promise of eternal life. If everyone is *already* enjoying eternal life, there seems no need for Jesus' noble sacrifice.

Today we stand at a critical threshold. The emergence of serious scientific research into various types of afterlife phenomena has begun to confound our established religions. A mere thirty years ago, a handful of scientists began to recognize that people around the world were having uncannily similar "hallucinatory" afterlife experiences. This insight sparked the first organized research into NDEs and PLRs, which then spawned grass-roots movements dedicated to researching these phenomena, followed by worldwide organizations which continue to grow larger with each passing year. If *any* model of the afterlife is going to be widely believed fifty years from now, it will have to recognize and convincingly account for the data emerging from this research.

Over the coming years, one can only assume that our advanced communication abilities will continue to more deeply integrate our cultural perspectives, transforming and unifying our collective vision of reality. Eventually, the day will come when all the different varieties of phenomenological afterlife data being researched today will be familiar to the majority of people. When that day arrives, only two possibilities are likely to remain: either there will be some model of the afterlife that successfully and convincingly accounts for all the data, or there won't be.

If such a model does emerge, it seems likely that it would eventually be accepted across all borders, becoming, in time, a single world religion.

When the world was fractured into a multiplicity of different isolated cultures, many different localized, nonintegrated afterlife beliefs existed around the world, each providing its own little sliver of humanity with its own unique vision of reality. But as human culture grows more globally integrated and more homogenous, a new uniformity of belief will also tend to establish itself on that new global scale, and humanity's separate conflicting beliefs will gradually become a thing of the past.

If, however, no model of the afterlife can be found that meets this challenge, if no model successfully and convincingly accounts for all our different modern phenomenological reports and classic afterlife traditions, then it seems inevitable that the human race will slowly, perhaps reluctantly, cease to believe in life after death altogether. So long as we keep hearing radically different and contradictory descriptions of the afterlife, our generation, and then our children's generation, and then *their* children's generation, will keep believing less and less in life after death as history marches on.

Since nature abhors a vacuum, a culture that cannot confidently hold a belief in life after death will eventually become a culture that *does* hold a belief in the *absence* of life after death.

And the culture that does not believe in life after death is a culture that will find it increasingly hard to respect love, law, and morality. We can already see the effects of this in our accelerating societal deterioration, and not only in the crime- and drug-infested sections of our cities. The deterioration is occurring at the top levels of society as well—often we no longer even pretend to expect our leaders to have any real integrity. Frequently, all we ask is that our own personal family/neighborhood/group be safe, and, if there *is* to be an inequity, then, we pray with less and less shame, let *us* be the ones on the right end of the gun.

This is a snapshot of a culture in the process of losing its balance. The rug on which we had been collectively standing to build this mighty civilization—our confidence in our own long-term safety and security—is already starting to slip out from under us. Our cultural advances have placed our traditional beliefs in question, and without anything to fill the gap, people are left floundering, unsure if anything they do makes a difference, unsure if human life, their own lives, the lives of others they see on the streets around them, are of any lasting value at all. Every year, more and more people are concluding that these lives are *not* of any value. Each year, we see more shooting rampages, more kids molested by religious authorities, more suicide bombings, all by people who have lost their belief in, and respect for, the value of human life.

This recent rash of public atrocities are just what would be expected from a culture that was losing its collective belief in life after death. They are, in fact, symptoms of the loss of our cultural belief in survival, which is not falling away because our traditional beliefs have actually been disproved yet, but because so many apparently contradicting reports have surfaced recently that no one feels much confidence in any single perspective on the issue. Planetary information exchange seems to have become the greatest enemy of mankind's faith in life after death, and therefore, the greatest enemy of our civilization's stability. The more we learn, it seems, the less certain we are.

However, we are not the first generation of human beings on this planet. We are not the first to ask these questions or seek answers to them. Nor are we the first ones to experience afterlife phenomena, or the first to consider their implications. We have at our disposal, a huge legacy from those who have gone before us. Many have worked ceaselessly, for thousands of years in every land, to find the same answers and the same understanding that we seek today. Death is the perennial human question. Many have walked these paths before us, having spent their lives trying to find answers of value and merit. Let us recognize that many who have come before us have had the same paranormal experiences being reported today, and asked the same questions we ask today. Knowing that these experiences are part of the human experience, and knowing that asking these questions is also part of the human experience, let us not turn away from what those who have come before us have to offer.

Let us also recognize that corrupting influences have also existed, and the original discoveries and messages of the sincere seekers of the past may have been edited or distorted. Knowing this, let us weigh the learning of the past in the light of the present, but let us not ignore outright what hundreds of generations died trying to learn and pass on to us. When we embark on this search for truth, we join an ancient and ongoing parade. Do not imagine we walk alone. Do not imagine we must invent the wheel from scratch all over again.

This book can, like the human psyche itself, be broken down into two distinct sections, one more left-brained, the other more right-brained. The first half of the book is more objective, factual, and analytical. Chapter 1 explores the belief systems of dozens of ancient cultures, including the Egyptians, Greeks, Hindus, Christians, Persians, Chinese Taoists, Hawaiian Kahunas, Australian Aborigines, Alaskan Inuit, Dakota Indians, Peruvian Incas, and Mexican Mayans, showing that these peoples all believed the human soul had two parts which sometimes divided from each other at death, never to be reunited again.

Chapter 2 explores how recent scientific discoveries substantiate, clarify, and elaborate upon these ancient reports about the two halves of the soul. This chapter illustrates why, if the mind did split apart at death, the nature of the human psyche would cause one half to experience something very much like reincarnation, while the other half would experience something very much like heaven or hell. One half of the mind would end up reincarnating again and again, each time jettisoning its memories at death by discarding its other half, which in turn would find itself unable to fully think straight, having become permanently trapped in a timeless heavenly or hellish dream-state.

Chapters 3–7 examine modern research into afterlife phenomena, including near-death experiences, past-life regression, ghosts and apparitions, shamanic soul retrieval, out-of-body experiences, and the reports of modern psychics and mystics, showing how the data emerging from all these seemingly very different information sources is consistent with, and even predictable by, the binary soul doctrine. And after reviewing, comparing, and analyzing the data presented in the first seven chapters, chapter 8 then issues a thirty-five-point challenge that any other afterlife theory must meet before it could be said to be as credible an answer to the mystery of death as the binary soul doctrine.

The second half of the book is more subjective, philosophical, and theoretical. Chapter 9 asks why the human psyche has a two-part compound structure in the first place, and explores mankind's ancient creation myths, as well as more modern material like Ken Wilber's work, the popular *Conversations with God* book series, and even the latest findings in astrophysics and quantum science for possible answers to this question. Chapter 10 looks for reasons that might explain why the psyche would break up into its constituent elements at death, and then charts the long-term personal and sociological consequences of such a division. Chapter 11 takes a fresh look at the Bible, revealing a recurring pattern within the various narratives that mirror the binary soul doctrine, suggesting that the Jewish scriptures were purposely designed to reflect and illustrate mankind's primary spiritual dilemma—afterdeath soul-division.

Seeking clues on how people might prevent their psyches from dividing in two at death, chapter 12 finds that modern science and ancient scriptures both point in the same direction, suggesting that the two halves of the psyche might be permanently cemented together via nothing more exotic than personal integrity and self-honesty.

Chapter 13 presents evidence that the many ancient religions that once subscribed to the binary soul doctrine were themselves all descendants of a far older parent culture from mankind's distant past, a culture known for erecting pyramids and mummifying their dead, a culture whose solution to mankind's spiritual dilemma was just that—to permanently unify and integrate the self, "making the two one."

Exploring the work of Carlos Castaneda and similar authors, chapter 14 examines the recent cultural re-emergence of Mexico's legendary Toltec religion, asking if it offers an authentic snapshot of the original teachings of that ancient pyramid religion, and, more importantly, asking if the ancient practices the pyramid religion once used to unify the two halves of the self have indeed survived into our era.

Chapter 15 starts off by explaining why the pyramid religion's solution to prevent afterdeath soul-division, the "Old Path" of self-integration (which is still the underlying goal of Buddhism, Judaism, and many other contemporary religions), was ultimately judged to be an insufficient answer to the full problem facing mankind. Although the Old Path did make it possible for the occasional rare individual to escape the self-destructive cycle of soul-division, it was never able to release more than a handful of humanity's teeming masses from this curse. This chapter then goes on to explain why a universal soul-rescue such as that reportedly attempted by the Biblical Jesus would indeed be the human race's only hope to fully escape from the ongoing nightmare of soul-division. And chapter 16 considers how long such an attempt might take to fully accomplish.

1

When We All Spoke One Language: The Single World Religion of Humanity's Past

And the whole earth was of one language, and of one speech.

—Genesis 11:1

The binary soul doctrine is probably as close as the human race has ever come to having a single world religion. Thousands of years ago, people all across the globe believed much the same thing about what happened after death—that human beings possess not one, but two souls, which were in danger of dividing apart from each other when a person died. After leaving the physical body, one of these souls was often expected to reincarnate, while the other was believed to become trapped in a dreamlike netherworld. Some of these cultures believed that the afterdeath division of these two souls could be prevented or reversed, while others saw the division as being inevitable and permanent.

Simultaneously present in numerous cultures at the dawn of recorded history, the binary soul doctrine may predate all currently known civilizations. This peculiar afterlife tradition not only seems to have saturated the entire Old World at a very early date, appearing in some of the earliest writings of

Egypt, Greece, Persia, India, and China, it somehow managed to jump the oceans as well, leaving yet more of its footprints in the cultural traditions of Australia, Hawaii, Alaska, the plains of North America, Mexico, Peru, and even Haiti.

Greece called these two souls the *psuche* and the *thumos;* Egypt called them *ba* and *ka;* Israel called them *ruwach* and *nephesh;* Christianity called them *soul* and *spirit;* Persia called them *urvan* and *daena;* Islam called them *ruh* and *nafs;* India the *atman* and *jiva;* China the *hun* and *po;* Haiti the *gros bon ange* and *ti bon ange;* Hawaii the *uhane* and *unihipili,* and the Dakota Indians called them the *nagi* and *niya.* The list goes on.

The most extraordinary thing about this ancient belief is not simply that it was so widespread, but that this lost model of the afterlife seems to be consistent with the latest findings in a number of areas of modern scientific research. For one thing, these cultures' descriptions of the two souls are strikingly similar to modern science's "right brain/left brain" descriptions of the conscious and unconscious halves of the human psyche, distinguishing between one part of the self that is objective, independent, masculine, logical, verbal, dominant, active, and possessing independent free will, and the other part that is subjective, dependent, feminine, fertile, emotional, nonverbal, recessive, passive, responsive, and in possession and control of the memory.

Even more interesting, the binary soul doctrine also seems to anticipate, even predict, many of the conditions being described in modern reports of near-death experiences, past-life memories, past-life hypnotic regressions, ghosts, apparitions, poltergeists, and other afterlife phenomena. These unexpected correlations carry profound and disturbing implications.

Egypt's Version of the Binary Soul Doctrine

Egypt, it seems, was convinced that the afterdeath division of the two souls could be reversed. For more than 2,000 years the Egyptian people united together in that mission, a whole people struggling as one against the greatest of enemies—death itself. They dedicated a huge percentage of their attention, wealth, and manpower to achieving a single goal, that of preventing and/or reversing the afterdeath soul-division of their leaders. Thanks to Egypt's unswerving faith in their ability to reverse this division and thereby guarantee eternal life in the next world, they left what is perhaps the most complete record of this long-forgotten belief system.

As with many of the cultures that subscribed to the binary soul doctrine, the mentality of ancient Egypt revolved around a dualistic perspective similar to China's yin and yang philosophy. Egypt's thoughts were dominated by the idea of united opposites; all reality, they thought, even including the human soul, was comprised of equal but opposite components that were dancing together in a delicate, tense balance. Even their language reflected this underlying assumption; not only was everything always either female or male, yin or yang, but their language often used a special grammatical structure called "the dual voice."

For instance, they called Egypt "The Two Lands"; their universe was called "The Dual Realities" or "The Two Truths"; they called their netherworld "The Great Double House"; their gods dwelt in "The Lake of Double Fire"; and their afterdeath judgment took place in "The Hall of Double Truth." This "dual voice" did not refer to two things, or even two halves of one thing; it referred to an integrated binary unit, two which are one, simultaneously separate and united, each part distinct on its own, yet incomplete without its equal-but-opposite, complementary partner.

Further reflecting this perspective, Egyptian mythology portrayed the universe as beginning when a set of divine twins leapt from the womb of space. The people of ancient Egypt thought of their gods as dualistic: Every masculine god had a feminine counterpart (except for one of their gods—Mut—who was actually seen as bisexual, transcending duality altogether). The Egyptians divided their gods into two groups, the "Lesser *Paut*" and the "Greater *Paut*." The highest god of Egypt was similarly differentiated into two divine elements or beings, Osiris and Ra, who were seen as two different aspects of the same being:

> Then who is he? It is Osiris.
> In other words: his name is Ra.
> —*Book of the Dead, Chapter XVII*

Horus, another high god, was also dualistic. The sun and moon were called the two eyes of Horus. Often called "Horus of the Two Horizons," he was the equal but opposite twin half of another god, Set, or Sutekh. Together, Horus and Set were often called simply "Those Two," or "The Rivals," or "The Two Companions." Constantly wrestling with each other, they were represented together as a single figure with two heads—the head of a man and the head of a jackal.

Just as Egypt perceived everything else as being composed of two parts, so too they distinguished two parts within the human soul as well. These two souls embraced the person's heart during life, but split apart from each other at death. Although Egypt named nine different aspects of the self in all,[1] only two of these, the *ba* and the *ka*, were thought to survive physical death and so could properly be called "soul" as the term is understood today. If and when these two parts of the soul successfully reunited with each other on the other side of death's door, they were then called the *akh*.

The *akh* does not seem to have been an additional, third soul that one also secretly possessed; rather, it was an entirely new kind of soul one could potentially *become*—the whole that was formed by the *ka-ba* union, a whole that was far greater than the mere sum of its parts. The *akh* doesn't seem to have existed at all prior to death, and after death, it merely had a chance of becoming fully functional, or "perfected," but only if all went well with the *ka-ba* union. The symbol for the *akh* was a stork, a bird often seen wading in the marshlands of the Nile, simultaneously at home in the air and on the land, a perfect symbol for the integration of diverse elements.

To the Egyptian way of thinking, it was natural, good, right, and true (a single word in their language, *Maat*) for all things to be "two which were one," and so, it was thought, all people should strive to follow this pattern. This was the double truth of nature (*Maati*). To be divided, on the other hand, to be "two which were *not* one," seems to have been the Egyptian definition of "sin." Although duality was expected, and differentiated binary systems were even appreciated, the two parts were ideally expected to work together smoothly, together forming a whole greater than the sum of their parts. Division, when the interaction and unity of the parts of the whole broke down, was seen as an abhorrent pathology in the natural system— duality taken to an unhealthy extreme. This attitude may explain why the cult of Osiris felt it was necessary to make a special point of forbidding the decapitation or dismemberment of any priests or worshipers of this god. Even the prayers during the annual festival of Osiris seem to reflect this condemnation of division:

> O grant unto me a path whereon I may journey in peace.
> I am righteous. I have not uttered lies willfully.
> I have not acted a double part (or, dealt doubly).[2]

The Legend of Osiris

The god Osiris, and his doctrine of eternal life, held center stage in Egyptian thought for more than 3,000 years, from pre-dynastic, literally *pre-historic* times until the Christian era. Egypt had many gods, each of whom needed to be revered and appeased when necessary. But no Egyptian god was ever worshipped like Osiris, who not only rose from the dead himself, but could make his followers rise from death as well. According to his legend, Osiris was killed by his brother Set, who cut him up into pieces and scattered them. But when those pieces were gathered and reassembled, Osiris not only found that he had been restored to divine and eternal life, but that he was then able to help others conquer death as well.

This model of death seems to be reflected in Egypt's doctrine of the division of the *ba* and *ka* souls after death, and the expectation that if these could be reunited, the person would then be fully reconstituted and perfected, transfigured into a divine being like Osiris himself. In fact, once the two souls of the deceased had reunited on "the other side," the departed person was then called an "Osiris." Egypt's annual ceremony honoring Osiris reflected this same theme: Priests would construct a figure of Osiris by placing a specially prepared paste into two halves of a mold, tying these two symbolic halves of Osiris together when the molds were formed.

These were very old concepts, even to the Egyptians. Many errors found in various copies of the Egyptian Book of the Dead reveal that the scribes who copied them were often uncertain just what those prayers were supposed to mean. This tells us that even as far back as 2000 B.C., the actual culture that originally gave birth to these theological concepts and treatises was already but a dim and flimsy memory, as far removed from those scribes as the days of the Twelve Disciples are to modern Christians, and every bit as mysterious.

Nonetheless, those prayers reveal surprises about ancient Egypt, strongly suggesting that Nile culture, so very long ago, was aware of a subtle truth that our scientists have only rediscovered and verified in recent years, that the human mind is differentiated into two distinct components: the conscious mind, which possesses the rational intellect and the autonomous free will, and the unconscious mind, which possesses the emotions and memory.

The *Ba* as the Conscious Mind

Just like the conscious and unconscious of modern science, both the *ba* and *ka* were considered integral elements of the person's self during life. In fact, both these two carried, independently of each other, the meaning of the self. The *ba* was the living conscious self. Just like the conscious mind of today's psychology, it was considered to possess autonomous free will, focused awareness, rational intelligence, and the ability to move and communicate. Like the conscious mind, the *ba* embodied the objective perspective, dispassionately viewing the rest of the world as objects separate and distinct from itself.

Like the conscious mind, each *ba* was the sole master of its own decisions, the lone witness of its own inner domain; the *ba* was the infinitely private and isolated experience of being the only person in the universe who was peering out through its own particular set of eyes. And like the conscious mind, the *ba* seems to have been conceived of as the source of intellect; while the *ka* was credited with making the body talk, the *ba* was what caused its words to make sense.

But in sharp contrast to modern science's conception of the conscious mind, the *ba* was also credited with eternal life—it was thought to permanently possess both the spark of life and the power of motion and animation. The *ba,* Egypt thought, could never die, never cease to exist, never cease to be conscious and aware. No matter what happened, it would at the very least always still be alive and aware of its own existence. But its sense of continuity, the coherence of its sense of self—that was a different matter. That was *not* guaranteed, and all the funeral rituals and prayers and mummification efforts of ancient Egypt had but a single purpose, to maintain the coherency of the *ba*'s self-experience while passing through the doors of death.

The *Ka* as the Unconscious Mind

The *ka* was not so lucky. It was possible for the *ka* to cease to exist. In the eyes of every Egyptian, one's *ka* was at grave risk.

What was at risk? Egypt's terminology has confused scholars for centuries, The *ka,* a different element of the person altogether, was somehow *also* considered to be the self. Actually, *ka* is an Egyptian word for "you";[3] this pun-like choice of words seems to emphasize the *ka*'s role in relationships. In many respects, the characteristics of the *ka* precisely match modern science's concept of the unconscious mind. Also like the right-brain unconscious, it was associated with dream activity during sleep. Like the mysterious unconscious, it was also thought to be able to work in secret, without its owner's knowledge.

A person's *ka* was even able to deceive or betray its owner, which sounds rather like Freudian slips, neuroses, and all the other ways the unconscious is still "misbehaving" today. Just as modern therapists teach their clients how to get the unconscious to work for them instead of against them, so Egypt thought the *ka* could either work for or against its owner. Like the subjective unconscious, the *ka* was also polarized toward a subjective or intersubjective orientation, providing one with the crucial ability to relate to and interact with others. Just as the unconscious is today, the *ka* was thought to be the source of one's subjective sense of belonging, one's sense of having a living connection with others.

Reminding us of the moral voice of the unconscious, the *ka* was also considered to be the source of the person's conscience. Like the unconscious, the *ka* was also considered to be moldable, programmable, changeable, and potentially unreliable. Just as popular culture today thinks of the unconscious as the equal but opposite dark interior to the conscious mind's lighted exterior, so too was the *ka* often depicted in Egyptian art as a blackened reverse image of the person.

The *ka* was often called the person's "double"; it seems to have been thought of as being, or embodying, the person's "pattern" by molding itself into a perfect image or likeness of the individual and his character. Reminding us that memory is stored in the unconscious, the *ka* was also thought to contain a record or model of all one's personal experiences, and thus, one's sense of self-identity; it contained the shapes of one's memories (on which the continuity and coherence of one's sense of self-identity depends, as any amnesiac will testify). It also constituted a complete database of a person's psychological disposition, containing the shape or pattern or reflection or memory of all one's needs, desires, fears, expectations, appetites, and emotions. In fact, the ancient Egyptian word *ka* still lives on in our language, in words like character and charisma.[4]

In short, the *ka* seems to have been the yin to the *ba*'s yang, the form that gave shape to the *ba*'s substance. The *ka* was closely associated with the concept of form and image, what allowed different shapes to be taken. Without the *ka*, the *ba* was unable to have any form at all; unable to manifest. Without the *ka*, the *ba* would be substance without form, text without context, potential without manifestation, being without identity, existence without self, rather like the Eastern religious concept of the impersonal, nonformed essence of one's being. Without the *ka*, the *ba* would be in just such a predicament. But unlike the Eastern religions of today, ancient Egypt saw this impersonal existence not as a desirable goal, but as the worst of all possible fates.

The Relationship of the *Ba* and *Ka* During Life

The *ka* had needs. It lacked something it could not do without: sustenance, an energy supply. The *ka* was not believed to inherently possess its own spark of eternal life force that could keep it perpetually energized and active and fulfilled, so it needed a source to supply this necessary nourishment. The *ba* was that outside source. The *ba*, which was thought to possess that eternally living spark of life force, was thought to reside inside the *ka* during one's human life; the *ka* held its *ba* within it just as a cup holds water, embracing it. In fact, the symbol for the *ka* was a pair of upraised arms, which seem to be stretched apart in a welcoming embrace, yet also raised up in a way that reminds one of a cup ready to be filled.

In the same way, the conscious mind can also be said to be contained, and therefore shaped, by the unconscious. By itself, the bare-bones conscious mind has no shape of its own, no unique personality, no subjective value system, except as it is "in-formed" through the memory shape of the unconscious; without the unconscious with its memory and emotions, the conscious mind, although aware, would be as blank and featureless as a sheet of white paper. Just as the *ba* was believed to animate the *ka*, so too the conscious mind animates and activates the otherwise dormant unconscious. It seemed, then as now, a partnership made in heaven, each supplying what the other needed.

Like a set of Russian dolls, the *ka* dwelt within the heart (or *ab*), and the *ba* sat inside the *ka;* this cozy arrangement sometimes blurred scriptural distinctions between the heart and these other two components. Like two embracing lovers, this union between the *ba* and *ka* was intimate in life; they were two conjoined beings that could not be separated prior to death. Even though the *ka* was sometimes thought to travel away from the body in dreams while the person was alive, such journeys rarely endangered the connection between the two.

The Division of *Ba* and *Ka* at Death

But once the person died, the *ba* and *ka*, which had until then known only partnership, having functioned as virtually a single unit all during the person's life, now found themselves separated, alienated, ripped apart from each other. This abrupt and disorienting rupture seems to have been associated with the *ba* experiencing a loss of memory; multiple chapters in the Egyptian Book of the Dead[5] pray for the deceased's memory to be returned to him after he has left the body. How was this memory to be restored?

By reconnecting the *ba* to its *ka*, which contained the full pattern and record of the person's life, including his memories and his subjective sense of self. Virtually all of Egypt's famous Pyramid Texts, as well as virtually the entire Book of the Dead, had but a single purpose: to cause the *ba* and *ka* to reunite again after they split off from each other at death. The Egyptians effected this reunion through the "Opening of the Mouth" ritual.[6] This ritual, it was hoped, would permanently bind the *ba* and *ka* to each other in the next world, thus guaranteeing the eternal continuation of the person's self-awareness and sense of identity after the transition.

It was thought, however, that this reunification could only be achieved in a physical body; the body seems to have been considered a necessary catalyst for their fusion. Ideally, this supreme spiritual transformation was supposed to take place well before the person's physical death (as is the case with many other religions), and many of Egypt's other religious rituals were devoted to doing just that. But the Egyptian people, for whatever reason, remained convinced for thousands of years that if the individual did not achieve this union prior to his death, it might still be possible to achieve it even after death, but *only if the physical body still existed.*

Reading the Book of the Dead over the deceased, it was hoped, would lead the *ba* and *ka* to return to the corpse, allowing them to finally consummate their union and achieve immortality. But Egypt seems to have worried about what might happen if their return was delayed. Since there was no way to be sure if or when the invisible *ba* and *ka* actually *had* returned and consummated their union, the remains of the deceased had to be preserved for as long as possible, so the opportunity for their reunion, at least, would always exist. Thus, it seems the practices of mummification and pyramid-building dawned in Egypt, not as the best and surest route to immortality their culture knew of, but rather as a last-ditch effort for the spiritually negligent.

The Transfiguration of the *Akh*

If this reunion was successfully accomplished, it was thought, the person would be transformed into an *akh*, something akin to a shining, glorified, immortal angel. Often called an Osiris (one whose parts have been reunited), the *akh* was thought of as the true, complete self in its fully awakened, perfected, and whole state after death. The word *akh* carried the sense of one who had been pulled back together, one who was now fully self-possessed, meanings which appropriately reflect the reunification of the *ba* and *ka*, and the reacquisition of one's past memories, personality, and sense of self-identity.

The Second Death

But if this reunification did not occur, the *ba* wouldn't mind or even notice. It would just flit away carefree and unconcerned to heaven, where it would still enjoy unlimited freedom and happiness, doing whatever it wanted and going wherever it pleased, and conversing with other *bas* in heaven. Meanwhile, the ghostly *ka* would be stuck behind, trapped in a feebleminded, cold, hungry, needy, and vulnerable state in the tomb. The *ka* was thought to have many very regular and pressing requirements after death, but, without the energy and animating mobility it received from its other half, its needs went unmet, and it would eventually disintegrate. If the reunification occurred, then all the *ka's* needs would be thereby instantly and eternally fulfilled. But failing that reunion, the *ka* would eventually perish in a "second death" which, to the Egyptian, was the worst disaster imaginable; the *ka* would be utterly disintegrated, made as if it had never come into existence.

Although the cult of Osiris forbade the dismemberment or decapitation of any of his followers, Egyptian legend warned that those unfaithful to Osiris would suffer that very fate; the headsmen of Osiris, the legends declare, were eternally busy. This would seem to be yet another representation of the idea that a soul-division occurs at death, but this particular detail of the Osiris legend suggests that soul-division was thought to be conditional: one would only "lose his head," or self-aware consciousness, if one failed to live up to the ideals of the cult of Osiris. If one's soul divided apart at death, it seems, the ancient Egyptians would have claimed it was his own fault, having spent one's life *acting a double part.*

A Common Model of Death

This ancient tale of dividing souls, or something very similar to it, seems to turn up in afterlife traditions around the ancient world. The specific details were often quite different from one tradition to another, but the core message was always the same, that human beings possess two separate and distinct souls which can and often do divide at death, each going off into a different afterlife experience. Although these cultures were otherwise very different and often separated by thousands of miles, they consistently described their two souls in very similar ways, amazingly anticipating modern science's descriptions of the conscious and unconscious.

Often, these cultures came to value one soul more than the other. When this occurred, the characteristics of the lesser-valued soul were seen as less real, more illusory or temporary. While the more-valued soul was invariably seen as being completely immortal, the lesser was often thought to disappear after death, sometimes seeming to cease to exist very quickly after death, other times seeming to fade away very slowly. But these cultures disagreed on which soul was the more important and more immortal. Some cultures, such as Hinduism and Islam, held that the objective, dispassionate, conscious-mind-like soul was the "true self," while the emotional, subjective unconscious-mind-like soul was held up as illusory. But other cultures, such as Christianity and that of the Australian aborigines, felt the opposite was true, that the innermost, subjective, personal, involved, emotional heart and soul of a person was her true self, and the objective, uninvolved, disconnected, analytical, masculine half represented all that was wrong and false with the world.

The strengths of the more-valued soul invariably dominated the cultural attitude of a particular society, while the strengths of the lesser were granted less significance. Those cultures that valued the conscious-mind-like soul more than its partner tended to put a lower premium on the subjective, personal, emotional experience of the individual in their society, while those cultures that valued the unconscious-mind-like soul put a lower premium on logic, science, and reason.

Of all the other binary soul doctrine (BSD) cultures, the ancient Chinese were one of the few who seems to have recognized that *both* halves of the soul were of equal value.

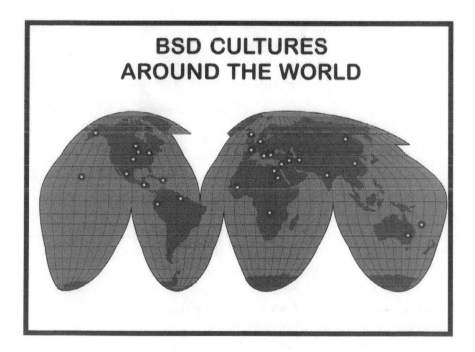

China's Version of the Binary Soul Doctrine

Like the Egyptians, the Taoists of ancient China were greatly concerned with ensuring the survival of the individual after death. Taoist philosophy paralleled Egyptian philosophy in many respects; as early as the "Warring States" period (475–221 B.C.), Taoists were teaching that all reality was comprised of and created by two equal but opposite interplaying primordial forces, yin and yang. But instead of leaving this concept in the abstract, they brought it down to a very personal level, maintaining that every person was an amalgamation of yin and yang souls.

At the moment of birth, they believed, these two components fuse together within the body, working together until they finally part company at death. Providing animation to the body and the mind, the *hun,* or yang soul, was conscious, active, intelligent, masculine, strong, ambitious, and dominant. Like the left-brain half of the psyche, it was thought to be particularly aware of the boundaries and differences between self and others. Like the dispassionate, objective conscious mind, it also excelled in nonattachment.

The *po,* or yin soul, was thought to take shape over the course of an individual's lifetime; being very impressionable and sensitive, it was molded by the person's environment. The *po* provided one's personal sense of self-identity, and was held to be what makes a person feel fully alive and real and present in the moment. It was thought of as earthy, only semiconscious, feminine, reactive, and passive, and was deemed responsible for all one's sensations, reactions, emotions, and instinctive impulses. After departing the dead body, the yang soul would return to heaven unchanged, sometimes returning to reincarnate later, while the *yin* soul became imprisoned in a dreary underground netherworld in a feebleminded state.

Like the ancient Egyptians, these Chinese Taoists also realized that an afterdeath soul-division would spell the disintegration of the known self, and they were just as anxious to ensure its survival. But unlike Egypt, which optimistically believed that this afterdeath division could be reversed after the fact, China felt the only hope revolved around preventing the division from ever occurring in the first place. They designed techniques to construct a "spirit body" by welding these two souls together while the person was alive, so they could no longer disconnect at death. Sometimes referred to as the "immortal fetus," this spirit body was believed to ensure the continuation of the personality and sense of self-identity.

The Taoists realized that although a human being was comprised of three distinct parts—body, *hun* (spirit), and *po* (soul)—there were only five different combinations these could be arranged in, since it was not possible for the animating *hun* to split apart from the body without leaving that body a lifeless corpse. The five possible combinations were 1. *hun* (spirit), *po* (soul), and body; 2. *po* (soul) with no *hun* (spirit) (and therefore no animated body either); 3. body with *hun* (spirit) but no *po* (soul); 4. *hun* (spirit) with no *po* (soul) or body; and 5. *hun* (spirit) and *po* (soul) with no body.

The first, with body, *po*-soul, and *hun*-spirit, would be the living. The second would be those with *po*-souls, but no *hun*-spirits, no source of animation, which are ghosts. The third would be bodies with *hun*-spirits but no *po*-souls—animated bodies without any sense of personal identity (the traditional name for such creatures would seem to be zombies). The fourth would be animated disembodied spirits without any objectively visible form or subjective sense of personal identity (which would seem to correspond to poltergeists). The fifth would be animated disembodied spirits with a cohesive and uncorrupted sense of their own self-identity and memories, which would seem to correspond to Taoism's immortal fetus, as well as Egypt's *akh*, and Christianity's angels or saints.

The Incan and Toltec Versions of the Binary Soul Doctrine

The Colombian civilization of the Incas, which covered much of present-day Ecuador, Peru, Bolivia, and Chile, held a philosophy strikingly similar to those of Egypt and China. Like ancient Egypt, the Incas built pyramidal religious monuments and mummified their dead. Like Egypt and China, the Incas subscribed to a dualistic philosophy that included the idea that people possess two souls which divide at death.

The religion, culture, and philosophy of the Incas revolved around the central idea of trying to harmonize and reconcile the equal but opposite forces of reality. Their supreme being was Viracocha, an androgynous being whose symbol was a two-headed serpent. The binary structure of reality so dominated their thoughts that they divided their villages and territories into two halves, calling one half *hanan* ("high, superior, right, masculine") and the other half *hurin* ("low, inferior, left, feminine").

At death, one soul was thought to return to its place of origin in heaven, while the other soul remained with the corpse. The soul that remained behind was thought to have many needs, and it was thought necessary (just as it had been in Egypt) for the physical body to be preserved for those needs to be fulfilled.

The Inca's neighbors to the north, the ancient Toltec civilization of Mexico, also subscribed to a version of the binary soul doctrine. Believing that the whole world was comprised of two equal but opposite forces, they called it *Omeyocan*, the place of duality. They also believed that each living

13

human was comprised of two mental halves, which they called the *tonal* and the *nagual*; they thought that the purpose of human existence was to integrate these two.[7]

Greece's Version of the Binary Soul Doctrine

When we peer back into the dimmest, most distant traces of the ancient civilization of the Greeks, we discover the binary soul doctrine already in full flower. In Homer's *Iliad* and *Odyssey*, Greece's oldest literary texts, two distinct types of souls are distinguished—the *psuche* and the *thumos*. To the Homeric Greeks, a person was only fully human when body, *thumos,* and *psuche* were functioning together as a cohesive whole. Thought to be free, unencumbered, and immortal, the *psuche* held the spark of life, and while it could not exit the body without causing the death of the individual, it was thought to be able to reincarnate. While it was not thought to possess any feelings or emotions, it was thought to be the center of all abstract intellectual thought. The other soul, the *thumos,* possessed one's feelings, emotions, needs, and urges.

Death shattered the unity of *psuche* and *thumos* in two stages. First, the two souls detached in unison from the body when its functions ceased, and shortly thereafter, they separated from each other as well, an event called the "second death." One soul disappeared into the air while the other soul, transformed into a shadowy replica of the living person, descended into Hades. There, these phantoms of the dead continued to exist, but it was a flavorless, unhappy, and dismal netherworld, and their thoughts were confused and oblivious.

The souls of the dead were portrayed as extremely weak and barely conscious in Hades, but able to gain enough strength and presence of mind to temporarily think, move, and speak if they were somehow able to acquire a little sustenance from the living. Homer's hero Odysseus, for example, makes a special offering to attract the souls of the dead. Any soul having access to the offering could then hold a rational conversation with Odysseus for a few moments, but without sustenance all the other wraiths of the dead remained without reason or understanding.

India's Version of the Binary Soul Doctrine

The Vedas are the oldest scriptures in India. Dating back to around 1000 B.C., these documents, the foundation of all Hinduism, provide us with the oldest available snapshot of Indian beliefs about the human soul. The story

14

they tell was already familiar to much of the world—that people possessed two nonphysical, psychological, potentially immortal soul-like elements, the *asu* and the *manas*. Like Egypt's *ba*, the *asu* was active, conscious, sentient, and immortal, carrying the spark of life. Like Egypt's *ka*, the *manas* was thought to hold one's internal feelings, emotions, and subjective perception, providing the ability to perceive and comprehend relationships with others. After death, the *asu* could reincarnate, but the *manas* was vulnerable and could be greatly harmed by death; if it separated from the animating and cognizing *asu* after departing the body, it would become inert and lifeless.

Modern Hinduism still teaches that two different entities coexist in the human body, the *atman* and the *jiva*. Deepak Chopra, perhaps the most well-known apologist for Hinduism today, writes "many people might wonder why the soul has to be divided in this way . . . the distinction between them is absolutely necessary."[8] During life these two are integrated deeply together, but after death they divide, after which the *jiva*, or astral-emotional body, is thought to deteriorate.

The *atman*, or inner witness, is the objective conscious self, the part of one's inner being that is eternally unchanging and observant. The *jiva*, on the other hand, is the more familiar, personal, subjective self which is always changing, but may or may not be eternal. *Atman* is to *jiva* as substance is to form. These two are intimate partners in life, and just as Egypt's *ka* was associated with form, so too the *atman* needs the *jiva* in order to take on form and definition, and thereby experience life on earth. The *jiva* gives the inner witness the sense or experience of having a subjective self with personal limitations and boundaries; it defines our sense of personal identity, telling us where we stop and the rest of the universe begins. Often thought of as a mirror that reflects the *atman* back to itself, the *jiva* is sometimes said to be an illusion, that all one is seeing or experiencing is a partial, limited reflection of the *atman* itself.

Strongly associated in Hindu thought with subjective awareness, the *jiva* provides all personal psychological experiences such as feelings, desires, likes, dislikes, and memories, as well as all subjective impressions, perceptions, and interpretations. The *atman*, on the other hand, is closely associated with an objective perspective; even the empirical subject himself is perceived as an object from the point of view of the *atman*, which sees everything, even itself, through dispassionate, unattached, objective eyes. When viewed from the perspective of the *atman*, the *jiva* seems to be a fraud, nothing more than an impermanent, haphazardly built structure of mental and emotional habits. Similarly, however, the detached, emotionless, disassociated perspective of the *atman* also seems to be a lie from the personal, subjective, deeply involved, connected-to-everything perspective of the *jiva*. Each seems false from the perspective of the other, yet each needs the other to experience anything at all.

Since the *jiva* is so closely associated with change and form, modern Hindu thought is conflicted over whether it is eternal, or whether, unlike the *atman*, it does eventually cease to exist. Opinions range all the way from the assertion that the *jiva* is ever-changing yet eternal, to the opposite idea that one's *jiva* disintegrates at the end of each lifetime and then another entirely new and different *jiva* is acquired at the start of the next incarnation. Those who feel the *jiva* is doomed usually regard it as false, an illusion, and insist that in the final analysis, the *atman* is the only true self that exists. This ancient attitude towards the *jiva* rejects, denies, and ignores all personal, subjective experience as illusory and ultimately unreal.

Recently, however, many social commentators have been suggesting that this traditional attitude is responsible for much of India's current poverty and disease. Leo Buscaglia, one of America's new-age gurus, would probably criticize this teaching for a different reason. He obviously wouldn't like to hear that people lose their personal emotional selves at death, not after spending years teaching that this is the *most* important part of a person—the part that makes us all truly and fully human.

Although the *atman* and *jiva* coexist in the same body and may even reincarnate together, the relationship between them is not thought to be fixed and unchanging. On the contrary, it is believed that these two parts of the self can be brought into a closer, more intimate and permanent relationship than what nature alone provides. Over the centuries, Hinduism has developed a set of spiritual practices that are intended to do this, which are called yoga, meaning "union." Typically, however, these efforts do not usually seek a balanced integration, treating these two as equal partners the way the Chinese did, but tend instead to magnify the perspective of the *atman* while ignoring or disregarding the experience and perspective of the *jiva*. The Hindu sage tries to avoid being possessed by his emotions, and seeks to walk through life attentively, unselfishly, and objectively, avoiding any and all subjective perspectives, behaviors, attitudes, and judgments. Nonattachment is favored over involvement, and a disconnected objectivity is preferred over any subjective sense of being personally involved with the rest of the universe.

Hawaii's Version of the Binary Soul Doctrine

> The kahunas had a number of beliefs which they did not
> keep secret. For instance, they shared with the common people

their knowledge of the fact that man has two souls or spirits instead of one. The early missionaries thought this a most droll and idiotic concept, worthy only of heathen and savages. To them, man had but one soul, and their job was to save it if possible. As they arrived in Hawaii in 1820, and the subconscious was not discovered by Freud until over half a century later, they can hardly be blamed for laughing at the kahuna beliefs.*

—Max Freedom Long[9]

Max Freedom Long, the first Westerner to study Huna, the indigenous religion of Hawaii, was convinced it had somehow evolved from an early form of Hinduism. This traditional Polynesian religion was first introduced to the civilized world in the early 1900's when sensational news reports began to circulate saying that Hawaiian priests, known as *Kahunas*, were somehow able to kill people simply by "praying" them to death. Long discovered that the explanation these priests offered for these supposed abilities seemed to revolve around a binary model of the human psyche much like that of modern psychology.

Hawaiian thought called their two souls the *uhane*, which was thought to be masculine, intelligent, and possessing free will, and the *unihipili*, which was thought to be feminine, emotional, and possessing the memory. Like Egypt's *akh*, the Hawaiians named a third, higher sort of soul, the *aumakua*, which was also created out of the two binary souls when united into a singular unit. The plural of Egypt's *akh* was *aakhu*, which even sounds a little like Hawaii's *aumakua;* and just as the ancient Egyptians called the company of their gods the *Paut*, the Hawaiians called the company of their gods the *Poe Aumakua*, the "Great Company of High Selves."[10]

The ancient Polynesians believed that their two souls might split apart from each other at death. If this happened, they said, the *uhane* would lose its memory and sense of self-identity, ending up as a ghost wandering in great confusion. The *unihipili*, meanwhile, would still recall its memories very well, but would become a different sort of ghost—feebleminded and behaving in an automatic and suggestible fashion.

It is interesting that today's two most commonly reported categories of ghosts seem to correspond with these two Hawaiian spirits. Poltergeists commonly display their free will, moving and throwing things around, but they are almost never seen visually, nor do they act out any scenes from their past;

---

*Reprinted from *The Secret Science Behind Miracles* by Max Freedom Long (1965). ISBN: 0875160476. DeVorss Publications: www.devorss.com

similarly, the *uhane* would still have its own independent free will, but no memory of its past, nor any self-image or sense of personal identity. Haunting ghosts, on the other hand, usually don't display independent free will, almost never moving or throwing things about, but they often display a self-image or other identifying characteristics, and frequently seem to be reviewing or reenacting scenes of their past memories, just as a *unihipili* might be expected to do.

Kahuna sorcerers claimed to be able to trap, manipulate, and control these separated *unihipili* souls, using them like invisible slaves to perform magic, commanding them to do their bidding much as a hypnotist controls the thoughts and actions of his or her subject. They could only do this to the *unihipili* souls, however, and not *uhanes*, because *uhane* souls still possessed free will, and so were not as suggestible. But the separated *unihipili* souls had no objective intelligence of their own, nor any independent willpower to resist. This made them the perfect hypnotic subjects, completely vulnerable to the commands of the Kahuna. As many as three enslaved *unihipilis* would be used at a time, being ordered to attach themselves to the *uhane* soul of the intended living victim. This would cause the *unihilipis* to sap the strength of the victim's *uhane* like invisible parasites. Those victims who were "prayed to death" in this way, it was said, reported a consistent symptomatology: a numbness would begin in their toes and move upwards, killing them as it reached their chest.

Persia's Version of the Binary Soul Doctrine

Zoroastrianism, the indigenous religion of Persia prior to the introduction of Islam, is yet another echo of mankind's early dualistic perspective. The Supreme Being, Ahura Mazda, was thought to have created two equal but opposite twin spirits who together ruled the world, Spenta Mainyu and Angra Mainyu. In much the same way, the soul of man was thought to have been designed with this same binary nature; the two parts of the soul were called the *urvan* and the *daena*, and just like the two primordial offspring of the original Creator, these two souls were thought of as twins.

Thought to exist before birth, the *urvan* survived death unharmed. It was conscious, active, and verbal, and was free to make its own independent choices and decisions. Meanwhile, the *daena* was, like Egypt's *ka*, also conceived of as the person's own image or self. Paralleling both the Egyptian *ka* and the Chinese *po*, Persia's *daena* was also thought to grow and develop over the course of one's life, being created or molded by the thoughts, words, and deeds of its *urvan*, becoming a mirror image of the person's earthly life. The *daena* contained the person's conscience, as well as a perfect memory of the person's life experience.

After wandering alone for three days after death, the *urvan* would again encounter its *daena*, in the form of a beautiful maiden[11] at a place called *Chinvat peretu*, the "Bridge of the Separator" which led to the Zoroastrian heaven. But the *urvan* could only cross this bridge if its *daena* did not convict it of unrighteousness. This encounter between the *urvan* and *daena* was critical; the nature of the afterdeath "conversation" of these two halves of the soul, when the *urvan* would find itself confronted by the full memory record carried within the *daena*, would determine the entire afterlife experience of the individual. Immortality required the successful reconciliation of the *urvan* and *daena* after death; if the *urvan* had been good and honest in life, it would pass through this judgment safely to live in heavenly bliss with its *daena*, but if not, it would fall into a gray, shadowy netherworld.

Judaism's Version of the Binary Soul Doctrine

At the time the Old Testament was being written, there seem to have been two primary soul concepts in the Jewish language. Ancient Israel held that people are comprised of two spiritual elements—a *ruah* and a *nefesh*. In the Hebrew text of the Old Testament, the word *nefesh* appears 451 times, being translated each time as "soul," and the word *ruah* appears 271 times, being translated each time as "spirit." The *ruah* was active, strong, conscious, intelligent, and communicated with words. It was immortal, pre-existing the person's birth and surviving his death unharmed, always "returning to God who gave it." But the *nefesh*, which embodied one's emotions, memories, and sense of self-identity, was vulnerable and could be greatly harmed by death, becoming trapped in a weak and feebleminded state in *She'ol*, a dark, underground, dreamlike netherworld.

A third concept also existed, but it was used far less often, and this rarely used term overlapped both those two primary concepts. The *neshamah*, which appears only three times in the Old Testament, is translated both as soul *and* spirit, suggesting that the ancient Hebrews may have seen this rarely mentioned soul element as the union of *nefesh* and *ruah*, paralleling their close neighbor Egypt's concept of the *akh* being the union of the *ba* and *ka* souls. Besides these three terms, no other Old Testament word is usually translated as soul or spirit.

More recent Judaic thought has raised the number of soul-elements to five; today's Kabbalistic teachings hold that people possess no less than five distinct souls, adding new concepts named *Hayyah* and *Yehidah*. Even so, these modern teachings still hold that death brings a soul-division, with the *nefesh* splitting away from the *ruah*.[12] Interestingly, although Christianity and Judaism both started out sharing this binary soul concept, they soon took opposite approaches. Judaism increased the number of their soul concepts from two to five, while Christianity reduced the number of their soul concepts from two to one, eventually thinking that soul and spirit were one and the same thing.

Christianity's Version of the Binary Soul Doctrine

By the time Christianity arrived on the scene, Greek ideas about a two-part soul comprised of *psuche* and *thumos* had saturated the Mediterranean area, and were the soil in which Christianity took root. And while most Christians today assume that the terms *soul* and *spirit* are synonyms, Christianity was originally in accord with Greek thought on this issue, distinguishing between these two parts of the self just as unequivocally as the rest of the Hellenized world. Further agreeing with the Greek model, one New Testament passage reveals that it was openly taught in the early days of the church that the soul and spirit were capable of dividing from each another:[13]

> The word of God is living and active
> and more powerful than any two-edged sword,
> and cuts so deeply it divides the soul from the spirit.
> —Hebrews 4:12

We can be fairly sure that the early Christian church continued to more or less openly subscribe to some form of the binary soul doctrine at least into the fourth century. While addressing the Apollinarius controversy during the Second Ecumenical Council of 381 A.D., the church again accepted and re-approved (albeit implicitly) the dogma that human beings are comprised of three parts: body, soul, and spirit.[14] However, when the Fourth Ecumenical Council rolled around 500 years later, the church made an explicit about-face on this point, bluntly declaring:

> Though the old and new Testament teach that a man or woman has one rational and intellectual soul, and all the fathers and doctors of the church, who are spokesmen of God, express the same opinion, some have descended to

such a depth of irreligion, through paying attention to the
speculations of evil people, that they shamelessly teach as a
dogma that a human being has two souls, and keep trying
to prove their heresy by irrational means using a wisdom
that has been made foolishness. Therefore this holy and universal synod is hastening to uproot this wicked theory now
growing like some loathsome form of weed.[15]

Perhaps without intending to, however, the above statement no less
bluntly declared that the binary soul doctrine (BSD) managed to survive
inside Christianity for eight full centuries, apparently finding the intellectual
culture of the church a consistently warm and nurturing home in which to
grow. Indeed, this doctrine was thriving in the church even as late as 869 A.D.,
having become so popular and widely accepted by that time that it seemed
to be *"growing like a weed."*

In addition, a number of modern archaeological discoveries have provided seemingly unimpeachable proof that the BSD played a more central
role in early Christianity than it does in today's church. The Gnostic Gospels,
a nearly 2000-year-old cache of lost and forgotten Christian scriptures
unearthed in 1945 in Nag Hammadi, Egypt, reveal that early church teachings[16] once credited supreme relevance to the distinction and interaction
between the soul and the spirit. These lost works return again and again to
the issue of division, mysteriously insisting that Jesus somehow divided into
two halves when He died on the cross (Gospel of Philip 68:26–29), that all
people are in danger of such a division (Gospel of Thomas 11), that the division of the soul and spirit was the origin of death (Exegesis on the Soul
133:4–9), and that "making the two one" is the key to achieving eternal life
(Gospel of Thomas 22). Yet another early Christian work, the Gospel of
Mary, was unearthed in 1896 after also having been lost for nearly 2000 years.
And again, just like the Nag Hammadi scriptures, the Gospel of Mary also
seems to reflect the binary soul doctrine:

Peter said to Mary: "Sister, we know that the Teacher
loved you differently from other women. Tell us whatever
you remember of any words he told you which we have not
yet heard." Mary said to them: "I will now speak to you of
that which has not been given to you to hear. I had a vision
of the Teacher, and I said to him: 'Lord, I see you now in this
vision.' And he answered: 'You are blessed, for the sight of

me does not disturb you. There where is the *nous*, lies the treasure.' Then I said to him: 'Lord, when someone meets you in a moment of vision, is it through the soul that they see, or is it through the spirit?' The Teacher answered: 'It is neither through the soul nor the spirit, but the *nous* between the two which sees the vision.'"[17]

Nous, of course, is the ancient Greek term often translated as "intellect" or "mind." Its use here clearly shows that at least one branch of early Christian anthropology included a BSD system of two primary souls with a third element in between them. This inclusion within the Gospel of Mary is especially important, for, when considered alongside similar passages found within the Nag Hammadi scriptures, it shows that the BSD was not a minor, little-known, or insignificant stream of thought within early Christian theology. One of the most disturbing criticisms of the Gnostic branch of the early church was that it had no clearly defined or agreed-upon theology, that its literature was just a hodgepodge of disconnected assertions, that anyone was free to make up anything he wished. But on the contrary, here we find that the same theme—the BSD—can be found in a number of different early Gnostic scriptures. It seems in fact to be a common thread that may have connected the whole movement.

Many now-unfamiliar gospels and scriptures were widely read and accepted as authentic in the early church. Although only four gospels ultimately made it into the approved canon of the Bible, far more than that were written by the early fathers of the church:

> Many have undertaken to compile a narrative of the things which have been accomplished among us, just as they were delivered to us by those who from the beginning were eyewitnesses and ministers of the word.
>
> —Luke 1:1–2

There were, in fact, two fairly distinct bodies of teachings circulating in early Christianity:

> And when he was alone, those who were about him with the twelve asked him concerning the parables. And he said to them, "To you has been given the secret of the kingdom of God, but for those outside everything is in parables;

so that they may indeed see but not perceive, and may indeed hear but not understand."

—Mark 4:10–12

Gnostic scriptures such as the Gospel of Thomas, the Gospel of Truth, the Gospel of Mary, and the Gospel of Philip were widely read, shared, circulated, approved, and honored by first-century Christians, and also by second- and even third-century Christians. Only in the fourth century, only when all first-hand eyewitnesses to Jesus' ministry had been dead and gone for more than 150 years, did the authorities of the church conclude that they knew better than those who had personally seen Jesus in the flesh, that they know better than the generation who had been taught by those eyewitnesses. And so, in the fourth century, the authorities of the church decided to condemn and destroy all Gnostic literature.[18]

Other Christian Versions of the Binary Soul Doctrine

The Mandaean religion, a small but still-living relative of early Christianity, believes even today that living people possess both soul and spirit, and that these two elements of the self split apart after death. A small religious sect in Iran and Iraq, the Mandaeans are also known as "The Christians of St. John," as Nasoraeans, and as Sabians. Their belief system resembles a mixture of Christian Gnosticism and Zoroastrianism, but the actual origin of the Mandaean faith is not fully known. It has been theorized that they came from a mountainous region north of Babylonia and Persia, but more recent scholarship places their origin in Palestine or Syria. Much like the ancient Egyptians once did, Mandaean priests still celebrate a ritual called the *masiqta* three days after burial, the aim of which is to reunite the person's soul and spirit in the afterlife, thus creating a new "Lightworld" body for the deceased that will allow him to live among the blessed dead.

Manichaeism, a once vigorous but now dead offshoot of early Christianity, also believed there were two distinct components to the human soul. The largest known sect of Gnosticism, Manichaeism spread out over most of the known world in the first millennium A.D., from Spain to China, but disappeared from the West in the tenth century, and from China in the fourteenth century, and today it is extinct. Dualism was central to Manichaean teaching, as was reincarnation. Salvation was effected via an inner knowledge, or "gnosis," although actual liberation was only thought to take place when a person with gnosis dies.

The *nous,* according to Manichaeism, was the half of the self that was immortal and invulnerable, while the *psuche* was the personal part of the self, which was extremely vulnerable and in immanent danger of being destroyed during the death transition. It was thought that a special emotional catharsis during life would unite the *psuche* with the *nous,* thereby saving it from destruction at death.

During the tenth to fifteenth centuries, yet another incarnation of Gnostic Christianity arose—Catharism. Occasionally called "The Pure Ones," the Cathar's message of love, tolerance, freedom, and equality between men and women was very deep, exacting, and hard to follow. This new "heresy" was, once again, based on a mixture of Christianity, reincarnation, and the BSD. Like the Egyptians, the Chinese, and so many others, the Cathars also believed both that the universe was comprised of two opposite primary forces, and that people possessed two entirely different spiritual components within themselves as well. Besides a physical body and a soul, the Cathars taught that everyone also possesses a spirit, which, they held, is always near God. Salvation in the Cathar religion meant the unification of one's soul and spirit, which would free the person from the need for further reincarnations. Salvation consisted of liberating the soul from the body prison, leaving the material world to come back to the Kingdom. But death alone was not the answer; this salvation was only available through a special baptism, which the Cathars believed to be the very same "Baptism of Fire and the Holy Spirit" mentioned by John the Baptist in the Bible.

For the Cathars there was thought to be no ultimate judgment where God would decide if one's soul should be sent for eternity to Paradise or Hell. On the contrary, they believed a soul could be saved only if it regained the knowledge (gnosis) of its divine nature; and only the baptism founded by Christ would allow man to reach this knowledge. The Cathars said they'd inherited their special baptism, and the knowledge it provided, directly from the Apostles, who in turn had received it from Christ Himself. It was directly transmitted person-to-person by the "laying on of hands." To witness such a baptism, the legends declare, was a remarkable and breathtaking event. This baptism, the Consolamentum, was believed to produce a permanent union between the soul imprisoned in the body and its spirit, which remained in Heaven. Without that baptism, the soul would just end up passing back into another physical body after death.

Unfortunately, Pope Alexander III pronounced the Cathars to be anathema in 1179 (in other words, burnable). What followed became Europe's first instance of genocide. The Cathars had been centered in Gascony and

Provence in France, but since this "heresy" was first discovered by the Catholic church in the county of Albi, the church referred to all the Cathars simply as "Albigenses," and the subsequent campaign to wipe them out has come to be known as the Albigensian Crusade. Not a war, but a massacre, it began at Minerve in 1210 with the burning alive of 140 Cathars at a huge stake, 140 people who never raised a single sword to defend themselves. The Catholic Church continued this war, on and off, for many years, continuing to burn Cathars until 1321. To the student of the BSD, this ancient atrocity is particularly distressing; with the death of the last Cathar, a primary path to achieving the union of soul and spirit might well have vanished from the earth altogether. Did that direct line transmission of Jesus' own "Baptism of Fire and the Holy Spirit" come to an end in fifteenth-century France, or has some remnant of it survived, still being handed down from one generation to the next?

Albeit without any "Baptism of Fire and the Holy Spirit," the binary soul doctrine was reintroduced yet again to mainstream Christian theology in the 1750s, when Emanuel Swedenborg founded the "New Church." Swedenborg taught that each person's spirit is composed of two distinct components that split apart from each other at death. After this division, they maintain, the soul's "inward element" goes on to experience an eternally unchanging afterlife in heaven or hell, while the "outer element" falls into a permanently dormant state, never to be heard from, felt, or seen again.

About a century later, the Jehovah's Witnesses emerged as yet another Christian denomination that distinguishes between the soul and spirit, believing that at death, the spirit returns to God, while the soul, or "personal self," entirely ceases to exist until it is recreated at Judgment Day.

Islam's Version of the Binary Soul Doctrine

Ancient Islam called these two souls the *ruh* and the *nafs* (notice the linguistic similarity to Israel's *ruah* and *nefesh*). Like modern Judaism and Christianity, most people in Islam today also assume that these are synonyms, just two different terms for the same thing—a singular, nonbinary human soul. But the binary soul doctrine also has its share of supporters in Islam, who maintain that these terms originally referred to two very distinct elements within the human constitution.

Like Israel's *ruah*, the *ruh*, or "soul," carried the life force, the free will, the rational intellect, and the ability to communicate. The *ruh* was thought to be essential for life; when it departed the body, the body became a corpse.

And like Israel's *nefesh*, the *nafs*, the "self" or "ego," was associated with one's feelings, needs, desires, instincts, personality, and sense of identity. People, it was thought, are born without a *nafs*, which was thought to grow and develop as life progressed, in response to one's personal subjective experiences and choices in life. The *nafs* is often compared to a blank canvas given at the start of life, upon which one paints a picture of her life, beautiful or ugly, depending on one's choices and environment. The *nafs*, then, seems to contain, or be molded into, a record of one's experiences in life, a record of one's memories. The *nafs* also contains one's moral sense; it distinguishes between right and wrong, it can be pleased or displeased with its owner, it can be self-accusing, and it can act as a watchdog over the person's behavior in life.

Thought of as an intertwined pair of opposites, the *ruh* and the *nafs* are said to be naturally engaged in a battle for the possession and control of their common child, the heart. Mohammed felt that the *nafs* is a person's greatest enemy. Islam teaches that one should surrender one's sense of personal self, or *nafs*, and that an objective, nonattached approach to life is needed to accomplish this. It is taught that the *nafs* is unruly, emotional, desirous, and animalistic, and must be conquered like an enemy by the *ruh*. These two are thought to be in a constant war in life; an equal balance between them is not thought to be possible. Either the *ruh* will control and dominate the *nafs*, or vice versa. Those who fight their own *nafs*, trying to control its egotism and passions, are said to be fighting the "greater Jihad."

The *ruh* is believed to be an immortal soul that never dies, but at least some *nafs*, the scriptures declare, *will* taste death. Thus, it seems, these two elements may be able to divide from each other after death. When death comes to the *nafs*, the body returns to Earth and the *ruh* returns to Allah. But the *nafs* of those who sacrifice themselves for Allah, it is said, will never die.

Voodoo's Version of the Binary Soul Doctrine

Although the Caribbean religion known as Voodoo blends Christianity with traditional African religions, it still seems to display the ideas of early Egypt. Voodoo pictures the soul as being comprised of two distinct parts, the *gros bon ange*, or "big good angel," and the *ti bon ange*, or "little good angel." The *ti bon ange* is one's individual soul and contains all one's personal characteristics, personal experience, and personality. The *gros bon ange*, thought to enter the human body during conception, carries the spark of life, vitality, intelligence, and animating drive of the person. If it leaves the body, the body ceases functioning and dies, but if the *ti bon ange* leaves the body during life, the *gros bon ange* just becomes sluggish, and the person is now a living body without a subjective personality, a zombie, one of the walking dead.

When a person dies, both the *gros bon ange* and the *ti bon ange* continue to exist and function, but they divide from each other. A ritual known as *dessounin* is performed by the Voodoo priest to separate the *gros bon ange* from the body while keeping the *ti bon ange* with the corpse in the grave. Otherwise, it is thought, the *ti bon ange* might become a ghost that could roam and cause harm to the living. For a period of time after death, the *ti bon ange* is thought to be extremely vulnerable, but the *gros bon ange* is never vulnerable.

Tribal Versions of the Binary Soul Doctrine

The belief in a dividing binary soul is also found in many primitive cultures across Eurasia. The two souls of Asia's Tunguz tribe is a typical example, in which the *beye* soul is free and independent after death, returning to heaven to wait until it reincarnates again, while the *hanan*, or shadow soul, becomes eternally imprisoned in an dark netherworld.

The Khanty and Mansi of Siberia also believe in a binary soul system. One soul, the *lili*, is associated with the breath, the head, and the handling of raw intellectual data, while the *is*, or shadow soul, is related to a person's emotions and is particularly active during sleep. Like the Egyptian *ba*, the symbol for the breath soul is a bird, while the shadow soul is usually depicted as having the form of a human, just as did the Egyptian *ka*. The *lili* soul is thought to be reincarnated in one's own kin after death, while the *is* soul would either depart for a realm of the dead, or remain behind on earth as a shadowy ghost. This binary conception of the self is apparently part of a wider dualistic philosophy, since the social organization of the Khanty and Mansi is also based on a dual moiety system: half the society is designated *mos*, the other half, *por*.

The Saami, a subpolar people whose descendants now live in Norway, Sweden, Finland, and Russia, also subscribed to a binary soul doctrine prior to their introduction to Christianity. Besides the corporeal soul, which could not leave the body without causing the person's death, everyone also had a free soul, which could manifest outside the body and was thought of as the person's double. It was thought possible for malicious beings to capture a person's free soul, which would cause sickness and death. If the problem was caught in time, however, the tribe's shaman could undertake a spiritual journey into the realm of the dead to negotiate for the release of the afflicted person's free soul.

The Lost Secret of Death

Many Australian aboriginal tribes still believe that people possess two souls which divide at death. The true self, which pre-exists the person's birth, comes from a timeless, primordial, heavenly realm called *Alcheringa*, or "The Dreaming," and returns there after death.

> Australian Aborigines distinguish between our every-day experience and what they call the dreaming. The Dreaming is another level of experience, in which they participate in the life of their ancestors, and indeed the creation of the world, in I suppose we might call it a trancelike state, but that doesn't quite do it, because even in the midst of their ordinary life, half of their mind, you might say, is still on or in this dreaming state. . . . I was in Australia, basically giving a series of lectures at all the universities there, but using my spare time to come in touch with the aborigines, and so I sought out at every university the anthropologists who introduced me and put me in touch with them. And I did not in that entire swing meet an anthropologist who was not convinced that the aborigines had telepathic powers. They simply told me story after story, when they would be with them, and suddenly one of the persons would say, "I must go back to the tribe; so and so has died."
>
> —Huston Smith, Ph. D.[19]

The other soul, meanwhile, separates from that self after death, remaining behind on earth to take up residence in another human body. Mirroring this belief in double souls, the practice of double funerals are very common in Australia, just as they once were all throughout the ancient Middle East. Most religious efforts of the Australian aborigines revolve around trying to re-establish contact with and re-enter the sacred Dreamtime.

Situated in Australia's Northern Territory, the Walbiri (or Warlpiri) tribe held to a textbook example of the binary soul doctrine:

> Although Walbiri notions of the transmigration of Dreaming or spirit essences implied a kind of reincarnation after death, the process was wholly impersonal. People did not believe that the human person survived the destruction of the body unchanged. Rather, they took death to mark the end of the previously coherent person-

ality of the individual, which then disintegrated into its spiritual components. The Dreaming elements returned to their spirit homes, and the matrispirit [the second soul] dissipated completely. In consequence, the Walbiri did not regard with equanimity the inevitability of their own or their relatives' deaths. There was instead an elaborate complex of mortuary behavior. . . .[20]

The belief in a binary soul is also a common feature of African religions. Two souls often consist of one part which lives forever, and a shadow which only lives for an uncertain length of time after death, hovering around the mortal remains. The ancient culture known as Kush, located in what is now Ethiopia, believed in the *ba* and *ka* souls of Egypt, and preserved the bodies of their leaders in pyramidal tombs, believing this necessary to ensure the survival of the *ka*. Africa's present-day Mossi tribe believe that human beings have one masculine and one feminine soul, and that death divides these two. The Samo tribe calls their two souls the *ri* and the *mere*. The *ri* soul contains the person's thought and life force, reincarnating after death, while the *mere* soul, thought of as a perfect double of the person, becomes permanently trapped in a netherworld when it experiences a second death sometime after leaving the body. The Ba-Huana tribe credits human beings with two souls, the *bun* and *doshi*. The *bun* is the soul, or self, and survives death unharmed, while the *doshi* is a shadowy second self, or double, that tends to linger around on earth after death, haunting its enemies and persecuting its own relations if a proper burial is not made.

The binary soul doctrine also used to be very widespread in the Americas. Tribes from South America to Alaska believed in a corporeal soul that gave life, consciousness, and the faculty of movement, and a free soul that would find itself trapped in some realm of the dead after death. The corporeal soul provided the life force, and could not exit the body without causing the death of the individual. The free soul often left the body during life, in times such as during dreams, trances, and mystical experiences.

The Inuit (Eskimo) of Canada and Greenland believed in two souls; the *inua* held the life force and reincarnated into a new body after death, while the *tarnneg*, or double of the person, became a permanent occupant of the realm of the dead.

North America's Dakota Tribe called their two souls the *nagi* and the *niya*. The *nagi* soul held the power of movement and independent free will, and after death, it could either join the world of the spirits, or be forced to wander aimlessly. The *niya* soul, thought to contain one's conscience and memory, helped the person to relate to and interact with others. After death, the *niya* was thought to testify against the other soul in a great judgment after death, much like Persia's *daena* and Egypt's *ka*.

Deep in the rain forests of the northwest Amazon, the Maku tribe still sub-scribes to the binary soul doctrine. They believe that the world is composed of two equal but opposite fundamental forces, the hot force and the cold force. Like the Chinese yin and yang, they must always be kept balanced, or else health and prosperity will suffer. These hot and cold forces are also the basic components of human beings; we all possess one hot soul, or *baktup*, the Maku declare, and one cold soul, or *bowugn*. When we die, these two divide; the *baktup* soul becomes something akin to a ghost, hanging around and frightening people, while the *bowugn* soul shrivels up into a little ball and flies away to heaven.

Buddhism's Version of the Binary Soul Doctrine

Known today as the Pli cult, the pre-Buddhist religion of Southeast Asia recognized the existence of multiple souls, believing that they could and often did separate from each other, a tragedy which resulted in sickness or death. This belief system emphasized the need to maintain the unity of those souls, thereby preserving the integrity of the person they comprised. This belief system paved the way for Southeast Asia's acceptance of Buddhism, which also assumed that the personal self was comprised of a number of dis-tinct elements. But in sharp contrast to Thailand's early Pli religion, Buddhism insisted that the eventual disunion of these elements was inevitable.

Buddhism teaches reincarnation, but denies the existence of the soul, leaving one wondering what is being reborn. "Is it me or isn't it?" its students ask. "Is death total nonexistence, or do I survive in some sense? Most impor-tantly—do I survive as 'me'?" Buddhism maintains that the thing being reborn from one life to the next is "not the same, not different," which is pre-cisely what the ancient binary soul doctrine maintained; if a person survives death in a divided state, all his nonphysical components would still exist, but the "self" the union of the two parts had formed would no longer exist, at least not in any functional sense. What would remain after death would indeed be "not the same, not different."

It is often stated that Buddhism denies the existence of any permanent soul, but the truth of the matter is that Buddhism's conception of the self is not all that different from the binary soul doctrine. In the *Dhammapada*,

Buddha plainly speaks of the existence of two selves within each human being: One makes the transition from one life to the next, the other does not. Buddhist teachers often liken rebirth to a pure and unqualified consciousness passed from one life to the next like a flame passed from one candle to another. This is precisely what the binary soul doctrine suggests, that the conscious spirit, stripped of the unconscious with all its memories and feelings, is what reincarnates, nothing but an eternally open, conscious, living eye stripped of everything but awareness itself. This spark of consciousness is considered permanent and unending in Buddhism; the Dalai Lama said "Even in Nirvana, the continuum of consciousness goes on."

The Mahayana school of Buddhism teaches that another component exists, namely a subtle mind (*alayavijnana*) which receives and stores one's impressions of the past (memory and reactions to the past), from which proceeds one's subjective experience of existence. This element is virtually identical to the unconscious soul of the binary soul doctrine.

Traditional Buddhism recognizes five constituents, or *skandhas*, which make up a person: form, feelings, perceptions, volition, and consciousness. None of those, by itself, is anything we can recognize as the self, which leads Buddhists to conclude that there isn't any self at all, only these pieces. But these *skandhas* match up perfectly with the ancient world's three-part model of a human being; Buddhism's form, feelings, and perception are all functions of the unconscious soul, while volition and consciousness are functions of the conscious spirit. When they are all united, these five create the illusion of the existence of a self, but that's all it is, Buddhist thought insists, an illusion.

The ancient binary soul doctrine argues that the self, or ego, is the product of the interplay of conscious spirit and unconscious soul; when separated, they have no "fruit." Separated, there is no sense of self, no functional self at all. But the cultures of the ancient world that subscribed to the binary soul doctrine did not see this as a denial of the reality of the self; they realized that the forest and the trees *both* exist. Just because a whole was made up of parts did not refute the reality and existence of that whole.

Buddhism teaches, just as the binary soul doctrine once did, that the multiple components of the self divide from each other at death. The major difference between the two views is that Buddhism insists that these components can *never* recombine again to reconstitute that self. Consciousness alone, but no self, is transmitted from life to life. Of course, Buddhism acknowledges that, in addition to consciousness, memories of past lives are transmitted, since Buddha himself was reported to have recalled his own past lives. Such memories indicate that there *is* "something more" than pure unqualified consciousness being transmitted, that memory is also making the jump. And with the transfer of memory, all sorts of subjective personal material—feelings, emotions, likes and dislikes—make the jump as well.

Both consciousness and memory, it seems, are transferred from one body to another during rebirth, but in a divided state that apparently shatters, or at least temporarily dismantles, the self-aware ego between one life and the next. Yet so long as all the original pieces still exist, that self from an earlier lifetime could conceivably be reassembled, made to exist again, by recombining its pieces. Buddhist doctrine insists that no ego survives death, but ancient Egyptian belief would have argued that the self does survive, albeit in a temporarily disassembled state. If the pieces that made up the self were never reconnected after death, then Buddhist doctrine would be right, there would indeed be no permanent self, no eternal soul.

But if it remains possible for them to reunite? . . .

Reincarnation and the Binary Soul Doctrine

Many of the cultures around the world that subscribed to the binary soul doctrine were convinced that the conscious or objective half of the soul would reincarnate after death. Reincarnation also played a part in Egypt's belief system. Pythagoras, who is credited with introducing the concept of reincarnation into Greek thought, did so after studying it in Egypt, according to the Greek historian Herodotus (fifth century B.C.). The "*ka*-names" of three Egyptian Pharaohs also reflect a belief in rebirth: the *ka*-name of Amonemhat I was "He Who Repeats Births"; the *ka*-name of Senusert I meant "He Whose Births Live"; and the *ka*-name of Setekhy I was "Repeater of Births." Pharaohs sometimes claimed to have more than one *ka*, claiming, in effect, to possess multiple selves, identities, personalities, and so on; this suggests that these ancient Pharaohs claimed, just as holy men of the East do today, that they remembered their past lives and identities.

In what some believe to be the oldest Egyptian scripture dealing with the afterdeath realm, the Book of the Two Ways, the deceased comes to a fork in the road that presents two different paths. Both paths, the text declares, ultimately lead to the same destination—the abode of the gods—but each takes a different route and involves different experiences along the way. The longer path that passed over land, "The Cyclic Route of Osiris," took far more time, involving many cycles, or incarnations, while the shorter path called "The Route of Horus" required one to pass through fire, but was a far more direct passage to "life with the gods."

Some elements of the "Opening of the Mouth" funerary prayer in the Egyptian Book of the Dead are, curiously, suggestive of reincarnation. The priest performing the ritual plays the role of Horus, while the deceased is given the role of Osiris, Horus's father and predecessor. In this ritual, the priest addresses the deceased, saying "I have come to embrace thee, I am thy son Horus," and thereupon opens the mouth and eyes of the deceased. After opening the mouth and eyes of the deceased, the priest playing Horus says "I have established for you your two jaw-bones in your face which was divided into two parts."[21]

This scene would make more sense if it were a person trying to reawaken his own past-life self. One's past-life "face," or subjective-self identity, would indeed have been "divided into two parts" when the *ba* and *ka* split off from each other. If Osiris represented one's previous generation or incarnation, and Horus represented the person's current incarnation, the father/son relationship between Osiris and Horus in this ritual would be meaningful, especially if the current incarnation, Horus, was trying to reawaken, or bring back to life, his own previous-life self, "opening the eyes and mouth" of his own dead predecessor-self.

In the original legend of the death and resurrection of Osiris, after the divided parts of his being had been gathered and assembled, one more task still needed to be accomplished before Osiris was able to return to conscious life. Osiris's son Horus had to pluck an eye from his own face and give it to Osiris to eat. The return of Osiris to life, then, is *twice* associated with his son Horus. In the original legend, Horus aids his father by giving him his own eye to consume, and in the funerary rituals, Horus is specifically the one who personally "opens the eyes and mouth" of his father, and he accomplishes this by "embracing" Osiris in some fashion.

If Horus originally represented the reincarnated "next generation" of the same person, then the idea of Horus giving one of his eyes to his father Osiris to eat would be a simple and elegant metaphor for the reincarnated present self giving part of his conscious awareness to his past-life self, thus allowing his present-life self to share consciousness with, or "embrace" his past-life self, integrating the two just as the mind integrates vision from the two eyes in the head into a single visual image.

But if this ritual was originally meant to be used to reawaken one's past-life memories, how did it end up being used as a funerary prayer? Just how old *is* this ritual? No one knows. When this ritual first appears in the archaeological record, it was, even then, an extremely ancient artifact from a much earlier period.

In this first chapter, we have seen that dozens of cultures all over the globe, including virtually all the great civilizations of the ancient world, once believed in the binary soul doctrine. However, as amazing and unexpected as such a discovery might seem, it would remain little more than a curious coincidence if not for the fact that modern science seems to be arriving at many of those same conclusions all over again. Over the last century, science has not only reconfirmed mankind's ancient intuition that our mental beings come ready made with a fundamental binary structure, but is even describing the mind's two components the same way the ancients did, with identical functions and characteristics. What's more, the ancient teachings about these two souls dividing apart after death also finds some support from modern science. While our bodies are alive and healthy, the two communicate so intimately with each other they seem to form an indivisible singularity, but if the tiny piece of flesh uniting them, the corpus callosum, is severed or taken away, these two minds then function completely independently of each other—just as the ancients insisted they did at death, when the flesh is taken away altogether.

As we explore this modern re-emergence of the BSD in the next chapter, we will see how today's scientific findings substantiate, clarify, and expand upon the mysterious reports of the ancients, even reconciling reports long thought to be mutually exclusive. Modern science, as it turns out, is the very lens needed to bring those reports into sharp focus, showing their message to be just as modern, relevant, and urgent today as it was thousands of years ago.

2

Two Selves in Every Brain: Modern Science's Binary Soul Doctrine

I believe we have two minds, one associated with each
  hemisphere. . . .
The dichotomy of mind . . . is entirely normal—it is, in fact,
  the way we humans are made.
—*Harvard Professor and Psychiatrist Frederick Schiffer, MD*[1]

When the ancient Egyptians spoke of the *ba* and *ka*, it was, perhaps, only a belief. When the early Christians wrote of the soul and spirit, it was probably still a belief. When folk cultures everywhere referred to the head and the heart, when astrologers discussed the sun and moon in a person's chart, even when Freud and Jung described the conscious and unconscious, it was, at least arguably, only a matter of belief. But no more. Finally, in our age, we have moved from shaky faith to solid and secure knowledge on this issue.

Sigmund Freud and Carl Jung first introduced psychology's binary-mind hypothesis in the early 1900s, and while it was reluctantly accepted as valid by the scientific community for many decades, it was increasingly dismissed by later theorists, until, by the end of the 1970s, it was on the verge of being unceremoniously discarded by modern scholarship. But then neuropsychology came along and provided substantiating objective evidence for what had previously been a purely subjective hypothesis. After applying the most rigorous tests possible, modern man has again arrived at the conclusion that we are two-part creatures, that two entirely separate and distinct minds co-exist in the brain, one in the right hemisphere, one in the left. This conclusion was first made public in the 1981 split-brain study *Left Brain, Right Brain* by Sally Springer and Georg Deutsch, but neuropsychological studies since then have continued to support those conclusions. In his 1998 work, *Of Two Minds*, Harvard professor of psychiatry Frederick Schiffer wrote that "Ordinary people have two autonomous minds, each associated with one hemisphere,"[2] and:

> . . . we have discovered two intact minds in split-brain research and in psychology [and] we have found that in both cases, the two minds seem to interact in similar ways. . . . A number of authors . . . have turned to the split-brain studies to advance the notion that the right hemisphere is the site of the Freudian unconscious.[3]

Incredibly, the ancient religious concept that we all possess head and heart, soul and spirit, was reintroduced twice by science over the last century. Just when the world was about to forget about the binary soul doctrine, Freud and Jung gave it a new lease on life with a soft science, analytical psychology. And just when psychology was about to abandon the Freudian model, a hard science called neuropsychology came along to reinforce this binary model all over again. In every case, the two components were the same: One was conscious, objective, rational, masculine, and held exclusive access to the free-will decision-making ability; the other was unconscious or only semi-conscious, subjective, emotional, feminine, and held exclusive access to the memory. It almost seems as if, after science struggled to climb to the top of the mountain, in the end it found religion sitting there already, having patiently waited thousands of years for it to catch up.

The only question is not why the world keeps rediscovering these two, but why we keep turning away from the insight. Despite modern science's reconfirmations of the binary model of the psyche, many today still question if such a thing as this mysterious and invisible unconscious half of the psyche really exists. Yet, the evidence could not be closer.

Who has not awoken suddenly from a vivid and deeply involving dream only to find that, in that brief transition, their own mental wall came crashing down, removing them from the dream and blocking out all memory of it as well, leaving only the nagging suspicion that something which had a second ago been extremely important to them could no longer be guessed? Who has not felt the urgent rush of love, unbidden but irrepressible, rise up within from the unknown source of all feelings? Who has not had his own unconscious "buttons" pushed, turning him in one moment from a seemingly rational and objective figure into a wild and irrational creature of blind instinct?

Why do we keep questioning, denying, and ignoring the existence of the unconscious? Perhaps because it is frightening to admit that a part of our minds is unknown to us, a part we cannot control, a part which sometimes seems to control *us*. Yet, every time we say to ourselves, "Oh for crying out loud—what on earth made me do that?!" we realize that this other half of ourselves is still a force in our lives.

Split-Brain Research

Scientific research over the last twenty years indicates that each side of the brain is home to a separate and distinct mind, each of which has a different nature and function. It is possible to experience one's two minds separately; in his book, Dr. Schiffer relates an experiment anyone can do which confirms that we have two distinct minds. Dr. Schiffer covers the right eye of subjects and then interviews them about their personal lives and outlooks. Changing the covering to the other eye, he repeats the same interview. While not all subjects' responses betrayed a striking difference in outlook from one eye to the next, the majority did. When looking through the right eye (which stimulates the left brain), subjects' responses were more anxious and self-critical; through the left eye (stimulating the right brain), their responses were more happy and indicated comfort.

The Division of Labor

Modern science has not merely rediscovered humanity's two souls, but has greatly added to the scant information about them that had managed to trickle down to us through history. What modern science has added to our knowledge about the nature of the conscious and unconscious seems to explain a great deal about the afterlife traditions of the ancients and the reports of today's afterlife researchers.

The two halves of the mind see the world differently. They can both observe the same photograph and come away with radically different descriptions. The conscious and unconscious each act as filters, coloring and

interpreting the person's thoughts, data, insights, and perceptions in different ways. Each is blind and deaf and crippled without the other; by itself,
each gets only half the story.

Classic psychology has long held that the conscious and unconscious are
opposites in many respects. The conscious is active, while the unconscious is
reactive and responsive; the conscious seems to exercise autonomous free
will, functioning under its own initiative and volition, while the unconscious
functions automatically and instinctively; the conscious is objective while the
unconscious is subjective; the conscious is intellectual when the unconscious
is emotional.

Recently, neuropsychology has added depth to our understanding of
these dynamics, teaching that the left-brain conscious mind is verbally
oriented while the right-brain unconscious is nonverbal, thinking and com-
municating instead via images, symbols, pictures, gestures, and metaphors.
The left-brain conscious mind sees the differences and distinctions between
things, while the right-brain unconscious is geared to see the connections,
relationships, and similarities between things. The conscious sees the trees,
the unconscious sees the forest; the conscious reads the text, the unconscious perceives the context; the conscious notices the details, the unconscious grasps the meaning.

This division of labor seems to explain why the ancients insisted that *only
one* of their two souls possessed free will. Blind to the differences between
things, the unconscious does not realize the existence of choices, options,
and alternatives. Unable to realize the existence of choices, options, and
alternatives, the unconscious cannot choose one thing and reject another; it
has no word for "no." Unable to choose or decide, the unconscious cannot
exercise self-determination. Unable to exercise self-determination, the
unconscious lacks autonomous free will. The unconscious lacks autonomous
free will; it is like a machine running on automatic.

Dancing Partners

Remarkably like the yin and yang of classic Chinese philosophy, the conscious and unconscious seem to closely embrace in an ecstatic yet subtle dance.
The conscious always leads in this dance, doing so by making new choices and
decisions. Whenever the conscious mind initiates a move, the unconscious
responds. Whenever the conscious mind chooses or acts, the unconscious
mind reacts immediately in the form of feelings, impressions, connections,
associated ideas, and insights, that are then released into the conscious mind.

These two halves of the psyche remain bound together during life. They are always dancing in unison, and although one or the other may seem to have the upper hand from time to time, both are always involved in our experience at any given moment. Thus, when the conscious mind seems to have full control, such as when one is most fully awake and involved in logical thought calculations, the unconscious is still there in the background, still coproducing the mental experience. In the same way, when one is asleep and dreaming, and the unconscious seems to be fully in charge, the conscious mind still assists in generating one's dream experience.

The conscious and unconscious are so tightly intertwined in this dance, they give the illusion of being a single unit. Just as one's left and right eyes produce two separate and distinct visual images which are then integrated in the mind into a single vision, so the two halves of the psyche are so intimately integrated together in one's mental experience that they also seem to be a single unit, a single self. This explains why people commonly rebel against the binary soul model. This illusion of singularity is so persuasive that it has taken our most sophisticated scientific research to penetrate and expose the fact that it is not the truth of things.

Neither of the visual images the two eyes send to the brain contains three-dimensional depth perception. On its own, each is a flat, two-dimensional image. But the brain combines these two into a new thing that never existed before: a superior visual experience containing three-dimensional data. Our three-dimensional visual universe is the product of the integration of these two flat images, and it seems greater than the sum of its parts. In much the same way, each of the halves of consciousness is severely limited and inadequate, but when they function together, they produce something almost magical, something that never existed before, the fullness of human consciousness, a self-aware individual.

Wholeness vs. Partness in the Human Psyche

Most things are wholes unto themselves but also parts of other, larger wholes. Arthur Koestler came up with the word "holon" to refer to this dual nature. Individual atoms, for example, are autonomous wholes that are at the same time parts of other wholes—molecules—which are themselves parts of cells, which are parts of organs which are parts of creatures which are parts of families, and so on. These two different natures, wholeness and partness, are always in a state of dynamic, balanced conflict: one nature is concerned with preserving the holon's sense of wholeness (its independent distinctness and autonomy), while the other nature is concerned with preserving the holon's sense of "partness" (its interdependent, integral relationship to the world around it).

This functional dichotomy is reflected in the two halves of the psyche. The left-brain conscious mind is wholeness-oriented while the right-brain unconscious mind is partness-oriented. The conscious mind tends to recognize the distinctions and differences between things. The conscious mind tends to view itself as independent, separate, and autonomous, a complete whole unto itself. The unconscious, on the other hand, seems to always focus on the similarities and relationships among things, always carrying the implicit assumption that "I am interconnected with all else—I am a part of everything I see, and everything I see is a part of me."

It seems that the two natures of holons have manifested in the human psyche as two distinct spheres of consciousness; like everything else, it seems, the human mind is also a holon. Every holon, Koestler realized, is equally dependent on its wholeness and its partness for its continued survival. If a holon lost either its distinct autonomy (its wholeness) or its integral relationship with its environment (its partness), he warned, it would cease to exist. This has sobering implications for the dividing-soul doctrines of the ancients.

Form vs. Substance in the Human Psyche

Ancient Egypt credited the *ka*, or unconscious soul, with the ability to assume different forms, and the nature of the unconscious seems to explain this, as the unconscious excels at form-recognition. Because the unconscious is designed to recognize the connections, relationships, and similarities among things, one of its jobs is to recognize meaningful patterns within data. In other words, it seems to be the half of the mind that discerns form. The neuropsychological studies of the last thirty years show that the right-brain unconscious is far more adept at recognizing patterns, forms, connections, and relationships than the left-brain conscious. Thus, the classic philosophical dichotomy between form and substance seems to be embodied within the distinctions between the conscious and unconscious. The conscious is like an eye that only recognizes substance, the unconscious, an eye that only recognizes form.

The unconscious is receptivity itself; it receives, takes in, and stores as memory all the input it receives from the conscious mind. This makes it a perfect memory-machine, forming itself into a flawless record of all the person's experiences, both internal and external, all her memories, thoughts, deeds, impressions, convictions, desires, dreams, hopes, loves, hates, etc. In this, it is easy to see a possible origin for the curious fact that so many cultures specifically described the unconscious-like soul as being a perfect double of the individual.

Choice + Memory = Conscience

Many of mankind's early belief systems maintained that the unconscious-like soul contained (or produced) the conscience, an innate moral sense of right and wrong. The combination of two of the unconscious's chief characteristics—responsiveness and memory—seems to explain this connection. Like a mirror, the unconscious forces a part of us to always be looking back upon ourselves and our own past thoughts. Whenever the conscious mind makes any new choice or decision, the unconscious automatically responds by looking for relationships, patterns, and connections with what came before. Comparing that latest choice with the gestalt of that person's memories, the unconscious automatically evaluates the current decision in light of all one's previous thoughts, attitudes, impressions, perceptions, decisions, and conclusions on the matter.

The unconscious records all our decisions and conclusions, treating them as commands to be followed, carrying them out like a computer carries out its programming, or like a hypnotized person carries out the commands he or she is given. Thus, if the unconscious contains a memory that the person decided that "this is bad," then if at any later point the person does that "bad" thing, the unconscious will compare the present act and the previous judgment, and then release appropriate psychological material, i.e., bad or guilty feelings. Like a mirror, the unconscious always responds in kind, good for good, bad for bad.

This conscience function of the unconscious deceives many into assuming that the unconscious is actively judging our actions and decisions in life. In reality, the unconscious, throughout the process, functions automatically, without will or intent. Instead of our unconscious judging us, it seems, it is the conscious mind that makes the crucial judgments; the unconscious simply reminds us of them later on.

As we will see, this conscience function seems to be directly responsible for the intense "judgment" experience that so many have reported during NDEs, as well as the heavenly or hellish experiences that often follow.

Does the Mind Survive Death?

Although modern science has (re)discovered the existence of the conscious and unconscious minds, we still don't know what these are, or even *where* they are. Science has not yet fully defined the nature of the two halves of the psyche. Perhaps it never will; if, as the ancients seemed to have believed, these two inner components of the self are each divine and therefore infinite, they could arguably never be fully defined. However, while science cannot claim to know everything about them, it has at least been able to flesh out a few salient details, and these are perfect matches with humanity's binary soul doctrine, as well as our most common afterlife reports.

Of course, many today bluster that the conscious and unconscious are not infinite or immortal at all, but are simply physical phenomena produced by the physical brain, and they will cease to exist the instant the brain ceases to function. But in reality, it remains an open question in science whether or not the mind is produced by the brain, or whether the brain functions like a radio receiver.[4] Since this uncertainty remains, and the mind has not been clearly shown to be produced by brain function, it is justified to ask "How would the mind work if it continued to exist after the body died?," and to answer, "according to the same laws it did before."

In and of itself, the simple act of dying, merely leaving the body, would not necessarily seem to produce any changes in the laws governing the way the mind functions. Obviously, there might be some additional bit of crucial knowledge we are missing, which, if we had it, would allow us to see instantly that death *would* change the laws of how the mind functions. But as it stands today, are we not bound to assume that the operational running of the conscious and unconscious would follow the same laws they do now? If so, then after death the conscious would still possess free will and intellect, but not emotion or memory, while the unconscious would still possess memory and emotion but not free will or intellect.

One thing we do know about the way the psyche functions is that the two halves of the mind can only communicate and interact with each other through a tiny bit of flesh connecting the two hemispheres of the brain, a mass of nerves called the corpus callosum. Their partnership is dependent on this fragile connection. When this bit of flesh is severed, as has been observed in many split-brain studies over the last few decades, the two halves of the psyche still continue to function, but now do so independently of each other. Without that bit of flesh, their partnership is destroyed, and each is then forced to continue on alone, functioning as best it can without any further input from its partner. From that moment on, in split-brain patients, there is no longer just one person living in that human body, but two, neither of which can see, feel, or communicate with the other.

In death, of course, that bit of flesh would no longer be there.

When things die, they deteriorate, breaking down into their constituent components. Systems break down, then tissues, then cells. Perhaps the mind does as well, as so many ancient cultures believed. Perhaps this explains why so many religions still focus so strongly on the importance of integrity, of forging oneself into a solid integrated wholeness. If the union between the two halves of the psyche is dependent on the corpus callosum, as modern neuropsychology has seemed to prove, and if, as religions all over the world have insisted, and as modern science has (so far at least) not been able to disprove, the two halves of the psyche are *not* products of the physical brain, then at death, the two halves of the psyche would indeed seem to be in danger of being disconnected from each other, just like in the split-brain experiments—and just like the binary soul doctrine.

If the Mind Splits at Death?

If the two parts of the human psyche each survived physical death, but divided from each other in the process, what would happen? Where would they be? What would each experience? This doesn't seem so hard to figure out; each would lose what the other half gave it, and would be forced to rely exclusively on its own capacities.

When people died, their minds would divide into two partial, semi-human fragments. Both parts would still possess awareness of a sort, but vastly different kinds, and neither would enjoy the volitional self-awareness that we possess during life. In life, it is the *interaction between* the conscious and the unconscious, the objective and the subjective, that provides us with this self-awareness, that allows us to turn our attention back upon ourselves, to see ourselves and realize that we are conscious. The unconscious is rather like a mirror in this respect, always reflecting our attention back to ourselves, providing us with a subjective perspective. If the phrase "I AM," as uttered by JHVH in response to Moses's question, indicates self-aware consciousness, then the subjective unconscious mind, on its own, knows only the "I" but not the "AM," and the objective conscious mind, on its own, knows only the "AM" but not the "I." We need the two together to be able to say "Hey! I'm here, and I'm alive, and I'm free to choose as I wish."

After the division, one side, the conscious, would experience purely external awareness, seeing everything objectively. It would be like a computer that was able to recognize, identify, classify, and distinguish a million different things, but could never realize that it, itself, the subject perceiving all these objects, was there as well. Meanwhile, the unconscious would experience purely internal awareness, seeing everything subjectively, and could never glimpse anything "outside its own skin." Everything it saw and experienced would be a reflection of its own contents.

The Afterlife Experience of the Conscious Mind

After the division, the conscious half would lose everything it used to receive from the unconscious; although it would still possess free will, it wouldn't have the slightest clue what to do with it, remembering nothing, feeling nothing, and seeing nothing but random, meaningless chaos.

Why would it see only chaos? Alone, the conscious mind would have no reference for perspective, no context in which to understand its environment. Without the unconscious, the conscious mind would have no memory, and therefore no sense of form, system, connections, or context, leaving it like a newborn baby, unable to make out patterns in anything around it. Without context, instinct, or intuition, everything it observed would seem empty, meaningless, irrelevant—nothingness. By nature, the conscious mind perceives details, distinctions and differences, rather than connections and similarities, so it would see the trees but not the forest, the text but not the context, the data but not the significance. It would be aware of every speck of raw data, all in the sharpest clarity, but it would be blind to the patterns within the data. The data would have no meaning; it would seem to be chaos, empty of significance.

Without the unconscious's subjective, emotional perspective, the conscious mind would not feel related or connected to its environment in any way. It would feel completely isolated and uninvolved. In fact, without the unconscious, it would not experience any feeling or emotion whatsoever. Objective to the end, the conscious would then just be a bodiless, identityless, emotionless, historyless, uncomprehending point of pure, living awareness.

However, while the conscious would lose its memory if separated from the subconscious, it would still have free will, and so would remain free to make new choices and thereby move on to new experiences, never knowing or suspecting that any previous life had ever occurred. In time, such an amnesiac conscious spirit could be expected to drift innocently into new experiences, from which it would slowly build up a new sense of identity. Free as a lark, it would be likely to repeat this reincarnation-like pattern indefinitely, perpetually creating new identities and leaving behind a steady stream of discarded past selves, like a plant endlessly growing shoots that are pruned as soon as they are grown.

The Afterlife Experience of the Unconscious Mind

Is there a division in consciousness at death? Those who believe in reincarnation *already* believe so, that the part of the mind containing the memories is taken away before the spirit reincarnates again. But it is not usually taught that this memory-containing part then falls away into a netherworld. The memory-containing part is generally thought to be left in a state of dormancy.

But modern science argues that the unconscious mind, the half of the mind that stores memories, is *never* dormant. Freud's great discovery was his realization that a half of the mind exists that we do not naturally acknowledge and cannot easily reach, which is nonetheless very much active, running robustly outside of our conscious awareness. The world of science in the early 1900s was shaken up about Freud's discovery. Why? Because they were told that a part of their minds was beyond their ability to monitor and control.

When we sleep, the unconscious mind is dominant, but the conscious mind is still running and functioning as well. When we are awake, the conscious mind is dominant, but the unconscious is still running and functioning too. The parts of the mind do not *ever* become dormant, at least according to all the data our scientists have been able to study so far. If the unconscious was cut off and separated from the conscious mind after death, modern science suggests it would *still* continue to function. Energy, after all, cannot be destroyed, nor can it be stopped from continual activity, from "being" energetic.

An afterdeath division would affect the unconscious very differently than it did the conscious mind. The unconscious would lose all ability for objective thought, logical analysis, and discriminative reason, along with all ability to make new choices. However, it would still possess emotion and memory, it would still be reactive and responsive, and it would still see connections and patterns and relationships.

The unconscious would contain the complete and unedited memory of the person one *used to be* before the split of conscious from unconscious at death. Neither side would really be that person anymore, for that person was the product of the *union* of the two sides, and in a sense, once those two sides were no longer united, *that* person would no longer exist. The unconscious would at least contain a memory of the person it used to be, including every thought, belief, impression, and suspicion that had ever crossed the person's mind in life, but it wouldn't *be* the same person.

45

Without the conscious mind, the unconscious would no longer have any free will. It wouldn't be able to change its mind, make any new decisions, or be creative, original, or spontaneous in any way. But since the unconscious would now be cut off from its rational intellect as well, it would never *realize* it was not the same person. Unable to use reason or logic, unable to arrive at any new conclusions or make any new decisions, it would remain convinced that it was still the same person it had been prior to the division, and would never notice that anything had changed or that anything was missing.

Without free will, the unconscious would be unable to move in any way. It would have to "sit" perfectly still, with nothing left to do but fall back deeper into itself, deeper into its own center. Cut off from the input of the physical body and conscious mind, cut off, in effect, from all it had known outside itself, from all objective reality and external stimuli, it would turn its attention inward. There, it would rediscover everything the person had stashed away and forgotten inside his unconscious over the course of his life—abandoned memories, denied feelings, ignored ideals, betrayed insights, and rejected self-judgments.

Now, while we are alive, our unconscious is constantly reacting to all our choices and decisions. It is forever whispering to us, continually comparing those choices and decisions with our own inner sense of right and wrong. That's its job. But, while we're alive, we can consciously choose to block out those whisperings. The conscious mind is stronger, and can repress the unconscious. We can, and often do, choose to ignore these whisperings, pushing their messages back down, out of our awareness.

It is these repressed judgments and emotional reactions, this still-energized content of the unconscious, that we would be confronted with after death. If our unconscious found itself cut off from the conscious mind after death, that conscious mind would no longer be there to repress those judgments any longer, leaving them free at last to resurface into our awareness. Without the ability of the conscious mind to discriminate between one thing and another, the unconscious mind would not be able to reject, deny, or ignore any of its memories, or the feelings and self-judgments stored up inside them. It would not be able to hide from itself any longer. The unconscious would suddenly find itself face to face with *all* those repressed self-judgments, a lifetime's worth. Remembering all its memories at once, and feeling all the feelings connected with them, it would be swimming in them.

If it were possible for such an after-death mental division to take place, it would be tremendously important to let the voice of one's unconscious be heard and consciously acknowledged while one is alive. By so doing, one would release the charge of those feelings, reactions, and judgments. All the input which the unconscious generated but was never allowed to release into consciousness while alive, one's soul would end up swimming in after death. Although the judgments are experienced after death, the judging itself occurs during life. After death, we would finally find ourselves coming face-to-face with the self-judgments we had run from in life. Women, instinctively more in tune with their unconscious, understand this process and this need, and tend to be far less willing to repress and deny the feelings that arise from the depths of their souls, and far quicker to acknowledge how healthy and restoring it is to purge the unconscious soul of repressed feelings it may have bound up within itself.

Collapsing into itself, an unconscious mind that had become detached from its conscious half would become preoccupied with redigesting its own memories. Running on automatic, the unconscious would review and re-experience its memories, feelings, and self-judgments, and since the unconscious is automatically responsive and emotional in nature, it would also be expected to react emotionally to them. If those self-judgments were primarily favorable, the unconscious would generate even more positive feelings and emotions.

Since the unconscious would still remain actively functional, and since it is image-, form-, and pattern-oriented, it would then create dream images for itself out of those memories, self-judgments, and emotional reactions. If those memories, self-judgments, and feelings were more self-affirming than self-condemning, then the unconscious would create a dream-experience for itself that was filled with absolute positive emotion, pure pleasure and happiness. It would think it was in heaven. But if those memories, self-judgments, and feelings were more self-condemning than self-affirming, it would experience a dreamscape filled with absolute negative emotion, the pain of self-condemnation. It would think it was in hell.

Lacking any objective, external window into the "real world," this inner soul-searching would be the unconscious's entire experience. Since it would be cut off from all external input, the unconscious would remain in this dream-state permanently, and 100 percent of its experience would derive from its memories and dream-reactions to them. With no external input possible, and no decision-making ability available to make changes, this process would continue without interruption, compounding upon itself. One's afterlife dreams would keep growing stronger and more intense. Due to its absolute isolation from all outside stimuli, these experiences would come to fill the unconscious mind's field of awareness, and so would be felt on an absolute level of intensity. The unconscious could never awaken from these dreams, at least not under its own power, since it would have no independent volition of its own.

Caught in a circular pattern of automatic behavior, it could be expected to perpetually review its memories, react to them emotionally, and react to those reactions emotionally as well—all automatically, over and over, forever, squeezing every last drop of emotional content from its life memories. This virtually duplicates the classic afterlife scenario of an eternal heaven and hell that is always becoming evermore intensely felt and experienced. The pains of hell would grow evermore horrible, the bliss of heaven evermore delicious.

One of the things so satisfying about the binary soul doctrine is its suggestion that the universe doesn't punish us at all after death. The universe is, as they say, out of the loop. The characteristics of the psyche would, all by themselves, produce one's heavenly or hellish afterlife experience. The soul would automatically judge itself, and then pronounce and execute sentence upon itself, automatically sending itself to whatever heavenly or hellish experiences it feels it deserves, based on its own inner value system.

The Division Would Hide Itself

What is particularly interesting is that such a division would also hide itself. The division itself would never get reported by any eyewitnesses, only its *after-effects*. Neither of the parties involved would be aware that any division had occurred; each half of the mind would be prevented from understanding what happened because each would be functionally crippled after the division, lacking the mental capacities necessary to arrive at this realization. The conscious would not remember the division, and the unconscious would not be able to figure out that a division had occurred. Since memory is stored in the unconscious, the conscious mind would have no reason to think that anything had changed after the division; it would have no memory of anything prior. And, since the unconscious would have no rational intellect after the division, it would never analyze the data (its memories) and arrive at a logical conclusion. This would explain why reports both of heaven/hell netherworlds and of reincarnation have continued side-by-side down through the ages, keeping both legends alive, while the reports of the division itself got lost.

What's at Stake

If this afterdeath division does occur, death becomes far less hopeful an experience than the reincarnation scenario of the East or the heaven/hell of the West. Instead, we would be split apart, losing our very selfhood. If the two nonphysical components of individuals survive death disassociated from each other, the individual, as he knew himself in life, would no longer exist.

When a car is disassembled, and its parts are scattered across the world, does that car exist anymore? Its parts all still exist, and so one might say that technically nothing had been lost. But the car itself does not exist, for the unity of its parts, when they were together, created something special, something unique, that only existed *when* those parts were together. A person can disassemble a watch and examine its parts, but that won't tell anyone what time it is. We are not our components, nor any individual specific component, nor any relationship between those components. What we *are* is that which is created, and which *only* exists, when those components are functioning together as a unity.

Perhaps the secret of death hasn't remained elusive because it was too far removed from us, but because it was too close. Division is at the core of the human experience. What was a stunning revelation to Freud 100 years ago—that we are *all* divided—is, and has always been, humanity's surprised cry of discovery. It is hard to imagine being split apart at death. The mind rebels at the notion: how could a person's experience be in two "places" at once? But modern science informs us that we are all doing this already, right now. While one part of the mind is consciously aware of reading these words, another part of the mind, the unconscious, is off doing all sorts of who-knows-what on its own. Some parts of it may well be one's past-life souls, experiencing their own little dreams of being in heaven or hell.

The revolutionary message of neuropsychology is that the left-brain conscious and right-brain unconscious are *components* of the psyche, not merely *states* of awareness. There are only two components, only two elements in the equation, but there are an infinite number of different ways these two can mix together, and so, an infinite number of different possible states of consciousness. While we are alive, these two components are always intertwined, never allowing us to experience one or the other in a pure and undiluted state. It is not natural for either to be experienced completely independent of the other in life, any more than it is natural for male to exist without female, happiness without sadness, light without dark. Each defines the other, and it is not possible, in the universe of the living at least, to have one entirely without the other. To separate these eternal pairs is to violate the very nature of reality.

Yet the binary soul doctrine suggests that is precisely what death is.

3
Witnesses of Division:
Near-Death Experiences

[At one point] my consciousness must have pulled away from my body because I suddenly observed it from a short distance as it sobbed. I was completely unemotional as I observed my body. As I watched, I saw some shiny, clear object lift away from my body. It was obvious to me it was my ego. The moment my ego started lifting, my consciousness went back into my body and I felt distress, thinking, "It's my ego, it's my ego!", not wanting it to leave me. I felt like I had to have it or I wouldn't be alive. It pulled away from me anyway, and in it I saw all the things I had done wrong in my life. I was stunned because I thought all that was part of me and simply couldn't be separated from me.

—NDE-er Peggy Holladay[1]

Is there anyone who hasn't heard about near-death experiences (NDEs)? Raymond A. Moody, Jr., a physician from Georgia, stunned the world in 1975 when he reported in *Life After Life* that thousands of people had independently described having the same "afterlife" experience during close brushes with death. Since then, dozens of other published studies have confirmed and expanded Moody's early findings, giving rise to an NDE subculture which some have compared to a religious cult, making the classic NDE journey through a peaceful dark tunnel to a love-filled realm of light almost as familiar a part of today's cultural backdrop as "Monday Night Football."

Although many scientists have played the role of skeptic over the last twenty-five years, suggesting various explanations for this phenomena,[2] the full experience reported by NDE subjects has never been replicated in a lab. For example, many subjects who had been technically dead have come back to describe visual and auditory details of events that had gone on in the room when they were supposedly "gone." This occurs so regularly it's virtually a cliché within the NDE community. Some of these subjects were blind, yet during their NDEs they claimed they could see, and accurately reported visual data upon their return.[3] In addition, many subjects have returned possessing knowledge they had not possessed prior to the trauma, such as knowing that this or that friend or relative had died recently. They say, of course, that these friends met them "on the other side."

Science fails to account for such experiences.

On the opposite end of the intellectual spectrum, many of today's new-age thinkers assume that we create our own afterlife experiences, that our expectations become mental projections in NDEs, and those projections then become the experience we perceive. But the research does not support this; many subjects experience things during their NDEs contrary to their expectations.

For example, many who experienced trips to hell or confrontations with Satan come back not only terrified, but surprised; they had believed in neither hell nor a devil before the event. Other subjects have had experiences vastly out of alignment with their expectations, such as Jews meeting Jesus in the afterlife, or Christians meeting Krishna or the Buddha. Such reports are fairly commonplace in the research literature, and collectively they show that people do *not* simply meet their own expectations. Whatever is going on in NDEs, it is apparently a little more complicated, and a little more objective and reality-based than that.

When Raymond Moody, Kenneth Ring, Michael Sabom, and all the other now-almost-legendary figures of NDE research started publishing their findings, it seemed like the best news in the world. When we first heard scientific researchers report that people all over the world had experienced similar afterlife episodes, we collectively said to ourselves, "Hey, great! Today's scientific age is really paying off! Confirmation is coming in from all quarters that life after death is real!" It seemed that mankind's ancient afterlife traditions were not dead myths after all, but were still alive. Even in the present day, people are still reporting experiences strikingly consistent with afterlife reports written thousands of years ago.

But as time went on, this blessing became a curse. It eventually became clear that these reports were, in many cases, directly contradicting each other. If one set of research pointed in one direction, the next set seemed to point in a different one. Some NDE reports, for example, declared that hell and the devil are real, while others insisted just as strongly that they are not. Some reports defended reincarnation while others refuted it. Some said that the earthly personality is preserved and maintained after death, while others refuted this as well. Some people returned from their NDEs insisting that Jesus Christ is sitting in His heaven, and only those who honor Him will enter, while other NDE-ers insisted that *all* enter heaven after death, regardless of other considerations.

These inconsistencies and contradictions have recently become too much for the fledgling NDE community to bear. In the summer of 2000 a sort of religious war broke out among the NDE leadership, highlighting this interpretational schism.[4] So, as has happened so many times before whenever the question of life after death comes up, people are asking "Which one of these stories is true?" "How can *this* one be true if *that* one is true?" And, "Why should we believe in *any* of them?"

In the minds of many, the great shining promise of NDE research is in jeopardy; these inconsistencies shroud the phenomenon under a blanket of doubt. The original strength of NDEs, the reason people started paying attention to them in the first place, was because the reports seemed so much alike; but now that the inconsistencies and contradictions within these reports are becoming more apparent, that original strength seems to be eroding. So long as the NDE community remains divided over what these phenomena mean, the public is sure to harbor doubts about the value of these experiences.

The ancient world's binary soul doctrine, however, explains and resolves all these inconsistencies and contradictions, providing a valid scientific foundation for NDEs, a simple, scientifically definable condition which seems to underlie, *and substantiate*, the vast majority of phenomena being reported. The scenario emerging from NDE reports is completely in line with what the binary soul doctrine predicts; the archetypal NDE occurs in two stages, a dark stage followed by a light stage, and subjects' experiences during these two stages seem closely related to the two halves of the human psyche, as if each half was operating independently of the other.

In addition to this circumstantial evidence, there is also *eyewitness testimony* of the division. A number of NDE subjects claim to have split into two separately functioning mental pieces during their NDEs, pieces which do seem at least tentatively identifiable as the conscious and unconscious halves of the mind. However, the majority of NDE-ers don't recall going through such a division, a fact which seems, at first glance, to be at odds with the binary soul model. Nonetheless, the mechanics of the division, as illustrated in the last twenty-five years of split-brain research, seem to predict this outcome, that in the majority of cases, the split would never be noticed by the subjects.

Dark Stage, Light Stage: Circumstantial Evidence of the Division

> It was really, really dark, daddy, and then it was really, really bright.
>
> —Child NDE-er Mark Botts[5]

The two different stages of NDEs seem to be mirror opposites of each other in many respects. The first stage typically takes place in pitch-black darkness, and often seems dull, brief, and hardly worth mentioning, especially when compared to the far more spectacular realm of light in the second stage. Virtually all of the NDE research that has been published over the last twenty-five years has focused on the sensational light stage, such as *The Tunnel and the Light* by Elisabeth Kübler-Ross, *The Light Beyond* by Raymond Moody, *Embraced by the Light* by Betty Eadie, *Saved by the Light* by Dannion Brinkley, *Living in the Light* by Larry Rosenberg, *Closer to the Light* by Melvin Morse, *Beyond the Light* by P. M. H. Atwater, *Children of the Light* by Brad Steiger, *Lessons from the Light* by Kenneth Ring, *The Truth in the Light* by Peter Fenwick, and *Light and Death* by Michael Sabom, to name just a few.

After the subject leaves the body, he typically finds himself floating alone inside a featureless and empty black void or tunnel, in which no forms or shapes of any kind are seen. In this unbounded darkness, subjects experience an extraordinary tranquillity which usually includes a loss of emotional investment. Subjects always seem to feel detached and dispassionate during this stage of their NDEs. Nothing seems particularly important anymore; nothing seems to hold any personal meaning. However, subjects often feel extremely alert, intelligent, and curious during this stage, as if their logic and analytical skills had somehow gone into overdrive. This first phase of NDEs is often brief, sometimes coming and going so quickly it is almost overlooked in the subject's swift passage into the second stage's far more emotionally intense and spectacular realm of light.

In the second stage, NDE-ers describe conditions that seem the opposite of the previous stage. Instead of being in darkness with no light anywhere, they find themselves in a realm of brilliant light, in which no shadows exist. Instead of floating alone in a void, they now seem to be enveloped in a living, breathing universe teeming with other life forms. Instead of being unique and distinct, instead of seeming to be the only thing that exists in all the universe, they now find themselves interacting with many others much like themselves.

Instead of noticing a dry and distant lack of emotion, they now feel intense surges of emotion, usually either the sweetest of joys or the bitterest of miseries. Instead of being objective and detached, they are now subjective, involved in and affected by everything going on around them. Instead of feeling unconnected to anything, now they feel an intimate connection to the entire universe. Instead of feeling that nothing has any meaning, now they feel their eyes have been opened and they can see the meaning and patterns and purpose behind everything. And instead of experiencing sharpened logic and reason, in this phase they often *exhibit* just the opposite (without realizing it), displaying a diminished tendency to exercise critical analysis and discriminative reason.

In short, the first stage of NDEs seems to be experienced through the eye of the conscious mind, the second through the eye of the unconscious mind.

The Two Bardos

The Tibetan Book of the Dead paints a similar picture of what happens after death, also describing these dark and light stages. However, unlike the emphasis of modern NDE research, the Tibetans viewed the first stage, or Bardo, as the more important of the two. In this first stage, which they call "The Clear Light of the Void," the Tibetans believed the newly deceased would find himself in ultimate reality, experiencing pure Buddha-mind, experiencing himself as the only Being that has ever existed. For perhaps only the briefest of moments, the person discovers himself to be "The One Besides Whom There Is No Other." But if the subject does not recognize where and who he is during this brief and precious moment, he then passes quickly into the second stage, which the Tibetans held to be a place of pure illusion without objective reality. Most NDE researchers, on the other hand, tend to assume that this second stage is more real and important than the first stage.

Stage One: Complete Release in the Dark Void

> There was only blackness, as though I were suspended in outer space, unbroken by a single glimmering star.... The darkness continued in all directions and seemed to have no end, but it wasn't just blackness, it was an endless void, an absence of light.
>
> —NDE-er Angie Fenimore[6]

In the first part of their NDEs, subjects often find that they leave their bodies to enter a black nothingness, a void or tunnel that contains no visual forms or imagery of any kind. They often find that they can't see anything, including themselves, while they're floating in this unbounded night. They seem completely alone, seeing nothing but velvety blackness in all directions. They don't know where they are, where they're going, or what's going on. But this apparently isn't just an inability to perceive spatial forms; *all* pattern and form recognition seems to be inhibited in the first stage of NDEs. Subjects sometimes report feeling that they can't perceive any pattern or meaning or significance to *anything* while they are in this dark void: "I was in a place of emptiness, total emptiness. There was no feeling. There was no purpose or anything. My life was meaningless. My taking care of my house, my decorating, and so forth, all had no purpose." (NDE-er Rochelle)[7]

But despite this seemingly disconcerting situation, a peculiar indifference tends to set in during this stage. They're not upset about dying at all; on the contrary, they feel "detached," "dispassionate," and "divorced from what is happening" during this experience. "I didn't feel any emotion at all and was completely indifferent to what I saw," said NDE-er Alf Rose.[8]

This detached calm state is reported more than any other element of NDEs, being experienced by 82 percent of all subjects.[9] It may also be the most perplexing aspect of the phenomenon; our single strongest instinct is to avoid death at all costs, yet NDE-ers who discover they've failed in this often seem to have no reaction at all. Despite having just been unexpectedly ripped away from their bodies, their family, friends, loved ones, careers, possessions, plans for the future, and everything precious to them, the majority of NDE-ers inexplicably feel no distress, anxiety, or reaction of any kind.

Suddenly, without giving it a moment's thought, everything that they had put so much of their hearts and souls and selves into throughout all of their lives no longer matters to them:

> I realized that I must be dying and the odd thing was that I didn't mind in the least. I remember being very interested in the experience in a very unemotional academic way and feeling that it was quite an adventure—no regrets at all. While I was there, I was very surprised at myself for feeling like this. My husband and two-year-old son were everything to me, and I was shocked and amazed at myself for not minding the thought of leaving them, yet I was overwhelmed by a feeling of peace such as I had certainly not known in all my adult life. I knew how devastated they would be at my death but even this did not really move me. I felt extraordinarily comfortable, relaxed, and free of any cares at all.
>
> —NDE-er Jenny McMillan[10]

Many subjects seem to be in a state of absolute objectivity during this stage; they can't feel their own feelings, or relate to their own lives, or even see themselves at all. It's an absence of the subjective. When we become insensitive to our own hearts and souls, when we find ourselves cut off from our feelings, we become insensitive to everyone else's feelings as well; NDE-ers' dearest loved ones, the people who only a moment ago had been the closest and dearest and most precious things in all the world to them, now seem unreal, insignificant, and irrelevant to them while they're in this dark void:

> I felt a strange sensation of floating away, floating dreamily down a tunnel. I could see a light at the end of it, and I knew I was dying. I remember thinking about my other two children, and then reassuring myself that my mother would look after them. I was very comfortable, quite unafraid. I wanted to go. The thoughts about my family were the things that seemed unreal, not the tunnel or the sensation of floating.
>
> —NDE-er Daphne[11]

The simplest feelings of the heart often seem to be absent during this stage. Others' pain doesn't seem to matter much at all; NDE-ers often find they have no empathy for anyone during this first stage, feeling no love, concern, compassion, or mercy for the family and friends being left behind. This is reminiscent of the infamous unconcerned bliss of the opium addict. "My children only have one parent. It was quite right, of course, but I have to admit I hadn't thought of them at all."[12]

Many have remarked how peculiar this initial reaction seems to be. It doesn't seem to make sense that the average person who is losing everything most dear would react with a flat emotionless nonchalance. Feeling some degree of empathetic connection with others is widely considered a sign of mental health. In fact, if this detached reaction occurred in any other context, if anyone other than an NDE-er displayed this level of indifference, her utter lack of feelings and emotions, would be immediately identified as a sign of neurosis. "Neurosis . . . is like a continual shot of morphine."[13]

The peaceful, dispassionate serenity of this first phase, however, seems to have more to do with an absence of negative feelings and emotions than the presence of positive ones, and so seems to be in sharp contrast to the second phase of NDEs, in which subjects commonly describe the presence of intense and overwhelming emotions. The well-publicized "peace" of this first stage seems to be the interpretation subjects give to the sudden loss of all subjective emotion and feeling, understandably equating the absence of anxiety and distress with the presence of deep calm and inner peace.

In life, we are always burdened by two kinds of weight—the weight we feel from gravity and the far more exhausting weight of our psychological baggage. Over the years, most of us accumulate a volume of painful experiences. Buddha said, "Life is pain," and he was right. Life does include pain, and much of our success or failure in life has to do with how we deal with that pain.

Many of us, unfortunately, are not adept at dealing with the failures, disappointments, and frustrations we encounter in life. Instead of dealing with them directly and experiencing them fully as soon as they occur, many of us try to ignore them, sweeping them under the rug, denying the feelings. Like babies playing peek-a-boo, we seem to think that if we don't look directly at those feelings, then they aren't there. Of course, this doesn't work; this tactic allows these feelings to build up inside us, forming an inner mountain of grief and pain.

We usually try our best to ignore it, but every so often the pain catches us off guard, sneaking up on us when we're not looking, and we find ourselves staring in surprised amazement and horror at the looming emotional darkness inside us. At such times, most of us bury it again as quickly as we can, and try to forget we ever saw it.

Grief doesn't disappear just because we ignore it. It sits tight inside our unconscious minds, continuing to silently accumulate over our lives, like a kind of plaque in the arteries of the soul. The unconscious is the perfect preservative: anything deposited into the unconscious is preserved in its original condition. As years go by, grief builds up steadily. It weighs us down and inhibits us, in many ways too imperceptible for us to realize. The weight of this inner grief leaves footprints in our lives; the more grief we are holding inside, the more grief we are *holding back* inside, the more grief we are *hiding from*, the more we become cut off from our own authentic feelings and emotions. The more we become cut off from the feeling of being alive, of feeling human, the more difficult it is for us to feel and act free, to be spontaneous, wild, and crazy in life, and the more we become artificial, robotic, control freaks.

The mystery is that in the first phase of the NDE, this inner grief suddenly vanishes. Poof! *It's just gone.* This psychological weight, our unpaid emotional debt to ourselves, often seems to mysteriously vanish in the dark-stage experience, leaving subjects feeling marvelously light, peaceful, and calm. This sudden peace is mystifying to most people who experience it; they can't imagine why they suddenly feel so light and carefree and peaceful, largely because most of what had been weighing them down in life had been hidden inside their unconscious. Even when it *was* there, they didn't realize it consciously, although they'd been used to the *feel* of it being there. But people notice it when that weight is suddenly lifted during the first stage of their NDEs.

There's only one way that weight, which they spent the owner's whole lifetime building up, could be lifted in a single effortless stroke—if his unconscious was itself somehow lifted from him during the dark-stage experience, just as the ancient binary soul doctrine once maintained.

The dark stage, however, is not only a place of diminishment, but of increase. In the first moments of the first stage, just after they have left the body but before they have entered the dark void, NDE-ers often report an unnatural clarity of perception in which every detail seems to be magnified into precise crispness:

> I had never felt more alert and conscious. . . . Everything was vividly clear. All the details of the room were extremely sharp and distinct. Every nuance in the linoleum floor, every bump in the paint on the steel bed was magnified. I had never viewed the world with such clarity and exactness. Everything was in such extreme focus that it was overwhelming.
>
> —NDE-er Howard Storm[14]

This is exactly what the binary soul doctrine would have predicted. The conscious mind is geared to notice specific details, while the unconscious mind is geared to notice the bigger picture. With the unconscious out of the picture, the conscious mind's perspective would be greatly magnified, making everything seem unnaturally sharp, detailed, and distinct. Even one's own distinctness seems increased in the dark stage; NDE-ers find themselves conscious and aware but alone in this void, not even seeming to have a body, as if nothing else existed in all the universe except their own consciousness. Such a state would be the epitome of distinctness, experiencing one's consciousness as the only thing existing in the universe.

Subjects also frequently claim increased clarity and swiftness of thought during this first stage, reporting that they feel far more alert, curious, logical, objective, rational, analytical, and intelligent than normal. For example, one of Dr. Fenwick's subjects felt she had been given "the magic key to understanding pure logic"[15] during this first stage. However, while NDE-ers are acutely interested in observing what is taking place during this stage, their interest seems to be more out of a cold and dry academic curiosity rather than any sense of living attachment or meaningful personal connection. Recall Jenny McMillan's account: "I realized I must be dying, and the odd thing was I didn't mind in the least. I remember being very interested in the experience in a very unemotional academic way, and feeling it was quite an adventure—no regrets at all."

In fact, one's mind often seems like a cold, impersonal, unfeeling computer during this stage: "It was like all relations were cut. I know—it was like there was no love or anything. Everything was just so—technical."[16]

Obviously, something happens to the human mind in the first few moments after death. Something changes. According to twenty-five years of NDE research data, the mind doesn't work the same way after leaving the body. Many mental functions seem to be diminished, such as the ability to perceive spatial forms and images, the ability to feel emotion, distress, and anxiety, the ability to appreciate connectedness and value relationships, and the ability to sense purpose and meaning. But other functions seem to be increased, such as one's objective awareness, logical intellect, level of curiosity, and detail perception.

These are all *exactly* the sort of experiences one would expect to be reported by a conscious mind that had suddenly become divorced from its unconscious half. Without the unconscious, it would be as if all the conscious mind's feelings and emotions had disappeared. Without the unconscious, the conscious mind would no longer be able to experience or appreciate any subjective sense of belonging, relationships, or personal connections of any kind; it would feel unconnected to anything. Without the emotional perspective of the unconscious, it would experience no distress or anxiety on any level of awareness. Since normal life always contains some anxiety, some awareness of one's vulnerabilities, needs, limitations, failings, and other stressors, the sudden unanticipated dropping away of this angst-ridden underlying mental context would be experienced as a profound state of peacefulness.

At first, as the division began, one would notice that her perception of detail seemed more pronounced. But as the division continued, and the conscious mind became more alienated from the unconscious, the conscious mind would soon find itself unable to recognize any shapes, patterns, forms, or images at all. It would see only nothingness. On its own, the conscious mind would have no memory of any forms or images, nor any ability for form-, pattern-, or relationship-perception. This would leave the conscious mind lacking any orienting sense of context, leaving it like a newborn baby, unable to see patterns in anything.[17]

Without any sense of context, everything the conscious mind observed would seem to be chaos, and this would explain why subjects often report floating in nothingness during the first stage of NDEs (as also do some past-life regression subjects when regressed to a point in time in between lives, as we will see in the next chapter).

Yet despite these losses, the conscious mind would still remain conscious and aware. It would still be oriented towards perceiving details and the differences between things, and would still possess its objective rational intellect and analytical curiosity. All *these* abilities would feel as if they had been powerfully enhanced, by virtue of the conscious mind no longer being compromised by the unconscious and its illogical emotions, subjective impressions, and alien mental input.

Stage Two: Joy in the Realm of Light

> Everything went very dark for a few seconds. Then suddenly I was . . . filled with a thrilling sense of joy. A being was at my side, a being of light. Yet it wasn't like a light that you see, but rather felt and understood. It touched me, and my whole body was filled with its light.
>
> —NDE-er Kathy[18]

After the dark stage, many NDE-ers move on to a realm of light, which in many respects seems to bring opposite experiences. This second stage tends to be characterized by *increased* emotional intensity, an *increased* sense of connections and relationships, *increased* form, pattern, and meaning-recognition, but a *diminished* sense of separateness and distinctness and *diminished* tendency to employ logic or analytical reasoning. Instead of being in darkness, subjects are now in brilliant light. Instead of a lack of emotion, they now feel intensely powerful and moving emotion. Instead of being alone in a void, subjects now find themselves enveloped by a universe of fabulous forms and patterns. Instead of being dispassionate and objective, they now feel extremely subjective, affected by everything around them. Instead of seeming to be unique within their environment, subjects now find themselves interacting with many others like themselves.

They don't feel unconnected at all anymore; subjects now feel connected to the entire universe. Instead of being in a formless, patternless, meaningless limbo, subjects now see meaning, pattern, form, and structure everywhere. Often, they are overwhelmed by seeing *big* patterns of meaning. They feel they see "the big picture," finally understanding the pattern and context of all reality. This is the opposite of what they had experienced in the black tunnel, in which they couldn't see *any* patterns or forms or meanings or connections at all.

These are precisely the experiences that science would predict for an unconscious that found itself no longer united to its conscious mind. Feeling would seem greatly enhanced, absolute, and overwhelming. All the natural characteristics of the unconscious, such as emotion, memory, conscience, receptiveness, responsiveness, aesthetic awareness, and form-, pattern-, and relationship-recognition, would define the experience.

Subjects in the second stage would also exhibit a pronounced loss of certain abilities, which would correspond with the characteristics of the conscious mind. Without the conscious mind, the unconscious would lose its linear reason, abstract logic, objective perspective, free will, and verbal communication ability. No longer having any critical, analytical, or discriminative faculties, it would be condemned to accept as unquestionable truth virtually all thoughts, suspicions, and impressions passing across the mind's eye. Without its verbal ability, the conscious mind's communication would have to take place without words, using gestures, symbols, metaphors, analogies, and direct intuitive awareness instead.[19] Without the conscious mind's objective perspective, one would have a diminished sense of his own distinct independence, autonomy, and unique identity. The normal defining boundaries between oneself and others would seem diminished, even nonexistent. These are precisely what most subjects report during the second stage of NDEs.

Increased Emotional Perception

> Eventually I emerged from the tunnel as its end widened out and I found myself in a place that is impossible to describe. It was landscape without form, composed only of light and colour. I was met by a figure of light, and it can only be described as a "Jesus" figure. But I "knew" that the appearance of the figure was to make me feel comfortable in this new place. We did not speak to each other because words were not necessary. The figure led the way for me to follow. I just cannot describe the place or my feelings and emotions. I experienced absolute happiness, utter bliss, complete love, perfect peace, and total understanding.
>
> —NDE-er Allan Pring[20]

The first thing that seems to be noticed about the second stage is the intense flood of positive feelings and emotions that instantly envelop NDE-ers as they enter the heavenly realm of light, or the overload of negative emotions that envelops them upon entering the hellish realm of bewildered spirits.[21] Most reports describe extremely positive emotions, such as love and joy, but occasionally extremely negative feelings are reported in the second stage instead. There's usually no "middle of the road" emotional experience during this stage. Besides the obvious contrast between the emotionally vacant first stage of NDEs and the emotionally saturated second stage, it also seems significant that these second-stage emotions always seem to be abnormally extreme. No one seems to come back from NDEs reporting that they felt just "a little bit good" or "a little bit bad." No sliding scale measuring the relative degree of one's emotional experience during these episodes would be needed, for the feelings experienced during the second stage of NDEs always seem to be at maximum levels.

This is precisely what one would expect if the unconscious were operating independently of the conscious mind during these episodes. With the conscious mind out of the picture, the unconscious would no longer possess any discriminative capacity; it would no longer be able to distinguish differences between things or degrees of difference. The unconscious is designed to perceive the similarities between things, not the differences, and so is constitutionally blind to degrees of difference. So if the unconscious was registering fear, it would experience that fear in its most undiluted form. Similarly, if the unconscious felt love, that love would be experienced as infinite, unlimited in any way, shape, or form. And that is precisely the character of the experience that NDE-ers tend to report during the second stage of these episodes.

Diminished Detail Perception

If the unconscious were separated from the conscious mind, it would find that its ability to recognize and appreciate details diminished; the differences and defining boundaries between things would seem subdued or even nonexistent, while the connections and relationships between things would seem magnified or more evident. As it turns out, just such a nonspecific lack of definition and detail is encountered again and again in second-stage NDE reports (standing out in sharp contrast to the crisp detail perception encountered so often in first-stage reports):

I kept trying to define the entity's shape in concrete terms, but couldn't.

—NDE-er Wesley[22]

I seemed to float along a corridor towards, then into, all-enveloping brightness and light, with indefinable shades of pastel-like colors. There were what I can only describe as billions of shimmering forms with no outlines . . .

—NDE-er Mary Lowther[23]

The library was a building sort of like the Acropolis, that style. So I went in . . . I went to the section on people. I got to look at my book. I'll never forget it. You opened it up, like in the middle. If you flipped back, you got the past and if you flipped ahead you got the future. But most of it had this grayish film, so you couldn't read it.

—NDE-er Tommy[24]

There were light beings. Most of them didn't have clear definition . . . they were never vivid enough to see details . . . It was like looking through an opaque glass into a physical setting. It wasn't clearly defined.

—NDE-er Charles Nunn[25]

This peculiar deficiency in specific detail, sharp definition, and clear boundaries also appears in hellish second-stage reports. In the first stage of Howard Storm's experience, the reader will recall, he emphasized how all the details of his surroundings seemed to stand out in unnaturally sharp contrast. But as the second stage began, his reports begin to paint the exact opposite picture:

> All the while we were walking, I was trying to pick up some clues as to where we were going by what we were walking on. There were no walls of any kind. The floor or ground had no features. There was no incline or decline, nor any variation in texture. It was like walking on a smooth, slightly damp, cool floor . . . I also couldn't make out how much time was passing. There was a profound sense of timelessness.
>
> —NDE-er Howard Storm[26]

Increased Sense of Connections and Relationships

> I had no sense of being separate. I was in the light and one with it.
>
> —NDE-er quoted by Margot Grey[27]

NDE-ers commonly report feeling a profound sense of oneness with the whole universe, and this too is what one would expect if the unconscious were operating independently of the conscious mind. Seeing only connections but never any differences, the unconscious would instinctively see the universe as a perfectly interconnected, synchronized, and harmonized singularity. Having lost all ability to distinguish between things, it would only see the connections, similarities, and relationships among things, which would cause it to identify things as parts of groups or a whole that the conscious mind might have otherwise distinguished.

This is the way the unconscious processes information, and the effects of this natural process can easily be observed in dreams, which are well known for blurring and melding the identities of multiple individuals into a single dream character. It would be nothing unusual for one's Uncle Arthur to also seem to be one's high school Spanish teacher in a dream, even though in real life they had been distinct individuals.

In normal life, the conscious and unconscious operate together, one pointing out the differences between things, the other highlighting their similarities; only together can they provide us with a balanced and realistic perspective. But without the distinguishing, objective perspective of the conscious mind, the unconscious is blind to all distinctions, divisions, and inequities. On its own, the unconscious would be unable to distinguish between oneself and the rest of the universe, and so, it would identify the two together ("I and the universe are one"), forced to do this by the same inner programming that causes separate elements to blend together in dreams.

Diminished Appreciation of Objectivity

Just as the unconscious is polarized more toward the subjective than the objective, so too the second-stage reports from NDE-ers seem to emphasize subjective interpersonal values such as personal relationships, family, love, patience, and charity, while de-emphasizing or even ignoring more objective values, such as worldly and professional accomplishment. Yet it seems disingenuous to value the one above the other in a world where both are inescapably interconnected.

If centuries of scientists had not dedicated their lives to impersonal, objective accomplishments in medicine, or if legions of soldiers had not dedicated their lives to the task of halting the advance of Hitler, the world would be a far more angst-ridden and loveless place today. Yet we repeatedly hear, in the life reviews of NDE-ers, that their subjective, emotion-based relationships with others are accorded more meaning and significance than their objective worldly accomplishments, which, as one NDE-er reported, "meant nothing in this setting."[28]

Increased Receptivity and Inclusiveness

The right hemisphere has no equivalent of "no."
—Psychologist Robert Ornstein[29]

Because the unconscious does not have any innate ability for perceiving details or distinguishing the differences between things, it must accept all thoughts equally. If it was operating independently of the conscious mind as the binary soul doctrine suggests would be the case, the right-brain unconscious would find itself in a state of complete and total acceptance, rejecting nothing.

This is precisely the mindset found to be in operation in most second-stage reports. All people are loved and appreciated and accepted equally, with none being rejected or turned away. Even during the legendary life review, when all one's worst thoughts and deeds are paraded in public, the person herself is still loved and cherished and accepted unconditionally. The unconscious would have no choice but to do this; its own design would force it to accept everyone and everything, not necessarily due to any objective analysis, but due simply to the way it is designed to function.

Diminished Separateness and Autonomy

> There are other clues which point in the direction of right-hemisphere involvement. One is the deep feeling of unity, the loss of boundaries, both spatial and personal, which is often described in the NDE.
> —Psychiatrist and NDE Researcher Peter Fenwick[30]

If the unconscious was divorced from the conscious, one would also expect to see a lessening of one's sense of the distinctions between all things, including the distinctions between one person and another, and this too is a regular feature of the second stage of NDEs. Subjects consistently report that the normal boundaries between themselves and others have faded, in some cases becoming nearly nonexistent. Instead of retaining their own independent autonomy, they find now their psyches have become like a glass house, into which anyone and everyone can peer at will. All their thoughts and feelings are exposed to the universe, and nothing is hidden.

> There was no division between the inside and outside of my skin.
> —NDE-er Loretta[31]

In short, there no longer seems to be any such thing as separateness, which is precisely what one would expect to experience if the conscious mind, which provides our ability to perceive separateness and distinctness, was no longer functioning.

Increased Aesthetic Sensitivity

The right-brain unconscious, modern neuropsychology informs us, is oriented towards recognizing and appreciating life's artistic and aesthetic qualities. Because of this orientation, if the unconscious is separated from the conscious mind, its aesthetic appreciation and artistic sensitivities seem to be greatly magnified. And this is perfectly consistent with the reports of second-stage NDEs. Descriptions of the realm of light always seem to include comments about how beautiful everything is. Whether the subject of discussion happens to be the buildings, the natural scenery, or even the inhabitants of the realm of light, they are always too beautiful for words, which is what should be expected if one's aesthetic sense was turned up to full volume. In much the same way, observers of the realm of bewildered spirits also betray a similar intensification of their aesthetic sense, but in the opposite direction. Instead of everything seeming impossibly beautiful, everything in *that* realm seems impossibly ugly or horrific. Either way, the observer's aesthetic sense always seems to be registering at maximum capacity.

Diminished Verbal Capacity

> My brother, who had died a few years earlier, was gesticulating delightedly as I approached. Their faces were so happy and welcoming. Then somehow my mother became detached from the group. She shook her head and waved her hand (rather like a windscreen wiper) and I stopped, and I heard the doctor say, "She's coming round."
> —NDE-er Elizabeth Rogers[32]

If the unconscious separated from the conscious mind, it would lose all ability for literal, linear thought, and thus all ability to communicate verbally. Again, the weight of the reports suggests that verbal communication ability is often greatly diminished during NDEs. Words are seldom used during the second-stage experience, communication more often occurring via gestures, images, and direct intuitive comprehension. Even long after the NDE is over, words are still hopelessly inadequate to describe the experience. The ineffability of the second stage is so commonly repeated it has almost become a cliché; again and again researchers encounter comments like "no words were spoken" and "words were not necessary," and "the feeling was indescribable." Even the life review is "more often in the form of pictures than verbal memories."[33]

Increased Sense of Form and Pattern (The Big Picture)

> Everything fitted in, it all made sense. . . . It almost seemed, too, as if the pieces of a jig-saw all fitted together. You know

> how it is with a tapestry and all the interwoven parts, then when the tapestry's turned over you see how it all fits in place.
> —NDE-er quoted by Kenneth Ring[34]

The fact that the conscious mind has no capacity for perceiving form, while the unconscious does, seems to explain why the first stage includes little or no perception of any forms (even one's own self often seems to be formless) while the second stage is usually filled with all sorts of forms. But the form-perception of the unconscious would also seem responsible for another second-stage characteristic: the feeling that one has "total understanding," perceiving the full scheme of things.

NDE-ers often return with amazing stories (but precious little evidence) of having seen the big picture, instantly understanding the grand scheme of reality, seeing how all the pieces to the puzzle of reality fit together. This would seem to simply be form- and pattern-awareness on the grandest scale. However, upon returning to normal consciousness, the invaluable specific data associated with that pattern are found to be missing from memory. It is as if they had seen the forest without noticing a single tree. As commonly occurs with dream memories, NDE-ers tend to be left with very compelling feelings and impressions, but often little in the way of specific detail. The BSD would suggest that this is because the half of the mind that perceives details was more-or-less "off-line" during this stage of the experience.

> This feeling of complete knowledge did not persist after their return.
> —Researcher Raymond Moody[35]

> I seemed to understand everything, but most of the answers were wiped from me. But I do have tantalizing tidbits of information and vague recollections, just enough to thoroughly frustrate me.
> —NDE-er Jarod[36]

This makes sense from the perspective of the binary soul doctrine. Second-stage NDE memories *would* behave like dream memories if both experiences had originated from the same source—the unconscious. While the unconscious is the repository of memory, such memories are primarily the records of the data it receives from the conscious mind while the person was awake. The unconscious fares far worse at retaining memory of its own activity than it does at retaining the memory of what the conscious mind experiences; the memory of what one did while awake is far more readily accessible than the memories of what one dreams at night. And while the unconscious is always active, always busy with its own "behind-the-scenes" tasks, one generally has no memory of this activity of the unconscious.

> A couple of days later, I approached my patient with pad and pencil in hand for an interview. At his bedside I asked him to recall what he had actually seen in hell. Were there any flames? Did the devil have a pitchfork? What did hell look like? He said, "What hell? I don't recall any hell!" I recounted all of the details he had described two days earlier . . . he could recall none of it.
>
> —Researcher Maurice Rawlings[37]

In much the same way that one has trouble remembering the specific activities of the unconscious, NDE-ers often report similar memory loss of the specific details of their second stage experiences, and are often left with little more than memories of unnaturally powerful right-brain feelings that are attached to frustratingly few left-brain details.

Diminished Use of Reason

> One of the unique characteristics of our form of consciousness is that it is self-reflexive—meaning that mind can examine its own processes. We can ask, "How did I arrive at that conclusion? Do I really know my reasons? Am I being influenced by prejudice? Do I have grounds to believe this is true, or do I merely want it to be true? Am I being logical right now? Do my conclusions really follow from my premises? . . ." To live consciously is necessarily to be concerned with such questions, and it is our rational faculty—our ability to think, and even to think about thinking—that makes such questions possible. A less evolved consciousness does not and cannot question its operations.*
>
> —Nathaniel Branden[38]

---

*Reprinted with the permission of Simon & Schuster from *The Art of Living Consciously* by Carlos Castaneda. Copyright ©1997 by Nathaniel Branden.

Were the unconscious divorced from the conscious mind, it would no longer possess any logical reasoning ability, and second-stage NDE reports often suggest a lack of normal deductive logic and analytical reason in subjects' thought processes. Without the conscious mind, the unconscious would have no objectivity, and a lack of objectivity would mean an inability to tell the difference between truth and falsehood. The unconscious, by itself, has no concept of the word "no." The objective conscious mind is what throws seeds of doubt in the human psyche; without it, no doubt can be experienced.

The objective conscious mind discerns differences and distinguishes between them, accepting one thing while rejecting another. But without the logic and objectivity of the conscious mind, all thoughts running across the screen of the unconscious mind would be accepted equally, and then each and every impression, suggestion, hint, suspicion, and notion that entered one's head would seem to be obvious, compelling, and true. This is the dynamic that seems to take place during the second stage of NDEs.

> A doubtful message would be impossible to receive.
> —NDE-er quoted by Margot Grey[39]

NDE-ers regularly report an experience that seems to be direct and certain knowing; information received in this way is always felt to be 100 percent certain, despite having in no way been questioned, measured, analyzed, or independently verified. This attribution of certainty to one's perceptions is exactly the way the unconscious processes information. It does not critique it, or analyze it, or question it, but just accepts it without dispute or hesitation as absolute and obvious truth.

The dreamer who dreams that he can fly, or that he is walking naked into his place of business, or that his uncle has asparagus stalks for eyebrows, does not for a moment question the reality of these impressions at the time, but takes them calmly in stride, for there is no logic available in his thought processes at the time, no discriminative capacity to raise the red flags of doubt. Similarly, the hypnotized subject who is told she is a rooster does not argue or even consider questioning the fact, but instead expresses her "roosterness" with the sort of conviction that is seldom seen outside a traveling revival tent.

In much the same way, NDE-ers during the second stage regularly entertain thoughts and impressions which are never questioned at the time. Yet later, when the cold light of objective logic is brought to bear upon these "divinely inspired and therefore absolutely true" insights, one finds that the impressions of NDE-ers sometimes contradict those of others. For example, some NDE-ers insist that they received the "divine truth" that reincarnation is a false teaching, while others return from these paranormal episodes carrying the opposite message. Similar contradictions have occurred over other issues as well, such as the existence or nonexistence of the devil, the necessity or irrelevance of accepting Jesus, the permanent or temporary nature of the individual self, and the permanent or temporary nature of the hellish experience.

The loss of one's critical and analytical functions would also translate into a loss of curiosity, and this too is consistent with second-stage NDE reports. Just as curiosity often seems to be heightened during first-stage reports, it often seems to be just as diminished in the second stage. Having no doubts, subjects in the realm of light often feel no need to ask any questions:

> Once I fused with the light, I didn't have any questions.
> —NDE-er Jarod[40]

> I was so glad to be there, that there was nothing I needed to ask.
> —NDE-er Charles Nunn[41]

This mysterious absence of objective reasoning abilities during second stage NDEs seems to have much in common with how Hawaii's Kahuna priests described the afterdeath experience of the *unihipili* soul:

> Their ability to grasp new ideas proved far, far less than when they were on this physical level of life. The fact that on the other side we have very little vital force compared to what we have while in physical bodies, seems to make the difference between swift learning and sluggish inability to grasp unfamiliar ideas. All thought demands the use of vital force. Memories can be recalled and "remembered" with almost no vital force, but to make a new thought form is difficult. . . . The dead tend to stick tight to the things they believed, hoped for, or feared while alive.
> —Max Freedom Long[42]

Early Christians also believed that our reasoning abilities were taken away in the next world:

> It is not good for any man to fall into death. For a soul which has been found in death will be without reason.
>
> —The Teaching of Silvanius 105:1–6

A loss of one's critical and analytical functions also seems evident in second-stage reports of addictive behavior. We have read, time and again over the last twenty-five years of NDE research, that many souls in these second-stage realms still seemed to be enslaved to their earthly addictions, as if they had remained frozen in the behavior patterns they'd held at the moment of their deaths. Sex addicts, drug addicts, tobacco addicts, and food addicts have all been observed still desperately trying to satisfy their physical cravings, even though they now possess no physical bodies. They seem to be unable to intellectually grasp the simple fact that these cravings can no longer be satisfied.

> . . . the woman snatched at the lighted cigarette. . . . Again she grabbed at it. And again. With a chill of recognition I saw she was unable to grip it. . . . Then I noticed . . . a number of men standing at the bar seemed unable to lift their drinks to their lips. Over and over I watched them clutch at their shot glasses, hands passing through the solid tumblers . . . they would be cut off for all eternity from the thing they could never stop craving.
>
> —NDE-er George Ritchie[43]

This loss of analytical reasoning ability is perhaps most obvious in the second stage reports of the hellish realm of bewildered spirits. The inhabitants of this grey netherworld have repeatedly been described as being trapped in unfortunate and unpleasant conditions which they could get out of quite easily if only they tried. Yet they don't try, and they don't seem to grasp the fact that they could end their misery in a moment if only they tried. Such behavior points strongly to a loss of objective rational intellect.

Increased Memory

If the unconscious found itself separated from the conscious mind, it would seem likely to automatically experience a full life review much like that reported by NDE-ers. Without the conscious mind in the way, it would no longer be possible for the emotionally based mental input of the unconscious to be denied, ignored, rejected, repressed, minimalized, rationalized, or diluted in any way. Unbound at last, all the repressed emotions, forgotten memories, rejected insights, and unacknowledged self-judgments that had built up within the unconscious over the course of the person's life would spring forth, finally free of the restrictive influence of the conscious mind.

This dynamic would seem to explain the sudden, immediate, and total life review and self-judgment that so often occurs during the second stage of NDEs. Just as the binary soul doctrine would predict, these life reviews occur suddenly during the second stage of the NDE, releasing into full view all the memories of one's life, even private thoughts and feelings.

The judgment that occurs during this review is most typically experienced as being a self-judgment rather than a judgment that comes from a second party, just as the binary soul doctrine would anticipate. The dynamics of human psychology suggest that this judgment, although experienced during the NDE, would not actually have its origins in that moment, although it would certainly seem like it at the time. Rather, during the flood of memories, one would suddenly realize that one's own unconscious mind had been reactively judging her choices and actions all along, during every moment of her life. During the life review, one would finally come face to face with the sum total of all those past judgments about her behavior that her unconscious had generated over the course of her life, judgments which were originally refused recognition by the conscious mind.

People tend to keep many such self-judgments repressed, never allowing them to fully enter into their conscious awareness during life, causing these self-judgments to build up over the years, producing the psychological equivalent of a logjam (unless, of course, a person exercises extreme self-honesty, recognizing those self-judgments instead of repressing them). But after death, when the repressive conscious mind was taken away, all those judgments would be unbound, allowing the entire logjam to finally break, smashing into one's awareness in a single great convulsion, finally being acknowledged as they had been intended to do from their very inception. This would explain why the life review, which finally makes all these unconscious thoughts, feelings, and self-judgments starkly apparent, often makes people feel as if they have finally been revealed to themselves as they truly are for the first time. This sense of having been "exposed" is a very common theme in the second phase of NDEs; stripped of all one's illusions and denials and self-deceptions, one feels unaccustomedly exposed to oneself, as well as to all others in this realm.

Increased Reactiveness

If those memories, feelings, and judgments were primarily positive, the unconscious, being automatically responsive and emotional, would automatically respond to them by generating positive feelings and emotions. Since the unconscious is also very creative, constantly generating images, dreams, and fantasies, it could then be expected to automatically spin images, dreams, and fantasies to give shape to all those feelings, emotions, and self-judgments. If they were primarily positive, it would generate positive images, dreams, and fantasies to give them shape and manifestation, and in that unconscious' self-manufactured dreamworld, it would experience itself to be in heaven. However, if those memories, feelings, and judgments were negative, the unconscious's self-manufactured dreamworld reality would be hellish.

This process, however, would not necessarily seem to occur slowly or sequentially in a normal cause-and-effect, before-and-after pattern, since the unconscious is not known for operating in a step-by-step fashion. Instead, this sequential process could easily seem to occur instantaneously, moving directly from the life review to the final effect—experiencing the heavenly or hellish dreamscapes so familiar to second stage NDEs without any sense of the psychological processes that led from one to the other.

The "Realm of Bewildered Spirits" Explained?

The heavenly realm of light is not the only face of the second stage. Raymond Moody, Peter Fenwick, P. M. H. Atwater, Barbara Rommer, and many others have described a grey or hellish realm that subjects sometimes visit during the second stage instead, a place that seems to be home to hordes of bewildered, confused, and distressed souls. However, these two faces of the second stage seem, despite first appearances, to have much in common. In both, emotions and credibility predominate while reason and verbal expression seems diminished.

In the realm of light, communication often takes place using gestures, symbols, and direct mental comprehension instead of words. In the hellish realm, communication often seems to be absent, but when it does occur, it too relies more on images and gestures than verbal communication. Words

74

don't seem to work in either place, as experiences are often found to be inef-
fable—unable to be described in words. While the souls in the realm of light
are filled to overflowing with joy, love, happiness, and bliss, the souls in the
realm of bewildered spirits often seem "desperate and wailing," and suffering "intense" and "dreadful" emotions. Interestingly, while the heavenly and
hellish realms seem to produce the opposite emotions, the feelings are
equally intense in each.

The souls in the hellish realm seem to possess very low intelligence, initiative, volition, and vitality. Even more so than the souls in the realm of light,
they demonstrate virtually no intellectual curiosity. They seem so caught up
in their own misery that they are unaware of the presence of others. They
are, one might say, in a state of absolute subjectivity, unable to see beyond
themselves at all.

> These bewildered people . . . had sad, depressed looks;
> they seemed to shuffle, as someone would on a chain gang.
> . . . they looked washed out, dull, grey. . . . They seemed to be
> thinking, "Well it's all over with. What am I doing? What's it
> all about?" Just this absolute, crushed, hopeless demeanor—
> not knowing what to do or where to go or who they were or
> anything else. They seemed to be forever moving, rather
> than just sitting, but in no special direction. . . . They didn't
> seem to be aware of anything—not the physical world or the
> spiritual world . . . they all seemed to be bent down and look-
> ing downward . . . they all had the most woebegone expres-
> sions; there was no color of life. . . . There seems to have
> been a great array of them around.
> —NDE-er interviewed by Raymond Moody[44]

This realm of bewildered spirits, of course, is not unique to NDE reports.
In fact, it may be the single-most substantiated of all afterlife reports. This
realm has been independently reported by NDE-ers, OBE-ers, psychics,
seers, and shamans, and can be found in many netherworld traditions of
mankind's early civilizations, including Egypt, Greece, China, India, and
Israel. All these sources describe virtually the same place, with souls there in
virtually the same distressing condition:

> In the lower world I find . . . hundreds of other beings
> shuffling in a circle, all to themselves, all despondent, lost in

absolute timelessness. There is no growth or hope, just silent pacing.

—Sandra Ingerman, describing a journey into
the netherworld for a shamanic soul retrieval[45]

Men and women of all ages . . . were standing or squatting or wandering about on the plane. Some were mumbling to themselves. . . . They were completely self-absorbed, every one of them too caught up in his or her own misery to engage in any mental or emotional exchange.

—NDE-er Angie Fenimore[46]

Mankind's ancient legends of a hellish netherworld, it seems, are not merely empty myths, but a reality that is *still* being experienced and reported. Within a span of only two days, according to P. M. H. Atwater, the same hellish NDE vision was independently witnessed by four strangers:

A landscape of barren, rolling hills filled to overflowing with nude, zombie-like people standing elbow-to-elbow doing nothing but staring straight at [the NDE-ers].

—NDE-er and Researcher P. M. H. Atwater[47]

It seems that this dreary realm has existed for millennia with little or no change. While the realm of bewildered spirits has been described by many NDE-ers as "hellish" or "hell-like," it usually seems different from the fiery hell of Christian tradition. The Biblical hell, of course, is supposed to be a "lake of fire and brimstone," but the realm of bewildered spirits is usually described more like the netherworlds of Greece, China, and other ancient cultures—as a cold and barren place filled with semiconscious, naked, and starving automatons. Today, just as in the ancient Greek legends of Hades, the most common characteristics of the "hell" vision seem to be lifeless ghosts suffering anxiety attacks in suffocating expanses. The majority of NDE-ers still describe the hells they visit as hard and empty, with dulled or dimmed light, just as their counterparts were reporting thousands of years ago.

The souls there seem to display the characteristics one would expect of separated unconscious minds that no longer have access to their rational conscious halves. These beings seem to possess extremely low intelligence, no objective awareness, no intellectual curiosity, no verbal communication, and seem to be entirely caught up in their own emotions.

Have the souls in this realm lost all access to their conscious minds? At least one NDE-er seems to have thought so, feeling as if his conscious mind was too deeply buried within for him to successfully access it during a hellish experience:

> I wanted to call out but no sound would come. It felt as if my brain or consciousness was buried deep within me and was too deeply embedded for me even to make it work.
> —NDE-er quoted by Peter Fenwick[48]

NDE-ers frequently insist that these ghostlike souls can get out of this horrid place any time they wish, if only they tried. But they *don't* try, and furthermore, they can't seem to figure out that they could get out if only they would try. The inhabitants of this realm seem convinced that there is no way for them to escape.

> There is no way to escape, no way out. You don't even try to look for one.
> —NDE-er Thomas Welch[49]

This is not normal human behavior. Every prison on earth, no matter how bleak, rat-infested, and torturous, is filled with people who remain alert and vigilant for the slightest hint of a chance to escape. The contrast between this behavior and that of the souls in the realm of bewildered spirits could not be more striking. The fact that these lost souls have somehow lost their will to even *try* to escape strongly suggests the absence of the human spirit during these second-stage experiences.

During normal human life, no matter how desperate the situation, no matter how thoroughly imprisoned and inhumanly mistreated a group of inmates might be, the indomitable will of the human spirit prevents them from giving up entirely. Regardless of the circumstances, there are (on earth, anyway) always a stubborn few who never give up, who never stop scheming for a way out. We humans are proud of our refusal to give up in the face of insurmountable odds, and much of our art and literature celebrates this majesty of the human spirit. We thrill at movies like *Papillon, Cool Hand Luke, Rocky,* and *The Shawshank Redemption,* for they remind us of the infinite potential for self-determination within each of us.

If there's one thing that makes human beings godlike, it is our free will. You can do anything to a man, even strip his flesh from his bones and burn his wife and children, but you cannot change his mind—only he can do that.

What a man chooses, what he wills within the solitude of his mind, is his to control. In our volition, and our volition alone, we are infinite; in the autonomy of his will, each human being is a god.

But the mystery is, this inner infinity, this autonomous free will, seems to be entirely lacking in the realm of bewildered spirits. Although freedom is apparently right at hand, ripe for the taking, that indomitable will is nowhere to be seen. That particular puzzle-piece is clearly missing from the picture, and it draws attention to itself by its absence. This suggests a scenario much in keeping with the binary soul doctrine: these lost souls are now but partial creatures, human fragments that lack a huge portion of what they had once had, of what they had once been, of what had once made them whole human beings in life—their independent volition and rational intellect.

There is a conflict, however, between what the logic of the binary soul doctrine would tell us about this realm and what the reports of NDE-ers tell us. If these souls had divided in two at death, losing their left-brain conscious minds, they would no longer be able to make independent free will decisions, and so would be permanently trapped in that state, unable to *choose* to get out even if that was all it would take to escape. But NDE-ers frequently insist that these souls *do* still possess independent free will choice, and can leave this misery whenever they choose. This is a conflict of logic; only one or the other of these positions can be correct.

Many other (non-NDE) paranormal sources have declared that the souls in the other world do not have their conscious minds, but are functioning exclusively in and through the unconscious. This has been the position of Edgar Cayce, Emanuel Swedenborg, Rudolf Steiner, James Van Praagh, and Sylvia Brown. Yet if this is true, that would decisively rule out any free will in the other realm. Unable to realize the existence of choices, options, and alternatives, the unconscious on its own could not exercise self-determination, and would essentially be a mindless machine running automatically, which, as it turns out, is an accurate summary of most NDE-ers' reports of the behavior observed in this realm.

Yet NDE-ers themselves often insist that, although they witnessed no evidence of it themselves, the souls in this realm are not trapped, and can leave whenever they wish. However, in all the descriptions of the realm of bewildered spirits I have run across, I have yet to encounter a description of one of those lost souls actually *exercising* free will and choosing to leave that dreadful place. No evidence of that alleged free will seems to exist, except, it seems, in the steadfast conviction of NDE-ers themselves. Even though all their descriptions of this realm point clearly to the opposite conclusion, NDE-ers remain unaccountably convinced that those miserable souls are not trapped.

Why is this?

Neuropsychiatrist Peter Fenwick, President of the British Branch of International Association for Near-Death Studies (IANDS), has suggested that this unaccountable certainty is due to the fact that the right-brain, unconscious half of the mind processes all mental experience during NDEs. This would make sense for second-stage NDE phenomena—the unconscious has no capacity for doubt (no word for "no"), and so all thoughts running across the mind's eye at such a time would be bathed in the same conviction and certainty.

So it seems that even the NDE-ers' certainty that "these souls are free" tends to point, not to freedom per se, but to the likelihood that these souls of the dead possess only their unconscious and not their conscious minds. As happens so often in life, the report of the witness seems to tell us more about the mental state of the witness than about what was witnessed.

NDE-ers report two different versions of this hellish realm, giving us what seem to be two different perspectives of this place—one seen from the inside, one from the outside. Those who observe it from outside tend to describe it as a dark, cold, and dreary place, in which the occupants seem to be wandering aimlessly, each of them caught up in private thoughts and horrible feelings. But those who describe it from the inside describe a vastly different place. Each NDE-er who personally enters this hellish realm seems to describe a horrifying nightmare world of hideous tortures and gruesome visual imagery.

> What I saw was the most hideous, horrible thing! This was no nightmare! These horrible black things came out and were grabbing me. There were people screaming. It was unearthly voices, not earthly. It was horrible! These things were all over me and they were screaming. I think I was naked there, because I remember feeling very ashamed. Everything was dark. I couldn't tell where the screaming was coming from. Then I actually saw these things, like horrible human beings, like anorexics. Their teeth were all ugly and twisted. Their eyes were bulging. They were bald, no hair, and weren't wearing anything. They were naked! There must have been at least fifty, everywhere, all around me. They were grabbing at my arms and my hair, and were screaming, pitiful screams. . . . They were wet, like sweaty, and they smelled so foul, like a rotting thing, like death.
>
> —NDE-er Sadira[50]

> I was frightened, exhausted, cold, and lost. . . . The hopelessness of my situation overwhelmed me. . . . They began to tear off pieces of my flesh. To my horror, I realized that I was being taken apart and eaten alive, methodically, slowly, so that their entertainment would last as long as possible. . . . I haven't described everything that happened. There are things that I don't care to remember. In fact, much that occurred was simply too gruesome and disturbing to recall. I've spent years trying to suppress a lot of it. After the experience, whenever I did remember those details, I would become traumatized.
>
> —NDE-er Howard Storm[51]

But descriptions of this place as seen from the outside never seem to include this nightmarish imagery. NDE-ers in the realm of light sometimes find that they can peer over into the Realm of Bewildered Souls, looking in on it from the outside. When they do, they tend to describe the hellish realm as grey, dreary, and dull, its inhabitants wandering around aimlessly, but then, paradoxically, they describe these inhabitants as experiencing acute emotional distress, feelings that seem strikingly out of sync with the bland dullness of their apparent surroundings.

This discrepancy leads one to suspect that these technicolor scenes of vivid torture are in fact the psychological nightmares these souls are enduring in that realm, each of them caught up in his own private dream of hell. But when outside observers look in on this realm, they do not see those nightmares, but only the sleepwalking figures themselves, and the anguish of their dreams. The feelings these souls experience, it seems, are the common denominator, observable from either perspective. This suggests, as the binary soul doctrine would predict, that those feelings are the only true reality of this experience, and that all these visions of torture are just dream images giving shape to those feelings.

> The all-consuming physical pain was nothing compared to the emotional pain. Their psychological cruelty to me was unbearable.
>
> —NDE-er Howard Storm[52]

> I will never forget the pain. It wasn't physical at all. That's what was so terrifying. It was emotional, psychological, and spiritual pain.
>
> —NDE-er Jay[53]

Metaphorical Communication

. . . all along my near-death subjects have insisted that the words they use to describe their experiences are only analogies or metaphors used to indicate experiences that ultimately lie beyond all human language.

—Researcher Raymond Moody[54]

If one acknowledges the preponderance of parallels between the descriptions of second-stage NDEs and the characteristics of the right-brain unconscious, one is forced to consider the possibility that the entire second stage of the classic NDE is experienced solely by the unconscious while it is in a state of near or full disassociation from the conscious mind. If so, this would require one to drastically reevaluate all these second-stage descriptions, for the unconscious does not process or relate information the same way the conscious mind does.

The unconscious is not literal, logical, linear, or rational. It does not think or communicate the way the conscious mind does, and knowing this, one cannot accept its communications at face value the way one does with communications from the conscious mind, which is literal, logical, and rational. Instead, the unconscious mind "thinks" and communicates with metaphors, symbols, images, gestures, and so on, and any communication or input coming from the unconscious must be viewed as such.

Dreams are communications from the unconscious, messages generated within the unconscious to be released into our conscious awareness. So, some say, are the world's great myths. Both dreams and myths follow the same rules of operation in effect within the unconscious. They do not paint a literal picture of what they are trying to communicate, but instead take a nonlinear route, relating their message using metaphors, analogies, symbols, images, gestures, and so on. If, as the evidence suggests, the second stage of NDEs is experienced more or less exclusively by the unconscious half of the psyche, its descriptions of those experiences should then be viewed in much the same way people view dreams and myths—as messages that should not be taken literally, but that need to be translated and interpreted before they can be comprehended.

NDEs as Circumstantial Evidence of the Division?

Right on down the list, the two stages of NDEs reflect the two halves of the human psyche, the dark stage bringing the enhancement of the characteristics of the conscious mind and the diminishment of those of the unconscious, while the light stage does the opposite. The dark stage brings a decrease in emotion, connectedness, form-perception, and subjectivity, and an increase in autonomy, logic, reason, and objectivity, while the light stage brings the opposite.

An argument could be made that the first stage also includes some memory loss—remembering no wants and needs, one experiences oneself as *having* no wants, needs, or addictions in the first stage. The apparently equal but opposite second stage brings an increase in memory (and not just during the life review, either), and as this would of course include the memories of all one's earthly wants, needs, and addictions, one would experience oneself as still having all those wants, needs, and addictions.

An argument could even be made that there is some diminishment of free will in the second stage. Those still obsessed with desires for food, drink, sex, or other addictions find themselves unable to break free of those yearnings even though they find themselves no longer able to satisfy them. Such a diminishment of free will would be consistent with such a division, for the conscious mind holds the free will, and on its own, the unconscious would not. Free will depends on being aware that different alternatives exist. On its own, the unconscious could never choose to change its behavior patterns; it could never even grasp the fact that these behaviors were no longer capable of leading to fulfillment. Instead, the unconscious, on its own, would just continue to try, again and again and again, ceaselessly, just as the reports of second-stage NDEs indicate.

But Most NDE-ers Do Not Report Such a Division

Detail after detail suggests that the two halves of the psyche are operating independently of each other during these two stages, as if they were, as the ancients believed, in the process of splitting apart from each other in the moments after physical death. But such a splitting is *not* what most NDE-ers report, nor what they believe themselves to be experiencing during these episodes. The idea of their minds splitting apart is alien to them and absent from their interpretation of the experience.

Their impression, rather, is that these two stages occur one after the other, in the normal continuous progression of moments in time: first comes the dark stage, then the light stage follows it, the way time normally operates. Yet NDE-ers themselves contradict this interpretation, consistently insisting that time is not experienced normally during NDEs. Again and again reports declare that "time as we know it" does not exist during NDEs. If so, then the dark stage and the light stage may not necessarily be arranged in the assumed time sequence of "before and after," but both may in fact be occurring *at the same time*, independently of each other, just as the binary soul doctrine suggested thousands of years ago.

But if two halves of the psyche *do* split apart from each other during many NDEs, why is this not noticed and reported? One answer might be simply because if such a division did occur, neither side of the mind would realize it. The conscious mind would have no memory of it, and the unconscious mind would no longer possess the analytical tools necessary to figure it out. But the explanation may even be more basic.

Most of us, as we move through the days and weeks and years of our lives, don't consciously perceive that our minds have two distinct parts. Even though the differentiation of the self into two parts, conscious and unconscious, or spirit and soul, or right and left brain hemispheres, is a well-known truth both scientifically and theologically, the average person doesn't identify with this truth on a personal level. And so, since the average person is not experientially aware that these two parts exist within himself, then it is no surprise that the average person would not notice any change in the relationship between these two parts if such a change in fact occurred.

The Divided-Soul NDE: Eyewitness Testimony of the Division

> Our death . . . is likely to be different from what we might have imagined.
>
> —Researcher Kenneth Ring[55]

But some NDE-ers *do* recall this division. In 1978, David King, a teenager from Lubbock, Texas, wrecked his car on a country road, propelling him into an NDE in which he believes he experienced a total separation between the conscious and unconscious halves of his psyche. David described it as follows:

> I found myself outside the car crash and eventually the physical body. I was still in a mental frame of mind when my spirit did leave the body. Then I heard the voice of another soul behind me. It was the backside of who and what I was in spiritual form. We were one body in that spiritual form. The two of us were one together. I am still struggling to find the "wordage" to define the type of body we

shared together when I experienced the NDE. Then the separation occurred—we were in one body together prior to entering the light—and in two separate "spiritual forms" when we returned. I felt like I was "cut in two parts" and the "Spirit of God" passed between the two parts. What overwhelmed my mental process in the out-of-body part of the NDE was the realization that there was two parts to me, and these two parts had divided apart. I have had other NDEs, but all of them have centered on this same theme. The separation of two parts and the reunion of those two parts while in physical form. Moments after the "spirit" departed the body, there was a separation of the "soul." It was divided into two parts. I am still not sure what to call those two parts. For now—I stick to the "spiritual unconscious" and the "mental conscious." It is very hard to put it into words that make logical sense to others. That is one of the dramatic differences I see in my own NDE memories and what I have read of others.[56]

This is a rare example of a subject who actually remembers a soul-division taking place during an NDE. But David King is not the *only* one who remembers going through something like this. Reports of soul-divisions have been published by a number of NDE researchers; in fact, Dr. Peter Fenwick specifically includes "a splitting of consciousness" as one of the classic phenomena associated with the near-death experience in *The Truth in the Light.* Dr. Melvin Morse, another well-known researcher, reported two similar stories in his book *Transformed by the Light:* one man named Olaf Sunden experienced his own mind "splitting into two parts" during his NDE, and, in what Morse called a "Fear Death Experience" a high school student who split into two parts while swimming off the coast of California described it "literally like having two sets of eyes connected to the same brain."

Soul-division experiences also apparently occur during hellish NDEs.[57] On September 12, 1992, three days after having a mechanical heart valve put in her chest, a code blue was called on a Floridian named Maggie D.:

The experience was a bad experience. I went to hell, I really went to hell! Nobody can change my mind about that. In the beginning of the experience, I felt that something was underneath me, lifting me so I couldn't move, and was pushing or pulling me forward toward a dark brown door. I was sucked through this very huge clear wall of Jell-o-like substance into a dark, dungeon-type room, where all I could hear was wailing and crying and moaning.

There were thousands and thousands of people crying at the same time, and everyone was just in agony. It was so terrifying to hear them, like they were being chopped up or killed. Whenever they spoke, it wasn't the actual words, it was as if we had telepathy. I could hear them but their mouths didn't move. When I spoke, I also didn't have my mouth move, but I had the sensation that the words were being pulled out of me. I felt like I was shriveling up almost to nothing. I felt like I was just going to die right there. I didn't know what to do. I felt like I was really in hell, and I screamed that I had to go back, that I could not stay there.

The more I screamed, the louder these whines got, these whiney cries, and you could hear, like, crowds and crowds of people crying and screaming and whining. When I was in this hole, dungeon-type place, I didn't feel like I was over my body. I felt like I was standing next to it, directly next to it. . . . This other person . . . looked worse than I did. But I knew it was me!—another section of me was right next to me! I felt like I had half a body. I felt that other part had my other half, and it has never come back. Something in my spirit, or soul, or whatever you want to call it, was taken away from me, and it has never come back. And me—my emotions—listen—whatever that part is—is gone—I miss that part of me. It's never coming back. I know that.[58]

Maggie's soul-division experience is especially interesting, not only because it was a hellish NDE, but because she specifically identifies the divided-away part with her emotions. Like Peggy Holladay's split-soul episode (quoted at the beginning of this chapter), Maggie also felt that this other part was an integral element of her being that had somehow been separated from her. While Peggy perceived this as being that part of her that contained her personal memories, Maggie saw it as the part that had contained her personal emotions. As the Egyptians had done thousands of years earlier, Peggy and Maggie recognized this other part as another, second "self." Just as Peggy had cried out "It's my ego! I had to have it or I wouldn't be alive," so too Maggie insisted "It was me! I knew it was me!—another section of me was right next to me."

Maggie insisted that this state of soul-division continued after the NDE was over. This seems to be the exception rather than the rule; in most NDEs, the two parts are only temporarily divided, and once the episode is over, they bounce back together, thereafter enjoying an even closer relationship than they'd had before the NDE occurred.

P. M. H. Atwater, an internationally-recognized authority on near-death experiences, came across a rare soul-division NDE which included dual vision—the subject witnessed her own soul standing outside her body, and yet was also looking out of the "eyes" of that disembodied soul at the same time:

> I could see my spirit standing before me. My spirit was so beautifully perfect . . . It was so strange, for I could see my spirit and my spirit could see my pathetic body. I had not an ounce of color and I looked all withered and cold and lifeless.
> —NDE-er Jazmyne Cidavia-DeRepentigny[59]

As might be expected, having one's consciousness divide into two parts like this was a very confusing and disorienting experience. Atwater tells us that Jazmyne felt torn between two worlds during her NDE: one self wanted to remain on earth, while her other self just wanted to slip off into the light.

In her book *Blessing in Disguise*, Dr. Barbara Rommer presents a very similar case, in which a woman named Sadhana not only experienced soul-division, but then still experienced "being" both halves at the same time. After getting feverish from contaminated water in India, Sadhana's consciousness split apart into two independent units—she found herself observing reality from the perspective of two different nonphysical selves at the same time. She described it like this:

> I was laying down on the bed . . . tossing and turning, hair matting in the water of the sweat.
> The first thing was—I saw myself—sitting at the bottom of the bed, cross legged as we tend to do in India. And I *also* saw the body that was tossing and turning there. The one that was watching was totally relaxed and there was a total consciousness. The first body is called the watcher and the

second is called the witness, and is not cognitive and does not communicate with the other. The witness has no thought, but had total awareness, but does not cognate, doesn't understand. It's merely a witness.

—NDE-er Sadhana[60]

This is quite different from the soul-division episodes of Maggie, David, and Peggy, who were cut off from the mental input of their other halves during their NDEs. While Maggie, David, Sadhana, Jazmyne, and Peggy all recognized these separated parts as being essential elements of their beings, only Sadhana and Jazmyne apparently remained undivided enough to still be able to peer out through the eyes of both halves at the same time.

Sadhana not only seems to have temporarily experienced her mind being divided into two distinct and nonintegrated components, but the way she describes these two parts seems to be consistent with the conscious and unconscious. She credits the "watcher" self with consciousness, which sounds like the conscious mind. She also says it was extremely relaxed during the experience, which also seems to fit, since the conscious half of the mind seems to be the self that experiences the dark stage of NDEs, associated with a deep feeling of calm and peace.

Sadhana's "other" self, the "witness," fits the pattern, too. It does not communicate, has no thought, cognition, or comprehension. This sounds like the unconscious, which is nonverbal and nonrational, unable to communicate verbally or appreciate logic or abstract thought. Even the name she gives this self—the "witness," brings to mind the fact that the unconscious, while having no rational thought of its own, contains a perfect memory record of one's life experience. It is, in that respect at least, very much indeed a perfect witness of the events of one's life.

In her book, Dr. Rommer also included the case of an NDE-er named Eve who reported being split into three separate pieces during her NDE— one physical body and two other nonphysical components. Like Maggie, Eve also realized that both these nonphysical selves were of equal value and necessity. She found that she had to reconnect *both* nonphysical selves before she could successfully reenter her body.[61]

I have also encountered other NDE-ers who experienced a soul-division during their NDEs. One individual was thrilled when he first learned of the binary soul doctrine, exclaiming: "This explains so much. I have wondered these years why I saw these visions from more than one perspective, and why I felt literally torn apart during my NDE. This explains so much!"

To Be or Not to Be? Division of the Self

> Identity ceases. The "you" that you once were becomes only a memory.
>
> —NDE-er and Researcher P. M. H. Atwater[62]

What does this division do to the *self*? The ancient Egyptians and Taoists, the reader will recall, felt that this division would disintegrate the person's identity and selfhood, and understandably went through a great deal of trouble to try to prevent this dissolution. Today we sometimes hear a very similar message in the reports of NDE-ers:

> No words were spoken but my predicament was completely understood. I loved my wife more dearly than life itself and I could not leave her like this. I knew that we would never meet again because as individuals we would cease to exist. The concept is so very sad and it is utterly inadequate to say that it does not matter.
>
> —NDE-er Allan Pring[63]

But many in the NDE community hesitate to arrive at this disturbing conclusion. Kenneth Ring, for example, justified Peggy Holladay's soul-division experience (quoted at the beginning of this chapter) by arguing that the part of the soul she saw splitting away, the "ego" that carried Peggy's personal feelings, emotions, memories, and self-evaluations, was not her "real self," but was really just an invalid, worthless, "false self." This is not a new attitude; many traditions have taken this pro-division, partisan approach for millennia, dismissing the unconscious soul and all of its feminine, emotional, subjective characteristics as false, unworthy, and invalid. Indeed, from the perspective of the dispassionate, objective, conscious mind, the subjective emotional nature of the unconscious *does seem* to be invalid and false, a fact we see illustrated in Peggy's subsequent conclusions:

> I was completely unemotional. . . . I saw some shiny, clear object lift away from my body. It was obvious to me it was my ego . . . in it I saw all the things I had done wrong in my life. I was stunned because I thought all that was part of me and simply couldn't be separated from me. I can't tell you how happy I was when it dawned on me that "that was never me." That identity was never the real me.
>
> —NDE-er Peggy Holladay[64]

What made Peggy arrive at that conclusion? Once the conscious mind had separated from its equal but opposite other half, its design would automatically cause it to perceive its unconscious partner as an alien other, unreal and unrelated. The conscious mind would dispassionately view its own unconscious through the same lens it was seeing everything during that dark stage, from a disconnected, unrelated, unemotional, nonattached perspective.

> What is key about neurosis? It is the split self—a feeling self which is sealed away from an understanding self. It often happens that a person will start to feel but then "splits." He observes the self, rather than reacting. The real self begins to feel but the neurotic self splits away, aborting the feeling process. . . .
>
> —Dr. Arthur Janov[65]

The question to be asked is, can we accept assessments like Peggy's at face value, knowing how the components of the mind would be likely to function during such a division? Statements about the unreality and unconnectedness and worthlessness of *anything* during this stage, whether one was referring to one's body, family relationships, career, *or this other half of the self,* would inevitably reflect the cold, mechanistic, and computer-like (dare I say inhuman?) perspective of the left-brain conscious during such a division. Such statements would not necessarily reflect valid judgment at all.

After all, the unemotional half of the mind that casually dismisses the value of all family relationships in most dark-stage NDEs was the same half of the mind that just as glibly dismissed the value of this other self during Peggy's dark-stage experience. If we are to accept the assessment of Peggy's dark-stage mind that this other half of her being is worthless and false, we are forced by the same logic to conclude that all other impressions during this dark stage are equally accurate, which would be to say that all feelings, relationships, and attachments in life are without value as well. That is, after all, what most people report feeling during the dark stage:

> My mother, husband, and baby boy . . . would be sad at my death but I didn't feel despondent. In fact, it didn't seem to make much difference to me at all!
>
> —NDE-er quoted by Maurice Rawlings[66]

Of course, most NDE-ers usually return from the second stage with a very different perspective than they had during the first stage:

> Every person is sent to earth to . . . discover that the
> most important thing is human relationships and love.
> —NDE-er Howard Storm[67]

Famous relationship guru Leo Buscaglia would probably argue that one's innermost subjective emotions are the most precious part of human life, and without them, no afterlife would be worth the bother. Yet the part of the human mind in operation during the first stage of most NDEs would seem to strongly disagree with the above sentiment, and it was *this* cold, unemotional first-stage mind that concluded that the other half of Peggy's being was without value.

The Rebound Effect

> The Near-Death phenomenon seems to stimulate the
> brain hemisphere that was not previously dominant.
> —NDE-er and Researcher P. M. H. Atwater[68]

As we've seen, both circumstantial and eyewitness evidence suggests that a temporary division or disassociation of consciousness often takes place during NDEs. But then, paradoxically, these paranormal experiences seem to leave subjects in a state of improved or enhanced mental integration *after* the fact. NDE-ers often emerge from these episodes with healthier minds and more balanced, happy, and comfortable outlooks on life. They often feel more creative and effective, and sometimes even seem to have new psychic abilities.

Psychological health often seems to have dramatically improved; again and again in the literature, we read that men end up more in touch with their feminine sides, women with their masculine sides. Many who had previously been more right-brained, intuitive, and unconscious-oriented find themselves becoming more left-brained, analytical, and conscious-oriented, and vice versa. NDE-ers, it seems, enjoy a far stronger, closer, healthier, more balanced and fruitful relationship between the two sides of their psyches than they had prior to their experiences.

This seems like a paradox. Both the circumstantial and eyewitness evidence seem to indicate that the mind really does start to divide apart at death to at least some degree, but the aftereffects show the parts of the mind to be working in *closer* unison and integration than they had before. This suggests a "rubber band" hypothesis: if NDEs stretch apart the conscious and unconscious, might those two halves then snap back together into a closer, more integrated relationship afterwards? John 11:14–16 seems to suggest such a metaphysical law.

> Then Jesus told them plainly, "Lazarus is dead, and for your sake I am glad I was not there, so that you may believe. But let us go to him." Then Thomas said to the rest of the disciples, "Let us go also, that we may die with him."
> —John 11:14–16

This passage, which seems to depict one or more of Jesus' disciples contemplating suicide, has been a challenge for biblical analysts for millennia. But if in fact those disciples were fully expecting to not only recover from those brushes with death, but to benefit from them as well, it may be one of the earliest records of human awareness of the rubber-band effect of NDEs. The 36th chapter of the Tao Te Ching also suggests such a metaphysical law:

> What is to be shrunken is first stretched out;
> What is to be weakened is first made strong;
> What will be thrown over is first raised up;
> What will be withdrawn is first bestowed.
> —Tao Te Ching 36

It does seem like a paradox. By embracing death, NDE-ers have become more alive. By experiencing division, they become more whole (and that, perhaps, is what life is really all about). But if so, then what happens when it's not just a *near*-death experience, but actual death itself? If the actual event of "returning to life" is what snaps these divided halves back together in NDEs, then what happens to humanity's billions who don't return, but just remain dead? Does the division still miraculously rebound all by itself anyway, or, as seems more likely, would the process of division then just continue under its own momentum until it became total and permanent?

Near-death experiences, by definition, cannot answer that question.

4

Descendants of Division:
Past-Life Regression

> The soul is able to divide into identical parts . . . because of
> the dual capacity of all souls, part of our light energy always
> remains behind in the spirit world.
>
> —*PLR Therapist Michael Newton*[1]

The modern world is doubly blessed, for NDE-ers are not the only crowd of people who claim to have personal memories of traveling beyond death's door. There is also another group of first-hand experiencers, whose reports (fortunately for the rest of us) substantiate NDE-ers' descriptions in many respects. All this data is a new thing on the planet. Until the modern age, the only source of information we had about what happens at death was the pronouncements of a few eccentric seers, mystics, and prophets (who, if truth be told, did not always paint the most consistent picture about what we ought to expect).

But now, for the first time in history, we have two huge groups of first-hand experiencers—NDE-ers and past-life regression subjects—who comprise an army of witnesses reporting essentially the same story. Recent studies suggest that at least thirty million people around the world have had NDEs, and a million or so more have successfully accessed memories of previous incarnations via past-life regression. Together, that makes more people living today who have personal memories of what happens after death than the populations of Paris, London, New York, and Tokyo combined.

Past-life regression, or PLR, started taking off as a widespread practice at just about the same time NDE research began. The two fields are like brother and sister, like two eyes looking at the same phenomenon from slightly different perspectives. PLR, of course, is based on the concept of reincarnation; subjects are regressed in their memories, through hypnosis or other means, to what seem to be convincing recollections of previous lives and deaths.

PLR research, however, has one disadvantage compared to NDE research. It depends on a belief in reincarnation, and outside of that context, these apparent memories have no objective meaning, though they do have tremendous subjective value, often being quite the therapeutic miracle cure. But PLR research also has at least one striking advantage over NDE research; if their memories are to be believed, PLR subjects were not just "nearly" dead at all. While NDE-ers apparently return from the threshold of death without actually crossing it, PLR subjects seem to discover memories of having once fully crossed over into "the land of no return."

Past-life regression is amazing. It seems to quite literally raise the dead. The ego, the self, the person as he knew himself in a past life, seems to be reassembled, made to exist again, simply by reconnecting the conscious mind of today with the unconscious mind of yesteryear. When people are hypnotically regressed in their memories to previous lifetimes, they momentarily *become* their previous selves again. Those long-silent egos exist anew, able once more to speak with their old voices and think with their old minds, able to react and perceive as they had in the past, able to experience anew. *Alive again.*

In one experiment, a regressed subject was instructed to open his eyes and look around at the twentieth-century room his body was now sitting in. He did, and marveled at what he saw. Though simple, this act was stunning in its significance, for it went far beyond merely tapping past memories—it added *new* experience to the memory banks of someone long dead. It temporarily restored them to life. And so, it seemed to put the lie to the Buddhist doctrine that no ego survives the trip from rebirth to rebirth. It seems that an ego *does* survive, but it is a temporarily disassembled ego.

The New Face of Reincarnation

. . . we want to integrate Freud and Buddha . . . the profound discoveries of the modern West—the whole notion of

> a psychodynamic unconscious, which is really found
> nowhere else . . . can be integrated with the mystical or con-
> templative traditions, both East and West, for a more full-
> spectrum approach.
>
> —Ken Wilber[2]

Reincarnation cannot be what most people think it is. The concept of reincarnation most familiar to people today is an obsolete model of the processes
involved, failing to take into account modern science's discovery of the active
unconscious. The old world's outdated model of reincarnation would have us
believe that between one lifetime and the next, we lose our memories, but
other than that, we are essentially unchanged and unaffected by the transition.

For ages, the reincarnational traditions assumed that these abandoned
memories (which included the person's personality and sense of identity
from the past life, with all his likes, dislikes, hopes, dreams, worries, fears,
suspicions, passions, discoveries, realizations, and hard-won skills) just go
into some kind of cold storage, deep in the back of the mind, becoming dormant and nonfunctional. However, this is impossible. Modern psychology
has discovered that material deposited in the unconscious never becomes
dormant, but always remains active, perpetually running its own programs
and privately registering its own subjective experiences, for however long it
remains in the unconscious.

> . . . complexes in the subconscious do not change in the
> same way that they do in consciousness . . . they are not cor-
> rected, but are conserved in their original form . . . they take
> on the uninfluencable and compulsive characteristics of an
> automatism, of which they can be divested only if they are
> made conscious.
>
> —C. G. Jung[3]

Modern science's discovery of the psychodynamic unconscious points
directly to the binary soul doctrine. If the conscious mind reincarnated, the
contents of the past-life unconscious would neither cease to exist nor even
become dormant; on the contrary, the unconscious would continue to function actively, just doing so on its own, thinking, feeling, and experiencing its
own private dream-world reality. Cutting off the memories of a past life
between one lifetime and the next would simply result in two separate parts
of the mind continuing on independently of each other after that. Like a

worm cut in half, each half of the psyche would continue to live and function, neither part realizing that the other still existed.

Emphasis on the Void

> What manner of land is this into which I have come? It hath
> not water, it hath not air; it is deep unfathomable, it is black as
> the blackest night, and men wander helplessly therein.
> —Egyptian Book of the Dead, Chapter CLXXV

The data coming in from PLR research seems to have much in common with that of NDE research. Past-life regression reports have also been known to describe both the dark and light stages, and some PLR subjects also claim to have personally divided apart into two soul-pieces in between one life and the next. However, there are some formidable differences between these two sets of reports. NDE reports tend to focus more on the heavenly realm of light of the second stage, while PLR subjects tend far more frequently to speak only of the empty void of the dark stage. Most of the time, PLR subjects find themselves floating quietly alone in between lives, experiencing nothing in a peaceful, emotionless black void, which seems to be essentially the same void that NDE-ers briefly experience during the first moments of their experiences. This void doesn't fit any traditional notion of heaven or hell, but it does seem a lot like Western theology's idea of limbo. While the dark stage is usually very brief in NDEs, often overlooked altogether in the transition to the spectacular light stage, the dark stage seems to receive far more emphasis in PLR reports.

Both the dark and light stages occasionally appear in PLR reports. Like NDE reports, PLR reports also occasionally describe both these afterlife scenarios, and this agreement is of tremendous significance to all afterlife researchers because here two different sets of witnesses are substantiating each other's reports. But there are some huge differences between the ways these groups describe these afterlife experiences, and these differences may be clues pointing towards some important new realizations about the nature of death and the afterlife. There are two major differences; one has to do with the *frequency* of these dark void reports, and the other has to do with the *duration* of these experiences. In PLR reports, the dark void is more frequently described as the primary afterlife experience, and it also seems to last for a far longer duration than in NDE reports.

In most NDE reports, the predominant focus is the light stage, not the dark stage. The dark stage, or tunnel experience, is often glossed over, often barely mentioned at all. But in PLR reports, this pattern often seems reversed.

In the many different books on PLR research that have been published over the last twenty-five years, the dark stage is by far the most frequently mentioned afterlife experience. In fact, the vast majority of these published PLR reports *only* mention the empty void, and never say anything about a realm of light.

> Most past life regressionists thought our life between lives was just a hazy limbo that only served as a bridge from one past life to the next.
> —PLR researcher Michael Newton[4]

In the typical NDE, the void seems to be very brief, coming and going very quickly. But PLR reports often say that people float quietly alone in that empty darkness for years, even decades, before returning to life again in a new body. Many PLR subjects never catch so much as a glimpse of the second stage at any point during their between-lives experience; they never see the heavenly realm of light or the hellish realm of bewildered spirits. For them, the between-life experience is a bland, neutral, quiet, emotionless void.

Some PLR researchers maintain that the afterlife experience described in PLR reports is identical to those of NDE reports. But none of these researchers offer any explanation for why so many more PLR subjects seem to only experience the void in between lives, or why this dark stage, which comes and goes so quickly in NDE reports, seems to last so long in so many PLR reports.

There currently is a disagreement within the ranks of regression researchers about what occurs in-between lives. Some regression therapists find that the majority of their subjects usually only describe floating alone in the empty void between lives, while other regression therapists find that the majority of their subjects describe afterlife experiences inside the realm of light. Dr. Janet Cunningham, past president of the International Association for Regression Research and Therapy (IARRT), estimates that, "the majority of past-life therapists find the client going to a place of 'Light' after they leave the body at death."[5]

But many other PLR therapists would disagree. Many say that the majority of their clients never experience the light, but only the empty void between lives. For instance, Thomas Brown, a member of the IARRT and past-life therapist from Detroit, finds that the majority of his clients only experience the dark void in between lives. A number of other researchers also point towards the void as the afterlife scenario most frequently described by their subjects. In at least five books on past-life regression, *Life Between Life* by Dr. Joel L. Whitton and Joe Fisher, *Many Lives, Many Masters* by Dr. Brian Weiss, *Other Lives, Other Selves* by Dr. Roger Woolger, *You Will Live*

Again by Brad Steiger, and *You Have Been Here Before* by Dr. Edith Fiore, the void experience is emphasized.

The details of these reports are similar to the dark stage of NDE reports. Subjects hypnotically regressed to memories of being between lives often describe themselves floating in blackness, not knowing where they are, not seeing anything, not feeling anything or doing anything or experiencing anything. They usually feel unemotional, detached, peaceful, and alone. They see no form, pattern, or meanings. They experience no emotions and do not concern themselves with memories. Unlike the vibrant and thrilling realm of light experience, this afterlife experience brings a lessening or muting of one's emotions, and sometimes even of one's memory and sense of identity.

PLR Researchers: Whitton and Fisher

The dark-stage experience is the opposite of the intensely stimulating experiences most NDE-ers describe having in the realm of light. In *Life Between Life*, Dr. Joel Whitton and Joe Fisher describe the afterlife as a "timeless, spaceless glide" through pure nothingness, a "mysterious void between incarnations" in which identity, memory, and emotion all seem diminished. One PLR subject reported: "I felt no emotions. I felt no fear and no loneliness, although I seemed to be alone" and another reported "All cares and fears were left behind. Time and space were no more than a memory." Other subjects reported: "I'm walking in endless nothingness—no floor, no ceiling; no ground, no sky" and "I'm not aware of being anywhere" and "It's black."[6]

Whitton and Fisher maintain that during the between-life state, people often lose their sense of self-identity: They write, "The percipient loses all sense of personal identity" and "[One] surrenders one's sense of identity." This identity-loss apparently even includes losing memory of one's own name. Dr. Whitton asked one regressed subject: "What is your name?" only to receive the answer "I have no name." A number of PLR subjects have been unable to recall their names or identities while in this empty void. One of his subjects told Dr. Whitton, "In experiencing a past life, one sees oneself as a distinct personality which engenders an emotional reaction. [But] in the interlife there's no part of me that I can see."[7]

PLR Researcher: Brian Weiss

Another past-life researcher, Dr. Brian Weiss, has also heard frequent reports of this void between lives. When regressed to a point in time in between lives, his subjects often find themselves floating peacefully and emo-tionlessly in a black nothingness, seeing nothing, doing nothing, experiencing nothing, just waiting patiently, resting there until the next incarnation. Like NDE subjects in the dark void, these PLR subjects can't even see themselves in this realm. Again and again, when asked what they see, they reply, "nothing."

> "I don't see me anymore."
> "Where are you? What do you see?"
> "Nothing . . . just darkness."[8]
> Her death was peaceful this time. She was floating. . . .
> I wondered if Catherine could remember anything more after her death, but she could only say "I'm floating."[9]

PLR Researcher: Edith Fiore

In her book *You Have Been Here Before*, Dr. Edith Fiore repeatedly portrays the afterlife as one of no feeling, sensation, or sense of location. She asks a patient regressed to the afterlife, "And now what are you feeling?" and receives the answer, "Nothing." She asks, "Are you aware of any sensations, any feelings, any emotions?" and is answered, "No." She asks, "Do you feel any concern, any worry, any pain?" and is answered, "No." She asks another afterlife patient, "What are you experiencing now?" and receives the answer, "Nothing. I feel like I'm floating." She asks, "How do you feel?" and is answered, "I don't feel anything." She asks another, "Where do you feel you are?" and is answered, "I don't know where I am. I'm just . . . I'm just floating around." She then asks, "What are you experiencing?" and is answered, "Nothing." She then asks, "Does anything come to mind?" and is answered, "No."[10]

PLR Researcher: Brad Steiger

In his book *You Will Live Again*, Brad Steiger portrays the afterlife realm as one of waiting in an empty, black, emotionless, locationless void. He quotes one PLR subject as reporting, "In the spirit world, one did not sleep, never ate, never became tired. . . . The afterlife was painless, nothing to be afraid of. . . . There was neither love nor hate. . . . The spirit world was sim-ply a place where the soul waited to pass on to 'another form of existence.'"[11]

Steiger also reports that subjects don't see or feel anything in between lives. He asked one subject, "Now what do you see?" to which he replied, "Nothing." "What are you doing?" "Floating." When asked, "Now what do you feel?"

another subject answered, "Nothing. I can't see anything. I can't feel anything." When then asked, "Do you enjoy that?," this subject responded, "Well, I don't know. I can't feel nothing, how can I enjoy it?" When then asked, "Does it bother you?" he replied, "No. Why would it bother me? I don't feel anything."[12]

Another of Steiger's PLR subjects seemed to show more evidence of loss of memory and sense of self-identity while in this in-between-lives state. When asked, "What's your name?" he replied, "I don't know. I don't have a name."[13]

Steiger's subjects report spending a long period of time in this dark void. When asked, "What do you see?" one subject responded, "Black." When then asked, "What are you doing?" he replied, "Nothing." When then asked, "Where are you?" he replied, "I don't know, I'm just floating." When asked, "How long have you been just floating?" he answered, "Oh, I don't know. Been quite a while, I guess."[14] One subject insisted he had been floating alone in this empty void for more than ten years!

Some PLR researchers never encounter *any* reports of the light stage; all their subjects ever mention is floating in the void between lives. Steiger quotes one such regression therapist:

> The soul first rises to a level of consciousness that is very closely related to our physical world. When the soul is there, it can still see what's going on in the physical world. . . . The next step in soul progression would seem to be what the entities described merely as "floating," being unable to see what's going on in the lower levels. Subjects always seem very calm at this level. A higher step, I would assume, is when the soul describes itself as doing nothing. This may be the final stage before rebirth.
>
> Loring G. Williams[15]

PLR Researcher: Roger Woolger

In *Other Lives, Other Selves,* Dr. Roger Woolger asked a regression subject after his death, "So what happens next?" and the subject responded, "It's blank . . . dark . . . nothing." Woolger then commented, "Many years of guiding regressions have taught me about the phenomenon of 'overshoot' when moving forward in time in a past life. Darkness or lack of images is nearly always a sign that death has occurred."[16]

One of Woolger's subjects also reported spending a long stretch of time in the dark void: "I don't understand where I am," he said, "it seems to be a dark mist . . . I am totally alone . . . I remain here for a long, long time. It seems like an eternity." Yet another reports, "I find myself in a great aloneness. Nothing there, not even a sense of time." Woolger writes that 95 percent of his subjects' reports of the between-lives realm described this same peaceful void.[17]

PLR Researcher: Janet Cunningham

Dr. Cunningham has found herself in this void in between lives, and her description of this experience is exactly what the binary soul doctrine would have predicted. She seemed to possess little or no right-brain functions at all; all ability to think or communicate in metaphor and symbolism seemed to be unavailable to her thought processes. She found herself floating alone in this empty void, experiencing nothing but the vague sense of the presence of undefined "energy" that totally lacked any definition, form, or quality. During one such experience, when the regression therapist instructed her to use metaphoric language to describe what she was experiencing in this void, she couldn't. She reported, "my mind simply wouldn't go there—that was a little too right-brained for me to do at that time."[18] This inability to speak in metaphor stands in stark contrast to the tendency of NDE-ers to use abundant metaphor while describing their light stage experiences.

> You have to describe it in metaphors.
>
> —Kenneth Ring[19]

> My near-death subjects have told me that the words they use to describe their experiences are only analogies or metaphors. . . .
>
> —Raymond Moody[20]

Both Moody and Ring felt it important to point out that virtually all NDE reports of the light stage are metaphorical descriptions, and yet here we find that when a PLR subject tries to describe the dark stage, she suffers from a strange inability to use metaphors.

The same dark void seems to be experienced in NDEs and PLRs. It seems to be an experience of "subject without object." The subject experiencing this does not seem to sense the separate presence of anything else, no visible light, forms, body, emotion, issues, relationships, past, future, pressing needs or obligations or goals. No "other" of any kind. In this realm there doesn't seem to be anything else in existence except the person's own consciousness, shining alone, like a candle in the darkness. But that candle is the only thing there *is* in that realm, almost as if the candle were located in the darkest, emptiest reaches of outer space. And so, since that candle's light finds nothing else there on which it might shine its light, the one holding the light (or better yet, the one who *is* the light, the consciousness itself) still sees only darkness.

It is the function of the unconscious to reflect—like a mirror, it reflects consciousness back to itself, like the moon shining back the light of the sun. Only thus, via such a mirror, can the conscious mind, which possesses consciousness, actually experience "*self*-consciousness." Without such a mirror to reflect an image of itself back *to* itself, it remains consciousness without self-consciousness.

Many of the descriptions of the dark void have this quality. The subject often experiences no sense of self at all. In their book *Life Between Life*, Whitton and Fisher quote one of their subjects as saying "in the interlife there's no part of me I can see."[21] In the dark void, this mental reflection seems absent, suggesting that the subject having these experiences is a divided being—a conscious mind that has become "cut off," separated from its unconscious.

A Mental Shift?

> . . . the after-death state is very much like a dream-state, and its dreams are the children of the mentality of the dreamer.
>
> —Tibetan Book of the Dead

Some past-life reports mention the light stage. A number of PLR researchers, including Fiore, Newton, and Whitton and Fisher have published PLR visits to the realm of light. In most respects, these descriptions are in agreement with the descriptions emerging from NDE research, but there is at least one important difference. The nature of the relationship between the dark and light stages seems different between NDE reports and PLR reports. We need to look at these differences carefully.

Nature reveals herself by her exceptions. In NDE reports, the light stage usually seems to follow the dark stage, but the relationship between these two phases seems to be different in PLR reports. In PLR reports, the relationship is not always sequential. These two experiences don't always occur one after the other. Instead, they sometimes seem to occur simultaneously but independently of each other.

In PLR reports, visits to the heavenly realm of light sometimes are described sequentially, occurring after passing through a dark void, just like we hear in NDE reports. But also just like NDE reports, PLR subjects repeatedly insist that there is no time, no space in the space between lives. Dr. Whitton, a neuropsychiatrist at the University of Toronto, has performed hundreds of between-lives regressions. He is adamant on one point: there is an "utter lack of temporal sequence" in the realm in between lives.[22]

It seems, in fact, that the only point that virtually all our afterlife witnesses agree on is that time does not exist in the afterlife. The absence of time in the afterlife has been consistently reported by NDE subjects, PLR subjects, and psychics and mystics such as Edgar Cayce, Emanuel Swedenborg, Rudolf Steiner, James Van Praagh, Sylvia Brown, and many others. Can these witnesses *all* be wrong?

If they are right, and time does not exist in the afterlife, then *neither does sequence.* And if sequence does not exist, then these two experiences—the dark stage and the light stage—cannot occur one after the other. Instead, they must be occurring simultaneously but independently. If so, they represent two separate pieces of the human soul that have split apart and are having two distinct afterlife experiences. But if, on the other hand, one insists that these two experiences do occur in sequence, one after the other, then one must be willing to accept that all these witnesses were wrong about what they reported. And if we conclude that the one point that *all* our afterlife witnesses agreed on was wrong, then what faith can we have in anything else they tell us?

Some evidence suggests that both stages are experienced by *all* past-life subjects. The only reason we ever hear of one of these stages being reported more frequently than the other may have more to do with the hypnotic commands of the therapist than with the actual experiences of the subjects. In those reports where the light stage is reported in PLR reports, the hypnotist usually uses a certain command. Dr. Cunningham tells us:

> After a PL regression, the therapist guides the client beyond the death experience into the Interlife realm. . . . Even if the therapist is very careful not to give suggestions during a regression, it is not uncommon for the therapist to give the suggestion to move into the Light—or to move to the Higher Self beyond the death—or to move into spirit for the purpose of continuing the therapy.[23]

PLR Researcher: Michael Newton

Dr. Michael Newton is one of the few PLR researchers whose published reports *focus* on light stage experiences between lives. And his regression sessions *depend* on giving these sort of instructions to his hypnotized subjects. At first, when they are regressed to a point in time in between lives, his subjects usually report finding themselves alone in the familiar dark void. But then Newton commands the subject to shift gears in her mind, to transfer awareness to a different part of the mind, to what Newton calls the superconscious mind. When the subject does, she is able to recall his light stage experiences.

Shifting gears in the mind seems to support the binary soul doctrine. At the beginning of the between-lives regression, one part of the mind seemed to be experiencing the dark void. It was calmly alone in an empty blackness. Floating in the dark void was all it knew. It was unaware that anything else was occurring, and certainly didn't seem to know that there might be a different part of itself having fun in a realm of light. But then, the hypnotized subject's attention is made to shift to another part of the mind, a part that is having a very different experience in the Light Realm. After this mental shift is made, *that* new part of the mind seems as myopic as the first part was; it also seems to be unaware of the other part that is still, simultaneously, independently, experiencing itself floating alone in empty blackness.

These hypnotic methods seem to allow subjects to recall the afterdeath experience of *both sides* of the mind. I think it is very important for us to recognize that these hypnotic techniques allow people to do today what they *couldn't do* when these experiences were occurring—monitor the experiences of both parts of the mind at the same time.

What would PLR subjects report in the absence of such coaching? What if the therapist never tells them to imagine entering the Light? Would they then only report floating alone in the empty, imageless void during *all the time* in between one life and the next? Maybe so. Dr. Cunningham says: "In experiences when the therapist can simply let the person 'go,' it would not surprise me to have the client just continue to 'float in a void' in between lives."[24]

This seems to be what *is* occurring in the PLR cases that only mention experiencing the dark void in between lives. In the cases reported by Weiss, Woolger, and Steiger, the subjects are *never* instructed to shift gears in their minds, and so all they report experiencing in between lives is just floating alone in the empty void. The two different descriptions that we are able to access by employing this mental-shift command suggests that, as the early binary soul doctrine maintained thousands of years ago, two separate pieces of the mind experience separate afterlife experiences at the same time.

More Eyewitness Testimony of the Division

In addition to this circumstantial evidence, a number of well-known PLR researchers, including Goldberg, Newton, and Cunningham, also provide us with eyewitness evidence of an afterdeath soul-division. Like NDE research, some PLR subjects also specifically report that an afterdeath division of the soul sometimes occurs between one life and the next. In his recent book on past-life regression, *Peaceful Transition*, Dr. Bruce Goldberg writes:

> The mind is divided into two main components. One part is termed the conscious mind and consists of our analytical, critical, and basic left-brain activities. This part of our mind literally dies when the physical body crosses into spirit . . . . The other component of our consciousness is our subconscious mind . . . which is our creative, emotional, and right-brain function. The subconscious is . . . indestructible. It is what reincarnates into a new body when the physical body dies; it is our soul.[25]

Obviously, Dr. Goldberg is convinced that some sort of a mental division occurs at death. Like the binary soul doctrine, he identifies these two parts as the conscious and the unconscious. But Goldberg seems to believe that after this division, the conscious mind then dies off entirely. Of course, if such a division did occur, then from the perspective of the unconscious soul, the rational conscious mind would seem to disappear or die off. But if so, if the conscious mind really did die off and thereafter cease to exist, then where does the new conscious mind come from at the start of a new incarnation?

The chief virtue of any theory is its simplicity. Goldberg's hypothesis—that the conscious mind dies off at the end of one lifetime, and then at the start of the next lifetime, a new one is recreated out of pure nothingness—is less simple, and therefore less compelling, than the binary soul doctrine, which simply suggests that these two parts temporarily divide for a time, and then link back up again on down the road.

In his two books, *Journey of Souls* and *Destiny of Souls*, Dr. Michael Newton maintains that people's souls split into two parts between one life and the next. Half of a person's soul often remains behind in the netherworld, his subjects report, in a sort of dormancy or dreaming sleep; the other half of the person's soul travels back to earth to get reincarnated. Sometimes, Dr. Newton says, one part of the soul reincarnates, while another stays on earth and becomes a ghost; but more often, this left-behind part does not become a ghost, but remains in the netherworld realm in a noncommunicative, dormant, sleeping state.

Short-Circuited Schooling?

According to Newton's research, the interlife realm is a place where instruction and learning take place. The unstated assumption that goes with this is that the souls in this realm are not divided, at least not in the crippling way the binary soul doctrine presumes; otherwise the instruction would likely go unheeded. Yet much evidence emerging from PLR research over the last twenty-five years suggests that this occurs—the instruction *is* going unheeded! PLR case records are brimming with reports of individuals who have repeatedly made the same mistakes lifetime after lifetime, for hundreds or even thousands of years:

> One subject, a doctoral candidate in nutritional sciences, learned from past-life investigation that she had a 2,000-year history of being unable to contend with being abandoned.[26]
>
> Through past-life regression, Ben Gronzi re-experienced a succession of male and female lives in which he participated in vicious exchange by killing those who treated him badly. In this life, he has been plunged once more into a repugnant situation in which he has been tempted to opt for a violent solution.[27]

Such reports, which seem to be all too common in PLR literature, do not indicate learning taking place in between lives. The schooling may take place, but it does not bear fruit. Somehow, the learning process is thrown off track, and one is left asking, "What happened to the lessons learned?" Subjects seem to start the next life as ignorant as they were at the end of the last one, even more so, for they make the same mistakes again. The binary soul doctrine explains this phenomenon: Once the division occurs, the memories of the previous lifetime, and also of any interlife schooling, are lost.

Saving the Dead? Retrieving Soul Fragments via Past-Life Regression

Dr. Cunningham has published cases of soul-division emerging from PLR research. In the December 1994 issue of IARRT's *Journal of Regression*

Therapy, she reported four case histories of regressions that seemed to recover fractured pieces of the subjects' souls. She believes these regressions discovered "pieces" of the subjects' living consciousness that somehow split off at the end of past lifetimes, becoming "locked away" in netherworld experiences. When subjects had these lost parts returned to them, they reported feeling strangely different, as if some sort of indefinable inner shift had occurred.[28] In an article for the 1999 issue of the *Journal,* Dr. Woolger seems to describe something very similar:

> When consciousness leaves the physical body at death, it takes with it another kind of body, often called the subtle or energy body, and imprinted on that energy body are all the memories from that lifetime, but particularly the impressions of trauma. In fact, all psychological and emotional states as well as physical memories are somehow imprinted in this energy sheath and this is what is carried over after death.[29]

Woolger's report that the soul has two parts to it, one that contains the conscious awareness, the other emotions and memory, is in accord with modern science's description of the conscious and unconscious, as well as with the ancient world's different cultural versions of the binary soul doctrine. Woolger reports, just as the binary soul doctrine maintains, that the soul can divide into two alienated fragments of consciousness which then have simultaneous and independent experiences after death: one part can reincarnate anew, while another might find itself trapped in a hellish, nightmare dreamworld experience:

> The spirit may hover around the area of the death for centuries and that part of the soul, a fragment of the greater soul, will be stuck or lost in time. . . . With the help of the therapist or guide, the confused spirit can be reminded that the life is over. . . . By bringing the outside consciousness of the therapist into the story, we can usually help release the soul fragment. . . . When we do this work in the afterdeath realm, we are actually performing a kind of healing ritual, integrating a part of the soul which has been stuck in an unfinished death process, bringing back a lost part of the soul. . . .[30]

Just as the binary soul doctrine reported, these "fragments" that become trapped in the past seem to be the cut-off and discarded unconscious minds of the dead. They seem to possess full memory and emotion (which the unconscious does possess), but no rational intellect or independent initiative (which the unconscious does *not* possess). Like ghostly sleepwalkers, they seem to be stuck in their own emotional replays of memories of the past, but apparently cannot figure out that they are dead, nor do they ever choose to escape this unfortunate stasis on their own.

Meanwhile, the other half of the mind of the deceased, the half these "fragments" lack and so dearly need, the objective mind, seems to spend its time in between lives floating blissfully alone in a black nothingness, unperturbed by memory or emotion, oblivious to the ongoing distress of its other half.

5

Victims of Division:
Ghosts and Poltergeists

The duality of souls and . . . soul-division [and] splitting soul-
energy is particularly relevant to the study of ghosts.
—*Michael Newton*[1]

Ever seen a ghost? Unlike NDEs and PLRs, most of us have at least met someone who's had the experience. This makes sense; an NDE or PLR is one's own personal afterlife experience, but when we encounter ghosts, we are observing someone else's afterlife experience, and there's always going to be more of them than us.

Many people encounter these mysterious forms at some point in their lives. Ghosts and apparitions have been reported in all eras and cultures; they seem to be an integral element of the human experience. In fact, even though my circle of friends is small, at least half a dozen claim to have seen ghosts. My sister insists that our grandfather's spirit appeared at the foot of her bed the night he died, even though his deathbed was 500 miles away. Awaking the next morning, she'd thought it had just been a dream until she was told he'd passed away in the middle of the night.

Many families have stories like this. According to a survey conducted by the University of Chicago's National Opinion Research Council, 42 percent of all Americans, and a staggering 67 percent of widows, believe they've heard, felt, or seen ghosts of the dead.[2]

After-Death Communications

The vast majority of these encounters are not what people think of as "ghosts," however, but might more properly be classified as "after-death communications" (ADCs). In 1988, Bill and Judy Guggenheim began a private research project on ADCs, collecting, cataloging, and analyzing thousands of reports from around the world about departed souls who briefly reappeared to say goodbye to their loved ones or take care of other unfinished business on earth. The Guggenheim's research indicates that the vast majority of ADCs occur within the first year after the person's death; very few occur more than a few years after, and practically none after fifteen or twenty years (suggesting that something, possibly a later division, prevents them from occurring later).[3]

There are, of course, notable exceptions to this—apparitions of a very small number of religious holy figures have been reported century after century. In these apparitions, the religious figure always seems mentally whole and uncompromised; all mental functions seem intact and operational, and they seem oriented to place, time, and person. Of all the different types of afterlife phenomena, such apparitions are the only ones that appear to demonstrate "eternal life," showing that a person who physically died long ago still exists, and hasn't suffered any deterioration of his or her mental faculties even after extremely long stretches of time have passed.

A few others also seem to exist after great stretches of time, such as 1) ghosts, 2) poltergeists and possessing spirits, 3) the personalities that are briefly reawakened during past-life regression, and 4) the miserable inhabitants of the realm of bewildered spirits witnessed during NDEs. But these are, one and all, crippled personalities, dysfunctional beings, damaged goods, fractured psyches.

In most ADCs, on the other hand, the departed loved ones usually seem normal; they don't seem to be suffering emotional or mental disturbances; they act the same way they used to; they know who they are, and who we are, and what's going on in the world. Their characteristic mannerisms, memories, and intellectual skills all seem unchanged. In other words, they show little or no evidence of any soul-division.

> I had just gotten into bed and . . . was still awake when
> a cloud appeared right next to the bed. The cloud was all lit

up, and the rest of the room was all black. My grandmother was in this cloud! I could see her from her waist to the top of her head. . . . She was beautiful! She looked so radiant and so happy. I had never seen my grandmother look that beautiful because she was always a hardworking woman. Her hair was gray, but it was like she had just come from the beauty parlor, and she appeared years younger. I said, "Grandma!" She didn't say anything, but she was smiling at me and radiating love and peacefulness. It was as if she had come to tell me she was fine and everything was okay, and that she was in a wonderful place.

—Cindy, whose grandmother had died two years earlier[4]

As such, ADCs represent some of the best evidence that soul-division either does not occur in all cases, or at least doesn't occur immediately after dying in all cases. There are some peculiarities common to these reports, however. For example, much like NDE reports of the realm of light, deceased loved ones frequently (but not always) seem unable to communicate verbally in ADCs; instead, they rely heavily on nonverbal gestures, scents, or symbolic images to get their messages across. When they do "speak," the message is almost always very brief and one-sided; extended back-and-forth conversations during ADCs are extremely rare.

When ADCs include a visual apparition, the deceased's appearance is often subtly different, usually looking healthy and happy; however, the deceased often seems to be surrounded by light or glowing from within. This is similar to reports in many ancient traditions, such as Judeo-Christianity's angels and Egypt's *aakhu*, both of which were also described as having a radiance. An interesting difference, however, is that Egypt's *aakhu* were thought to be extremely rare (the ultimate spiritual success story), while shining ADCs don't seem rare at all today. The Guggenheims's research includes case after case in which the deceased was enveloped in a shining radiance, looking happy, healthy, and whole.[5]

Sleepwalkers from the Past

Real ghosts are another matter.

According to Rosemary Ellen Guiley, author of numerous books on ghosts and apparitions, the majority of ghosts haunt a single location, going through the same motions again and again, oblivious to the presence of the living.[6] Most of the time, ghosts seem tied to particular physical locations or physical objects, always showing up in or around the same buildings, roads, or vehicles again and again. While ADCs are usually only seen once (or in very rare cases a handful of times), and always by a close friend, relative, or associate, ghosts are often witnessed year after year (sometimes century after century), by people who never had the slightest thing to do with the deceased in life.

> A house in Cheltenham, England . . . was the site of a haunting by a female apparition on and off for more than 90 years. The majority of the sightings occurred between 1882 and 1889, but the phantom was viewed independently by at least 17 persons . . . a tall woman, dressed in black, holding a handkerchief over part of her face. . . . The ghost often passed down the stairs; she almost always paused in the living room before moving down the hall to the door to the garden, where she disappeared. On at least one occasion, one of the Despard daughters saw her in the garden. The phantom appeared to be solid . . . but she never acknowledged anyone's attempt to communicate with her.[7]

Sometimes just a ghostly face will be seen in a window, a mirror, or floating in mid-air, but most ghosts come complete with a fully clothed body. Each time they appear, these specters look the same, wearing clothing and hairstyles of the period in which they lived, often standing in the same spot or traveling the same route. In buildings whose floor plans were changed at some point, ghosts are sometimes observed moving along those previous floor plans, traveling through doorways or along staircases that no longer exist. It is generally thought that ghosts haunt locations that held emotional significance to them in life, such as their homes, places of business, or the place they died. While this theory is supported by the fact that so many ghosts seem to be seen reenacting emotionally traumatic scenes, in the majority of the cases, there is no way to be sure who the ghost was in life.

In addition to visual appearances, ghosts sometimes provide evidence of their presence by opening doors and windows or turning lights on and off. Peculiar smells and cold spots are also often reported, as well as strange sounds, voices, and footsteps. Despite the sounds that sometimes accompany hauntings, however, when these ghosts visibly appear they are usually silent, and almost never verbalize any intelligible speech.

Haunting ghosts often seem to be unconsciously sleepwalking, acting out memories from their past. They seem permanently frozen in time, oblivious to the present day, just doing the same thing again and again down through the ages. Noticing this, the famous parapsychologist F. W. H. Myers[8] suggested that they are not sentient beings at all, but just the unconscious dreams of the dead; others have suggested they are meaningless psychic recordings running on automatic, possessing no more independent awareness than a videotape of a man on TV. Pointing out that many ghosts seem to be enacting particularly unpleasant scenes, some theorists have suggested that emotionally traumatic events can somehow impress themselves upon a physical location.

However, emotionally traumatic memories are not the only thing ghosts are seen acting out; many of these tape-loop ghosts seem to reenact common actions, and others reenact presumably happy memories. Several people, for example, have reported seeing one phantom playing the piano at the Captain's Museum in Brownsville, Nebraska, and another has been repeatedly seen riding a roller coaster at the King's Island amusement park in Cincinnati, Ohio.

For nearly a century, many ghost researchers have concurred that these tape-loop ghosts were not really souls of the dead at all, but just some bit of discarded psychic rubbish left by the soul's passing into the next world. However, modern research into Alzheimer's disease has raised some doubt about this time-worn conclusion. The behavior of Alzheimer's patients seems to have a great deal in common with the behavior reported about these sort of ghosts. It is very common for Alzheimer's patients to wander mindlessly through their old behavior patterns, endlessly repeating old, habitual actions for no apparent reason. When they are in the middle of such "spells," they don't seem to realize that they are lost, they don't respond when addressed, and they seldom seek help on their own. These multiple parallels are suggesting to some modern ghost researchers that these tape-loop ghosts may not be empathy images after all, but the mentally ill (i.e., dysfunctional) souls of the dead.

Talking with Ghosts

Most ghosts make no attempt to communicate with others, acting as if they are unaware of the living. When communication is received from ghosts, it is almost always subjective in nature, using gestures, signals, images, and symbols—a classic right-brain formatting of information. There is a long history of the nonverbal nature of these entities; even the souls of the dead in Homer's *Iliad* are portrayed as being unable to speak properly. Haunting ghosts almost never use left-brain communication techniques such as codes or spoken or written language, or any sort of linear message format.

While the average person usually can't communicate with ghosts, some psychics maintain they can. In fact, psychics tend to divide haunting ghosts into two groups—those they can communicate with, and those they can't. Those they can't, psychics often claim, are not real beings, merely nonsentient memory-recordings. But to the average person, these two categories of ghosts seem indistinguishable. Both types appear at the same place every time they are seen, always wearing the same thing and doing the same thing, both seem equally caught up in their emotional memories, attitudes, and behaviors from the past. It seems unlikely that two separate kinds of phenomena could look and behave so much the same.

The binary soul doctrine suggests that both categories are living sentient beings, but the noncommunicative ones are functioning more exclusively through the right-brain, unconscious halves of their minds, which would cause them to have less objective awareness and be less able to interact with others. Such ghosts would be like comatose patients—alive, but imprisoned in their unconscious.

Those ghosts that can be communicated with often benefit from receiving new information. Sometimes psychics get through to these ghosts, explaining that they are dead and free to leave. Many ghosts are said to have haunted the same locations for 200 or more years, apparently never realizing that they are dead or that time has moved on. This suggests, of course, that somehow they've lost the ability to make even the most elementary logical deductions. Ghosts can apparently have the most obvious clues staring them in the face for centuries, watching their hands, legs, and bodies pass through solid objects, without having it cross their minds that they have died.

> The fact that many spirits do not know they are physically dead is difficult for most people to comprehend. However, there is a vast amount of evidence that such is the case.
>
> —Ghost Researcher Hazel Denning[9]

How long would it take normal people to watch their hands pass through solid objects before it dawned on them that something odd was going on? It would take about half a second while we're awake. But while we are asleep and dreaming, we might see it as the most normal thing in the world, never drawing the obvious conclusion. During sleep, we function through the unconscious, so all sorts of strange and bizarre things can occur and we take them in stride, never analyzing them. If in a dream, a milkman arrives at my door with two cows for me to milk, I would probably just think, "Oh, what a bother!" It wouldn't cross my mind that this would never happen in the "real" world.

The vast majority of ghost reports seem to describe beings suffering from diminished reasoning ability, cognition, and objective awareness. What's lost always seems to be the capacities of the left-brain conscious mind, and what's retained always seems to be more of the nature of the right-brain unconscious mind (emotions and memories) which seem to be magnified beyond normal levels. These conclusions are found in the reports of many ghost researchers, such as Robert Coddington and Hazel Denning.

In the tradition of the famous "ghost hunter" Hans Holzer, Robert Coddington uses a psychic in his attempts to help ghostly souls escape from their mental prisons. Coddington's wife, Marianne, lets these lost souls temporarily use her body and conscious mind to make verbal communication possible. They are often able to contact the ghost, explaining that it has died and is now free to move on.

Most ghosts described in Coddington's *Earthbound* don't seem to be evil. They don't seem to have deserved to become ghosts, but they did anyway. Their ghostly existence seems identical to many NDE-ers' descriptions of the realm of bewildered spirits: They were trapped in time, reliving their memories of traumatic events. When they finally awoke to consciousness in the psychic's body, seeing through Marianne's eyes, they were still under the impression it was the same time period in which they died, although in reality two, three, or four hundred years had since passed. They had been so caught up in their memories and emotional distress that they had remained oblivious to the external world for centuries. The picture Coddington's book paints of the subjective experience of ghosts seems in line with the binary soul doctrine.

Coddington tells us that many ghosts lack the ability to reason, calling them "confused," "disoriented," and "unaware." Because they cannot think logically, he says, obsessions that exist at the time of death can "continue unchanged and unresolved for a hundred years." Coddington believes that ghosts are sleepwalkers acting out their dreams and memories: "The unaware ghost seems to be immersed in its own repetitive nightmare of events, now past, oblivious to present reality." Ghosts are often obsessed with continuously reviewing their emotions and memories, he maintains, much like a computer locked into a repetitive cycle; the consciousness of the ghost remains locked in time at the moment of its death, never progressing beyond that instant. Coddington writes: "Their perceptual awareness [was] frozen in the moment of the physical demise, [and] need[ed] to be 'awakened.'"[10]

Dr. Hazel Denning, another modern-day ghost researcher, reports much the same in *True Hauntings,* noting that many ghosts are essentially insane, often remaining in a disassociated state for centuries.[11] Coddington and Denning repeat the same refrain we've heard for centuries: ghosts often don't realize they're dead. Sometimes, well-meaning people like Coddington and Denning can help, but even when a psychic communication channel has been made available, haunting ghosts still often resist reprogramming the interpretation of their situation, as if their minds were locked computer discs that won't allow any new data. Like psychiatric patients with fixed delusions, sometimes no amount of new data or logical argument can dissuade these ghosts from their mistaken beliefs about what happened to them and where they are now. Sometimes ghost rescuers get lucky; like the unconscious mind of a hypnotized person, ghosts sometimes accept new input, especially when it doesn't conflict with their previous programming.

The haunting ghost, the reader will realize by now, closely fits the binary soul doctrine's profile of a disembodied unconscious mind that has lost its conscious half. It would be trapped in a fixed dream world formed out of its memories and emotions, and would not have any objective awareness, analytical reason, or ability to communicate verbally. Ghost reports seem to be the other side of the coin from dark void reports. NDE and PLR subjects who find themselves in the dark void report being liberated from their memories, emotions, and grief, but ghosts seem immersed in them. Each seems to be the missing half of the other.

The Bible repeatedly uses a curious phrase in relation to the afterlife, "treading the winepress," which seems an apt metaphor for ghosts who retread their memories over and over. Like winemakers pressing grapes, ghosts seem to be squeezing out every last drop of emotional content from their memories.

The Poltergeist

Besides apparitions of the newly dead and the haunting ghosts, there is the poltergeist, the most feared of all ghosts. While other ghosts might seem merely eerie, poltergeists are loud, mischievous, willful, and destructive. While they seldom appear visually, these mysterious entities tend to make a lot of commotion: objects float in midair, furniture moves around, fires ignite, lights flash, puddles of water appear out of nowhere, and showers of stones occur both inside and outside the house. These physical phenomena are often accompanied by raps, scratches, knocks, explosion noises, animal noises, laughter, whispers, and strangely mechanical- or artificial-sounding voices.

In many respects, the poltergeist seems an equal but opposite version of a haunting ghost. While ghosts tend to be more frequently seen than heard, poltergeists are far more commonly heard than seen. People often mention how strangely quiet the air seems to get when a ghost appears; and when a ghost does make audible sounds, they are usually nonverbal whistles, chirps, screams, or moans, all of which are subjective right-brain sounds that need to be interpreted by the listener.

The poltergeist, on the other hand, seems to be more of a no-nonsense, left-brain communicator; many have been known to employ a sophisticated linear communication code consisting of knocks, raps, and scratches, and a number have even been known to use language, sometimes speaking and occasionally even using the written word. While haunting ghosts' communication attempts are usually limited to nonverbal signals, gestures, and images, poltergeists virtually never resort to symbol or metaphor to get their messages across; they're just not that subtle.

While the haunting ghost seems tied to a particular place or physical object, poltergeists usually have a connection to a living person, their focus subject. Sometimes the poltergeist seems linked to a location and a person, and the disturbances only occur when the focus subject is at the focus location. But this is not a hard-and-fast rule; some poltergeists have not been tied to a particular location and were able to follow their focus subject from place to place; other poltergeists have not had a focus subject at all.

The general consensus among parapsychologists today is that poltergeists are not disembodied entities at all. Instead, these disturbances are held to be the unintentional and unconscious manifestation of the focus subject's own psychic ability. There is no ghost at all, these researchers maintain; all the trouble is being unconsciously caused by the focus subject and no one else. However, this theory fails to account for all the facts. A number of poltergeist cases have had no focus subject at all, which has led other researchers to ask if a focus subject is simply leaking psychic energy that disembodied entities occasionally discover they can use. If so, then the focus subject is not the author of the disturbances, but takes on the role of victim, while the poltergeist would be a psychic parasite.

Whereas haunting ghosts seem to be subjective, introverted, and self-oriented, caught up in their own private memories and emotional turmoil, the poltergeist usually seems objective, extroverted, and other-oriented, not particularly interested in its own memories or emotions at all, but attentive to the memories, emotions, and reactions of others. While most haunting ghosts never notice the presence of others, poltergeists always seem to be aware of what's going on around them in the real world. In fact, many researchers have remarked that poltergeists seem to like having an audience and getting attention from others, almost as if they feed off the attention and emotional reactions.

Many poltergeists have demonstrated the unnerving ability to read the thoughts, memories, and history of others, but they rarely seem to reveal any well-defined thoughts, memories, or histories of their own. In fact, even in the rare cases when poltergeists communicate verbally, as often as not their statements are incoherent and meaningless, like a parrot mixing and matching phrases it has heard, without any insight into what they mean.

While the haunting ghost is known for its fixed and consistent behavior, poltergeists are known for being unpredictable and inconstant. Ghosts tend to be seen again and again at the same place, doing the same thing in the same clothes; many even adhere to a specific timetable, appearing at regular intervals, or on the same anniversary date year after year. But poltergeist manifestations tend to be erratic, appearing suddenly, carrying on for anywhere from a few weeks to a year or two, and then inexplicably stop just as suddenly, usually never resuming again. Poltergeists, in short, seem to exhibit much more free will than the typical haunting ghost does.

While ghosts often seem to require the presence of an especially sensitive or psychic person (someone with a well-developed unconscious mind) in order to be seen, poltergeists seem to need the presence of a fully conscious person (someone with a strong conscious mind) in order to manifest. Very often, some members of a group will be able to see a ghost while the rest of the group will be blind to it. Many feel that the more psychic a person is, or the more tuned in they are to their own unconscious, the easier it is for them to perceive these entities.

Poltergeists, however, are another matter. Everyone in the vicinity is usually aware of all the commotion going on. However, the poltergeist usually needs its focus subject close by to create these disturbances, and when the focus subject is not present, no phenomena occur. The focus person not only needs to be present, but also needs to be fully awake for these phenomena to occur; when asleep, nothing happens. This suggests that just as the manifestations of ghosts are dependent on the presence of a living person's unconscious mind, so too the manifestations of a poltergeist are somehow dependent on the presence of a living person's conscious mind. Yet the ghost does not seem to *need* the unconscious, but the conscious: ghosts seem trapped inside their own dreams, and can only be freed by the introduction of left-brain logic, reason, and objectivity.

Similarly, the poltergeist does not seem to *need* the conscious, but the unconscious: poltergeists seem to crave and feed upon the emotional reactions of those in its presence, and virtually all the poltergeist's behavior can be viewed as cries for such feedback. It is almost as if poltergeists are all jumping up and down, waving their arms and screaming "Look what I can do! Look at me! Here I am!" Yet they remain uncertain of the truth of that statement, and seek independent confirmation of their existence from others.

Why would a poltergeist be insecure about its own existence? Poltergeists are usually not seen visually, and this seems to be a recurring theme, a strange sense of hiding surfaces in many aspects of poltergeist phenomena. For instance, they usually seem to act in secret: many researchers have noted that poltergeists move objects, yet no one ever seems to actually be watching the object as it first starts to move. Inevitably, the object is spotted *after* the movement has already begun.

This is just part of a larger theme; all other clues to the poltergeist's nature and identity also seem strangely absent. While a haunting ghost gives every indication of having a definite identity, poltergeists often seem to have no clear identity of their own, sometimes presenting no identity at all, and other times offering a variety of different, mutually exclusive identities:

> Although the poltergeist initially communicated with a rapping code, it quickly acquired the power of speech, which progressed from a squeak, to a whisper, to a loud shrieking. When those present asked the entity who or what it was, it gave several contradictory replies, one of which was: "I am a spirit from everywhere, Heaven, Hell, and the Earth. I'm in the air, in houses, any place at any time. I've been created millions of years. That is all I will tell you." Another reply was: "I am the spirit of a person who was buried in the woods nearby and one of my teeth was lost under the house. I've been looking for that tooth."
>
> —Alan Baker[12]

118

The same thing occurs when poltergeists try to use a visual image to represent their personal identity. Most of the time, of course, poltergeists don't manifest visually at all, offering their audience no specific likeness to wrap their minds around. But when they do, more often than not, poltergeists present themselves in a number of different, mutually exclusive forms, often visually manifesting as a variety of living people, dead people, devils, demons, and purely imaginary creatures, or occasionally just as a shapeless, featureless dark shadow.

> At the age of thirteen, an epileptic girl in the Midlands, England, began to have hallucinations of people. At first she saw an old man, who was taken to be her long-deceased grandfather. Then, in 1971, she repeatedly saw a young girl who claimed to have been strangled in 1808 and who wished to be buried in consecrated ground. . . . Involvement of the rest of the family and of friends began when they witnessed ostensible poltergeist phenomena such as doors and curtains opening and shutting, objects moving. . . . Apparitions . . . then began to be seen by others, both singly and collectively. These were not only of dead persons, but also of persons known to be alive. Dogs, bears, birds, and devilish "horny things" were also seen—a coldness was usually experienced in the part of the body nearest to the apparition. Shared apparitions sometimes appeared, to different observers, to be differently dressed.
>
> —J. F. McHarg[13]

Again and again in poltergeist reports, the entity seems to insist "This is who I really am," only later to deny that identity and offer a different one instead, and later another, and yet another after that. Many commentators have suggested that poltergeists are liars who like to have fun with their audiences. But are they lying about who they are, or do they *just not know*?

> We have seen that poltergeists are frequently influenced by what people say; in the Enfield case, one investigator visiting the house mentioned that he had just come from a case where the poltergeist caused fires; the Enfield poltergeist immediately acted upon the suggestion. The Dagg poltergeist did not seem to be sure whether it was supposed

to be a devil or an angel; it seemed quite prepared to be whatever people wanted it to be.

—Colin Wilson[14]

In one study, more than 80 percent of poltergeists did not seem to present any clear personal identity.[15] Poltergeists often seem uneasy about the concept of self-identity; in fact, one of their favorite tricks is destroying all portraits and photographs in a given house. Do photos and portraits disturb poltergeists because they are reminders of something these entities lack?

While the haunting ghost seems constitutionally incapable of presenting a false image of itself to others, the poltergeist seems comfortable and adept at doing this. In fact, while the haunting ghost may not know anything else, it is at least clear about its own identity, about who it is. But at least as often as not, the poltergeist leaves us not only with questions about its true identity, but wondering if it knows who or what it is.

Why? Poltergeists seem to be able to see inside our minds and memories as easily as we peer through a glass window.

Like the original Hydesville poltergeist in the home of the Fox sisters, it seemed to have intimate knowledge of the people who came in, and of their private affairs . . . When people bandied words with it, as many did in mockery, it taxed them with all the things they had done in their lives which they were least willing should be known or spoken about.

—Colin Wilson[16]

This leads one to ask if poltergeists are confused. Does it seem to them that they are disembodied nobodies[17] in a universe of mental mirrors? Is their existence one of having no unconscious, no personal identity, no memories, no sense of self, no sense of perspective or context, yet being able to peer into the depths of any being they stumble upon, each of which does have a well-developed sense of self? Would such beings not become evermore confused, wondering each time "Is that me? Is that who I am?" With no sense of context, might they occasionally decide to try on some of these various identities as their own, just to see what it's like to have a personal identity? Some poltergeists seem to say, with each new "self" they encounter, "Yes. This is me," only to change their minds when the next "self" is spotted.

But other poltergeists seem to recognize the fallacy of that approach, and instead insist "No, that is *not* me." Many poltergeists act like children in their terrible twos, infants in the earliest stages of discovering and defining the boundaries between themselves and the rest of the world. As all parents know, children who have just learned the meaning of the word "no" tend for a time to embrace it as their dearest friend, wielding it against all others, for it makes them feel they are someone, allowing them to define where others stop and they themselves begin. In his book *Poltergeist: A Study in Destructive Haunting,* Colin Wilson's description of these entities also reminds one of two-year-olds: uninventive and suggestible dimwits who lack the ability to reason and have no sense of purpose or right and wrong, but are very persistent and demand a lot of attention.[18] Indeed, the tricks poltergeists perform often remind one of a precocious child who is simply experimenting with all the different ways it can interact with the world: "The tea button on the dispenser attached to the wall was continually being pressed by some unseen force, which did not stop until the dispenser was empty."[19]

Poltergeists are known for being antagonistic and quarrelsome, but are they merely testing limits, trying to establish the boundaries of their own sense of self, boundaries which they feel they lack? The instincts for self-actualization and self-determination are aggressive ones; is the poltergeist's apparent aggression a misunderstood attempt at self-realization?

Of course, the reader will by now realize that many of the classic characteristics of poltergeists are what one would expect from a disembodied conscious mind that has lost its unconscious. It would have no sense of identity and no sense of right and wrong, but it would still be active and willful, and would still be able to communicate through language and other linear codes. (One might object that the poltergeist often seems stupid, while one of the primary qualities of the conscious mind is rational intelligence. However, while every child is born with a conscious left-brain mind, it takes many years of practice to harness and use that inherent intelligence.) Being objective and other-oriented, the poltergeist would observe that most other beings possess well-defined identities, and would realize that this was something it lacked. Feeling unsure about its own identity, it might seek feedback from others to substantiate and redefine its own sense of self. Having no well-defined sense of perspective, context, or self-identity, it would at times become confused and disoriented when observing the inner mental depths of others.

But since the conscious mind focuses primarily on the differences and distinctions between things, the poltergeist would focus most of its attention on the differences and distinctions between itself and everything else it observed. In its mind, it would seem alone and alienated from its environment, and its actions would illustrate that perspective, emphasizing that it was different from those around it, behaving divisively and destructively rather than relatedly and supportively. The poltergeist, then, would be the ultimate alienated being.

Another thing which suggests that poltergeists are disembodied conscious minds is the fact that, in a number of cases, the poltergeist's voice seemed strangely artificial or mechanical. As it turns out, this same observation has been made by NDE-ers in the dark void of the first stage. In P. M. H. Atwater's *Beyond the Light*, one NDE-er encountered beings in the dark void who communicated with "a clicking sound . . . they were jeering and tormenting, not evil, exactly, but more mocking and mechanistic."[20] Similarly, poltergeists often use knocking or rapping codes to communicate; their voices have also been described as artificial or mechanical; and they have also been described as more jeering and tormenting than evil. Like poltergeists, the dark void has also been shown to have strong left-brain conscious mind characteristics.

The binary soul doctrine paints a simple picture that after death there would be only three possible types of human survivors: isolated conscious minds, isolated unconscious minds, and united conscious/unconscious minds. As it turns out, the reported manifestations of discarnate entities similarly fall into three parallel categories—ghosts, poltergeists, and whole persons who are bodiless. Again, like NDE research and PLR research, the data emerging from ghost research also seems to describe the scenario predicted by the binary soul doctrine.

We know that something happens at death. We know that whatever it is, it somehow is responsible for producing reports of ghosts, poltergeists, ADCs, angels, past lives, NDEs, dark void experiences, heavens, hells, multiple souls, dividing souls, possessions, memory loss, emotion loss, life-reviews, and all the rest. We know that a single phenomenon—death—is somehow responsible for all of this. The binary soul doctrine is one explanation, perhaps the only explanation, that accounts for all these phenomena, and it does so with a single, simple if: If the conscious and unconscious halves of the psyche do split apart after death, then virtually everything being reported about NDEs, PLRs, ADCs, ghosts, poltergeists, and apparitions becomes predictable.

6

Healers of Division: Shamanic Soul Retrieval and Out-of-Body Rescues

Almost everyone I have ever met suffers from some sense of incompleteness and emptiness. They sense that parts of themselves are missing and that they are cut off from a deep connection with life. For some people, this feeling of incompleteness and alienation causes great suffering. For most, the sense of not being fully alive is a continual, low-grade pain often masked with drugs, entertainment, compulsive sex, and addictions of many other kinds. . . . Contemporary psychology, like shamanism, recognizes that parts of the self can become separated, leaving the individual estranged from his or her essential self. Many current therapies understand that if trauma is too severe, parts of the vital, feeling self will split off to lesson the impact of the trauma.
           —*Shamanic soul retrieval expert Sandra Ingerman*[1]

Ghost hunters like Hans Holzer, Robert Coddington, and Dr. Hazel Denning are not the only people trying to rescue the lost souls of the dead. Other groups have made similar claims, such as shamans (sometimes called witch doctors) and out-of-body experiencers (OBE-ers). Curiously, both groups believe that the souls of the living sometimes divide or fragment into pieces; they claim to be able to rescue the lost souls of the deceased, and believe they can retrieve split-off soul fragments of the living.

Much as the binary soul doctrine maintains, many modern OBE-ers have reported that one part of the self often seems to get stuck in the past, frozen in the moment of its death, while another part of the self goes on to reincarnate. Many OBE-ers claim to be able to hunt down these ghostlike souls of the dead, reuniting them with their reincarnated other halves, thereby restoring them to wholeness and full awareness.

Soul Retrieval Experiments at The Monroe Institute

Often called "astral projection," out-of-body experiences have been reported for millennia. Clear references to this phenomenon appear in many ancient Hindu scriptures, and there are even a few passages in ancient Egyptian works which suggest that the Children of the Nile knew about OBEs. According to modern reports, most OBEs occur spontaneously and involuntarily. Quite to their bewilderment, and for what seems to be no good reason, people sometimes suddenly find themselves standing or floating outside their bodies.

As one might imagine, many react with panic when this happens; afraid they are in the process of dying, people struggle and squirm desperately to crawl back inside their bodies. But occasionally, this phenomenon is viewed with more objective eyes; it has, for example, been explored by a number of researchers over the last century, such as Hugh G. Callaway, Sylvan J. Muldoon, and Hereward Carrington.

No modern exploration into the OBE phenomenon, however, approaches the scientific sophistication of Robert A. Monroe's thirty-seven years of research. Working in the communications industry in 1958, Monroe had been conducting sleep-learning experiments when he began to spontaneously experience his first OBEs. Eventually learning how to induce and control these experiences with his own specially designed audio technology, he founded The Monroe Institute in 1971, a nonprofit educational and research organization dedicated to the study of OBEs and other altered states of consciousness.

Since 1971, thousands of people have come to Monroe's OBE mecca in Virginia, and many claim to have achieved astral projections there, thanks to Monroe's patented Hemispheric Synchronization ("Hemi-Sync") process. Feeding a certain tone into one ear and a different one into the other, Monroe discovered, forces the brain to try to synchronize them together (much as the brain also instinctively blends the sight of our two eyes together into a single image). As the two steady tones combine together in the listener's mind into a wavering binaural beat, the two hemispheres of the brain become more synchronized, working more as a balanced and integrated team than they usually do. This, somehow, seems to produce OBEs.[2]

What Monroe reports about his own OBEs seems familiar to the student of the binary soul doctrine. When out-of-body, Monroe insists, one's thought processes are different: "When out-of-body . . . we don't have total consciousness as we like to think of it."[3]

The OBE-er, however, usually retains his or her full memory while out of the body, Monroe reports, even though one's intellectual and analytical abilities are often diminished and communication is usually nonverbal. The person is bound neither by time nor distance, but, as is so often reported in NDEs, one's thoughts and feelings seem exposed. Clearly, these details match the binary soul doctrine's expectations for a separated unconscious mind. In fact, much of Monroe's success in generating and controlling OBEs might be attributed to his realization that such a divided state does tend to occur during these experiences: "The trick is to get both left and right brain into simultaneous and synchronous action, nudging the left brain more and more into taking part in the There activity. You should never abandon one for the other."[4]

Monroe seems to have felt that, left to its own devices, only one half of the mind tended to participate in the OBE. It is interesting that Monroe's research arrived at essentially the same conclusions that "primitive" shamanic cultures entertained for millennia: that people have two souls, but only one of them is a free soul that can wander from the body during life.

In addition to his Hemi-Sync technology, Monroe tried to compensate for the missing left-brain conscious mind in yet another way—providing an alternate left-brain substitute during the process. He noted:

> The Institute's investigations led to a path being taken which ran in the opposite direction to that followed by some others involved in mind research. Almost the whole effort has been and is directed to the utilization of left brain methodology, of the intellectual, analytical portion of the mind, to explore the right brain, the intuitive, abstract side. . . . Outside the booth, a technician operates the audio and various items of electronic measuring equipment and records the subject's brain waves and other physical responses, while

125

a monitor is in voice communication with the subject in the booth. The stereo headphones worn by the subject give the effect of the monitor being inside the subject's head. As such, the monitor becomes a surrogate left brain of the subject.[5]

During his thirty-seven year career as an OBE pioneer, Monroe wrote three books describing what he experienced. Writing his last and most ambitious work—*Ultimate Journey*—in 1994, he described trips deep into spiritual realms where he repeatedly met souls of the dead. Monroe's descriptions of these entities reminds one of similar reports from other sources: confused, disoriented beings who had remained trapped in the moments, memories, and emotions of their deaths for 300 years or more, semiconscious ghostlike entities unable to move forward, unable even to figure out that they'd died. While he could communicate with these discarnates, Monroe discovered that he was frequently unable to convince them of the nature of their imprisonment.[6]

In what seemed to Monroe to be a bizarre twist, sometimes these lost souls would turn out to be *his own!* He would occasionally encounter what seemed to be one or another of his own past-life souls during these journeys, lost parts of his being which had somehow become trapped in the past, unable to move forward, even though some *other* part of his self had apparently reincarnated again and again. When he encountered and freed these souls, they became reincorporated inside his mind, inside a previously unfamiliar level of his own being he called the "I-There." In many respects, Monroe's description of this level of his being seems similar to mankind's legends of the mysterious "third soul"—the fullness of the complete self, undivided, uncompromised, and whole, yet highly differentiated, organized, and integrated:

So . . . what am I? Beyond the barrier there were hundreds and hundreds of what appeared to be waving beams of multicolored light. Uncertainly, I reached out and touched the nearest one. A rich male voice rang out in my mind. "Well, well! Curiosity pays off again, Robert!" I pulled back quickly, but the chuckling stayed with me. Immediately another brightly colored beam, mauve in color, came close. This voice was female! "Of course! You're not all male, Bobby!" That was only the beginning. The process was repeated again and again. . . . I realized that every beam of light was one of me, one of my I-There personalities complete with a different life experience. Lodged with my I-There was a corresponding life pattern of each personality in great detail.[7]

Everyone has an "I-There," Monroe maintained, and this secret, hidden aspect of our being has a single purpose: to collect and reintegrate our lost past-life souls until we are completely whole.

> The major task of my I-There was to pick up previous life personalities who had been overwhelmed by Earth Life System addictions or various belief systems so that the essence of the personality was unreachable ... all such "rescues" took place in what we would label the past. ... We are gathering together the parts of us, up and down in time ... I cannot—we cannot—leave until we gather all in.[8]

Monroe's conception of the I-There and its purpose seems eerily similar to the single-minded purpose of the early Christian Gnostics, who, nearly 2,000 years ago, wrote:

> [Jesus said], "Verily I say unto you, no one will ever enter the kingdom of heaven at my bidding, but only because you yourselves are full. ... Therefore I say to you, become full and leave no space within you empty."
> —The Apocryphon of James 2:28–33; 3:34–37

> Then, if one has knowledge, he receives what are his own and draws them to himself ... consuming ... death by life. ... Raise up those who wish to rise, and awaken those who sleep.
> —The Gospel of Truth 21:11–15; 25:15–19; 33:6–8

In 1991, Monroe initiated a new program called "Lifeline" to help others do this, training people around the world how to seek out the lost souls of humanity's dead and guide them to consciousness and freedom. Even though Monroe himself admitted that this method of soul-rescue is inefficient (usually they have to be rescued one at a time), it seemed the only option available. Countless millions of cast-off souls of humanity's dead seem to be frozen in eternal, unchanging, dreamlike experiences, Monroe and his students discovered, and there seems to be no one else to rescue them.

Like Monroe, his students also found that while they were seeking out the lost souls of others, from time to time they too would find parts of themselves—their own past-life souls. After attending Monroe's Lifeline program in 1995, Frank DeMarco described such an experience in his book *Muddy Tracks*:

> I discovered another lifetime in which a little girl died, disoriented and tormented, at age eight. That motherless child lived within me, affecting me—here, now—from the time I was a child until I was able to retrieve her and bring her to a place of safety. She had left this life disoriented and lost, and until I was able to rescue her, a part of me—a part of the individual living out this lifetime—was disoriented and lost as well. I had a motherless child crying within me all those years, though I was never consciously aware of her, and certainly never considered that this might be a past life resonating within me. After I rescued her, that motherless-child feeling ceased to exist. In rescuing her, I had rescued myself.[9]

Monroe's students have also reported another dynamic at work: sometimes during these journeys, they run across broken-off fragments of their own souls from the present lifetime!

> What surprises many participants, however, is that while they are engaged in their mission they discover that at the same time they are retrieving lost parts of themselves. These may appear as past-life selves . . . others may appear as fragments of current life personalities, aspects which had fled or been torn away from the Core Self; for example, child selves who had escaped from the trauma and pain of physical or emotional abuse in their families and now seek to be reunited.
> —Robert Monroe[10]

Shamanic Soul Retrieval

While Monroe's discovery that it is possible to seek out, recover, and reintegrate lost pieces of our own souls from past and present lifetimes seems a new discovery, nothing could be further from the truth. This is precisely what shamans have been claiming to do for millennia.

Of course, shamans don't rely on sophisticated audio technology to induce their otherworldly trances; usually they use drumming ceremonies (although both methods rely on an audible rhythmic beat). Nor do they seem to have trouble synchronizing the two brain hemispheres. Perhaps this is because shamans start out more mentally integrated than the average person. Often called Wounded Healers, shamans often were ushered into their professions via life-threatening illnesses, which may well have included an NDE. If so, then, thanks to the rubber-band effect common to NDEs, they probably emerged from their illnesses deeply integrated, spiritually sensitive individuals.[11]

Many shamanic cultures subscribed to the binary soul doctrine, believing people possess two souls in life, a corporal soul that always stayed with the body during life, and a free soul that was able to leave the body to explore other realms. It is this free soul, or parts of it, that shamans believe can fracture off during life. When this happens, the shaman uses his own free soul to go traveling in "nonordinary reality" (much as OBE-ers travel in astral realms), seeking out and recovering the lost fragments of others' free souls.

Although beliefs like these were once held across much of the globe, being found in Siberia, Central Asia, Indonesia, China, India, the Philippines, Africa, Australia, and North and South America, shamanic soul retrieval recently seemed on the verge of dying out as a living tradition. Then psychologist Sandra Ingerman, anthropologist Michael Harner, and their Foundation for Shamanic Studies gave shamanic soul retrieval a face-lift, revealing this ancient practice to be based upon a sophisticated understanding of psychological dynamics.[12] It is now being widely touted as a powerful supplement (if not an out-and-out alternative) to conventional psychotherapy. Once closely guarded secrets, traditional soul retrieval techniques are being taught today in workshops across America and Europe.

Just as psychology maintains that people often waste much of their strength and vitality pining for lost parts of their emotional beings, shamanic cultures once held that soul-loss was the primary cause of illness and death. And just as shamanic traditions held that soul-loss usually occurred as a result of trauma, science recognizes that traumas often produce unhealthy psychological states of disconnection and disassociation. Shamanic traditions maintain that when a person goes through traumatic events (accidents, illness, abuse, attacks, anxiety, grief, or other stressors), the person can lose a part of his soul. It is thought that we often bring this fate on ourselves, by neglecting, denying, or rejecting aspects of our inner being.

The basic premise common to shamanism and psychology, is that when any aspect of the inner being feels itself to be in danger, that piece of the psyche might withdraw to allow the remainder of the self to survive the trauma. The soul part that sees itself in danger will not allow the whole psyche to go down in flames, so instead it goes off on its own to die a quiet death, thereby allowing the remainder of the self to continue. Soul-division, then, would seem to be an example of a selfless ideal, self-sacrifice for the greater good.

Operating on the level of the inner soul, however, this ideal results in elements of the self committing a sort of suicide. Still, as distressing as this would seem to be, such splitting of consciousness can be seen as a positive thing, as an effective survival mechanism that has been built right into the hard-wiring of the human psyche—a way for a traumatized person to escape trauma and therefore survive an ordeal. The traumatized element of the psyche flees to fight another day, or more literally, to confront the trauma another day.

The problems begin when the soul fragment *doesn't* come back on its own to confront the trauma again. After the event has passed, if soul loss persists, the person finds himself feeling as if some undefinable part of him is missing. The experience, memory, and emotions of the trauma remain stored in a disengaged fragment of the consciousness, a subself or subpersonality, a little subject that has become separated and isolated from one's center of consciousness. Soul loss usually manifests as some form of dissociation: people feel disconnected from the world, as if they're watching their lives from the sidelines.

In dissociation, segments of the personality separate from one's main consciousness. Disassociated people often complain of feeling dead inside, as if they were sleepwalking through their days. They often feel ungrounded and disconnected, and may appear expressionless, their reactions delayed or suppressed. They may complain that they're just "not all there," that something is "missing" inside. When people lose parts of their beings, shamans warn, it tends to prevent them from being able to find satisfaction or success in life. Soul loss is a real illness, they say, causing real emotional pain, and even physical disease and death.

Ingerman believes that most people today suffer from some degree of soul loss; most of us don't feel totally whole, she points out, and few of us live as fully as we could. Psychologists have long recognized that we seem to spend a tremendous amount of energy looking for lost parts of ourselves. Without inner wholeness, we feel an emptiness inside that aches unrelentingly. When people lose soul parts, shamans teach, they usually react either by trying to numb themselves to avoid feeling that nagging inner emptiness, or, no longer sure what belongs in that inner void in the first place, they try to fill it with something else—anything else. Psychologists agree—when people don't feel whole inside, they instinctively spend a great deal of time and energy trying to fill that void. Some of our favorite ways seem to be starting relationships with others who mirror our missing parts, or seeking evermore money, power, sex, food, drugs, excitement, or other addictions.

When shamans journey into nonordinary reality to find and retrieve lost parts of other people's souls, they report (just as the binary soul doctrine predicts) that these lost soul parts are not dormant at all. On the contrary, they seem to be like autonomous, self-aware subjects still engaged in experiencing their own parallel reality. However, so long as they remain separated from the person's conscious self, these soul parts do not seem to progress at all, but remain frozen in the same state of emotional and intellectual development they were in when they first split off from the person's living mind.

The soul part that split off when a child was four years old will still act and think like it did when it was four, and believe itself to be four, even if the rest of the person has grown up to be a cane-toting senior citizen. These alienated fragments do not seem to grow or mature until some healing takes place and the missing piece is finally restored. This alienated shard of the soul is usually a complex package of personal qualities, abilities, and feelings, with a consciousness of its own, and even an ongoing life in its own fantasy world.

The part of the soul that was lost as a little child will still be there playing in the school yard, or perhaps shivering in fear under the stairs, still hiding from an impending punishment that already occurred forty years earlier. It is the job of the shaman to try to make these split-off soul parts understand the reality of their predicament, convincing them to return and rejoin the rest of the person's living mind. Often, however, the split-off soul part will have no idea what the shaman is talking about, believing itself to be the whole person, complete unto itself!

If and when the soul part does return, the person feels strangely different at first, but is usually unable to define what has changed. However, within a few days or weeks after the soul retrieval, the memories associated with that lost soul-piece begin to reemerge within the person's waking consciousness. When the soul part returns, its memories return with it. These memories were lost when the soul fragment split off, and the living person hasn't had access to them since. Once returned, the memories generally require psychological attention to work out, because they usually include traumatic feelings and emotions that need to be dealt with and integrated, often the very feelings that caused the soul fracture in the first place.

The integration period can also bring emotional pain for another reason, since *additional capacity to feel emotion* returns with each soul part. Things which the person hadn't been able to feel at all before, now come right to the surface. Once it hits the subject that this soul fragment is a real part of his inner self that had been lost and forgotten for years, the grief of having lost it often hits with great force. Feeling and accepting this grief is the beginning of the process of reintegration. The soul retrieval ceremony itself is not the full cure for the person's problems, but it does allow the person the chance to integrate lost aspects of the self.

Ingerman believes that most people suffer from some degree of soul loss, and that most of us probably have multiple pieces missing:

> Most of us have more than one part of ourselves missing. We have experienced a series of traumas at different periods in our lives, causing many pieces of our essence to leave. . . . I worked with Sherry, who experienced soul loss during the breakup of her marriage at age twenty-eight. She also lost her soul at age four when she felt abandoned as her own parents divorced. I found the four-year-old Sherry, still in her room . . . trembling with fear. The twenty-eight year-old part was with me, and she gently picked up the four-year-old part and held her to her heart . . . a happy duo returned to the forty-year-old client lying on my floor waiting to reunite with her lost essence.
>
> —Sandra Ingerman[13]

Like Osiris, people today may also be fractured into many pieces. The shamanic vision of the free soul suggests that it is like a pane of glass, shattering into fragments at the slightest mishandling. When a person undergoes soul retrievals, they are urged to take loving care of their returned soul-pieces, or those fragments will flit away again. People undergoing successful soul retrieval sessions emerge feeling more whole and complete, more alive and present in the moment, more in touch with their memories, emotions, and intuitions, much the same way NDE-ers feel upon emerging from their paranormal journeys. Soul retrieval is viewed by shamans as a much-needed path towards the most urgent of all spiritual goals—wholeness: "Our goal in doing soul retrievals is to fill people up with their own selves, so they have the energy to create their lives in a meaningful way."[14]

Like Robert Monroe, however, shamans who practice soul retrieval despair that the burden of all that needs to be done outweighs their resources. There are far too many people with divided souls, and far too few shamans to ever repair all the damage.

Both schools of thought on soul retrieval, Monroe's scientific version and the traditional shamanic version, agree about something of vital interest to the student of the binary soul doctrine: Soul-division is not something that occasionally occurs at death, but is something that is probably *already* occurring in most of us, again and again throughout our lives. And the fact that trauma seems to be the trigger 1) suggests that the *ultimate* trauma—death—would be likely to produce the ultimate in soul-division, and 2) explains why many religions have felt it so important to prepare people emotionally for death, to minimize the potential for it to be experienced as a traumatic event. The less one's death is experienced as a trauma, the less likely it would result in the full soul-division described by the binary soul doctrine.

Soul-Division During OBEs

NDE-ers are not the only people who have witnessed their own souls dividing apart and lived to tell the tale. Eyewitness cases of soul-division also frequently occur in OBE reports. Rosalind Heywood, a clairvoyant member of the Society for Psychical Research, wrote in her book *The Infinite Hive* about a divided-soul OBE she had one night while tossing about in bed. She had been arguing with herself about whether or not to wake her husband up to make love. During this inner dispute, she reports, she split apart into two distinct selves, a pink-clad self that wanted to wake the husband up, and a white-clad self that did not:

> I did something very odd—I split in two. One Me in its pink nightie continued to toss . . . but another, clad in a long, very white, hooded garment, was now standing, calm, immobile and impersonally outward-looking, at the foot of the bed. This White Me seemed just as actual as Pink Me and I was equally conscious in both places at the same time. . . . Pink Me was a totally self-regarding little animal, entirely composed of "appetites" . . . "I shall do what I like," she retorted furiously, "and you can't stop me, you pious white prig!" She was particularly furious because she knew very well that White Me was the stronger and could stop her. A moment or two later—I felt no transition—White Me was

once more imprisoned with Pink Me in one body, and they have dwelt as oil and water ever since.[15]

Heywood included a second example of this phenomenon in her book: a woman who split in two after giving birth to a baby. One self continued to lie in bed while the other stood by its side. The standing self, she remarked, seemed to be unfeeling and unemotional.

Dr. Celia Green, head of the Oxford Institute of Psychophysical Research, in Oxford, England, also reported two soul-division cases in *Out-of-Body Experiences*. In the first case, an exhausted waitress suddenly found herself floating above her physical body, looking down at it as it was walking home after a long day at work. For a time, her body continued to walk along while she floated above it, thinking "so that's how I look to other people" (this dual activity suggests that both halves were functionally conscious).[16] Another OBE-er in Green's book mentally bifurcated during an illness; this subject called these two parts his "Top Me" and "Bottom Me." The Top Me was relaxed and peaceful, calmly observing the suffering and discomfort of the Bottom Me.[17]

And in his *The Personality of Man*, G. N. M. Tyrell described a similar division of consciousness during an OBE. A Mrs. Willett was arguing with herself over whether or not to open another person's mail or deliver it to the intended recipient. Suddenly, she found that she'd split apart into two separate beings, which she simply called "Mind Number One" and "Mind Number Two." After the split, Mind Number One delivered the mail, while Mind Number Two found itself in a state of confusion: "Mind Number One got my body up and walked it across the room to the door. . . . But Mind Number Two (which was 'me' as I know myself) couldn't make out why it was that I was there."[18]

Tyrell also reported the split-soul OBE of a professor of anatomy at Dublin. Sir Aukland Geddes experienced his consciousness splitting into two separate selves during an attack of acute gastroenteritis, reporting: "My consciousness was separating from another consciousness which was also me."[19]

Unlike the other cases, Geddes and Heywood specifically experienced their conscious self-awareness dividing into two selves. Once the division was total, they still felt equally present in both selves at the same time. Heywood insisted: "I was definitely both 'mes,' and conscious in both places simultaneously. There was no sense of a third 'me' linking the two."[20]

Four of these six soul-division episodes clearly point to the conscious and unconscious. Heywood's White Me self was stronger, desireless, objective, and seemed to appreciate the abstract concept of justice (not wanting to disturb her husband's sleep for purely selfish reasons) while her Pink Me self was weaker, emotional, subjective, and needy. The subject who called his two halves Top Me and Bottom Me seemed to follow this same pattern; his Top Me was just as dispassionate and objective as Heywood's White Me, while his Bottom Me was just as needy and subjective as Heywood's Pink Me.

Willett's Mind Number One and Mind Number Two also seem to fit science's pattern: Like the conscious mind, one self was willful and intent on justice, while the other was like the unconscious mind, muddled, confused, and disoriented. Even in the case of the childbirth mother, one of the two selves stood out as abnormally unemotional and detached. These peculiar details all fit the pattern of the left-brain conscious and the right-brain unconscious, supporting the binary soul doctrine.

Many more examples of divided-soul OBEs can be found in published case reports, but few researchers or theorists have dared to explain this perplexing mystery. One who has is an Australian named Robert Bruce, an exciting new authority in the field of OBEs.

Robert Bruce and the Mind-Split Effect

If you read the enormous number of case histories available on out of body and near death experiences, you will find many accounts hinting at perceptions of duality which indicate symptoms of the mind split effect at work. . . . This is the natural mind-split effect which always occurs, but is very seldom noticed, during sleep and all types of OBE. . . . At the moment of separation, as the real-time body projects free of the physical/etheric bodies, the mind appears to split or reflect a complete copy of itself into an "exterior" subtle body. From this moment onwards both copies, one internal and one external, continue to record their memories separately. Neither will usually be aware of the other's presence or existence, apart from the occasional vaguely shared feelings and remote perceptions of each other.

—Robert Bruce[21]

Robert Bruce may understand these soul-division reports far better than Robert Monroe ever did. Bruce is a phenomenon. In an era when so many of our spiritual leaders are accused of padding their pockets, brainwashing their flocks, cheating on their wives, visiting prostitutes, and/or molesting children, Robert Bruce is an uncommon reminder that true spirituality always goes hand in hand with simple integrity. A natural mystic who has enjoyed spontaneous OBEs since childhood, Bruce is a true "salt-of-the-earth" type, humble, warm, and genuinely likable. An internationally respected mystic, he has provided the world a free OBE consulting service from his home "down under" via the Internet since 1992. And while his web-based OBE advice has earned him much appreciation, it's really his openness, his sense of humor, and his sensitive and insightful poetry that have truly touched people's hearts around the world.[22]

Having had spontaneous OBEs for as far back as he can remember, Bruce made it his personal mission in life to understand this uncommon yet apparently "natural" phenomenon; eventually learning how to control the process, he has (like Monroe and others) explored many of the breathtaking realms available only to the astral traveler. All in all, Bruce has spent twenty-five years (so far) experimenting with and studying this obscure paranormal phenomenon, gaining invaluable experience which he organized into his widely celebrated OBE tutorial *Astral Dynamics*.

Much of what Bruce reports about OBEs resonates strongly with the binary soul doctrine. Like Monroe, Bruce says that one's mind seems to work rather differently during OBEs. It is common for OBE-ers to be plagued by vagueness of thought after leaving the body, Bruce reports, and indeed, the other OBE-ers one meets up with while out of body often seem to be mindless sleepwalkers. "Many of the people found here seem to be half-asleep and wandering astral projectors. They are usually not aware of where they are or what they are doing . . . I stopped and spoke politely to several people, but . . . I could not get any real sense out of anyone."[23]

During astral projection, Bruce reports, everything seems abstract, metaphorical and symbolic, all too often with a frustrating lack of specific details. Again and again, Bruce's descriptions of his OBEs seem right-brain oriented. For example, one might find himself in an astral realm filled with feelings of love, understanding, and acceptance, intuitive impressions, and beautiful metaphorical imagery, he says, but no words can be spoken there. Or one might find himself in a place filled with infinite love but without a sense of one's separate individuality.[24]

Bruce believes he has, like shamans, and like the "Voyagers" of today's Monroe Institute, journeyed to the realm of the dead, who seemed to be suffering from similar afflictions.

Spirits I have spoken to in this situation do not seem to be aware of the length of time that has elapsed since they passed over, or of many details concerning their afterlife since that time. Memories of their earthly life also seem vague, much like a half-forgotten dream. Many spirits seem to be aware only of their present reality, that of being in one place, the hospital scenario, for an indeterminate length of time. Some spirits do have vague memories of coming from other dimensional areas, but have so far given me only very sketchy details. Often they will speak of a warm, brightly lit, interesting place where they have many friends and loved ones, but with little more detail than this. The most common response I get from asking spirits what it's like where they come from is: "It's really very lovely there and everyone is so nice. I don't understand this. I'm very sorry. I know it well and can picture it in my head, but I just can't describe it to you."

—Robert Bruce[25]

Of course, these descriptions seem to agree with the binary soul doctrine's expectations for a separated unconscious mind. The emphasis on feelings, visual images, and metaphors, combined with a lack of detail and a vagueness of thought, suggests that the right-brain unconscious mind is the dominant player in these experiences, with the left-brain conscious mind relegated to a subordinate position. The idea that a division of consciousness occurs during OBEs is central to Bruce's discoveries.

A lifetime of experiments convinced him that the key to success in OBEs doesn't have as much to do with getting out of the body as with how one slips back in. We all engage in astral projection, Bruce maintains, but don't remember it. Night after night, we all project ourselves naturally out of our bodies, but almost always lose all memory of these journeys before waking. Each night, as we emerge from our bodies, seems to us to be the first time we've done it; because we don't remember previous experiences, we are condemned to repeat the process again and again, never being able to learn or progress.

Sounds a lot like reincarnation, doesn't it?

Being able to remember these nightly journeys, Bruce insists, has everything to do with how one reenters the body. To learn how to properly reenter the body, one must first realize that the mind splits into two components during OBEs, and during reentry these two parts must rejoin properly, or the memories of the OBE will be erased during reentry. Bruce, it seems, has rediscovered the binary soul doctrine.

While Bruce maintains that the mind splits into two parts during OBEs, he believes that one part always stays inside the body. However, we have seen that this isn't always true, at least not during the OBEs that occur during NDEs. In chapter three, we read about David King, Maggie D., and Peggy Holladay, all of whom had NDEs in which *both* halves of the mind separated from the physical body.

Once the two halves of the mind have separated from each other, Bruce maintains, both record separate sets of memories from that point on until they are rejoined. The half of the mind remaining in the body will have its set of memories for the time period, and the other half of the mind floating around outside the body will have its own quite different set for the same period. The problem is that when the two halves rejoin at the end of the OBE, unless the reentry is done properly, only *one* of those two sets of memories will survive. The other set will be erased.

The mind-split almost always occurs during OBEs, Bruce maintains, but is virtually never noticed. Either the person's in-body memories survive, leaving her convinced that no projection took place, or, less frequently, the OBE memories survive and erase the in-body memories for the same period of time. Either way, the mind-split itself is never noticed. Just like the after-death division of consciousness of the binary soul doctrine, the nature of the mental division automatically shields itself from view, trapping people in repeating cycles of fruitless behavior and experience.

But there is a way around this problem, Bruce believes. In order for the memories of the OBE to be preserved, one must make a special effort to get the two halves of the mind to make contact with each other *prior* to reentry, "downloading" the memories of the OBE half of the mind into the half that resides in the body during the OBE:

> The separateness of the mind-split effect and memory recording will continue until reintegration occurs. Upon reintegration, or waking, only one set of memories will usually be retained. . . . The successful "downloading" of projection memories . . . appears to be the real key to successful and repeatable OBE. . . . One way of cementing projection memories is to make contact with yourself during an OBE. Keeping in mind the nature of the mind split, agree with

yourself to try and make contact from both sides of the projection, from both physical and projected sides. . . . Once contact is made, memories will flood both ways and will become cemented—making a strong and lasting impression upon the physical brain. . . . The projected double can periodically return to its physical counterpart and download (top up) its projection memories. If this is done, I suggest no more than a few minutes interval between each memory download.[26]

This whole process seems remarkably similar to the ancient Egyptian practice of getting the *ba* and *ka* to link back up with each other after having split apart outside of the body. Some Egyptian texts held that the *ba* and *ka* periodically rejoined this way, temporarily reconnecting once each day after death. Of course, this apparent parallel raises as many questions as it seems to answer.

Why wouldn't the *ba* and *ka* stay together permanently after death if they were able to reunite? Are they sometimes unable to stay together for longer than brief periods? Do some people find themselves unable to reunite their *ba* and *ka* into an indivisible *akh* after death, yet still find they are able to maintain some degree of personal continuity by this repeating process of memory exchanges such as Bruce outlines?

The Egyptians seem to have thought so. Their scriptures describe three different possible relationships between the *ba* and *ka* after death: permanently united, permanently divided, and in this ping-pong, back-and-forth state of perpetual reunion and redivision. Robert Bruce may have given us the key to understanding yet another piece of the Egyptian afterlife puzzle.

7

Conquerors of Division: Psychics and Mystics

Let's not confuse the terms soul and spirit, for they are not the same.

—Edgar Cayce[1]

It may not be necessary to personally have an NDE or PLR, or be visited by an apparition, ghost, or poltergeist to acquire first-hand knowledge about what happens on the other side of death's door. Every generation also produces a handful of psychics and mystics who, although they have seldom had any personal afterlife experiences, claim to provide accurate information about death and the afterlife. Of course, history's most famous psychics and mystics, such as Abraham, Jesus, Buddha, and Mohammed, went on to found (or transform) major world religions. But in addition to these luminaries, every age always has its own share of lesser-known seers as well.

A list of the most celebrated figures over the last few centuries might include Emanuel Swedenborg, Edgar Cayce, Rudolf Steiner, Daskalos (Stylianos Atteshlis), Don Juan Matus, and James Van Praagh. Each seems to have at least partially overcome the mental division that prevents the rest of us from acting in this world and the next at the same time. And when these mystics did peer across the veil, each came back describing circumstances and phenomena consistent with the binary soul doctrine.

In many respects, Swedenborg, Cayce, Steiner, Matus, and Van Praagh report the same story, supporting the binary soul concept. Besides the physical body, they all agree, human beings are composed of two other nonphysical components. Cayce and Steiner use the same terminology for these two, referring to them simply as the soul and spirit. Swedenborg calls them the "inward" and "outward" elements of the soul; Matus calls them the *tonal* and *nagual;* Daskalos the *psychical* and *noetical* bodies, and Van Praagh the astral and mental bodies. Each of these visionaries associates one of these two components with right-brain characteristics, and the other with left-brain characteristics.

Swedenborg, Cayce, Steiner, Van Praagh, Daskalos, and Matus maintain that in addition to losing one's physical body at death, most people also have another major element of their beings taken away from them during (or shortly after) the transition. Steiner declared that the soul and spirit divide at death; Swedenborg said the same about the inward and outward elements of the soul; Daskalos taught the same about the *psychical* and *noetical* bodies, and Van Praagh has written the same about the astral body and mental body. And while Cayce didn't declare that the soul and spirit divide at death, he did report that they switch positions with each other on the other side, which from the subject's point of view would probably seem to be the same.

Emanuel Swedenborg

Emanuel Swedenborg (1688–1772) is one of the most well-known seers of the last few hundred years, perhaps even more famous than Edgar Cayce or Nostradamus. Although Cayce left behind a world-famous educational institute in Virginia (The Association for Research and Enlightenment, or ARE), and people across the globe still pore over Nostradamus's 500-year-old prophecies every time another international incident occurs, Swedenborg's visions founded a religion. Today, congregations of his Swedenborgian "New Church" can be found all over the world.

For most of his life, Swedenborg had been a level-headed, no-nonsense scientist, but at fifty-six he found himself going into trances and having bizarre visions of heaven and hell. These unnerving experiences lasted for the rest of his life, and, scientist that he was, he carefully recorded them, eventually writing a number of books on religion and the afterlife.

In many respects, Swedenborg's reports of heaven and hell match up quite nicely with what is reported today by thousands of NDE-ers. Swedenborg reported that the recently dead undergo a memory review of their life, recalling every small detail, shortly after departing their bodies.

Like NDE-ers, Swedenborg also mentioned the curious fact that much of the phenomena that occurs in the next world is experienced visually. He maintained that everyone's experience of heaven or hell is unique. And like NDE-ers, he reported that it sometimes seemed that he was being given great insights into the larger patterns of reality, but upon returning to this world, he could recall none of the specific details.[2]

Swedenborg was a more direct advocate of the BSD than most NDE-ers are today. He maintained that the human soul is composed of two parts, one inner and one outer. He variously described these two as the inward thought and the outward thought, or the inward aspects and outward aspects, or the inward elements and outward elements. And like the BSD, he associated one part to thoughts and speech, and the other to feelings and emotions. "We may gather from this that we have two thought processes, one more outward and one more inward, and that we talk on the basis of our more outward thinking and feel differently on the basis of our more inward thinking. Further, these two thought processes have been separated."[3]

While they are alive, he reported, every human possesses both parts. But shortly after death, a person's "outward thought" is ripped away, never to be returned. This loss produces many consequences. While we are alive, we are able to think and weigh and judge and choose and decide for ourselves, reforming and re-creating ourselves and our opinions, attitudes, and preferences as we please. But after the "outward thought" is removed, we are no longer able to do this. He said:

> After death we can no longer be reformed by being taught the way we could in this world, since the outmost level, made up of natural insights and affections, is then dormant and cannot be opened.[4]
>
> [The dead] can no longer be changed for the better by the path of thought or of understanding what is true.[5]
>
> There is no repentance after death . . . there is no way to change anyone's life after death.[6]

After this division, we remain permanently frozen in whatever attitudes, beliefs, and desires we embraced at the moment of our death. Without the "outward thought," one could no longer think logically.

> In the other life they are deprived of their ability to reason.[7]
> Evil spirits who have become irrational . . . have by

divine compulsion been faced toward people who were in the light of truth. Then they understood everything like angels and admitted that they were true and that they understood everything. However, the moment they turned back toward the love proper to their own intentions, they did not understand anything and said just the opposite. I have even heard some hellish people saying that they knew and recognized that what they were doing was evil and what they were thinking was false, but that they could not resist the gratification of their love and therefore of their will. This moved their thoughts to see evil as good and falsity as true.[8]

Nor, according to Swedenborg, can a person who has lost this outward thought exercise any independent free will.

All spirits can be led wherever you want as long as they are kept in their dominant love. They cannot resist even though they know what is happening and think that they will refuse. . . . Their love is like a chain or rope tied around them, with which they can be pulled and which they cannot escape.[9]

Without logic or free will, the person is doomed to remain permanently frozen in a steady and unchanging state, knowing no further emotional growth or psychological evolution for hundreds or even thousands of years.

After death we remain the same forever in regard to our volition or dominant love. I have been allowed to talk with some people who lived more than two thousand years ago, people whose lives are described in history books and are therefore familiar. I discovered that they were still the same, just as described.[10]

After death, our ruling affection or love awaits each one of us. This is never rooted out to eternity . . . our own eternal quality is that of our ruling affection or love.[11]

In life, the "outward thought" represses the "inward thought," Swedenborg wrote, but after death that repressive influence is removed:

Everyone's deeper levels are allowed a certain freedom in the other life, being no longer constrained by outward considerations, for their worldly purposes. Then people are outwardly what they are inwardly.[12]

[The dead] come into the state of their deeper concerns in the other life . . . they are separated from the more outward factors that constrained them in the world. In short, they lose their rationality.[13]

Interestingly, Swedenborg maintained (as the worldwide spread of the BSD also indicates) that an ancient worldwide church once existed long ago, a religion similar to Christianity and based on the same truths. But this single world religion eventually self-destructed, he said, due to mankind's own failings:

I have talked with some people who were in the early church. (By "the early church," we mean the religious culture [that prevailed] after the flood over many kingdoms, throughout Assyria, Mesopotamia, Syria, Ethiopia, Arabia, Libya, Egypt, Philistia as far as Tyre and Sidon, and the land of Canaan on both sides of the Jordan.) People then knew about the Lord who was going to come, and they absorbed the good qualities of faith; but nevertheless they did fall away and become idolaters. They . . . are in a sorry state. They have . . . practically no rational thought. They said they had been there [in the next world] for centuries.[14]

Edgar Cayce

Dubbed the "Father of the New Age Movement," Edgar Cayce (1877–1945) was the most famous psychic of the twentieth century. Cayce's psychic feats are legendary, and virtually all modern spiritual or parapsychological seekers discover his work sooner or later. Cayce was able to enter trances in which he would answer questions on everything from history to religion and the supernatural. He was best known as a medical diagnostician; in his day, his name was repeatedly plastered on newspaper headlines across America, crediting him with releasing hundreds of people from ailments that medicine had failed to cure.

Cayce deserves credit for reintroducing the subject of reincarnation into Christian conversations. A devoted churchgoer, Cayce's trance statements surprised many by insisting that reincarnation be integrated into the teachings of Christianity. His readings consistently supported both Christianity and the doctrine of rebirth. Therein lies a dilemma, for according to conventional thought, reincarnation and Christianity are irrevocably incompatible. Resurrection, not reincarnation, was the cry of the church. How did Cayce reconcile the apparent contradictions between the two?

Many assume he never addressed this issue; while he insisted that the two truths could be reconciled, he never explained how. However, when one plugs the binary soul doctrine into the picture, one instantly sees how reincarnation and resurrection could both be true. One half of us, the spirit, could reincarnate again and again, while the other half of us, the soul, might not arise again until it resurrected.

Cayce taught a distinction between soul and spirit; he did not see them as two extremes on a sliding scale of consciousness, but as two separate components of the psyche. He specifically identified the unconscious with the soul. "We have many phases of mind. We have the mind of the spirit consciousness, of the physical sub-conscious, or soul. We have the mind of the physical body, through which any or all of these may manifest."[15]

Not only did Cayce associate the soul with the unconscious, but, like modern science, he asserted that this unconscious soul is the half of the mind that possesses the memory. He perceived the soul and spirit as two different parts of the same whole *self*, distinct, yet united together. Like two sides of the same coin, they comprised unity. "The soul and spirit are one, yet distinct—even as the Father, the Son, the Holy Spirit is one, yet is the manifestation of a force that is capable of manifestation in the varied planes of development."[16]

Cayce taught that both the soul and spirit initially survive the death of the physical body: "In the separation of the soul and spirit from an earthly abode, each enter the spirit realm."[17] After that, however, he felt that the soul held far greater relevance to one's afterdeath experience than did the spirit. According to Hugh Lynn Cayce, "Edgar Cayce said that the subconscious mind becomes the consciousness the moment we step out of this body."[18] And Harmon H. Bro wrote of him, "The unconscious mind [the soul mind] . . . became the functioning mind when one died."[19]

Cayce seems to have felt that the relationship between the two halves of the psyche was inverted on the other side. Although they may not have been any more divided than in life, in the next world that division seemed different.

After leaving the body, Cayce maintained, the unconscious mind suddenly finds itself raised to the top, becoming the more present, immediate, and dominant mental influence; the conscious mind finds itself pushed into the background, hidden from view, just as the unconscious had been in the world of the living:

> When the soul passes . . . the soul body, with the mind, the subconscious mind . . . is then as the sensuous [conscious] mind of the soul body; the spirit being that as the subconscious mind.[20]
>
> When the body physical lays aside the material body . . . that called the superconscious [becomes] the consciousness of the entity, as the subconscious is to the physical body. The subconscious [becomes] the mind or intellect of the body.[21]

Cayce reported that the dead were not able to think in quite the same way as the living. Unless a person had achieved enlightenment during life, he would not be able to fully comprehend what had happened to him once he was on the other side:

> (Q) Will he know he was [Morton Blumenthal] on earth, an individual with definite personality and character, and will he be able to realize that which he was and that which he has become?
>
> (A) When he, [Morton Blumenthal], has reached that perfect realization of these consciousnesses of personae and personalities of individuals, and of self (to which he may develop), he will become able to attain such superconsciousness in a spiritual plane, as has been outlined. At present, no.[22]

Cayce taught that the dead possessed a lower level and amount of free will, choice, and intellectual comprehension than did the living, just as would be the case if they had lost their rational conscious minds. Cayce lamented that although the invisible shades of the dead sometimes came to attend his lectures, they were not able to understand the new ideas and concepts he was presenting as easily as the living. "There were lessons which the living faced and grasped, because of their freedom of will and choice, in a different way than could the dead."[23]

Also in keeping with the BSD, Cayce taught that God did not judge our souls after death, but that we would be judged by our own subjective judgments of our memories. This judgment occurred in and through the unconscious mind:

> The Cayce source insisted that each man was judged by God only in terms of his own ideals.[24]

(Q) What form of consciousness does the entity assume after death?

(A) That of the subconscious consciousness, as known in the material plane, or the acts and deeds, and thoughts, done in the body, are ever present before that being. Then consider what a hell digged by some, and what a haven and heaven builded by many.[25]

Humanity's great spiritual challenge, Cayce believed, revolved around a division or alienation between the soul and spirit. Awakening some unity between these two was, in his view, the goal of life. Making the two one would accomplish something on the order of the East's enlightenment:

(Q) Explain what the divide between the soul and spiritual forces is? How manifest, and how we may study self to gain the approach to that divide.

(A) This [is] of the spiritual entity in its entirety. The superconscious [is] the divide, that one-ness lying between the soul and the spirit force, within the spiritual entity. Not of earth forces at all, only awakened with the spiritual indwelling and acquired individually.[26]

Cayce's words fall in line with the binary soul doctrine. There is a division between the soul and spirit, but when this division is overcome, one finds a new psychological element where the division had stood, almost like a third soul—a "super-conscious." And finding this "super-conscious," he believed, was essential in man's quest for immortality.

Eternal life is a given, Cayce taught, insisting that the spirit within each of us lives forever. But acquiring certainty of that eternal life is another story. Cayce held that our subjective awareness of our continued existence is dependent on our relationship with God. We will never know immortality until we know God: "Continuity of Life, then, is being conscious of our oneness with God"[27]

This certainly raises the stakes. If Cayce is right, then none of us can hope to become aware of our immortality until we embrace our psychological wholeness. A person cannot hope to know oneness with God (or oneness with anything at all) before he knows oneness with his own self. This raises a crucial question. If "making the two one," or overcoming the division between soul and spirit, *is* what life is about, but one failed to do this, then what could happen in the worst-case scenario?

Cayce's answer is consistent with the BSD. The spirit, he insisted, is immortal, invulnerable, and indestructible, and so is never in danger, regardless of what one does or doesn't achieve in life. But the soul, the part which holds the memory, *is* changeable and vulnerable, according to Cayce. He taught that all spirits would be reunited with God at the end of time, but some would do so lacking memories of some (or even all) of their past lives. For some, all soul memories would be missing, destroyed, gone. "Some who continue to reject [God's] ways will be returned to their original estate with Him—without consciousness of what they have been and done, won and lost."[28]

Some souls could become lost forever, just as religions around the world have warned: "There was in very fact, in the hearts and experience of men, an 'outer darkness' from which even God would not save them forever."[29]

Rudolf Steiner

> Man has three parts to his nature . . . man consists of body, soul, and spirit.
> Through his body man is able to place himself for the time being in connection with things; through his soul he retains in himself the impressions they make on him; through his spirit there reveals itself to him what the things retain for themselves.
>
> —Rudolf Steiner[30]

The teachings of Dr. Rudolf Steiner (1861–1925), founder of Anthroposophy, also echo the binary soul doctrine. A natural mystic who, like Swedenborg, could peer at will into the next world, Steiner taught that human beings are three-part creatures comprised of body, soul, and spirit. He credited the soul with the traits of the right-brain unconscious, such as subjective feeling, emotion, memory, and responsiveness, and the spirit with the objective intellectual and cognitive abilities of the left-brain conscious mind. In a healthy person, Steiner maintained, the soul and spirit interpenetrate each other during earthly life, comprising a fruitful unity. The soul nourishes the spirit with the memories it has assimilated, and the more nourishment the soul brings to the spirit, the more enriched the spirit becomes.[31]

But at death, this unity dissolves. At first, the soul and spirit stay together as they leave the physical body, but eventually they split off from each other. This only occurs, however, after the soul has become one with an area of the afterlife Steiner called the "soul world" or "astral world."[32] Once this merging process is complete, the spirit would find itself separated from its soul, and would then finally be free to travel into the "spiritual world," its own proper area of the afterlife. This realm is inhabited by many other individual separate spirits engaged in abstract intellectual pursuits:

> [When] the soul is absorbed into its own world . . . the spirit rises to the regions where it lives entirely in surroundings of its own nature."[33]

The afterlife of the soul, then, is one of pure unity without any separate individuality, while the afterlife of the spirit preserves one's separate nature: ". . . [T]he soul will . . . merge into and become one with [the soul world] . . . It ceases to exist as a[n independent] being . . . and the spirit is set free by it . . . the spirit is in bondage until this last moment. The spirit can feel free of the soul only when the soul itself has become one with the general soul world."[34]

After spending time in the spirit world, Steiner believed, the spirit reincarnates. But while the spirit only temporarily visits the spirit world between earthly lives, the soul remains permanently trapped in its own world after death.

James Van Praagh

In many respects, James Van Praagh's (1959–) descriptions of the afterlife is a textbook example of the binary soul doctrine. More of a psychic than mystic, Van Praagh claims to be able to communicate with the dead. But like many mystics, Van Praagh insists that two parts of a person's soul survive physical death: an astral or emotional body which contains all one's emotions, yearnings, and memories, and a mental body, which contains one's logic, intelligence, and reasoning abilities. While we are alive we exist concurrently in both these nonphysical bodies, which "intermingle and are dependent on one another, and make us whole beings." But in death this wholeness is shattered when we "shed our various bodies."[35]

This soul-division doesn't occur immediately at death, Van Praagh maintains. When we first depart the physical body, for a time our psychological being remains unaltered. Eventually, however, a change does occur, when the dead "stop thinking with [the] earthly mind." Sooner or later, the dead experience a "complete sloughing off of the old earthly memories and patterns of thinking . . . releasing the earthly patterns and lower elements of the emotional body. . . . As these old remnants are left behind to disintegrate in the lower astral regions, a spirit goes through another death of a sort. Hinduism and spiritualism actually call this a second death, when the lower bodies . . . are cast off." Memory, emotion, and desire all belong to the astral body, and so of course when that body is discarded the dead find they have "cast off [their] past earthly memory patterns, behaviors, and desires."[36]

Clearly, Van Praagh falls into the camp which holds that the emotional half of the soul is lost at death while the intellectual half continues on, rather than vice versa. In fact, Van Praagh seems to go a bit farther in that direction than Steiner. While Steiner merely held that the emotional soul merged with the general soul world, Van Praagh holds that the emotional body actually disintegrates and completely ceases to exist after dividing from the mental body.

Daskalos

> Absolute Beingness is the one God, beyond time and space, Who is expressed as Christ Logos and Holy Spirit . . . Absolute Beingness is Total Reality, within which we can distinguish two Natures: . . . the Christ Logos and the Holy Spirit.
> —Daskalos[37]

Known to his students as Daskalos and to much of the rest of the world as the Magus of Strovolos, Dr. Stylianos Atteshlis (1912–1995) of Cyprus may have been one of Christianity's greatest mystics. Although he was never well-known in America during his lifetime, he was legendary in Europe. Over the course of his life, he is said to have publicly healed hundreds of people in the name of Christ. Like holy men of Eastern traditions, he claimed to possess full awareness of his past lives, to be able to read minds, and to be able to leave his body at will.

Daskalos taught a unique form of Gnostic Christianity to thousands of people who flocked to him from all over the world. His teachings embraced Christianity, reincarnation, and the binary soul doctrine. Like the Egyptians, the Chinese Taoists, and many other adherents to the BSD, Daskalos taught that all of reality is comprised of a primordial duality, a single all-encompassing unity built out of a pair of complementary partners. Daskalos envisioned the Christian Trinity to be just such a united duality. God the Father, Daskalos taught, is the all of all, in which all that exists lives and breathes and has its being. But God the Father was Itself comprised of a divine duality, one half of which Daskalos called Christ Logos, and the other the Holy Spirit. The interactive relationship between these two, Daskalos taught, is the creative force that produced (and is still producing) the whole universe. "There is no part of infinity which does not contain both the Holy Logos and the Holy Spirit. Nevertheless, they are not separate gods, but expressions of one and the same absolute Lord."[38]

Further following the classic BSD description, Daskalos identified the Christ Logos as having virtually all the typical left brain/conscious spirit characteristics, such as reason, intelligence, self-awareness, and will. He suggested also that this half of the duality was dominant over its partner, the Holy Spirit, which is "in service to the Christ Logos" (just as the unconscious soul is in subjection to the conscious spirit). Daskalos closely follows the familiar BSD pattern in describing the other half of the duality. Omnipresent, receptive, conserving, fertile, and all-fulfilling, the Holy Spirit is "the Orchestrator which keeps the universes in harmony," and is closely related to the human unconscious.

Human beings contain both these elements within their beings; the Christ Logos provides us with thought and reason, while the Holy Spirit provides us with instinctive intelligence in and through the unconscious. Just as God is a being of three parts, so too are humans. Besides the physical body, we possess two nonphysical components during life, a *psychical* body and a *noetical* body. Like the right brain/unconscious soul of the BSD, the *psychical* body is related to art, poetry, emotions, needs, and desires, but does not have much common sense. Meanwhile, the *noetical* body is related to thought, intelligence, rationality, and abstract intellectualism, but does not possess much concern or empathy for others. As the Holy Spirit is subservient to the Christ Logos, and the content and character of the unconscious mind is shaped by the conscious mind, so the *psychical* body is built or shaped by the *noetical* body. During life, these *psychical* and *noetical* elements remain closely conjoined, but shortly after departing the dead body, they divide, in the event he recognized as the "second death" mentioned in the Bible and other ancient scriptures. ". . . the psychic body is discarded at the time of the so-called 'second death.'"[39]

In Kyriacos C. Markides's biography of Daskalos, *The Magus of Strovolos*, he describes *Erevos*, an afterdeath experience strikingly similar to the "separated conscious spirit" predicted by the BSD. In *Erevos*, Daskalos taught, one's memories would be removed: "When one enters there one ceases to remember, reflects no impressions, yet one knows that one exists."[40]

In *Erevos*, the person becomes more sober and reasonable, in line with what the BSD predicts for a conscious spirit that had become separated from its unconscious soul after death. Without the reflective unconscious, the separated spirit indeed would, as Daskalos curiously reported, "reflect no impressions," yet still remain conscious and aware.

After a person dies and reincarnates, a living part of his being does not go along on the new incarnation, but becomes separated from that part of the self, remaining behind to live an entirely separate existence. This is the part of the self that carries all the memories of the past life. This part Daskalos saw as being not a dormant database of memories (as conventional reincarnation theory maintains) but a still-living, completely separated portion of the earlier self, now living an independent existence. What once was a single person has divided into two separate elements, each having its own distinct afterlife experience.[41] This *is* the BSD.

Daskalos believed that the familiar personal self we know during our lives on earth is formed out of the combination of the *psychical* and *noetical* bodies. Usually this personal self is perishable, unable to survive death. "Our temporary selves are flawed, because they are perishable, but there is an immortal part of them, which . . . we can discover and with which we can establish continuous communication."[42]

There was a way for people to ensure that their known earthly selves *would* survive: by "making the two one." As we have heard in so many other variations of the BSD, this could only be achieved by perfecting the *psychical* and *noetical* bodies during life, building a closer, more balanced, integrated, and unified relationship between them. "The central task of each Soul is to reunify the self."[43]

> The aim of every human being is to "shape" [the psycho-noetic body], to make it perfect.[44]
> Knowledge provides the motive for the creation of the requisite will, which together with right-thinking will

develop the small shapeless psychic and noetical bodies, until they are assimilated with the permanent personality. At that point the permanent personality will become one with the temporary personality as a single unity.[45]

In this way, an individual could achieve personal immortality. The aim of human life is to develop a person's *psychical* and *noetical* bodies, shaping them into a perfect unity called the *psycho-noetic* body.[46] If the *psycho-noetic* body is made perfect, it will provide a person with supernatural abilities, including the ability to achieve OBEs at will. More importantly, it would unite the person with his secret, underlying, third-soul-like "permanent personality," ensuring the survival of the known self into eternity.

Don Juan Matus

In the 1970s, an anthropology student named Carlos Castaneda began writing about his apprenticeship with a Mexican sorcerer named don Juan Matus, who taught what we could call a form of the binary soul doctrine he said had been handed down from the ancient Toltec civilization. Don Juan and Castaneda claimed to be able to perform all sorts of supernatural feats, many of which revolved around OBEs. However, don Juan and Castaneda seem to have been *made*, not born, psychics. Their mystical abilities did not spontaneously manifest on their own, but were the hard-won rewards of adhering to a demanding spiritual discipline. In don Juan's Toltec teaching, the two halves of the human self were called the *tonal* (which seems analogous to the left-brain mind) and the *nagual* (which seems related to the right-brain mind). The goal of life was to integrate and unite these two together.

> Don Juan had told us that human beings are divided in two. The right side, which he called the "tonal," encompasses everything the intellect can conceive of. The left side, called the "nagual," is a realm of indescribable features: a realm impossible to contain in words. . . . We are divided in two . . . our time was divided between normal states of awareness, on the right side, the "tonal," where the first attention prevails, and states of heightened awareness, on the left side, the nagual, or the site of the second attention. . . . Our task of remembering, then, was properly the task of joining our left

153

and right sides, of reconciling those two distinct forms of perception into a unified whole.[47]

If these two halves of the self were not united during life, don Juan taught, after death one would find his own conscious awareness being stolen away. But if a person did successfully unite his *tonal* and *nagual* sides in life, he would then find himself able to achieve OBEs at will, as well as perform other supernatural feats, not the least of which was surviving intact when one passed through the doors of death.[48]

Consensus or Contradiction?

Each of these seers came back from his mystical journey reporting much the same thing—that human beings possess two psychological elements in life which seem to divide at death. But after that point of agreement, they diverge slightly in their subsequent reports. Cayce and Swedenborg focus on the afterdeath experience of the unconscious soul, while ignoring or downplaying the experience of the spirit. But Steiner and Van Praagh report the afterdeath experience of the conscious spirit instead, downplaying the experience of the soul. Don Juan Matus states that the afterdeath loss of the personal self, the whole that the two psychological elements made when they were together, is the major issue to address, while Daskalos says that the continuing presence of an underlying third soul (which the average person never knows in life at all), is the most important message of the story.

From the perspective of the BSD, however, one can see that each of these reports data about the same processes, yet none was presenting the *whole* story.

But perhaps the full picture only comes into focus when all the reports are integrated into one composite model.

8

That's Why They Call It a Blind Spot: Cognitive Illusions in Afterlife Experiences

The victims of the best con men never even realize they've been conned.

—Contemporary folk saying

In chapter 1, when we read about cultures that once subscribed to the binary soul doctrine, we learned that many of our modern religions, as different as they now seem, originally painted much the same picture of what happens after death. In chapter 2, we discovered that science subscribes to a similar model of the human psyche, and that if the mind actually did survive death but split apart in the process, as the ancients believed, such a division would account for both the traditional Eastern and Western models of the afterlife. In chapters 3 through 6, we found that the data emerging from modern research into NDEs, PLRs, OBEs, ghosts, and poltergeists conforms well to the binary soul doctrine. We have seen, in chapter 7, that many statements of humanity's most famous and celebrated psychics and mystics are also in accord with this hypothesis.

Yet, despite this wealth of evidence, many in the field of afterlife research object to the split-mind model of the binary soul doctrine being used to explain the data coming in about NDEs, PLRs, ghosts, poltergeists, and so on. I wonder if this isn't because most people are in denial about the existence of the unconscious. Although the unconscious accounts for at least half of the human mind, most people never take it into account in their attempts to explain any of the conditions or experiences in their lives. Without this crucial piece to the puzzle, we often find ourselves scrambling to come up with alternative explanations for situations life throws at us. And then we defend those explanations, sometimes even in the face of tremendous evidence to the contrary.

> He was wrong. She was wrong. They were wrong. No, I didn't say that. If I had said that, I would have been wrong. I would have been wrong. Isn't that right?
>
> —Mr. Waturi, from the motion picture *Joe vs. The Volcano*

We sometimes find ourselves doing mental gymnastics to reassure ourselves that our minds are still whole and undamaged, that our interpretation of things is accurate and reliable, that *we are not wrong*. We *all* do this. We all have blind spots. We are all expert at deceiving ourselves.

In fact, whenever we get to know another person, sooner or later we come to identify some of their blind spots, yet often it never crosses our mind that we may have our own. We end up on intimate terms with the blind spots of our husbands, wives, bosses, and friends, but miss our own.

> Why do you look at the speck of sawdust in your brother's eye and pay no attention to the plank in your own eye? How can you say to your brother, "Let me take the speck out of your eye," when all the time there is a plank in your own eye?
>
> —Matthew 7:3–4

So long as people do not acknowledge the existence of the unconscious (and all that implies), they will oppose the binary soul doctrine, and with just as much force as they use daily to maintain the division within their own psyches. To acknowledge the BSD is, in the long run, the same thing as acknowledging the existence of one's own unconscious, and the majority of people on the planet seem to spend the majority of their effort avoiding that very acknowledgment.

There are psychological experiments that reflect this. In one such experiment, a patient's nonverbal right brain was surprised with a provocative picture that elicited a laugh. But when the patient was then asked what made her laugh, the verbal left brain had to respond, but all it could come up with was "Doctor, you have a funny machine."

> Her statement demonstrated that her left, speaking mind had not the slightest idea why she was laughing. Her giggle was precipitated by the very distinguished Professor Roger Sperry, who had placed a provocative picture of a nude woman in among the words being flashed to his patient's right-sided mind. Her left-sided, speaking mind had no idea why it was laughing; it could only feel that something was "funny." It is interesting that she did not say, "Gee, I have no idea why I am laughing." Instead, she tried to fabricate a reason to gloss over the situation.
>
> —Fredric Schiffer[1]

The patient's left-brain mind did not know what had made it laugh, but instead of postulating/acknowledging the existence of an unseen/unfelt other side, it offered groundless speculation as fact. It did not know why it had laughed, but instead of admitting that it did not know, it just invented an answer out of thin air. Why? Because the *last thing* that occurs to us is that our integrity has been compromised, that we are less than whole. In fact, we usually prefer to invent and cling to any other explanation before that one, for it threatens us at the most basic level.

Cognitive Illusions in NDEs

Although the binary soul doctrine provides a consistent and logical explanation for most of the afterlife phenomena reported today, it is not accepted by many NDE-ers. The division of the two parts of the human psyche is not something most NDE-ers usually recall, so they say, "The binary soul doctrine must be false. I certainly didn't split apart into two souls at death. No division occurred in me!"

But the objective researcher must ask how reliable such conclusions are. Most people never even consciously "experience" the presence or existence of their own unconscious in the first place. While they may have learned of its theoretical existence in school or through other cultural sources, most are not really aware of having *ever* personally experienced the existence of the unconscious within themselves.

Nonetheless, a huge chunk of the human mind is partitioned away within the unconscious, and that other, alien part leads a largely independent existence, thinking its own thoughts, dreaming its own dreams, living inside its own rich and complex imaginary world, while we go about our business in the "real" world. Each of us carries this other world inside, a shadowy and fantastic realm teeming with figures, melodramas, grievances, and fears that exert their influence over our every word and deed.

Since most people tend to be so unaware of the ongoing functioning of their unconscious, how can anyone be sure that the disassociation between the conscious and unconscious does not expand after we die? Since most people don't notice the unconscious much when they are alive anyway, why should they notice changes in it after they die?

How Might the Division Hide Itself?

NDE-ers declare almost unanimously that they experienced no division of consciousness during their NDE (although a very small minority, as we saw in chapter 3, do remember undergoing such a division). Logic forces us to conclude that one of two things must be true: either 1) all of the other correlations between the BSD and the data emerging from modern afterlife research must be an incredible series of consistent but meaningless coincidences, or 2) NDE-ers actually do experience such a division, but most do not recognize it as such, neither as it occurs, nor after the fact.

Is this possible? Could NDEs be so bizarre and traumatic that they would cause people's minds to generate a cognitive illusion that masks some portion of what happens during these episodes? Is it possible that the NDE so twists and distorts the psyche that afterwards most people cannot wrap their minds around it?

Perhaps. Going through an authentic NDE probably would ask the mind to perform tasks it had never performed before, to go places it had never gone before, to process data it had never processed before. NDE-ers seem to undergo an experience so alien that there is nothing similar in their earthly experience to compare it to. When they emerge from these journeys, their minds try to process what they had just gone through, trying to organize the data of the experience into some meaningful pattern. But that would be a problem, wouldn't it? There *would be* no such pattern in their memory banks, the experience being for them uncharted territory. Their minds would have never encountered anything like it, and would have no clue how to correctly organize the data.

After these NDE-ers wake from their odysseys, their minds would back-track excitedly over the event, racing to organize and interpret the alien memory data in the cognitive models most familiar to them, even though those models probably would be incorrect and inappropriate to the situation. Even if their minds had been divided into two separate streams of conscious experience during the event, after the fact the NDE-er's mind probably still would interpret this unfamiliar experience the only way it knew how: as a single unbroken experience. This would create the cognitive illusion of having had an unbroken experience when in fact the experience was nothing of the kind.

This is the bizarre twist of perception that one must assume to be true if all the other logical correlations between the BSD and modern afterlife phenomena are to be credited as anything more than mysterious coincidence. But this is, admittedly, asking a lot. Besides the few-and-far-between NDE-ers and PLR subjects who do recall having experienced the division predicted by the BSD, and besides the BSD accounting for the rest of the afterlife data, the division lacks any direct "smoking-gun" evidence. Nonetheless, for the BSD to be correct, a cognitive illusion such as that described must occur, an illusion which masks the occurrence of the division itself. Without such an illusion, the BSD's otherwise compelling ability to account for the other aspects of afterlife reports becomes a meaningless curiosity.

NDE-ers usually reject all of this, claiming to have experienced no division at all. What the BSD interprets as two independent streams of consciousness simultaneously experiencing two independent streams of thought (one part of the mind experiencing the dark void or tunnel, the other simultaneously experiencing the realm of light), the NDE-er interprets as a simple before-and-after sequence of events, the dark tunnel experienced by the same mind that *later* experiences the realm of light.

Of course, if there was an illusion, it would not be recognized *as* an illusion—the victims of the best con men never realize they have been conned. So if NDE-ers did experience this illusion, they could not be expected to be aware of it. So how can we tell when an illusion exists? What are the earmarks of a cognitive illusion? What clues us in to the fact that we have been stumbling around under an erroneous assumption?

The Time Dispute

When one's perception of reality conflicts with or contradicts other established evidence, one can be sure that her mental constructs are off the mark somewhere along the line. That's precisely what we encounter when we compare NDE-ers' descriptions of the "before-and-after" sequence of the dark and light stages with NDE-ers' reports of the absence of time in the other world.

The virtually unanimous NDE report that there was a "before-and-after" sequence to the dark and light stages contradicts other, equally unanimous reports by NDE-ers that time does not exist during NDEs. If this is true, if time is not experienced during NDEs, then all that occurs during these inner experiences occurs at the same time, making it impossible for any *sequence* of events to occur, thereby ruling out the familiar interpretation of the NDE as "first came the dark tunnel, and then came the realm of light."

There's no way around it. Either the time report is mistaken, or the sequence report is mistaken. It doesn't matter that the majority of NDE-ers include both in their reports; no matter how many people are under the impression that two plus two equal five, it doesn't and never will.

Inconsistencies in cognitive models, such as the NDE-ers' sequence/no time contradiction, are often the only clues we have to help us discover these illusions. Cognitive illusions are very common, the by-products of the mind trying to make sense of the data it is encountering when that data is inconsistent with its previous experiences, or when that data triggers preexisting programming in the mind. The simplest cognitive illusions are when the mind finds itself spontaneously finding faces in random patterns, such as clouds, rumpled bedding, or whatever.

But perhaps the two most interesting things about cognitive illusions are they are often very strong and difficult to overcome, and that they are products of the *unconscious mind's* way of thinking, its compulsive, automatic, and simpleminded way of jumping to conclusions when it is organizing raw data into patterns and models. Cognitive illusions are often so strong that even when the rational mind realizes the pattern it thought it was seeing is an illusion, that illusion often still stubbornly persists, continuing to be generated by the unconscious mind. One finds he cannot easily stop "seeing" the pattern, even though he realizes it is an incorrect interpretation of the data. Massimo Piattelli-Palmarini's 1994 book on cognitive illusions notes:

> A cognitive illusion is not an ordinary blunder; it does not originate in guesswork but from the formulation of a potent although mistaken intuitive judgment that, at least at first sight, convinces us within ourselves. It convinces us, but it also enters into conflict with other facts or other judgment,

that are also compelling. Another element crucial to every illusion is the weakness of our will. . . . We may know perfectly well that the St. Louis Arch is exactly as broad as it is high. Yet, the truth is that our will does not control our eye; rational knowledge does not enter into our sense of visual organization. An optical illusion is the product of a low-level mental process, of the kind that is simple, rigid, stupid, specialized, and totally impervious to any intervention from a higher form of mentation, reason, or knowledge.[2]*

An Example of a Cognitive Illusion

These illusions are compelling, and even after one is confronted with evidence that her cognitive assumptions are mistaken, the illusion is often so strong that one still argues in favor of it. Here's an example:

Imagine that you bet five dollars on a game of three-card monte; if you guess which of three overturned cards in front of you is the queen of hearts, you win. But after you make your choice, the game manager does something unexpected. Instead of immediately telling you whether you are right or wrong, he lifts up one of the two other cards that you didn't choose, showing you that the queen was not there. And he gives you the opportunity to change your choice. There are now only two cards left to choose from, and you know that one of them is the queen. Is it to your advantage to stay with your first choice, or to change your choice to the other card, or does it make no difference?

Virtually everyone answers that it would make no difference, intuitively "knowing" that there must be a 50/50 chance that either card could be the queen. And since it would make no difference, they do not change their original choice. And everyone who answers this way, surprisingly, is dead wrong. Why?

When you originally made your choice, you would have had a one-in-three chance of choosing the right card. Let's say in our first example that you *did* choose the right card with your original choice (which, of course, you would do one out of every three times you played this game). So if you chose the right card, but then you chose later to *change* your original choice, that would be a mistake and you wouldn't win the five bucks. Thus, 1/3 of the time, deciding to change your original choice would be a mistake.

---

*From *Inevitable Illusions* by Massimo Piattelli-Palmarini, copyright © 1994 by Massimo Piattelli-Palmarini. Reprinted by permission of John Wiley & Sons, Inc.

Let's say instead that you *didn't* originally make the right choice. After all, you only had one chance in three to get it right, so 2/3 of the time you are going to pick the wrong card. So, having picked the wrong card, if you then chose later to *change* your original choice, you end up picking the *right* card. Thus, choosing to change your original choice would be the correct choice 2/3 of the time.

Surprisingly, choosing to change the original choice turns out to be wrong only 1/3 of the time, and right 2/3 of the time. Unless you were aided by psychic powers when you made your original choice, you will win the five bucks 2/3 of the time when you change your original choice, and end up with the five bucks only 1/3 of the time when you don't change your original choice.

This goes against every intuitive sense we have about this, doesn't it? Every fiber in our beings (in our unconscious) tells us that it should be a straight 50/50 chance. We *know* it *has to be* 50/50. But despite that confidence, our interpretation of the situation is not correct. The mistaken conclusion that the 50/50 odds is a correct interpretation is a cognitive illusion.

Evidence of Cognitive Illusions

Cognitive illusions are often amazingly strong, and even after they have been logically proven wrong, people still defend them passionately, which is all the more curious when one considers how little thought went into these conclusions. We jump into them without thinking and then hold to them desperately. But anyone who bothers to test the three-card monte trick 50 or 200 times will eventually admit that the 50/50 model, as right as it *seemed* to be, was just a cognitive illusion.

Cognitive illusions are real, and we are all vulnerable to them. Cognitive illusions like the one described above *always* originate in the intuitive assumptions of the *unconscious* mind, and these are strong. Even when the conscious mind's rational intelligence reveals them to be illusions, they remain persuasive. But they are at odds with the conscious mind's logic, and it is precisely this conflict which eventually exposes them.

Thus, the logical conflict regarding the time sense during NDEs helps to expose a possible cognitive illusion that the mind may resort to when it tries to formulate models to interpret the NDE data. Now, since we have recognized the logical conflict between the sequence/no time models, we have been alerted to the possibility of a cognitive illusion within the NDE interpretation. Does this prove that the mind splits during NDEs? No, but it does bring us one step closer to it.

From the perspective of the BSD, the death experience is ripe for cognitive illusions. Since they are automatically generated by the unconscious, and since cognitive illusions can fight to perpetuate their erroneous perspectives even after the rational mind has exposed them, imagine how persuasive they would be when that conscious mind is removed from the picture altogether, as the BSD postulates. The weakness of the will is also crucial to cognitive illusions; if the conscious mind, which holds the will as well as the intellect, is absent during an NDE (as the BSD suggests), conditions are simply ripe for cognitive illusions to occur. In such a case, we would have no defense against cognitive illusions. Without the discernment of the conscious mind, they would seem utterly real and persuasive.

Some Apparent Memories of NDEs Not Accessible Even via Hypnosis

Another reason to suspect that a cognitive illusion occurs during NDEs is the fact that all those great insights and visions of "the big picture" that are so common during the light stage of NDEs don't seem to be quite "complete." Not only do NDE-ers typically report being unable to recall any specific details of those marvelous insights and sweeping visions after returning to waking consciousness, but even when they have been placed under deep hypnosis they *still* cannot recapture those insights.[3]

Researchers had hoped for great breakthroughs if some of the details of those experiences could be remembered under hypnosis, but, as the BSD predicted, the details don't seem to be there at all. They don't seem to have *ever* been there. It is as if NDE subjects had an experience of seeing a great universal pattern or form, but a form without substance, as if the unconscious was functioning independently of the conscious mind. They saw a forest without any trees.

NDEs Are Not Illusions

If the lens of our perception splits in two during NDEs, does this mean that our entire perception of reality is all illusion, all of it fractured and invalid from that point on? If those who have reported NDEs have all been in disassociated states during their experiences, can any aspect of their reports be trusted? Can *either* half of the psyche be trusted to provide a valid picture of reality when they are divorced from each other?

One good reason to consider trusting their separate input might be the obvious parallel between the two halves of the psyche and the two eyes of the face. One integrates the input from both sides of the psyche in much the same way as one integrates the input from both eyes. When a person closes one eye and peers through the other, is that single eye's vision invalid? Of course not. Each eye on its own still provides accurate data. Yet each eye alone cannot provide a person with as full and rich and living a picture of reality as they can when together. Each eye alone can only offer a two-dimensional image. Only together does the real magic happen, marrying the flat, two-dimensional input of each eye to produce something more, something new: true three-dimensional depth perception. In the same way, the experience of each side of the psyche on its own does provide us with accurate data. Each on its own has an equally valid perception of reality. But which dimensions one perceives and experiences seems to depend on whether one is only looking out of one side, or only out of the other, or out of both at the same time.

The NDE itself, then, does not seem to be unreal or an illusion; the only illusion involved would seem to be the mistaken impression that no division has occurred. Other than that single qualification, the BSD would not seem to violate or compromise any of the perceived value or reality of the NDE; it does not suggest that anything experienced within the NDE is an illusion or false or unreal in any meaningful way. The only illusion the BSD suggests occurs is that when the mind splits apart, neither half notices it. The split is covered up, hidden, whitewashed, and the individual assumes the mind is not split. After the mind splits, each half is still registering valid experience. But by having half of our vision removed, we find ourselves able to see things we were previously blind to. It is, in effect, a simple filtering process.

We may all be familiar with a similar sort of filtering process. Once when I picked up a new set of eyeglasses, I noticed a display on the counter for polarized sunglasses. There was an apparently imageless picture in a frame, and a pair of polarized glasses customers could put on to look at the picture. When I did, I found myself viewing a brilliant and detailed scene, where before I'd seen nothing. The scene was there inside the picture all along, but it couldn't be seen until part of the visual data was filtered out. By putting on the glasses, part of the visual data reaching my brain was filtered out, and a new visual experience revealed itself.

The BSD suggests the same dynamic is occurring during NDEs. Those realms are already right here, right now, but we can't see them until part of our normal mental perception is filtered out. So in that respect, the temporary division of the conscious and unconscious during NDEs is good, in that it assists us to see what we otherwise would not. But too extreme a division may cause one to end up like those miserable sleepwalkers in the realm of bewildered spirits.

Variations in Timing and Quality

The data suggests that the soul-spirit division can occur at any point in time between death and rebirth; it doesn't seem to always occur at the same time for everyone. Some seem to experience the division very soon after leaving the body, while others might not experience it until just before rebirth. Actually, the division usually seems to begin shortly after death; in some, it quickly reaches a maximum state of disassociation, while others seem to remain only very partially divided until shortly before their next incarnation.

Ghosts and those in the realm of bewildered spirits seem to be examples of people who quickly reached maximum division, while those in the realm of light appear to have a far milder form of disassociation.[4]

Many PLR researchers report that many people in between lives exist in the exact state the BSD predicts: memoryless, emotionless, floating in nothingness. Others have functional minds, with free will, logical processes, and memory/identity intact. In other words, they haven't experienced any division. Yet when those people reincarnate, they lose their memory of those past lives, which is clear evidence that a disassociation has occurred. The time when the division occurs varies from one person to the next; it seems to be able to occur anytime from the very end of one's life until right before the beginning of the next.

Similarly, the degree of division is a variable. Some people come into their present lives with only a thin veil separating them from their past-life memories. Often memories and behavior patterns seep through from one lifetime to another,[5] which suggests that the division taking place between incarnations in such people is nearly nonexistent. Apparitions and visitations of the recently dead, often reported by family members shortly after the death, suggest that such souls are not suffering from any afterdeath division at all. These visitors from the next world, unlike other categories of afterlife phenomena, seem to have all their wits about them, with functional minds, logic, memories, and senses of identity still intact. These souls have apparently not experienced the division predicted by the BSD. The question is, have they permanently avoided it, or has it just not caught up to them yet?

The Otherworld Is Psychological

The characteristics of the psyche tie in so perfectly with classic and contemporary afterlife reports that it seems the psyche's innate characteristics actually *produce* the afterlife experience. The discoveries of the functions of the two sides of the psyche account for the descriptions of the afterlife reported for millennia, in every part of the world. It seems to perfectly exemplify the idea that "what you are will produce your experience."

Some will be disappointed by this suggestion that our experiences in the Great Beyond will be fashioned directly from the stuff inside our psyches today. Many are counting on being left alone to drift into oblivion when they die, becoming a part of everything and nothing. The question is, will the unconscious leave *itself* alone?

Everyone used to fear that, after death, God was going to punish or reward us based on how good or bad we were in life. But in recent years many have started to wonder if perhaps the Ruler of the Universe doesn't care about our petty anthropocentric concepts of good and bad. What good or bad thing could any of us little humans do that would ever disturb the Creator? Many today feel it absurd to imagine that the universe wants to reward the good and punish the bad. And perhaps they are correct. Perhaps it is only we humans who care about such things.

But that doesn't let us off the hook, not if the afterlife is psychologically based. If it is we ourselves who create our own afterlife experiences, then we *do* need to watch out for an afterlife which rewards the good and punishes the bad and gives a damn if we cheat on our taxes or kick our dog, because *we* give a damn about those things. At least we do deep inside, and if what's down inside creates our afterlife experience, we'd better give a damn *now* about what is going on in the recesses of our minds before we die and it is too late to do anything about it.

This is one of the most satisfying qualities of the BSD: it paints a picture of the afterlife in which our Creator doesn't directly punish or reward us at all. The rest of the universe is out of the loop, and we are in control of our destinies. The characteristics of the psyche by themselves produce all our afterlife experiences. The soul automatically judges itself, and then automatically pronounces and executes sentence upon itself, automatically sending itself to whatever heavenly or hellish experiences it feels it deserves, based on its own inner value system.

Reconciling the Four Faces of Death

Anyone can make stories about what might happen after we die, but no one would believe that those stories necessarily resemble the facts of the situation. Fortunately, we don't need to make up stories. There is already a sizable body of reports about the afterlife from every corner of the globe. Those reports consistently fall into four categories: 1) ghosthood, 2) a dreamlike netherworld, 3) reincarnation, and 4) apparitions of the dead.

Virtually all of humanity's afterlife reports fall into these categories, and this sparsity of variations has been used as an argument for the veracity of these reports. The argument goes like this: If people were making up reports of the afterlife, there should be a variety of types of afterlife reports, since human imagination is infinitely creative. Instead, we keep seeing the same four models of the afterlife reported.

Consider the old story about the blind men and the elephant. If five blind men feel an elephant and each one describes something different (I felt a wall, I felt a snake, I felt a rope, I felt a blanket, I felt a tree) it seems that every report contradicts the others, and no information is validated. But if you then send 50,000 more blind men up to feel that elephant, and you get 10,000 people saying they felt a wall, another 10,000 saying they felt a snake, another 10,000 saying they felt a rope, another 10,000 saying they felt a blanket, and another 10,000 saying they felt a tree, you can be sure that each of those reports is more than imagination. Something there can somehow simultaneously seem to be a wall, snake, rope, blanket, and tree. This is how it is with humanity's afterlife reports. Each report is repeatedly and independently validated in all lands and at all stages of history. Whatever the afterlife is, it can seem to be all these things. And until we can figure out *how* it can simultaneously seem to be all of these, we can be sure of only one thing: We do not understand death.

There have been many attempts to explain the mysteries of death and the afterlife, to account for the reports humanity has received through the ages. Any attempt to explain these reported phenomena needs to be comprehensive; ideally, the correct answer should, by itself, explain all the different kinds of phenomena reported.

NDEs, for example, are not the same as PLRs, but both seem to be genuine firsthand reports of afterlife experiences, just from different groups of witnesses. I have long been convinced that both sets of witnesses are reporting accurate data, but their interpretations of the experience is in question. These two groups of witnesses have each had, I am convinced, genuine afterlife experiences, but none have experienced the whole, nor do any of their partial experiences grant them the necessary insight to understand how their different experiences fit together into a single complete picture of the afterlife. Still, if the testimony of these two groups cannot be reconciled, this casts doubt on both sets of reports.

Likewise, if the two cannot be reconciled with reports of ghosts and poltergeists, then all three sets of reports are in doubt, and if all three cannot be reconciled with the reports of those who claim to have encountered and/or interacted with psychologically healthy apparitions of the dead, then all four sets of reports are in doubt. Fortunately, the BSD explains, reconciles, and integrates all four.

Many other researchers have tried to explain these reports in other ways. Usually they introduce another new hypothetical assumption to account for each afterlife-related phenomenon. Ghosts? Oh, that's because of *this*. Reincarnation? Oh, that's because of *that*. Heaven and hell? Oh, that's because of this *other thing*. Memory loss after reincarnating? Oh, that's something else yet. The devil? Oh, that's another story entirely.[6] Legends of binary souls? Oh, that's something else still. And before long, one's model of death and the afterlife is a bewildering maze of unsubstantiated assertions involving poorly defined elements such as shells and sheaths, and "soul body number one" and "soul body number two" and so on.

The BSD, on the other hand, provides us with a simple model that elegantly illustrates how death can take on all these different appearances.

We know that something strange happens at death. We know that whatever it is, it is responsible for reports of ghosts, past-lives, NDEs, heavens and hells, multiple souls, dividing souls, devils, possessions, memory loss, life-reviews, emotion loss, haunting ghosts, lost spirits, angels, and all the rest. We know that a single phenomenon—death—is responsible for all of this.

The BSD succeeds in explaining all reported phenomena with one single, simple "if." If the conscious and unconscious survive death, but divide in the process, then all the above follows logically, immediately, without our need of a single additional assumption. I know of no other explanation which can make this assertion, and I certainly know of none, besides the BSD, which can do so based solely on already-existing scientific knowledge. I know of none, besides the BSD, which can stand on actual evidence.

The demand for evidence, for validity claims, which has always anchored genuine and progressive science, simply means that one's own ego cannot impose on the universe a view of reality that finds no support from the universe itself. The validity claims and evidence are the ways we attune ourselves to the cosmos. The validity claims force us to confront reality. They curb our egoic fantasies and self-centered ways. They demand evidence from the rest of the cosmos.

—Ken Wilber[7]

Any theory worth its salt must stand on two legs: 1) objective evidence, and 2) the laws of reason. The BSD does this. It is based on the psychological discoveries of science, it is reflected in a great number of humanity's ancient traditions about the afterlife, and it obeys the law of Ockham's Razor, showing that a single assumption can explain all the phenomena reported.

Ockham's Razor: The maxim, one of the most ancient and universally accepted laws in logic, that assumptions introduced to explain a matter must not be multiplied beyond necessity.

The simplest explanation, science discovered long ago, is the best one. If one explanation, containing a single assumption, will explain a set of data as well as another explanation that contains multiple assumptions, then the less complex explanation is superior to the more complex one, and more likely to be correct. This is exactly what the BSD does; with a single assumption (that the human psyche survives death but divides apart in the process), it predicts virtually all the afterlife phenomena reported today.

Thirty-Five Questions

However, most people would still prefer *not* to believe in the BSD. It is, after all, a terrible prospect to be dis-integrated after death.

"It is not just an idea," he said. "It is a fact. And a damn scary one if you ask me."

—Don Juan Matus[8]

169

As near as I have been able to tell in my fourteen years of studying humanity's traditions and reports about the afterlife, there is no equal to the binary soul doctrine. Nothing else comes close to accounting for all the data that it explains.

How else are we to account for the fact that there exist two mutually exclusive accounts for what happens after death (reincarnation and heaven/hell), each of which is still a living tradition that continues to be reported in past-life regressions and near-death experiences? How else do we account for ghosts? For the loss of memory between reincarnations? For the loss of feeling, emotion, and memory between lives reported by past-life regression subjects? How else do we account for the loss of feeling and emotion reported by NDE-ers immediately after leaving their bodies? For the occurrence of the life review? For the world-wide doctrine of a dual soul that split apart at death? For the fact that science has recently discovered two halves to the human psyche which seem virtually identical to that ancient dual-soul system? How else do we account for the fact that modern science credits the conscious and unconscious with precisely the traits necessary for one half of the soul to experience a reincarnation-type experience, and for the other to experience a heaven/hell type experience?

To my knowledge, the BSD is the only hypothesis that has ever presented any sort of intellectually consistent solution to these mysteries, and is certainly the only hypothesis that simultaneously generates solutions to *all* of them from a single assumption.

Of course, no one wants to believe that such a division awaits us after death. This model of death and the afterlife is so abhorrent that we might all prefer to forget we ever heard of it. But can we afford to? If anyone found an alternate explanation that was equally simple and all-encompassing, we would all run to it in a heartbeat. But the BSD seems to have no worthy rivals. It is alone on the field.

For any alternate explanation to be as sound, it would have to demonstrate that some other single cause would produce all the phenomena listed below. Although we may want to reject the BSD because it seems abhorrent, to do so without providing an equally successful alternate explanation would betray the search for truth. Here are thirty-five questions the BSD answers:

1. Two very different stages of experience are commonly reported in NDEs—a dark stage followed by a light stage. Why is this? The BSD explains it.

2. These two stages seem to be mirror opposites of each other in many respects. In the first stage, when the subject has just left the body, the experience is typically described as floating alone within a black void or black tunnel, experiencing perfect calmness and peace, a loss of emotional investment in one's past life, a loss of all sense of connection to anything else, and often, a hyperalert awareness with sharply enhanced logic and reason. In the second stage, NDE-ers describe conditions that seem to be polar opposites of the previous stage. Instead of being in total darkness, they are now in brilliant light. Instead of floating alone in a void, they now seem to be enveloped in a living universe filled with forms of all types. Instead of being unique, they are now interacting with many others like themselves. Instead of noticing a lack of emotion, they now feel intense emotion. Instead of being objective, they are now subjective. Instead of feeling unconnected to anything, now they feel an intimate connection to the entire universe. And instead of experiencing a sharpened sense of logic and reason, they now often seem to exhibit the opposite. Why do these two stages hold such opposite qualities? The BSD explains it.

3. NDE-ers often describe the first stage as taking place in a black nothingness, a realm devoid of forms or imagery. They often find that they can't see anything, including themselves, in this realm of unending emptiness. Why is this? The BSD explains it.

4. A strange loss of emotions and a sense of disconnectedness tends to take place during the first stage of NDEs. Subjects tend to characterize their psychological state during this phase as one of complete indifference and emotional detachment; they inexplicably feel no distress or anxiety of any kind. Why is one of the most consistently mentioned features of near-death experiences a flat emotional state immediately after leaving the body? The BSD explains this.

5. Reports of increased clarity and swiftness of thought are common during the first stage. Subjects often mention a heightened sense of objective intellect, feeling far more alert, curious, logical, rational, and intelligent than normal during this phase. Why is this? The BSD explains it.

6. The second stage brings an intense flood of feelings and emotions that always seem to be abnormally extreme. No one seems to come back from NDEs reporting that they felt just "a little bit good" or "a little bit bad."

The feelings experienced during the second stage of NDEs always seem to be at extreme, absolute levels. Why is this? The BSD explains it.

7. NDE-ers regularly report an experience that seems to be a direct, pure, and certain knowing; information received in this way is always felt to be 100 percent certain, despite having been in no way questioned, measured, analyzed, or independently verified. This information is not questioned, but accepted without dispute or hesitation as absolute and obvious truth. Why is this? The BSD explains it.

8. NDE-ers during the second stage regularly entertain thoughts and impressions which are never questioned. Yet later, when the cold light of objective logic is brought to bear upon these insights, one finds that some NDE reports sometimes contradict others. Some NDE-ers insist, for example, that they received the "divine truth" that reincarnation is a false teaching, while others return from their NDEs carrying the opposite message. Similar contradictions have occurred over other issues as well, such as the existence of the devil and the primacy of Christianity. Why is this? The BSD explains it.

9. Inhabitants of second-stage realms seem to remain frozen in whatever behavior patterns they held at the times of their deaths. Even though they now possess no physical bodies, they still seek to satisfy their physical cravings, seemingly unable to intellectually grasp that these cravings can no longer be satisfied. Why is this? The BSD explains it.

10. The recently deceased often can't figure out that they are dead, despite an abundance of glaring clues pointing in that direction. They remain unaccountably befuddled, seemingly unable to perform even the simplest logical deductions. This loss of analytical reasoning ability is perhaps most obvious in the reports of the hellish realm of bewildered souls, who are trapped in unfortunate and unpleasant conditions of their own making, which they could get out of easily if only they tried. Yet they don't try. Why is this? The BSD explains it.

11. Second-stage NDE-ers commonly report feeling a profound oneness with the universe. They see the universe as a perfectly interconnected, synchronized, and harmonized singularity. Why is this? The BSD explains it.

12. The reports from second-stage NDE-ers seem to emphasize subjective interpersonal values such as personal relationships, family, love, and patience, while de-emphasizing more objective values, such as worldly and professional accomplishment. In the life reviews of NDE-ers, their subjective, emotion-based relationships are accorded more meaning and significance than their objective, worldly accomplishments. Why is this? The BSD explains it.

13. NDE-ers report that the normal boundaries between themselves and others fade. Instead of retaining their own independent autonomy, all their thoughts and feelings are exposed to the universe and nothing is hidden. In short, there no longer seems to be any separateness or privacy. Why is this? The BSD explains it.

14. In the realm of light, everything is always incredibly beautiful. In much the same way, observers of the realm of bewildered spirits display an intensification of their aesthetic sense, but in the opposite direction. Either way, the aesthetic sense of the observer always seems to register at maximum capacity. Why is this? The BSD explains it.

15. Verbal communication ability is often greatly diminished during NDEs. Words are seldom used during the second-stage experience, communication more often occurring instead via gestures, images, and direct intuitive comprehension. Even after the NDE is over, words are still inadequate to describe the experience. Even the life review is experienced more often in pictures than verbal memories. Why is this? The BSD explains it.

16. The first stage of NDEs typically includes little or no perception of any forms (even one's own self seems to be formless) while the second stage is usually filled with forms of all sorts. Why is this? The BSD explains it.

17. NDE-ers often report memory loss of second-stage experiences. Again and again, NDE-ers have reported that momentous insights and revelations were received during the experience, but upon returning to normal consciousness, this invaluable data is found to be missing from memory. They are left with very strong and compelling feelings and impressions, but often very little in the way of actual specific detail. Why is this? The BSD explains it.

18. During the life review, all the repressed emotions, forgotten memories, rejected insights, and unacknowledged self-judgments that had built up within the unconscious over the course of the person's life spring fully forth *en masse*. Why is this? The BSD explains it.

19. The judgment that occurs during this review is most typically experienced as being a self-judgment rather than a judgment that comes from a second party. The life review often makes people feel as if they have finally been revealed to themselves as they truly are for the first time. This sense of having been "exposed" is a very common theme in the second stage of NDEs; stripped of all one's illusions and denials and self-deceptions, one feels unaccustomedly exposed to oneself, as well as to others. Why is this? The BSD explains it.

20. Many researchers have described a grey or hellish version of the second-stage NDE realm which seems to be home to hordes of bewildered, distressed souls. Deeply unconscious, these beings possess extremely low intelligence and vitality, appearing washed out and confused. These bewildered spirits show no intellectual curiosity about where they are, nor any inclination for communication, being caught up in their own emotional misery, unaware of the presence of others. Why is this? The BSD explains it.

21. The ghostlike souls in this grey realm seem to be trapped in easily escapable misfortunes, situations which they could get out of very easily if only they tried. But they don't try. During normal human life, no matter how desperate the situation, no matter how imprisoned a group of people might seem to be, the indomitable will of the human spirit refuses to let them give up entirely. But in the grey realm described in NDE reports, that will is nowhere to be seen. Why is this? The BSD explains it.

22. The heavenly and hellish realms visited during the second stage of NDEs seem, despite first appearances, to have much in common. In both, emotions and credibility predominate while reason and verbal expression seems diminished. Why is this? The BSD explains it.

23. NDE-ers have described what seem to be two very different perspectives of the hellish realm—one seen from the inside, and one from the outside. Descriptions from inside can be frightening, with horrifying visual imagery.

But descriptions of this place as seen from the outside never seem to include this nightmarish imagery. Why is this? The BSD explains it.

24. The two stages of NDEs reflect the two halves of the human psyche, the dark stage bringing the enhancement of the characteristics of the conscious mind and the diminishment of those of the unconscious, while the light stage does the exact opposite. Why does this parallel exist? The BSD explains it.

25. Why do NDE-ers insist that time does not exist in the "other world," and yet also insist that the dark or tunnel stage of their NDE occurred *before* (indicating a time-sequence) the "realm of light" stage occurred? The BSD explains it.

26. Individuals who have undergone past-life regression have often reported spending time in an emotionless black void very similar to the dark void of the first stage of NDEs. But unlike the reports of NDE-ers, the past-life regression subjects claim to have spent years, even decades, in this empty limbo. After this NDE-like void, the next thing many regressed subjects recall is reincarnating again into a new body, without ever experiencing anything like the classic "Realm of Light" of the second stage of NDEs. Why this discrepancy? The BSD explains it.

27. For PLR subjects, memory loss often seems to be a part of this experience. Many subjects don't remember their own names or anything else about their previous life while they are floating in this void. All they remember doing is floating calmly alone in this void, losing all sense of personal identity. Why is this? The BSD explains it.

28. Haunting ghosts seem to act like mindless recordings stuck on automatic replay, repeatedly reliving their memories. They seem to possess no objective awareness, rational intellect, or verbal communication ability. In the rare instances when they do communicate, it almost always takes the form of pictures, images, and symbolism. Why do ghosts have these characteristics? The BSD explains it.

29. Psychics often describe souls of the dead who seem to be suffering from extreme confusion, often unable to perform the elementary deductive

logic necessary to figure out that they have passed on. Psychics also maintain that entities in the other world tend to be nonverbal—in lieu of verbal communication, spirits as well as ghosts often communicate by pantomime. Why is this? The BSD explains it.

30. Sylvia Brown, Edgar Cayce, and Rudolf Steiner identified the unconscious as the "spirit mind," the mind used in the realm of the dead. Why is this? The BSD explains it.

31. James Van Praagh reports that two personal elements survive physical death: an emotional body and a mental body. But after declaring that the union of these two makes one whole, he says that wholeness is irreversibly shattered after death. The mental body continues on alone after this division, leaving the emotional body to deteriorate. Why is this? The BSD explains it.

32. Robert Monroe, founder of The Monroe Institute, also taught that one part of a person would be left behind in the realm of the dead while another part went on to reincarnate, and placed tremendous emphasis on the importance of collecting up all these lost parts of the self, reintegrating them back into one's present psyche. Why is this? The BSD explains it.

33. Why do some NDE-ers believe that death brings the end of the individual personality? The BSD explains it.

34. NDE subjects often return with enhanced psychologies, more balanced, healthy, and creative outlooks on life, and sometimes even with new psychic abilities. Why is this? The BSD explains it.

35. Why does the Near-Death phenomenon seem to stimulate the brain hemisphere that was not previously dominant? The BSD explains it.

This Answer Really Works?

The simple cause-and-effect connections between mankind's afterlife reports and the binary soul doctrine are stunning in their implications. All the different afterlife phenomena that mankind has been reporting down through the ages were predictable all along, through nothing more esoteric than basic psychological dynamics. An afterdeath division of the conscious and unconscious would provide a cogent scientific explanation for all the most commonly reported afterlife phenomena, experiences which actually seem to be built right into the hard wiring of the human psyche.

The ancient binary soul doctrine even seems to finally solve the riddle of mankind's two afterlife scenarios (reincarnation vs. heaven/hell), explaining at long last why the world has so stubbornly held onto these two seemingly opposite and incompatible doctrines—because two very fundamentally different afterlife experiences *really were* being experienced. The unconscious soul was having one type of experience, and the conscious spirit having a radically different one. Together, this scientific discovery and the once-widespread binary soul doctrine from which it sprang suggest that human religion originally began as a science, a hard knowledge, a discipline which once explored the psychological mechanics of an eternal mind—a mind which, while it could not truly die, could nonetheless become profoundly fractured.

More Questions

As is often the case with discoveries, this one seems to raise as many questions as it answers. Why do our two souls have to divide when we die? And for that matter, why do we have two souls in the first place? More importantly, is the division permanent? When the conscious mind goes on to reincarnate, does the unconscious still stay behind in its heaven or hell? If so, then where does the new unconscious for the next lifetime come from?[9] Does everyone living today have multiple, long-forgotten past-life unconscious souls still engaged in their own private heavenly or hellish experiences deep within their psyches? And if so, will these discarded parts of our beings ever be reunited and made whole again? Do some people die without ever dividing at all? If so, how might this be accomplished?

And why do the majority of mankind's ancient reports of the realm of the dead seem to describe a hellish realm, while today most NDE reports describe a heavenly realm? Are relatively fewer hellish experiences experienced today than in humanity's past, or is it that fewer are reported than are experienced? If fewer *are* being experienced, what caused the change? Is it significant that the vast majority of the hellish reports date from before Christ, while most of the heavenly reports appear after?

9

Why We Have Two Souls: The Divine Dichotomy and Our Binary World

These two come paired,
but distinct by their names.
Of all things profound,
Say their pairing is deepest,
The gate to the root of the world.

—Tao Te Ching 1

People often react very negatively to the idea that we are double beings, that the human soul is binary in nature. It rarely occurs to them that this is just the reaction one would expect if the soul was bifurcated. To be dual, after all, is to be duplicitous and double-dealing. To have two parts to the self makes it possible for one hand not to know what the other is doing. It paves the way for violated integrity, unintentional falsehood, self-betrayal, and self-deception.

Plus, it just seems odd. *Why* do we have two souls?

Perhaps the answer is as simple as this: because that's the way *everything* is made—with two parts, two equal but opposite complementary components. The ancient Egyptians certainly thought so, as did the Chinese. One has but to step outdoors for a moment to be reminded that the world, and everything in it, has a two-part, binary form. Looking at a tree, we are reminded that the root structure beneath the tree looks just like the branch structure above it. When we look at the form of that tree's leaves, or the form of practically any living thing, we notice that its shape and body are symmetrical, having equal but opposite right and left sides.

Such symmetry seems a hard and fast rule of this world. We see it in the equal but opposite natures of the sexes, of day and night, of summer and winter; in the positive and negative poles of electricity and magnetism; in the dualities of life and inanimate matter, of plants and animals, and in the natural law that for every action there is an equal but opposite reaction.

We see it in the double-helix of the DNA molecule that splits down the middle during reproduction, the two halves becoming complements to each other. Although equivalent, these copies are not identical, but equal opposites, just as a mold and a cast contain inverted forms of the same image.

Indeed, we see this duality in the makeup of the universe, composed of matter and antimatter. Cosmologists speak of virtual particles constantly appearing and disappearing in the universe. According to quantum field theory, pairs of virtual particles, one positive and one negative, appear together in the primordial vacuum, move apart, then come together again and annihilate each other.

While we once thought that space and time were quite separate things, we've since realized that they are but two sides of the same strange coin. In the same way, we once thought that matter and energy were separate, until Einstein cleared up the issue with the $E=MC^2$ equation. We see the universe's duality in the nature of light itself, which somehow manages to be both a particle and a wave at the same time, two equal-but-opposite, seemingly mutually exclusive natures. As if to drive the point home to the modern age, the machine that has completely revolutionized the world in the last few decades—the computer—does nothing more complicated than distinguish between ones and zeros.

We even see this duality in the laughably unequal way men's and women's clothes sizes are measured.

We see the universe's immanent duality smiling out from behind science's struggle to incorporate all the laws of physics into a single equation. For more than half a century, our scientists have unsuccessfully tried to integrate and reconcile two seemingly equal but opposite theories; each, on its own, seems obviously and indisputably true, and yet the two seem irreconcilable. Quantum theory addresses the laws that govern how things work on the scale of the extremely small. We know quantum theory is correct. Relativity theory addresses the laws that govern how things work on the scale of the extremely large. We also know that relativity theory is correct. The "Holy Grail" of science's modern quest is the grand unified theory, which, it is hoped, will reconcile and integrate these two together into a single complete picture that accurately describes the universe. The problem is, relativity theory simply does not seem to describe the same universe as quantum theory; no matter how our scientists twist and squirm to try to make these two perspectives interface, they seem to have nothing in common, as if each were describing a separate and unrelated universe. And yet, impossibly, they are both here in the same one.

Yet one particularly strange duality in the physical world seems to have a special purpose: The sun and moon seem designed to function as *symbols* for this immanent duality. Every schoolchild learns that the sun and the moon are vastly different from each other, that the sun is immensely larger than the earth, and unimaginably far away, while the moon is smaller than the earth, and incredibly smaller than the sun. The sun is *65 million times larger* than the moon, yet to an observer on the surface of our planet, they appear to be the *exact same size*. This is a mere trick of perception, of course, yet it is an extraordinary trick to have pulled off.[1] For this illusion to occur, we needed first of all to have just a single moon orbiting the earth, instead of the multiple moons that so many other planets possess. And that moon had to be just the right size, shape, and distance from the earth, a coincidence of mind-staggering improbability.

But the duality of the sun and moon does not stop there. Even when science was figuring out that the sun and moon are not the same size after all, we were discovering that they are equal opposites in many other ways. The sun produces its own light, while the moon only reflects light; the sun is unimaginably hot, the moon ridiculously cold; the sun is active, the moon passive; the sun is what we orbit, the moon is what orbits us. The sun is eternally renewing itself; its nuclear fires making it fresh and eternally new, living forever in the present moment. The moon, on the other hand, does not renew itself, but contains, in its crater-pocked surface, an unedited and unbroken record of its history from its earliest times.

The sun's visual image is constant and unchanging, appearing to the naked eye to be the same day after day, while the moon regularly changes, cycling from new moon to full moon and back again. To ancient observers, it seemed there was only one sun, but a plurality of moons. While the sun was always the same, never changing, the moon appeared to come to life and grow, then wither, die, and disappear altogether. When another fresh moon finally appeared a few days later and began to grow larger again, the ancients thought it was, indeed, a whole new moon (thus the term).

The sun and moon seem perfect symbols for the soul and spirit of the binary soul doctrine. The sun reflects the everpresent, living-in-the-moment, vibrant conscious spirit that never changes, and is the same lifetime after life-time, but which never saves any memory record of its past history. The nightly moon reflects the unconscious soul that seems entirely new and different in each subsequent lifetime, a soul that can grow or shrink, be born or die, a soul which does not supply its own light (energy) but which does record its own past history.[2] In many places around the world where these parallels were taken seriously, astrologers began to report that the sun in one's horoscope chart reflected one's conscious spirit, the moon one's unconscious soul.

Doesn't it seem that the same Intelligence that designed us to have two sexes, two brain hemispheres, two eyes, two legs, two parts to the psyche, and so on was thinking along the same lines when It decided to plant us on a planet with two huge attention-getting, equal but opposite looking lights in the sky? Our planet has only one moon, a fact that astrophysicists consider very unusual and hard to explain. The fact that the sun and moon appear to be the *exact same* size in the sky is even more difficult to explain away by chance, but is consistent with the overall bipartite nature of the universe experienced by human beings. If these parallels are not coincidence, and the sun and moon were purposely designed to be the ultimate and obvious symbols of a universal duality that exists both in the world at large and also within our being, then what are we to make of the solar eclipse, when the two seem to unite,[3] casting an otherworldly spell over the whole land?

A God Divided?

Duality seems to be so fundamental an element of our observed and experienced reality that it permeates every conceivable facet of human experience. One could never compile a comprehensive catalog of all the evidence, even though I have assembled a token sampling in this chapter. Fortunately, as the saying goes, you don't have to inspect every blade of grass to know which way the wind is blowing.

It seems to have always been this way. Thousands of years ago, religious teachers taught that the universe was created by the fundamental distinction between inside and outside. Hundreds of years ago, philosophers maintained that everything is composed of form and substance.[4] A generation ago, politicians divided the world into democratic and communist halves. Today, we still look at the world and see it divided into rich and poor, brave and cowardly, master and slave, scientific and religious, Democrat and Republican, black and white, up and down, hot and cold, left and right, and on and on. Some argue that conscious awareness itself depends on such dualities; we cannot know what "happy" is until we have also experienced "sad." Existence has no meaning if it is not contrasted with nonexistence. Pleasure has no meaning unless there is also pain. There is no up without down, no male without female, no exterior without interior, no singular without plural.

This is all certainly true, but it is not the whole story, because it is not merely the world we observe that reflects this duality, but also the world that we human beings *create* that carries this ever-prevalent stamp of duality. It is not merely inscrutable Nature, but our own selves, that have created the Pepsi/Coke, Ford/Chevy, Democrat/Republican, liberal/conservative, labor/management, urban/rural, East Coast/West Coast, AC/DC, AM/FM, UHF/VHF, VHS/Beta, analog/digital, Windows/Mac, Netscape/Internet Explorer, Rock/Country, pro-life/pro-choice, paper/plastic, fiction/nonfiction, quality/quantity dualities of this world. Everything we create seems, independent of our will, to become stamped with this same dualistic nature. This makes sense to me. If nature makes everything dualistic, and it made us, then we must be dualistic. And if we are dualistic, then everything we make will carry that same imprint as well. Creations reflect their creators.

> There is a crack in everything God has made.
> —Ralph Waldo Emerson[5]

Through the ages, people around the world recognized the universal stamp of duality on the universe, preserving this precious insight by inserting it into their creation myths. At the dawn of creation, many cultures taught, there originally existed a pair of gods, sometimes thought of as a set of twins, other times as brother and sister or husband and wife, who were usually conceived of as having equal but opposite natures. From this original divine pair, all the rest of creation emerged.

A common variation on this theme held that a single god existed at first, but then that singular being divided into (or differentiated into, or created) two beings, from whom the rest of creation then sprang. Such stories can be found in abundance all over the globe; it is one of the most common themes in mythology, and perhaps *the* most common theme in creation mythology. Near-Eastern creation myths described this original primordial state as an egg with "twin male and female waters intermingled." Indeed, even the Bible's familiar Adam and Eve story fits this pattern, with Eve having been created by dividing away from Adam's body.

Tracking this division is anything but an academic exercise. Opposites pervade every facet and level of the reality we experience, up to and including our selves—and even beyond that. Duality characterizes our perspectives and ability to perceive; for are we not made of mind and heart? Conscious and unconscious mind? Objective and subjective awareness? Active and passive, male and female elements? Soul and spirit? In each case, we find we can never quite get a handle on any of these sets; we can never completely identify or define them. No matter how hard we look at them, we can never fully wrap our minds around any of these sets of components.

That would make sense if they were infinite, echoes of a primordial division of an infinite being.

Nor is this notion of a primordial division merely an obsolete and archaic concept. On the contrary, it is near and dear to the hearts of many today. Neale Donald Walsch has resurrected this idea within his widely read *Conversations with God* series. At the dawn of creation, Walsch reports, God divided Himself into two equal but opposite halves, in a primordial event he calls the "Divine Dichotomy."[6] Ken Wilber reports much the same thing, declaring that spirit manifests in this world in two diametrically opposed ways, which he calls the "Right and Left Hands of God," or the "Masculine and Feminine Faces of God."[7]

While many different sources agree that this Primordial Division somehow occurred, they do not all agree on its value. While some, like Walsch, hold that the Primordial Division was a beneficial and necessary development, others feel it was a dreadful calamity. Such is the message of the best-selling 1975 work *A Course in Miracles* (widely known as ACIM). A publishing phenomenon, ACIM has been a profound success, inspiring a worldwide movement and numerous schools built in its honor. A disturbing yet deeply moving work, ACIM is purportedly a modern communication from Jesus Christ, a psychological reinterpretation of Christianity's entire conception of history. What really happened at the biblical Fall, ACIM says, was that the human mind was split apart into two opposing elements. We willfully initiated this division ourselves, violating our own integrity by deciding to ignore, deny, and reject part of our own being. And ever since then, the human mind has been disassociated, in an insane war with itself that prevents effective communication between its two halves.

This divided mind, ACIM maintains, is the source of all unhappiness, sickness, and death: So long as our minds remain split in two, peace of mind is impossible and death is inevitable. Unlike most New Age teachings, ACIM openly declares that death is a serious problem for humanity:

> You do pay a price for death, and a very heavy one.[8]

Part of that price is that this divided mind prevents us from learning (which would explain the repetition of life mistakes so commonly found in past-life regression research):

> You cannot learn . . . with a split mind, because a split mind has made you a very poor learner. . . . The learning situation in which you placed yourself is impossible.[9]

With the mind fractured in two, each half of the psyche seemed to take on opposite functions and characteristics, one half paying more attention to the connections and similarities between things, while the other focuses more on distinctions and differences (the ACIM reported this division of labor in 1975, six years before Sally Springer and Georg Deutsch's groundbreaking 1981 work *Left Brain, Right Brain* said much the same thing). But being unable to tolerate knowing that our minds are divided and our integrity compromised, we take great pains to avoid acknowledging this, instead projecting our inner division out onto the world we observe:

> A split mind is endangered, and the recognition that it encompasses completely opposed thoughts within itself is intolerable. Therefore the mind projects the split, not the reality. Everything you perceive as the outside world is merely your attempt to maintain your ego identification.[10]
>
> The mind always strives for integration, and if it is split and wants to keep the split, it will still believe it has one goal by making it seem to be one. . . . As you look in, you choose the guide for seeing. And then you look out and behold his witnesses. This is why you find what you seek. What you want in yourself you will make manifest. . . . The mind then sees a divided world outside itself, but not within.[11]
>
> You . . . made one substitution . . . fragmentation for wholeness. It has become so splintered and subdivided and divided again, over and over, that it is now almost impossible to perceive it was once one, and still is what it was. That one error, which brought truth to illusion, infinity to time, and life to death, was all you ever made. Your whole world rests upon it. Everything you see reflects it.[12]

As ACIM recognizes, the universe and everything in it, even our own souls, does indeed seem to come with a ready-made binary structure. Unfortunately, this insight into an all-encompassing duality has not answered the question this chapter started with—"Why do we have two souls?"—but has merely changed it to "why is *everything* so dualistic?" And it is at that point that we are forced in this work to leave the realm of solid evidence and venture cautiously into the realm of conjecture.

Is ACIM right? Many spiritual traditions, like ACIM, take this universal duality to be a horrible error that must be corrected and reversed. However, many other traditions (Walsch's work is but one example; innumerable creation myths around the world reflect others) feel that God Himself is dualistic, and, reasoning that His Creation must therefore be as well, find nothing wrong with either. But, as is so often the case, the truth may lie somewhere in the middle. Modern biology, of all things, reminds us of that unique concept Egypt embraced so very long ago—that true virtue is not to be found in either unity exclusively nor duality exclusively, but only in the integration of both together: the two that are one.

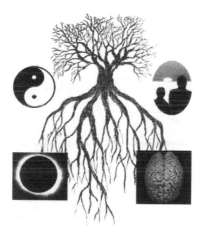

**All things have been created in pairs
so you may reflect on it.
—Quranic verse 51:49**

Taking a Cue from Nature

All natural and healthy growth processes proceed by dif-
ferentiation-and-integration . . . that is how nature creates
higher unities and deeper integrations.

—Ken Wilber[13]

Differentiation is the first step towards growth in all living systems. First differentiation occurs, then the differentiated elements integrate together, forming complex systems. The same thing happens when an acorn grows into an oak tree as when an embryo grows into a man or woman. One cell splits into two, then four, then sixteen, and as they divide, the cells differentiate into different forms, and those various forms integrate into marvelous organisms of complex depth and integrity. In human reproduction, a single cell multiplies and differentiates into many other very different types of cells, forming tissues and organs and systems, which all become integrated perfectly together to form a being of far greater depth, sophistication, and capacity than the single-celled embryo from which it sprang.

After the different parts have finished differentiating, the natural tendency is for them to then try to reunite and integrate with each other. This integration does not require the differentiated elements to sacrifice any of their own unique natures, but only that they achieve a balance among themselves. Achieving the balanced integration of opposing forces seems to be the trademark of the universe. When human beings finish differentiating into mature males and females, the natural tendency is for these to re-integrate. And when that happens, a magical event occurs, creating a new element—an embryo. Again and again, we see that the processes of differentiation and integration work together to produce healthy growth.

This magical process is not limited to reproduction. Two eyes eventually form as our bodies develop in the womb, differentiating from what was once a single-celled, undifferentiated homogenous embryo. When those eyes are functionally mature, they integrate together as well. We don't observe two separate fields of vision when we open our eyes; we find that the two fields magically integrate together into a single, vastly superior visual experience. Whenever such integration occurs, magic takes place. Instead of just ending up with a pair of flat, two-dimensional fields of vision, we now experience a single three-dimensional field, something that neither eye was able to provide on its own. The newly created whole proves greater than the sum of its parts. So once again we find that the processes of differentiation and integration produce greater depth, sophistication, and advancement. In a word, *growth*.

But *what* is growing? Observing that duality seems to be a universal feature of reality, many philosophers have suggested that God divided apart into two halves at the dawn of Creation, and that those parts have been trying to reunite ever since. Since God was infinite, His two parts would also be infinite, they reasoned, which would explain the infinite variety of dualistic pairs we observe in the world around us. Eventually this Divine Dichotomy will reunite, and Creation will fall back upon itself and cease to exist. Some thought that this division/reunion was only going to occur once, and our species just happened to evolve into existence right in the middle of it. But other philosophers said that this was a cyclic process, with division and reunion occurring over and over forever.

If these philosophers are right, then what is God doing? If the processes of nature are any indication, then we can only assume that God is *growing*, using the very same processes of differentiation and integration that we see used in the world around us.[14]

The Name of the Game

What does this mean for the binary human soul? It suggests that the differentiation of the human psyche into two parts is but another example of the same growth process of differentiation and integration that we observe taking place everywhere else in the world. If so, this suggests two further things:

1. The human race is, at present, only halfway through this process. We seem to have finished the process of differentiating the psyche into two distinct elements, but we have not finished reintegrating what has been differentiated.

2. It suggests that we are unfinished products. The ultimate destiny and nature of the human species would be as different from where we are now as three-dimensional sight is from two-dimensional sight.

It suggests that it is just as possible for the two halves of the human psyche to form a balanced, integrated singularity as it is for the sun and moon to join so perfectly together in the sky that they seem to be a single light. And that the result will be just as stunning and unfamiliar.

It's not like we haven't been *trying*. Both on the levels of the individual and the collective, humanity has been struggling for a long time to integrate its two halves. The call to integrate these halves is not new, but has been repeated in culture after culture for as far back in time as we care to look. This call comes in two forms: one is to integrate at the level of the community, and another to integrate at the level of the individual.

Our struggle for integration takes many forms, such as science vs. religion, reason vs. faith, head vs. heart, intellect vs. emotion, logic vs. intuition, left brain vs. right brain, form vs. function, objective vs. subjective, art vs. business, career vs. family, work vs. play, responsibility vs. freedom, law and order vs. right and wrong, West vs. East, capitalism vs. communism, corporation vs. individual, and so on. But underneath all these struggles, one can see the soul and spirit wrestling each other for dominance. Being equal but opposite, the two parts within us seem to be in inevitable conflict with each other; but underneath that conflict (or within it), the two seem to follow a natural compulsion to try to integrate with each other, to achieve perfect balance.

The next logical step in our development would be to achieve the same integration in the "sphere of the individual" that we are just now starting to have some success at in the "sphere of the society." Granted, we haven't perfected this integration in the sphere of society yet, but we're a lot closer than we were just a hundred years ago. In the last century, we've seen a remarkable integration of male and female roles in society, as well as an integration of Eastern and Western thought and practices. We should take great hope in these developments, because nothing can occur on the level of the collective that is not also occurring on the level of the individual. We should celebrate the fact that we have taken steps closer to the goal of achieving integration between our two halves.

Is Something Broken?

Still, doesn't it seem that it's taking longer than it should to make the jump from differentiation to integration? Granted, we don't have any similar examples at hand to compare our own species' progress to, but in most of the examples of differentiation and integration that we *are* able to observe, the integration seems to occur either alongside the differentiation, or immediately following it. Humanity, on the other hand, seems to have become stuck in the middle, all dressed up with no place to go, more or less fully differentiated but apparently nowhere close to achieving integration.

We are far from balanced.

The unhealthy imbalance in our system is reflected in the domination and repression of women by men, the domination and repression of the unconscious by the conscious, the domination and repression of our emotions by our will, the domination and repression of our intuition by our reason, the domination and repression of the poor by the rich, the domination and repression of religion by science, and so on. We seem to have been stuck like this for at least a few thousand years, if not far longer. In the next chapter, we will explore possible reasons why we might have become caught in the middle of such a stagnant pathology, as well as some of its more long-term consequences.

10

Why Would Our Souls Divide at Death? The Pathology in the System

When the situation was manageable it was neglected, and now that it is thoroughly out of hand we apply too late the remedies which then might have effected a cure. There is nothing new in the story. It is as old as the sibylline books. It falls into that long, dismal catalogue of the fruitlessness of experience and the confirmed unteachability of mankind. Want of foresight, unwillingness to act when action would be simple and effective, lack of clear thinking, confusion of counsel until the emergency comes, until self-preservation strikes its jarring gong, these are the features which constitute the endless repetition of history.

—*Winston S. Churchill*[1]

Like all living things, the human species is in the process of growing, and, also like all other living things, we use the same process of differentiation and integration to propel us. But perhaps unlike other creatures, we've reached a point in our evolution where the majority of our growth is now taking place in the mental (or spiritual) sphere instead of merely in the physical. The processes of evolution, it seems, are attempting to make our inner beings richer, deeper, and more complex.[2]

But we are only halfway there so far. Our minds have achieved differentiation, but not yet integration. The differentiation process begins at birth, and by the time we are adults, our minds have differentiated into two distinct units of consciousness. This is a normal example of the natural growth process, no different from the way a single cell, the fertilized human egg, differentiates into all the thousands of different types of cells in the adult human body.

As newborns, psychology teaches, our psyches are like a single cell, existing in a pre-differentiated or non-differentiated state. Neither the conscious mind nor the unconscious mind has yet emerged; both are still melded together in the infant mind. It is important to note that this is not a form of integration. Neither the conscious nor the unconscious yet exists; none of the qualities of either has yet emerged. The mind of the infant, our experts tell us, is predifferentiated; it cannot yet distinguish between subject and object, self and mother, or body and environment, but instead experiences an incomprehensible reality without specific boundaries, qualities, or definitions.[3] In the infant's mind, the mental lenses through which adults observe the world have not yet been formed. There aren't any separate elements to join together into any functional synthesis or working relationship, but instead a simple homogenous mental field that robs any potential elements of their unique character, dignity, and function. Fused impotently together in this fashion, the two halves of the mind cancel each other out, allowing neither to operate successfully.

In time, these two quite different spheres of consciousness, the right-brain unconscious and left-brain conscious, do emerge within the child's mind, as distinct elements of the psyche. In other words, our minds do successfully differentiate; our minds successfully complete the first stage of the growth process. This first step occurs automatically, without anyone's choice or assistance.

But what of the second half of the equation of the universal growth process—integration? The struggle towards integration seems to be what the rest of life is all about. We have these two sides within us, and we find we are always confronting the necessity of trying to integrate them, making them function in unison.

It is common for humans to feel they are divided. Our inner life is immediately distinguishable into thinking and feeling, analysis and emotion, head and heart; the experience of the two are different and distinguishable. The head and heart frequently have battles; we get conflicting signals from them, drawing us in different directions. This is the challenge of being human, to surmount that conflict. Unfortunately, many never do, but merely mask and repress it, remaining secretly divided all their lives, a condition that they hide even from themselves, until they die and can hide from it no longer.

When Freud discovered the existence of a secondary, sub-level of the human psyche in the beginning of the 1900s, he was dismayed, and throughout the rest of his life he remained convinced that this binary structure was evidence of pathology, and that the human mind was dysfunctional. Folk wisdom would agree, holding that "everyone is mentally ill to some degree," and that "we only use 10 percent of our full mental capacity."

We certainly all have our unique mental blind spots. When something is inside a person, whether we're talking about a liver, spleen, tumor, or the unconscious, it affects that person, regardless of whether or not he or she "believes" in it, regardless of whether or not anyone acknowledges its existence. In fact, *not* believing in it gives it more power over the person. The more a person remains unaware of those forces that affect and influence him in this world, the less control and authority he wields over his own life.

> Unconscious phenomena are so little related to the ego that most people do not hesitate to deny their existence outright. Nevertheless, they manifest themselves in an individual's behavior. An attentive observer can detect them without difficulty, while the observed person remains unaware of the fact that he is betraying his most secret thoughts or even things he has never thought consciously. It is, however, a great prejudice to suppose that something we have never thought consciously does not exist in the psyche.
> —Carl G. Jung[4]

Most people aren't even aware they have an unconscious; it is no more real to them than the tooth fairy or the Easter bunny. Considering that science discovered the existence of the unconscious about 100 years ago and has been building temples to it ever since, this is pretty strong evidence of the strength of the division. Even after a century of confirming research, the average person still goes around in his life ignoring, discounting, or overlooking the fact that half of his own mind is AWOL, mistakenly assuming he is the uncompromised master of his own psychological domain. In reality, the average person is still divided; half of his being is foreign to him.

When we fail in the task of reconciling and integrating our two inner selves, our minds tend to splinter and scatter. This can lead to anguish and

191

stunting, in the individual and in society. We are constantly confronted by this struggle to resolve the relationship between these two halves, and all too often, we choose disassociation instead of integration. Instead of trying to get the two elements to work together in some sort of balance, we frequently identify exclusively with one side and disassociate from the other. What this does is raise the stakes, changing a healthy differentiation into an unhealthy division. The two parts then no longer interact well at all, but instead begin to splinter apart.

In many, perhaps most people, the differentiation of conscious spirit and unconscious soul suffers from this pathology, progressing from differentiation into full-blown disassociation. Communication between the two halves fails, throwing the system into dysfunction. Instead of being integrated, the components of the system split apart, resulting in fragmentation, repression, and alienation.

Psychology has a term for this disassociated state: neurosis. And there is abundant evidence that this mental illness is ravaging our species, like mold sweeping through a petri dish. We pay our sports stars and entertainers (on whom nothing of much consequence depends) millions of dollars, but force the true heroes of our culture, our teachers, librarians, police, and firemen (on whom almost everything of consequence depends), to scrape by in virtual poverty. Our priorities seem inside-out and backwards; some people spend more money on tennis shoes than on feeding their children. We regularly destroy huge food surpluses, callously ignoring the many thousands around the world who go to bed hungry each night.

In America, the richest country in the world, more than half of all teenage girls have some sort of eating disorder, while the rest of the populace enthusiastically saturates their bodies (and the rest of the planet) with deadly toxins. Our appetites are betraying us. The most popular beverage in the world carries a label on its side that declares it to have no nutritional value. Many who have conquered the outer world end up getting brought down by their own inner wars; we've seen so many exalted public figures destroyed by sexual indiscretions that it's become a cliché.

We seem to do everything we can to avoid what's going on inside us. Today we have more kinds of addictions than there are names for. We find ourselves using ever-greater amounts of evermore powerful drugs and pain killers (and other distractions) to mask the ever-increasing pain and dissatisfaction we endure in life.

Why are we so dissatisfied? Perhaps because we have built a society in which the workings of justice are having less and less to do with right and wrong, and more and more to do with who can afford the best lawyers for the longest stretch of time. But we accept this in our stride. We accept a society in which criminals are set free every day on pointless technicalities, while well-meaning people who are trying to make a positive difference in the world are being hamstrung.

Our collective insanity knows no limits. Not only have we all apparently agreed to allow 10 percent of the population to control 90 percent of the wealth and power, but when given half a chance, many of us opt to freely give even more of our own power and wealth away.[5] Some of the primary causes of death in our culture are heart disease, cancer, diabetes, drug abuse, AIDS, and gang violence, all of which are largely preventable ailments. We could easily avoid a great many of these deaths, but instead we seem to do about everything we can to hasten them. Judging by our actions, an outside observer could only conclude that the human race has a death wish . . . but we don't want to think about that. Instead, we focus all our attention on worshipping youth, and hide all our old and sick people away inside invisible institutions where they won't remind us of any unpleasant inevitabilities. And as the average individual member of our species is still divided within himself, still at war with himself, so too our collective, our culture and society, has pretty much *always* been at war with itself. After 6,000 years of so-called civilization, we still haven't quite figured out how to live in peace with each other (something every other species has done); every generation, if not every decade, seems to write yet another attempt at global domination and/or genocide into the history books.

How crazy are we? The repulsive sideshow that is daytime television catalogues some of the more disturbing examples of our collective insanity, but even so, it is alarming how very "far-out" the guests of those shows have to be nowadays to successfully perform their primary function: making the rest of us still feel relatively normal.

The craziest thing is that we all know these facts already. Everyone reading this list can probably add a few more items. There is nothing in this discussion that is not common knowledge. We also know what it means, how these facts add up, but we go through our days as if we didn't know, as if everything was okay. But everything is *not* okay. We are a very sick species.

A question no one seems to ask is *why?* Why are our minds (and therefore our culture) still divided, unbalanced, and unintegrated? What prevents the two halves of the psyche from reintegrating *automatically?* From every other example of the differentiation/integration process that we observe in nature, it seems that integration should occur on its own as soon as differentiation has been achieved. But instead, we find that the vast majority of human beings fail to achieve this integration. We can only assume that something has come along to prevent the integration process from occurring on its own. What is getting in the way?

Original Sin: Rebellion

> Why do we get sick? Because we are already sick and don't know it. Neurosis is the key illness of our day. It has so many manifestations that it seems like dozens of ailments. It is the most intangible and insidious of diseases because it has no single location, no focus, no smell, no look, no obvious structure; to make matters worse, the person is not only unaware of his illness but will deny its existence when confronted with its possibility. Once the neurosis sets in, however, it is only a matter of time until symptoms appear, either physical or mental.
>
> —Arthur Janov[6]

The separation, or division, or alienation of conscious from unconscious, Freud discovered, is comprised of nothing of real substance whatsoever, nothing but pure resistance, raw determination, in other words, an act of will. It almost seems as if an original rebellious act of will, a conscious choice to push away the unconscious from the conscious, was deposited at some point in history into the human unconscious like a seed into a field, effectively programming the unconscious. Once that programming was installed, of course, the unconscious would have automatically carried it out forever, or at least until a new act of will overturned it. The unconscious accepts all commands given to it, and carries them out without question or hesitation. Until that original programming is changed, the unconscious secretly yet persistently urges the conscious mind to push it away.

Left to its own devices, the unconscious would be *all for* integration; it is forever generating responses to the input it receives from the conscious, and emitting those responses back "upstairs" to be received and experienced by the conscious. But the conscious is forever pushing this mental input away. Why? It certainly doesn't recall anymore why it ever started resisting. But once it originally decided to do this, that decision would have fallen into the unconscious, coloring everything that came out of it afterwards.

After that first rebellious decision, an underlying thought would have been attached to every message rising up from the unconscious: "These messages from the unconscious are beneath me; they are unworthy of being noticed or respected, and deserve to be ignored." And hearing this subversive message over and over, day in and day out, the conscious mind indeed would be likely to respect those messages a little less than it otherwise might have done, becoming a little more willing to reject or overlook them when convenient (which is often, as these messages are frequently moral admonitions).

> The self can fail in the integration . . . this pathology forms a lesion in consciousness that tends to infect and distort all subsequent development. Like a grain of sand caught in a developing pearl, the malformation "crinkles" all subsequent layers, tilts and distorts them.
>
> —Ken Wilber[7]

This decision to sabotage our ongoing integration process, this investment in division, this detour in our evolutionary path, would be reflected in every thought and impression and interpretation rising up from the unconscious, coloring every feeling the unconscious emits, like a barrage of subliminal suggestions. Once the original seed-distortion is implanted in the unconscious, the unconscious grows them like weeds.

The Cycle of Rebellion

> You belong to your father, the devil, and you want to carry out your father's desire. He was a murderer from the beginning, not holding to the truth, for there is no truth in him. When he lies, he speaks his native language, for he is a liar and the father of lies.
>
> —John 8:44

From the decision to rebel, in seven brief steps, humanity's whole evolutionary momentum came to a screeching halt, diverting us into a holding pattern of fruitlessly repeating cycles of behavior:

1. The original rebellious decision to resist and prevent the integration of conscious and unconscious had to have been a conscious decision.

2. That decision would have been automatically accepted by the unconscious as an authoritative command, and would have been immediately carried out.

3. All subsequent messages from the unconscious to the conscious would have carried a subliminal encoded reminder of that original decision.

4. Those reminders would be constantly whispered into the conscious mind as subversive suggestions.

5. The conscious mind would frequently reaffirm its decision to follow those suggestions.

6. Those subsequent decisions to divide again and again would reinforce and strengthen the force of the original decision, building up a wall of resistance between the conscious and unconscious.

7. The pattern would continually repeat itself.

The Western religious tradition that all people carry a flaw within them from Adam's "Original Sin" seems to be in agreement with Freud's assertion that *"We are all . . . malfunctioning."*[8] Even in the Bible, it seems, we find reason to suspect that the human psyche, as it currently exists, isn't working properly, isn't functioning the way nature intended. Was it we ourselves who originally chose this divided, repressed, self-betraying, disassociated mental state? We may never know; the memory of that event has been lost. All we can be sure of is that now, quite without intending to do so, we seem to do all we can to perpetuate that divided state. What's more, if reincarnation is true and we've all lived multiple lifetimes already, then we've probably been doing this for quite a while; we've all probably spent a very considerable amount of time and effort blindly reinforcing that division, building up an old and very thick psychological wall of resistance between our two halves.

The Division Response

One way in which we can become unconscious [is by] receiving a series of psychological blows that cannot be integrated . . . the memory of such an event remains well hidden, as does its meaning. All of the pain and its attendant memories become unconscious. The person then walks around in a semi-coma for the rest of his life and isn't even aware of it. He is as unconscious as if someone hit him on the head. Great parts of himself are inaccessible. He cannot learn from his past history because it is buried in his mental archives. He will repeat patterns over and over because he is unconscious.

—Arthur Janov[9]

How do we perpetuate the division? How do we maintain the wall that separates the two halves of the duality, the wall that even today continues to keep the conscious and unconscious at arm's length from each other? The answer is simple to the point of being embarrassing: by dividing ourselves. By betraying our integrity. By rejecting, denying, and ignoring parts of our own inner beings. By being different on the outside than we are on the inside. By rejecting by our outer actions that which our souls urge. Every time we push aside the input from our soul, rejecting it as impractical, too "bleeding-heart," or too painful, we further alienate the unconscious soul from the conscious spirit.

We seem to do this in many ways, and for many apparent reasons. We might seem to disassociate because of some physical or emotional trauma, or perhaps because of some moral conflict. But the underlying reason is always the same: because we have an unconscious predisposition to do this, an automatic knee-jerk reaction we blindly follow without realizing it. Whenever our stress levels get too high and our sense of self seems to be in some kind of jeopardy, we run the risk of succumbing to the unconscious lure of disassociation. Both yesterday's shamans and today's psychologists know that disassociation is a common response to emotional or physical trauma, causing parts of the developing self to split off from the rest of the psyche. The ancient Hebrews, however, knew that violating one's own sense of morality was *also* a sort of trauma that could trigger the division response.

The unconscious is the source of mankind's moral sense, our innate, instinctual awareness of right and wrong. When we violate our own inner standards, the unconscious always tries to tell us that what we did was wrong (as in the cliché "I knew in my heart that it was the right [or wrong] thing to do"). This moral awareness, it seems, preexists inside the mind prior to any cultural influences. The reflective nature of the unconscious causes the mind to always try to look back upon itself, comparing its own chosen actions with its inner ideals.

The unconscious is always reflecting our choices, judgments, and aware-ness back in our faces. It is forever showing us "this is what you are," "this is what you did," "this is how you felt about this then, but then this is how you acted here, and the two don't match up." It is always comparing us to our-selves, showing us the inconsistencies and contradictions. When the uncon-scious finds an inconsistency, this inconsistency is registered and noted, and one's sense of integrity, wholeness, and self-esteem suffers—a sort of trauma. This seems to be a built-in self-monitoring mechanism, one apparently designed to ensure that we are true to ourselves, that we truly honor those ideals and goals and values we embrace inside.

However, we often prevent this inner comparison from occurring, side-stepping the mind's built-in self-correcting mechanism, by refusing to acknowledge the whispering voice of conscience, by denying the validity of all thoughts coming from that side of the mind.

> I might lie to myself. I might try to conceal aspects of my own depth from myself. I might do this intentionally, or I might do it "unconsciously." But one way or another, I might misinterpret my own depth, I might lie about my own inte-rior. . . . My unconscious is the locus of my insincerity, of my being less than truthful with myself, less than truthful about my subjective depth, my interior status, my deep desires and intentions. The unconscious is the locus of the lie.
>
> —Ken Wilber[10]

When the inner man is not aligned with the outer man, this produces a schism in the psyche, a division, a loss of integrity, a neurosis which virtually everyone on the planet has experienced.

> All have sinned.
>
> —Romans 3:23

Those Broken-Off Pieces of the Self Are Not Dormant

One of the greatest breakthroughs of Western science has been the dis-covery of the psychoactive unconscious. When fragments of the psyche split off from the main self they do not die, disintegrate, or cease to function at all, but carry on their "lives" behind closed doors, in various degrees of isolation from the rest of the mind. Amazingly, when the conscious mind pushes these rejected elements away, the split-off little bits and pieces still subjectively experience themselves to be actively involved in their own private ongoing realities. Psychologists and shamans around the globe observe that each portion still seems to subjectively experience its own imaginary world. However, so long as they remain cut off from the greater self, they seem unable to evolve, remaining fixed at the level they were at the time of the original division.

What's more, these split-off fragments sap our energy in two ways: they drain energy from the system by continuing their own thought processes, and it takes energy to keep them exiled from the rest of the system.

Consequences of the Division

Our resistance to integrating our two halves has produced seven consequences for humanity:

1. Division is the history of the world: Humanity sees and experiences all of reality as being binary.

2. Self-alienation: Humanity remains a polarized, alienated species without integrity, which ensures the perpetuation of all sorts of social ills, including crime, war, and insanity.

3. Disintegration of the self at death: The self disintegrates at death, as the unconscious soul becomes trapped and exiled.

4. The horrors of amnesia: The conscious spirit continues to lose its memories between one life and the next, which results in alienation from God and a fear that no justice exists.

5. Caught in a repeating cycle: The conscious spirit remains caught in a repeating cycle of experience that consumes all our energy and attention, preventing us from further growth.

6. The threat of Armageddon: We risk a collective mental breakdown of Armageddon-like proportions if and when all the repressed contents of the full unconscious, containing all our past-life memories and souls, should ever be released all at once back into our conscious minds.

7. Responses to the pathology: Humanity has responded to this pathology by
building pathways to escape from it.

1. Division Is the History of the World

> From virtually the inception of every major knowledge
> quest, East and West alike, the various approaches have
> fallen into one or the other of these two great camps, inte-
> rior versus exterior, Left versus Right. We find this in psy-
> chology (Freud vs. Watson), in sociology (Weber vs. Comte),
> in philosophy (Heidegger vs. Locke), in anthropology (Taylor
> vs. Lenski), in linguistics (hermeneutics vs. Structuralism),
> and even in theology (Augustine vs. Aquinas)!
>
> —Ken Wilber[11]

So long as humanity's mind remains divided and unintegrated, so long
as the mental lens through which we observe the universe remains cracked,
the universe will appear divided and cracked as well. The history of civilization could be described as battle between right-brain-oriented groups and
left-brain-oriented groups, men and women, science and faith, East and
West, and on and on. In every conflict, the two sides seem to align with opposite halves of the human psyche. In each battle, we are convinced at the time
that we are embroiled in a new or different issue, but in fact they are all
reflections of a single conflict, the one going on inside our heads.

2. Self-Alienation: The Face of Evil

> As it turns out, those who are inhibited seem to inhibit
> both their laughter and their tears. It is ultimately their entire
> spectrum of emotionality that is trampled by repression.
>
> —Arthur Janov[12]

The unconscious is not only the source of our moral balance, but also of
our emotions. So when the unconscious is repressed in order to avoid its
moral judgments, a person often finds that he is becoming cut off from more
and more of his own human feelings. It is a classic cultural image that the
most evil people seem to feel no emotions, for in the process of silencing the
voice of morality, they block the voice of the unconscious, and so become cut
off from their feelings.

Everyone has met people who seem alienated from their own souls. When people violate their sense of right and wrong and repress the input from the unconscious, they push their souls away from themselves, or at least from their conscious awareness. Thus, when you find a person who has chosen a life which violates commonly accepted limits of moral behavior (a serial murderer, rapist, gang-banger, or even a ruthless businessman), it often seems that these people do not experience the same level of emotions that most people do. By consistently violating their own moral sense and repeatedly pushing away their own unconscious messages, they have alienated themselves from those messages and from most of the other feelings that normally rise from the unconscious. Each time we reject the input of the soul, the gap between the soul and spirit, between conscious and unconscious, grows wider, and we cut ourselves off from most of the feelings associated with being human.

> Psychopaths do not experience feelings like fear of punishment, empathy with other people, sympathy for their victims, shame or remorse. . . . These results suggest a general deficit in processing emotional information. The decreased emotional responsiveness was found to be specific to psychopaths. . . .
>
> —Dr. Sabine C. Herpertz[13]

When someone is alienated from their feelings and conscience, they are said to have a diagnosable mental illness, to be a sociopath or psychopath. But what this is, is the illness called evil.

> Much of the evil in the world comes from the fact that man is hopelessly unconscious.
>
> —Carl G. Jung[14]

Try as it might, the conscious cannot block *all* the input from the unconscious. The conscious cannot completely repress the unconscious; its messages always find a way to leak through at least a little. When the unconscious is being repressed, it will send powerful warning signals that something is wrong, and these are usually experienced as an unfocused, nagging anxiety or fear. And that would seem to be why deeply disassociated people are often paranoid, but otherwise seem to experience little in the way of normal human emotions.

There is a direct connection between a lack of personal integrity and the prevalence of social disorder. Our social problems could not be successfully treated by anything that did not address the root of the problem: our lack of personal integrity. Thus, any proposed financial or political solution to the ills of society that does not strike at the root of the problem, providing a way for people to reintegrate their divided psyches, can never hope to actually improve the problem. Instead, all proposed solutions that fail to heal humanity's fractured soul will merely shuffle social problems from one group to the next to the next, giving a mere temporary appearance of solving the problem until the new problems generated by the previous "solution" make themselves cruelly apparent.

3. Disintegration of the Self at Death

> If a holon fails to maintain its agency and its communions, then it can break down completely. When it does break down, it decomposes into its subholons: cells decompose into molecules, which break down into atoms, which can be "smashed" infinitely under intense pressure. The fascinating thing about holon decomposition is that holons tend to dissolve in the reverse direction that they were built up.
>
> —Ken Wilber[15]

It's only natural to assume that one's "self" is a unity, an indivisible singularity, but the evidence suggests otherwise, that the "self" we experience in life is the product of multiple, separate components. This reminds us of modern science's neverending quest to find the first, smallest building block of matter. Each time scientists find a new "smallest" particle, before too long, they seem to discover that even that particle is itself composed of even smaller parts. It seems, after decades of search, that there may be no such thing as a smallest building block of matter. Is the same true of the self?

Freud's revelation that human consciousness is fundamentally divided went against all our assumptions, rattling the scientific community with a counterintuitive surprise that it has not recovered from even today. But much evidence exists that during life, the two halves of the psyche are operating simultaneously yet independently. It is not merely a back-and-forth, first-one-and-then-the-other relationship. It seems that each side is continuously operating, and the only issue is how well or poorly they interact with each other at any given time.

The findings of modern research into ghosts, poltergeists, NDEs, PLRs, and other afterlife phenomena, as well as the testimony of innumerable ancient belief systems, suggest that the same thing is true after death. When we die, our fundamental self sometimes splits into pieces. This is a frightening outcome to face, even more so today than it would have only forty years ago; in the last few decades our culture has embraced afterlife "mythologies" which have maintained that everything is fine and there's nothing to worry about. Few realize that this denial of death's dangers is a new message, and does not find much support in mankind's oldest teachings, which always held the opposite, that one's situation after death could prove to be unfortunate.

And it doesn't seem to merely be a switching of which "eye" we look out of in life and death; we do not simply look out of the conscious mind in life and the unconscious in death. On the contrary, both elements seem to function on both sides of death's door. Again, the issue is not which portion is functioning, but how well the two interact. There seems to be a very real experiential division both in life and in death, in which both sides of the psyche are crippled by being estranged from each other. The neurotic behavior of ghosts, the miserable automatons seen in the netherworld by NDE subjects, the partial loss of subjective feeling and emotion at the early stages of NDEs, the loss of emotion and memory between lives by PLR subjects, and many more phenomena point to an afterdeath division taking place, and not merely to a switching of psychological points of view.

Where is the self after the division? One might as well ask "If a person has a favorite car, and he dismantles that car and ships its various parts all over the planet, where is the car now?" Does it exist or doesn't it?

Psychology tells us that we each possess a conscious and an unconscious mind and that while we're alive they are united (if not entirely integrated) in the body. But after death, these two sometimes seem to separate. This concept is hard to grasp. The psyche is the lens through which we have seen and experienced all life and reality, so to imagine any alteration in that lens is perhaps as difficult as a man blind from birth trying to imagine a painting, or a woman deaf from birth trying to imagine a symphony, or a monkey trying to imagine a black hole. Yet the evidence does seem to point in that direction.

What would it feel like to have one's conscious and unconscious minds divide at death? Both halves would go on, from our perspective, in a crippled state. The spirit would know no emotion, memory, context, meaning, or subjectivity, and the soul would know no rationality or objectivity. Yet neither part would realize that anything had happened. The spirit would not remember anything prior to the division, and the soul would lack the intellectual capacity to figure it out. Each would be intellectually crippled, albeit in different ways. This seems to explain why so many ghosts and spirits exhibit reduced mental capacities after death. The soul, the part feeling the guilt, doesn't seem to reincarnate, but apparently sits and stews in its own juices. The spirit, knowing nothing of its past, and certainly feeling nothing like guilt, seems to reincarnate out of sheer ignorance.

However, the spirit does not get off completely scot-free. Both the soul *and* spirit meet up with the fruits of the person's actions: the soul by experiencing heaven or hell; the spirit, by entering another earthly life formed by its past actions. Both parts are forced to confront the consequences of the person's choices.[16]

The only problem is, once the two parts of the psyche have divided, neither is able to realize that this division has happened. So while, technically, justice is served, the all-valuable lesson that justice might have taught is lost. Both sides suffer, and nothing seems to be gained by that suffering. In the end, both parts find themselves where they started.

Why would we divide at death? If the mind is independent of the brain, then leaving the body would not seem likely, in and of itself, to produce any changes in way the mind functions. Perhaps there is some additional knowledge we are missing, and if we had it we would see instantly that death *would* change the laws governing how the mental system functions. But as it stands today, without that crucial data, we can only assume that the functioning of the psyche would follow much the same patterns it does now. This means that if we have spent most of our lives alienating the halves of our psyche, pushing away the input of the soul from the spirit, then this could be expected to continue after death. If people's minds do split apart, it doesn't happen all of a sudden at death, but takes place over time during life.

This makes sense. Psychology has discovered that most of us are profoundly divided in life. What reason is there to assume that this division would be miraculously healed at the moment of death? The afterdeath division of soul and spirit, it seems, is the climactic event in a lifetime of division. If people split into pieces at death, it can only be because they were *already* fractured long before they died, but never noticed it before. Indeed, most afterlife witnesses never recognize the division for what it is even after the fact. The division of the halves of the psyche after death is as well hidden as it is during life.

The fact that nature uses the processes of differentiation and integration to produce new, more advanced and evolved structures and organisms tells us something, that it was trying to build something special when it decided to differentiate the human mind into a complex, integrated system. But what was it trying to build?

The union of an objective conscious mind and a subjective unconscious mind produces something unique in the world: self-aware consciousness, a being aware of its own autonomous existence, a sentient creature capable of self-determination. This may be what nature's experiment called humanity has been trying to achieve all along. Unfortunately, nature's experiment seems to be enjoying a very low success rate; most human minds seem to fail the integration process, self-destructing at death. God, one might conclude, is growing minds; death is their test.

Some would argue on the other hand that any apparent division is an illusion, that underneath appearances, the halves of the psyche always remain united. Of course, it is difficult to conceive of a division when one is speaking of nonphysical elements. The only thing that seems to be clear is that after death, the two elements function more independently than they had during physical life. The division, then, is a functional, experiential division, and any assertions on the nature of the division beyond this would seem to be speculative at best.

Perhaps this division ultimately *is* an illusion, but if so, it's a good one. Why would such an illusion exist? Again, every time we embrace division, we reinforce the illusion of division. Every time we push away the input of the unconscious, or choose to ignore the moral outrage we hear coming in deafening whispers from our own inner souls, or are not true to our own ideals but instead turn from them in shame and horror, we promote and strengthen the illusion that we can be divided, that we can run from parts of our own inner selves. The only power that this illusion has is whatever we give it.

This means that such an illusion would not disappear at death. Why? Momentum. The law of inertia. We push this illusion a little further every day, every time we refuse to acknowledge and honor the voice of the soul. Every time we do something we know we shouldn't, every time we act differently than we feel, we betray ourselves, deny our own nature, split ourselves. Thus, the division, from our perspective, does seem very real, and simply dying is not going to immediately solve everything. Illusion or not, it looks like we will be as afflicted by this division in death as we let ourselves be during life, and it will probably take as much effort to tear down the wall that divides the halves as we have put into building it up.

4. The Horrors of Amnesia

> Unfortunately, when the gates in the brain shut down against pain, they also shut out our history with it. . . . We are bereft of exactly the kind of memory we need to resolve the

unfortunate and crippling effects of those old traumas. We
never repress with impunity. There is always a price to pay.
—Arthur Janov[17]

Perhaps the greatest tragedy that comes from dividing at death is that it
robs us of our memories. My nephew recently turned one year old, and we
have found delight in watching him learn to walk. We look forward to watching him learn to talk, to use a toilet, to read, learn social skills, and, in time,
learn a trade or profession. And while each step will be challenging for him,
they will be joys for us. But what a waste if this is the tenth, or fiftieth, or four-
hundredth time he has had to relearn all these skills. And what a tragedy if
we *all* spend the majority of our lives re-struggling to learn the same damn
things over and over again, only to have them taken from us at the end of
each lifetime.

An ass which turns a millstone did a hundred miles
walking. When it was loosed it found that it was still in the
same place. There are men who make many journeys, but
make no progress towards a destination. . . . In vain have the
poor wretches labored.
—The Gospel of Philip 63:11–21

I don't know who you are. I don't *want* to know. I have
worked all my life to find out who *I* am, and I am tired now,
you hear what I'm saying?
—Nelson the Limo Driver in the
motion picture *Joe vs. The Volcano*

We lose many precious things when we lose our memories between lives.
We lose identity, which we have struggled long and hard to discover. In losing our memories, we lose our triumphs, achievements, loves, and hard-won
spiritual advancements. Think of the struggles we go through to get where
we are now, emotionally and spiritually. This is all lost if we lose memory.
Think of all the people we have loved, and think of losing contact with them,
losing even the memory of ever having known them.

We also lose hope of ever having certainty about a grave matter—justice
in the universe. If there is any justice in this world, it apparently comes as
karma, working itself out from lifetime to lifetime. This is our only hope;

we've all been around the block enough times to know that justice does not always catch up to people in a single lifetime. Evil people often escape punishment, and all too often, good people never seem to get a break. Seeing this, some brave souls still hold out hope that divine justice might yet be secretly working, that everyone gets precisely what they deserve in the long run.

Perhaps. But without our memories of previous lives, we can never know for sure, and so we find ourselves craving justice in this world, but uncertain if our cravings will ever be satisfied. Thus we anxiously try to take justice into our own hands, spending billions each year on lawyers, court cases, and wars. This quest for justice consumes a *huge* amount of time and resources. I'm not sure if all that effort has brought us any closer towards seeing true justice in the world.

If we didn't lose our memories between one life and the next, we'd know who we are, we'd know what we deserved, and we'd know everything we'd struggled to learn in the past, all our hard-won skills and wisdom. We'd also know who we'd loved and who we'd hated, and we'd know how each of those relationships had worked out in the past. All in all, we'd start out our lives with a much better understanding about why a great many things in the world are the way they are. We'd be way ahead. But instead, we have to enter this world with a blank slate each time, forcing us to spend most of our time playing catch-up, relearning the same skills and discoveries, and guessing about most things as we go along.

5. Caught in a Repeating Cycle

If the self represses or disassociates aspects of itself, it will have less potential left for further evolution and development. And sooner or later, this will drag development to a halt. . . . By the time the self reaches adulthood, it might have lost 40 percent of its potential, as split off or disassociated little selves, little blobs, little hidden subjects, and these little subjects tend to remain at the level of development that they had when they were split off. . . . These disassociated selves, these little hidden subjects that are clinging to lower worldviews, will take up a certain amount of your energy. Not only do they use energy themselves, your defenses against them use energy.

—Ken Wilber[18]

After the division of the soul and spirit at death, both halves become trapped in a circular pattern of repetitive behavior and experience. To the unconscious soul, this means perpetually reviewing and redigesting its memories and emotions in a dreamlike netherworld. But to the conscious spirit, it means going through lifetime after lifetime making the same mistakes. The literature of PLR research is brimming with reports of people who have repeated the same unfortunate behavior patterns lifetime after lifetime.

If I burn my hand on a hot stove a hundred times while trying to reach for a pan, immediately forgetting each time after the fact that the incident had occurred, I will keep burning it. Yes, I will carry the scars from the past, but nothing will draw me out of the cycle, nothing will teach me to grab a pot holder first, and I will keep burning myself again and again. If we were able to carry our memories with us from one life to the next, we would realize that we'd tried this or that approach to a problem already, and since it hadn't worked, we would try a different tack the next time. But without that memory, the learning process is stymied, so we keep trying the same stupid things, causing ourselves and others untold grief and misery, and getting nowhere useful at all.

We certainly don't evolve *spiritually*. Anyone who studies the history of the twentieth century will realize that humans are still bloodthirsty and ruthless. Here at the summit of human development, do we see evidence of a lessening of spiritual darkness, or an intensification of it? We see horror after horror, from atomic warfare to Hitler to Stalin to despot after despot ravaging the globe. If we have been spiritually evolving all this time, our history is a poor indicator of it. And after some 40,000 years on this planet, if this is all the farther we have proceeded through spiritual evolution, we are at best standing still, at worst, going backwards.

Judaism, Christianity, Islam, and Hinduism all hold that mankind *has been* going backwards. Judaism and Islam hold that the state of man at the Garden of Eden was perfect, but we have been falling farther and farther away from that perfection ever since. Christianity agrees with that assessment, while adding that a liferope has been thrown in the person of Jesus Christ. Hinduism declares that we are in the spiritually lowest era in human history thus far. Human history started off well, according to Hinduism, with humanity advanced and enlightened, but with the passing of each successive Age, the enlightenment meter falls a notch, and this present age, *Kali Yuga*, is the worst period in human history.

Why? Perhaps because every time we learn anything, it gets taken away from us. The current mechanics of reincarnation offer zero hope of progress. At the end of every life, all we learn, achieve, struggle for, and love is mercilessly deleted, leaving us back where we started. That's not progress. That's trapped. And that is exactly what we are. So long as we all continue to divide at death, we remain trapped like rats in a cage.

In fact, the *only* thing that changes at all under such circumstances is that the number of our past-life souls trapped in the deepest levels of the unconscious keeps increasing. At the end of each lifetime we unceremoniously toss another used worn-out *self* into the holding cell in the backs of our minds. Which may prove, one day, to be our biggest problem of all.

6. The Threat of Armageddon

> Primal Pain can be dampened, re-channeled, and diverted, but it cannot be erased. It cannot be cajoled or encouraged out of existence. . . . Once something is impressed into the system, it cannot be extinguished. Thus a feeling, "I am not loved," never leaves once it is set down in early childhood. It remains pristine pure and resembles Freud's immutable id-unconscious because it lasts forever and is unchanging. Life experience, being loved by hundreds, will never change that feeling one iota. . . . The painful feeling remains stored, waiting for its chance at consciousness and resolution. The organism is waiting for its chance to return to health and to its evolutionary destination.
>
> —Arthur Janov[19]

Something psychology discovered in the last century completely changes how we must look at reincarnation. We thought we could violate our own integrity and betray our own deepest selves with impunity, but now it looks like we were wrong about that. Psychology discovered that the unconscious is not dormant but is always active, and that everything we toss inside it stays there, perfectly preserved. For years, probably lifetimes, we have been dumping all our unwanted feelings and memories into what we thought was a garbage disposal in the back of our minds, but now our scientists tell us it was a high-security vault.

Discovering that all this discarded material remains active somewhere down deep in the backs of our minds is a frightening thought. What if a day comes when it refuses to stay buried any longer? Imagine undergoing 10,000 years of psychoanalysis in an instant, vividly experiencing, feeling, and reliving all the repressed pains, feelings, and memories of a hundred lifetimes at once. If the barrier holding this repressed material ever collapsed, an unimaginable flood of emotions and memories would swell up in a thunderous roar, crashing ferociously upon the landscape of the person's mind.

If this happened on an individual basis, it would result in inconceivable psychological trauma, insanity, and possibly death. But if it happened to everyone on the planet at the same time, it would produce devastation of Armageddon-like proportions. Our minds would be invaded by hordes of confused, desperate, and mostly uneducated strangers, our own past-life selves. The flood of their thoughts, emotions, and memories would rage mercilessly through us, and the world we are familiar with today would fall, never to rise again.

7. Responses to the Pathology

> The low and middle selves often are at war, divided by divergent purposes and drives. Seldom are the two lower selves well enough united to cause an automatic union. . . . Most failure to progress when following the paths of religion has come from a lack of understanding that there is a division to be considered.*
>
> —Max Freedom Long[20]

At some point in history people began to add two and two and realized that this pathology exists. As soon as they figured out what was going on, people began to look for a way out of it, a way to avoid all the horrendous consequences of their inner division. The remnants of the binary soul doctrine found in cultural traditions tell us that this desire to conquer humanity's division once came close to uniting the world in a common vision and purpose. Conquering this division was once seen as humanity's highest priority.

Seemingly, spiritual paths and religions started out as attempts to resolve that pathology. In culture after culture, we hear the same message: "we are divided, and we must try to heal this division."

One culture, however, not only taught about this division on an intellectual level, but in some seemingly miraculous way, even the tribe's *history* came to reflect the division, precisely mirroring mankind's ongoing saga of soul-division. In the next chapter we will see how, like an actor playing a part, a dusty desert tribe somehow became a living, breathing, reflection of the human soul as described by the BSD.

---

*Reprinted from *Growing Into Light* by Max Freedom Long (1955). ISBN: 0875160433 DeVorss Publications: www.devorss.com.

11

Message in the Messenger: The Encoded History of the Jews

> The only way for there to be lasting peace is for there to be two states living side by side at peace with each other.
> —*President George W. Bush, April 23, 2002*

As we observed in chapter 1, the inventory of cultures that were once at least partially familiar with the binary soul doctrine is extensive. "Partially familiar," however, would seem to be the key phrase here; the majority of other cultures, in contrast to the Judeo-Christian tradition, seem to have been unfamiliar with the *complete* scope and long-term potential of mankind's situation. Most cultures do show evidence of having known about mankind's two souls and their division, but displayed little concept of how these divisions ever started in the first place, or if there would be an end to them.

As I discussed in *The Division of Consciousness*, the Judeo-Christian tradition once possessed unique insights into these aspects of the binary soul doctrine. More so than any other tradition in the ancient world, Judaism saw "the big picture," understanding what was going on in the long term. Or perhaps it would be better to say that Whoever created Judaism understood what was going on, and put that knowledge directly into the history of the Jewish people, using their lives as the paper He employed to write His message to the world. The pattern was there, mysteriously encoded both in the history and the sacred texts of the Jewish people, but there is little to suggest that anyone comprehended the meaning.

In *The Division of Consciousness*, I explored some of the more obvious parallels between the binary soul doctrine and the Bible. In this present book, I had intended to focus on the parallels between the BSD and data from paranormal research. However, the fact that the history of the Jewish people has continuously reaffirmed the pattern of the BSD seems too paranormal to ignore; from the perspective of the binary soul doctrine, the events in the history of Israel repeatedly parallel the life-cycle of the human psyche:

1. An infant's psyche starts off whole and undivided, but differentiates into two equal but opposite elements as the child grows to maturity.

2. In most people, the masculine, intelligent, cerebral left-brain mind asserts its dominance over the feminine, emotional, earthy right-brain mind by the time the child reaches adulthood.

3. At death, these two divide, the left-brain conscious mind continuing on unharmed to reincarnate, the right-brain unconscious exiled and imprisoned in a netherworld wilderness.

Amazingly, many of the most famous stories of the Bible, Adam and Eve, Cain and Abel, Isaac and Ishmael, and Jacob and Esau, follow this very same pattern:

1. One entity gives birth to two entities which seem virtual opposites from each other.

2. One of these, the younger or smaller one, has characteristics in common with the conscious spirit, while the other, the elder or larger one, has characteristics in common with the unconscious soul.

3. These two interact and conflict, and from their conflict, the elder/larger entity is condemned and banished into exile.

Of course, one could argue that this pattern was intentionally designed into these stories by human authors, that these stories are not historic reports at all, and that all we are observing is an oft-used literary tool, repetition, intended to drive home a point. But the same pattern also turns up in the later history of the Jews, in events which are *not* in doubt, such as the division of the kingdoms of Israel and Judah, and in the division of Gnostic Christianity and Roman Catholic Christianity, two more dividing pairs which also seem to be variations on the same archetypal theme.

Throughout Jewish history we find this same story repeated, as if history itself were trying to hammer home a single thought, or perhaps as if it were trying to ensure that a single image would be preserved across the ages, by repeatedly offering it up in a variety of seemingly different reports.

The Division of Adam and Eve

The first human, according to the Bible, was originally a single whole being, until a part of him was divided away,[1] effectively cutting him apart into two separate beings: Adam and Eve. After this division, the two interacted and conflicted over the forbidden fruit, which resulted in Adam being given dominance over Eve, and in Eve being cursed with suffering during childbirth. Thus, after the division and the conflict, the figure most symbolic of the masculine left-brain conscious mind, Adam, is granted dominance over his feminine counterpart, who is forced into subservience and cursed with suffering. This pattern is repeated again and again in subsequent stories. However, this is one of the few times in these biblical stories where the figure most symbolic of the feminine right-brain unconscious mind is not specifically discarded into exile; in all subsequent versions of this pattern, exile plays a part.

The Division of Cain and Abel

Eve gave birth to two offspring, Cain and Abel, who, like Adam and Eve, were opposite symbolic archetypes. The firstborn, Cain, was a gentle farmer of the land, while his younger brother Abel was an aggressive herdsman. As one who coaxed crops from the land, Cain's profession made him earthy, reactive and responsive; Abel's profession, requiring him to slaughter livestock, paints him as more decisive and willful. Thus, like his mother Eve, Cain is symbolic of the passive and earthy right-brain unconscious, while Abel, like Adam, symbolized the active, self-assertive left-brain conscious. As in the Adam and Eve story, we see that the figure symbolic of the left-brain conscious is favored over his partner. Abel received favor from God while his brother did not, and when this happened, Cain's response was emotional and reactionary, again like the unconscious soul.

213

When the two interacted and conflicted, Cain, symbol of the unconscious, was condemned and exiled, another piece to the puzzle that recurs in subsequent versions of this story pattern. Exile, Cain's punishment for murdering his brother, has always stuck out like a sore thumb in this story, because the more typical Old Testament "eye-for-an-eye" sentence would have been Cain's execution. But perhaps Cain could not be executed because that wasn't the message this story was meant to deliver; the unconscious soul is not killed or destroyed after dividing from the conscious mind at death. Like Cain, it is merely sent into exile.

The story had to reflect that theme, and does, but at the cost of settling for unequal punishment. But that unequal punishment also serves a function: It calls attention to itself, thus suggesting there is more to the story than meets the eye. The fact that the younger of the two was preferred over the elder, and that the elder was sent into exile, are two elements that recur in all these stories. In the same way, the conscious spirit is also ever-young, always reincarnating and renewing itself, while the unconscious soul preserves the memory of the past, thus knowing what came before (as would an elder brother), but is sent off into exile after death.

The Cain and Abel division uses the same outline as the Adam and Eve division, but adds two new elements: the younger is preferred over the elder, and the elder is sent into exile. In subsequent appearances of this story pattern, additional elements are added, each building upon the pattern of the earlier ones while introducing new details. And invariably, the recurring details make sense from the perspective of the binary soul doctrine.

The Division of Ishmael and Isaac

After making his covenant with God, Abraham fathered two sons, Ishmael and Isaac, who again are archetypal opposites. This pair conflicted through their different mothers when they were infants, and later through their descendants, the Arabs and Jews, respectively. And once again, the younger Isaac won out over his elder brother Ishmael, who was sent into exile. Abraham's blessing went to Isaac, despite the tradition in those times that the elder son would receive the inheritance. Again, this incongruity suggests there is more to the story below the surface.

These two brothers again seem to be symbols of the conscious and unconscious. Like the emotional, earthy, and unruly unconscious, Ishmael was portrayed as animal-like and uncivilized (Gen. 16:12). And while the texts do not provide much data on Isaac, the most famous story about him reports that he was originally marked for death, but in the end a sheep was sacrificed in his place. Similarly, although the conscious spirit is responsible for making all decisions during one's life, it is not the conscious spirit, but the unconscious soul that is punished by death, while the conscious spirit is allowed to continue on unharmed, reincarnating again and again. The additional elements this story adds to the pattern are: the figure symbolizing the unconscious is portrayed as earthy, emotional, and animalistic; and the figure that symbolizes the conscious is allowed to continue on only because another was sacrificed in his place.

The Division of Jacob and Esau

The same pattern appears again in the story of Isaac's twin sons, Jacob and Esau, another pair of equal opposites. Esau was the firstborn, and so originally owned the birthright, the favored status and inheritance, until he gave it away to his brother in exchange for a small favor.[2] Esau was an earthy, instinctive, animal-like man of little intellect (like the unconscious soul). His brother Jacob was the opposite, very intelligent and clever (like the conscious spirit). Jacob used his cleverness to rob Esau of his birthright and blessing, thereby gaining dominance. Modern psychology reports that the conscious mind similarly uses its abilities to dominate the instinctive, earthy, and subjective unconscious.

For the first time in these stories, the preferred younger brother is identified with left-brain attributes of intelligence and cleverness. Again, the older brother is diminished while the younger is exalted. In fact, the figure who represents the right-brain unconscious is not only rejected in favor of his brother, but is forced to be his brother's subordinate, as the right-brain unconscious is the subordinate servant of the left-brain conscious mind. And like the elder brothers Cain and Ishmael before him, Esau was condemned to exile: "Your dwelling will be away from the earth's richness, away from the dew of heaven above. You will live by the sword and you will serve your brother. But when you grow restless, you will throw his yoke from off your neck" (Gen. 27:39–40).

The Division of Jacob's Children

Like the children of Adam, Abraham, and Isaac, the fate of Jacob's children also followed this pattern. Interestingly, the pattern of the younger child's dominance holds true, both for Jacob's twelve children and their offspring, the twelve tribes of Israel. Jacob's youngest son, Joseph, was divided from his eleven brothers, and during the prolonged drought that followed the separation, found himself exalted above them, granted a high governmental position in Egypt. Through this position of power, he was able to save his brothers from starvation and death.

This again fits the pattern of the binary soul doctrine. Each person has only one conscious spirit, but may have many unconscious souls from past lifetimes. Yet it may only be through the intercession of that one conscious spirit that those past-life unconscious souls can be rescued from death (see appendix A).

Jacob's first wife, Leah, had six children, the first four of which were Reuben, Simeon, Levi, and Judah, in that order. In accordance with the pattern, the eldest child, Reuben, was condemned (Gen. 49:3–4), while the next three children were highly elevated. Indeed, "highly elevated" is an understatement, for of all the children of Israel, only the descendants of Simeon, Levi, and Judah have survived into the modern era; all Jews living today credit themselves as being descendants of those three men.

The tribes of Judah and Simeon made up the southern Jewish nation ("Judah"), which survived while all the tribes of the northern nation ("Israel") were taken into captivity by the Assyrians, never to be seen again.[3] The remaining tribe, descended from Levi, was one of priests, and as they lived within the southern nation, they too survived. Again we see the pattern: the elder child is condemned and taken away while the younger is saved and blessed.

The Division of the Kingdoms of Judah and Israel

For a brief shining moment, the Jewish nation was a single kingdom, whole and undivided. Israel's idealized king, the man "most like God's own heart," was David, whose great accomplishment was the original union of Israel's twelve loosely affiliated tribes into a single nation. David was the only Jewish king who treated both the northern and southern lands equally and justly, thereby preserving their unity and autonomy. Shortly after David's reign ended, however, the nation was split into two parts; ten tribes splintered off to rule the northern provinces, while the remaining two tribes in the southern kingdom of Judah remained loyal to David's dynasty. Weakened by this division, the ten northern tribes were conquered by foreign invaders from Assyria, who marched the entire population into captivity, never to be seen or heard from again. After that, the only remaining descendants of

Abraham, Isaac, and Jacob lived in the southern kingdom of Judah. From that point on, they were known as Jews.

Thus it becomes clear that even the *political* history of the Jewish people is aligned with the binary soul doctrine. Whether by design or coincidence, the patterns match: as the human psyche splits into two at death, with the larger unconscious part cut off and sent into exile, so the Jewish nation once split itself into two parts, the larger/elder of which was then cut off and sent into exile.[4] After all these uncanny parallels, can there remain any doubt that the history of the Jewish people is somehow being purposely designed to reflect the pattern of the life cycle of the soul?[5]

The Division of Christianity

The pattern also holds true for the two versions of Christianity derived from Christ, namely that of the elder (the earlier Gnostic, subjective, loving, intuitive teachings of John, Thomas, and the other original Apostles) and of the younger (the later, more authoritarian, objective, and legalistic teachings of Paul).

Both schools of thought descended from the same messenger, but split and started to conflict shortly after Christ physically left the scene. And as the previous pattern would lead us to expect, the elder, right-brain oriented teaching of the Gnostics was the one to become condemned and drop from view, while the younger, more authoritative left-brain teachings of Rome became dominant.

Yet in the end, will the birthright and rightful dominance of the elder be reestablished?

An Unexpected Barrenness

Other relevant patterns emerge from these stories. Again and again, we encounter parents that are barren at first, and it is only after enduring great trials that they are finally able to conceive and give birth. Adam and Eve, Abraham and Sarah, Isaac and Rebekah, and Jacob and Rachel were *all* unable to have children at first.

At first, for the unspecified amount of time they resided in the Garden of Eden, Eve was barren; she had no children until after she and Adam were condemned for disobedience and exiled. Then Abraham's wife Sarah was also barren, and couldn't get pregnant until after she first asked her husband to sleep with her handmaiden as a substitute wife. Isaac's wife was also barren until Isaac finally prayed to God for help.[6] And Jacob's wife Rachel was also barren until after she asked her husband to sleep with her maidservant Bilhah in her place.

Assuming that this consistent pattern is not accidental, one wonders why these couples were ever barren at all. Other couples might be expected to occasionally suffer from barrenness, but *these* couples were all supposed to have enjoyed the special favor and support of God. Why then were they all unable to produce offspring at the very time they were supposed to be their healthiest and most lucky? We will find a possible answer to this question in the next chapter.

The Wife/Sister Pattern

Another relevant theme is also repeated throughout Genesis, that of a wife also being a sister. On two occasions, Abraham tells the Pharaoh of Egypt, and then later the King of Gerar, that his wife Sarah is merely his sister (Gen. 12:11–20, 20:1–17). Isaac does the same thing a few chapters later (Gen. 26:7–10), deceiving the king of the Philistines into thinking that Rebekah is not his wife, but his sister. And in a variation on this theme, Jacob marries two women who are *each other's* sisters.

This recurring theme seems purposely designed into these patriarchal legends, yet this repeated identification of wives as sisters seems devoid of any significance in conventional theology. The binary soul doctrine, however, reminds us that the conscious and unconscious are both partners and siblings; to the conscious spirit, the unconscious soul *is* both its sister and its wife.

A Covenant of Division

The word of the LORD came to Abram in a vision . . . He took him outside and said, "Look up at the heavens and count the stars—if indeed you can count them." Then he said to him, "So shall your offspring be". . . the LORD said to him, "Bring me a heifer, a goat and a ram, each three years old, along with a dove and a young pigeon." Abram brought all these to him, cut them in two and arranged the halves opposite each . . . When the sun had set and darkness had fallen, a smoking firepot with a blazing torch appeared and passed between the pieces. On that day the LORD made a covenant with Abram and said, "To your descendants I give this land, from the river of Egypt to the great river, the Euphrates."

—Genesis 15:1–18

The moment Abraham and God entered into a covenant is the moment three religions were born: Judaism, Christianity, and Islam. That covenant was inaugurated with a bizarre ceremony in which living creatures died by being carefully divided in two, and then their halves were arranged opposite each other in a fashion that emphasized both their continued separation and their lost unity. This ceremony was obviously symbolic, but modern Judeo-Christianity hasn't a clue what these actions might have represented. However, from the perspective of the BSD, the ceremony was a perfect symbol of the fate of the soul and spirit at death.

It is striking how sharply this ceremony differs from the Egyptian rite performed during the feast of Osiris (mentioned in chapter1). The Egyptian rite started with two separate but opposite halves of an inanimate statue, and after binding the molded halves together, the priest pronounced the statue whole and alive. But Israel starts out with living creatures, cuts them into two equal but opposite pieces, and lays out the pieces in a way that emphasizes their separation and death. The two ceremonies could not be more opposite, and yet more similar. Both apparently held the concept of division to have some supreme theological significance, yet whereas Egypt's ceremony celebrates unity and wholeness coming forth from duality, Israel's celebrates duality coming forth from unity and wholeness. While Egypt saw division and disunion as the root of all evil, Judaism seems to have felt that duality and division were so good they deserved to sit center-stage in the most important religious ceremony in Jewish history, the one that cemented Abraham's eternal covenant with God.

Egypt, one of Israel's closest neighbors; was a powerful and magnificent nation, and must have had a huge influence on Israel's culture and intellectual climate, so it makes sense that both cultures accorded special theological significance to the same concept, the relationship between unity and duality. But why then did Judaism seem to approach it from such an opposite direction?

The First Letter

There is a kabbalistic teaching that says that the secret of the Torah is in the first letter. If you cannot understand the secret from the first letter, God, in His infinite mercy, repeats the secret, in greater detail, in the first word. If you cannot understand the secret from the first word, God, in His infinite mercy, repeats the secret, in greater detail, in the first verse. . . . We could find something fundamental about Genesis 1:1 if we could see how the first letter was like the first word and how both were like the entire first verse.

—Stan Tenen[7]

The Bible's first letter, first word, first sentence, first chapter, and so on, all have something in common, according to ancient Jewish tradition, and that common element, whatever it may be, is absolutely essential to fully comprehending God's revealed message to humanity.

The first letter of the Bible, the first letter of the first word of the first chapter of Genesis, is *Bayt*—the second letter of the Hebrew alphabet *(Alef-Bayt)*. Being the second letter in and of itself implies duality and therefore division, but the parallels to the binary soul doctrine go far deeper than simply that. In Hebrew, letters have meanings, and the meaning of the letter *Bayt* is "house," and what a house does and represents. So *Bayt* represents the separation, or distinction, between what is inside and what is outside. A house divides the inside from the outside. *Bayt*, in other words, represents the first possible distinction, the first division. It is perhaps not surprising that it has been mathematically proven that all of formal logic can be derived from this single distinction.

The Bible *begins* with this letter, this image—the image of division.

The division represented by the first letter of the Bible also has much in common with the division between the conscious and unconscious within the psyche. Like the outside of a house, the conscious mind is exterior, out in the open. And like the inside of a house, the unconscious is interior and concealed.

The First Word of the Bible: "The Fire Inside the Pyramid"

Although the first word in the Bible—*B'reshith*—is traditionally translated as "In the Beginning," that is not the only possibility. Stan Tenen of the Meru Foundation points out that this word also breaks down into *beth*, which means "in"; *esh*, which means "fire"; and *shith*, which means either "a thorn" or the number six; or, more likely, both a thorn and the number six: a "six-thorn." As Tenen explains, this is a simple and elegant symbol for a tent, or a pyramid. Thus, the first word of the Bible translates very accurately as "fire in the six-sided thorn," "the fire inside the tent," or "the fire inside the pyramid":

> A "six-thorn" as an archetype is readily identifiable with what mathematicians call a tetrahedron. (A tetrahedron is a pyramid shape, the first Platonic solid, with 4 triangular faces, 4 corners, and 6 edges. Tetrahedra look like thorns.) When we put a fire in a tetrahedral frame, we have an archetypal model of the relationship between inside and outside— a light in a tent.
>
> —Stan Tenen[8]

We can already see a repeating pattern. The first word of the Bible presents us with the same meaningful symbol the first letter did: a house, a symbol of the distinction and/or separation between inside and outside,[9] the most elemental distinction that can be made.

The First Sentence

> In the beginning God _____ the heavens and the earth.
>
> —Genesis 1:1

The first line in the Bible, of course, is usually translated "In the beginning God created the heavens and the earth." However, the Hebrew word that the author of Genesis chose for "create" was *bara*, which most readers will probably be surprised to learn means "to divide," to separate, to cut or cleave, both in the literal and idiomatic senses. Thus the first sentence in the Bible shows God *using division to create the universe* (reminding us of how Abraham's ceremony also used division to inaugurate his covenant with God). Thus we find, just as Jewish tradition maintained, the first letter, first word, and first sentence of the Bible indeed do all revolve around a single concept: division into two parts.

But the parallels of this first sentence to the binary soul doctrine do not end there. In the 1970's, physicist Stan Tenen discovered an astounding mathematical pattern encoded within the letter sequence of this first line of the Bible. The arrangement of the letters of Genesis 1:1, Tenen found, generates the pattern of a torus, a three-dimensional shape which not only acts as yet another perfect symbol for the distinction between inside and outside, but also suggests a dynamic interactive relationship *between* inside and outside.

Furthermore, he found that when viewed from different angles, this three-dimensional model casts astounding shadows that perfectly replicate all twenty-seven letters of the Hebrew alphabet. Tenen's discovery led to the founding of the Meru Foundation in California in 1983, a nonprofit organization that has spent the last twenty-five years exploring a variety of mathematical, philosophical, theological, meditational, and mystical offshoots of this discovery.

Did God implant a unique message into the Abrahamic traditions that He gave no other people or culture? Tenen believes his research demonstrates that Hebrew, Greek, and Arabic are indeed "sacred alphabets," and that the "Primary Distinction" of Genesis 1:1 may hold priceless gifts for both science and spirituality. While the jury may still be out on those issues, the student of the BSD cannot help but prick up his ears when hearing that the very first line of Genesis has a dynamic 3-D model of the distinction between inside and outside embedded mathematically within it, and will be paying very close attention to further developments from the Meru Foundation in the years to come.

And the Theme Is?

Just as Jewish tradition has held for generations, the theme of the Bible's first letter—the division of *Bayt*—does seem to be expanded upon in the first passage, then the first chapter, and then the first book. In the first chapter of Genesis, God divided the heavens from the earth, then the light from the darkness, and the water underneath from the water above, and the water from the dry ground, and the day from the night. In the second chapter he divided humanity into male and female. In the third He divided good from evil, and in the fourth we encounter the story of the division of Cain and Abel.[10] The theme seems to continue throughout Genesis; indeed, the whole of the Old Testament could be seen as telling a single story: the division of God and humanity.

Did He really divide all these pairs in two, or did He differentiate them one from another? Genesis sets before us this inscrutable symbol—the "house" of *Bayt*—as if asking this very question. Does this image show division, or merely differentiation? It seems to be a subjective distinction; what seems to one person to be division seems to the next to be differentiation.

Perhaps the universe doesn't even *have* a definitive answer to this question. *Bayt* seems to ask if the universe itself *is* a question, and suggests that who and what we make of ourselves is the answer—the only *possible* answer—to that question. For every yin, it is said, there is a yang; if the universe is a question, then perhaps *we* are the answer. Is it possible that no single definitive answer to the question the universe asks even exists? Perhaps the whole point of the universe is for it simply to *be* the question, to give us the opportunity to have a question to answer, and the whole point of our existence is to *be* the answer, to create an answer in and through our lives. We seem to find this same question asked all over again in the second verse of Genesis: "Now the earth was formless and empty, darkness was over the surface of the deep, and the Spirit of God was hovering over the waters."

This "deep" was pure formless emptiness, the ultimate unknown, the ultimate question. And right there alongside the ultimate question we find God, the Ultimate Answer Himself, hovering above it, staring, as it were, directly into its endless blankness, as if it were an empty canvas waiting to be filled with the strokes of His brush. If so, this would seem to emphasize our freedom, and the importance of our creativity; giving a new depth of meaning to the phrase "the truth will set you free."

The Division of God

Even if Judaism once revolved around the importance of an archetypal division, showing reflections of it again and again—in the first letter *Bayt;* in all the divisions God performs in the first chapters of Genesis, in the division stories of Cain and Abel, Ishmael and Isaac, Jacob and Esau, the kingdoms of Israel and Judah, and in the historical division of Gnosticism and the Roman Church—no other division seems as profound as that between the two faces of God. Jewish theology, it seems, once addressed the paradox of a unity composed of a duality by giving God two names and two "faces," and stressing the unity of the two. For millennia, the central Jewish prayer has been the unity prayer: "Hear, O Israel: The Lord our God, The Lord is one" (Deut. 6:4).

However, what practically no one realizes today is that in the original Hebrew, what is translated as "Lord" and "God" originally referred to two different names with different meanings. Like the conscious mind, one aspect of God (*HaShem,* often translated as "Lord") was singular, distinct, and highly focused, while, the other aspect of God (*Elohim,* often translated as "God") was, like the unconscious, seen as having perfect wholeness and all-inclusive totality.

The central message in this unity prayer was not simply that this *HaShem* and this *Elohim* existed at the same time, but that despite appearances, they were the very same Being. Stan Tenen explains it this way:

> Abraham realized that the inner world of consciousness and the Source of conscious volition (personal will) is a Singularity in meditation in the mind, and that the outer world is a panoply of All-There-Is. The Singularity in the mind is identified with the state of being (consciousness): the Four-Letter Name, "Lord." The panoply of "All-There-Is" is identified with the Five-Letter Name, "God." Abraham's discovery is that the inner Singularity and the outer Whole are in fact the same. The "Lord-God" is Abraham's discovery. It's this fundamental discovery that academic scholars, modern Jews and Christians, and just about everyone else, completely ignores. Without the distinction between inside and outside, conscious life cannot exist.[11]

12

Forging a Self That Won't Shatter at Death: Baptism into the Authenticity of the Third Soul

Whatever you bind on earth will be bound in heaven, and
whatever you unbind on earth will be unbound in heaven.
—Matthew 18:18

When we look back into humanity's most ancient cultures, we find again and again that people everywhere arrived at the same bizarre conclusion that humans have two souls which split apart at death. But some of the more sophisticated cultures, such as Egypt and China, were not satisfied leaving it at that, but struggled to prevent this division, devoting a great deal of their resources to solving the riddle. And in *these* civilizations, we find occasional mention of an even more mysterious "third soul" that was also sometimes said to exist, a soul that, if found, was supposed to make it possible for a person to survive death intact. This third soul was the key, not only to eternal life, but to an eternal *name*, an eternally coherent self-identity.

Opinions seemed to have differed over how one was supposed to go about acquiring this third soul. Sometimes it seemed to be a matter of finding it, as if this third soul had secretly existed all along but was hidden for some reason. But other times this third soul was spoken of as if it didn't exist at all until a person created one for himself. Either way, the third soul was accessed by somehow uniting the person's two souls.

In Egypt, this immortality-bestowing third soul was called the *akh*, and was created by joining the *ba* and *ka* souls together. It was thought that this union could be successfully achieved either before death or after. In China, the third soul was called the "spirit body," or the "Immortal Fetus," and was formed by integrating the *hun* and *po* souls together. Unlike in Egypt, the Chinese believed that this unification had to be accomplished while the person was alive. Hawaiians called their third soul the "High Self," or *aumakua*, which again was formed out of a union of the binary *uhane* and *unihipili* souls. In Persia the post-death reconciliation of the *urvan* and *daena* was seen as the key to a satisfactory afterlife, and the Mandaean Christians felt the same way about the reunion of the soul and spirit.

Throughout the ancient world, the acquiring of a third soul seems to have been the only recognized path to true personal immortality. Uniting a person's two souls was seen as the only way anyone was going to survive death intact and unchanged. Besides the few traditions that believed in a third soul, nearly every other culture on the planet seems to have taken it for granted that the "known self," the person as he had known himself in life (i.e., with both his souls), was essentially doomed: At death, that self was going to shatter into pieces no matter what, and there wasn't a thing anyone could do to stop it. That known self, that wholeness, would be lost forever, and the best anyone could do was to try to find consolation in the fact that at least some of its pieces would continue on.

But the Egyptians, Chinese, Hawaiians, Persians, and Mandaean Christians didn't think that was good enough. Nothing less than immortality of the personal self was acceptable as far as they were concerned. They wanted an eternal name.[1] And if the problem was division, they reasoned, the answer had to be unity.

It all boiled down to black-or-white simplicity as far as they were concerned. They saw their two souls as having only two possible kinds of relationship: either they were united or they were divided, and death did nothing but make this relationship more obvious. If a person's two souls were united before he died, they would remain united afterwards as well, and the person would remain whole. But if the two souls were not united, if one was unfortunate enough to die while his two souls were in a state of disunion, then those souls would begin flying apart from each other as soon as they exited the physical body.[2] The ancients seem to have felt that the most common relationship between the two souls in life was one of division; therefore the two souls were expected to divide at death unless special preventive efforts were taken.

"We are all . . . malfunctioning," Sigmund Freud said. Today, psychology tells us much the same thing: We *are* divided; the two halves of the psyche are somewhat alienated from each other in virtually everyone. In the psychiatric community, it is widely accepted that *everyone* is a little imbalanced, everyone is slightly off-center. No one walking around in this insane world, it seems, is completely sane; none of us is perfect. Every person we meet has a partially dysfunctional relationship between her conscious and unconscious minds; everyone has his unique blind spots, self-contradictions, and internal inconsistencies. This idea is nothing new; we can see it in the Western religious tradition that "all are sinners," that we all carry a flaw within us, that all are cursed by "Original Sin." Modern science even has a name for this state of partial self-alienation: neurosis.

The Wall That Grief Built

If the conscious and unconscious are separated, alienated, or disassociated to some degree in most people, why is this? What, if anything, is right now between heart and head, between unconscious and conscious, preventing or sabotaging their attempts at interaction and communication? And how do we overcome it? How do we unite the halves of our selves? How might we attempt to find or build our own "third soul"?

The Hebrew prophet Isaiah wrote that a great wall had been created in the spiritual world (Isa. 30:9–14) out of humanity's "sin." Freud is on record as saying that the only thing separating the conscious from the unconscious is "resistance."[3] And while these different attempts at explaining the barrier between the halves of the soul may both be correct as far as they go, they still leave us with a lot of questions about what this blockade is and what might be done about it.

But there may be another way to explain this partition, a more modern approach that helps expose its presence within us. Some modern psychologists speak of this wall in different terminology than Freud or Isaiah used, giving it a more familiar context for the modern mind. Instead of describing the wall as resistance or sin, some psychologists say it is grief. This approach helps us see that Isaiah's wall of sin and Freud's wall of resistance actually refer to the same thing. Stephen Levine says:

> Along the path of healing that leads into the heart, one
> is called upon to examine grief. Grief is the binding alloy of
> the armoring of the heart. As if touched by fire, the mind
> recoils at losing what it holds most dear. As the mind con-
> tracts about its grief, the spaciousness of the heart often
> seems very distant.[4]

These words paint a picture of psychological division, suggesting that one's grief can make the heart seem distant from one's conscious awareness. This division often exists inside a person without being noticed; many would sincerely insist that *they* have no such inner wall, *they* have never lost anyone, *they* are not grieving! But grief is not so simple.

Despite its public image, grief is not always a colossal and obvious sadness; in fact, most of the time it is subtle, insidious, and easy to overlook. *Everyone* has grief. It is an inescapable part of being alive. As we go through our lives, most of us accumulate a tremendous amount of unfinished business, including all our disappointments in our lives, in ourselves, in our unfulfilled hopes and dreams and potentials, in our unrequited loves, in all the unaddressed, unchallenged, uncorrected injustices that life feeds us on a daily—if not hourly—basis. Every moment of every day, we remain aware that "all this business still remains unfinished," experiencing this awareness as a sad draining fatigue in the backs of our minds. The First Noble Truth of Buddhism is that "Life is suffering."

Like the everpresent low-level radiation that astronomy calls "the background noise of the universe," our forgotten or ignored, yet still active grief over these disappointments shows up everywhere, as self-judgment, fear, guilt, anger, and blame ("road rage"), as a mercilessness with ourselves and others, even as a hesitation to let the rest of the world in close enough to touch us. Our unacknowledged grief shows itself in, and as, our fear of loss, of rejection, of death, of everything new, as ever-present fear of each new unknown corner in life. Our tendency to cling to things, to judge and condemn ourselves and others, is the day-to-day voice of this hidden grief, screaming from inside us about these unfulfilled needs that ache silently for satisfaction.

> Every emotional pain that you experience leaves behind
> a residue of pain that lives on in you. It merges with the pain
> from the past, which was already there, and becomes lodged
> in your mind and body. . . . If you look on it as an invisible

entity in its own right, you are getting quite close to the truth. It's the emotional pain body.

—Eckhart Tolle[5]

All this repressed fear, grief, and anger is unhealthy to the extreme; many psychologists point to underlying tensions such as these as the origin of a great many medical ailments. No one represses without consequences; there is always a price to pay. Indeed, many neurotics are highly functional, seeming to be fine until a heart attack drops them in their prime. Hidden pressures in the mind take time to do their damage, but like dripping water, they keep wearing away our foundations until we finally plunge through.

The number one killer in the world today is neither cancer nor heart disease. It is repression. Unconsciousness is the real danger, and neurosis the hidden killer. Repression, a stealthy, hidden, intangible force, strikes many of us down. It does so in so many disguised forms, cancer, diabetes, colitis, that we never see it naked for what it is. That is its nature, diabolic, complex, recondite. It is all pervasive, yet everywhere denied because its mechanism is to hide the truth. Denial is the inevitable consequence of its structure.

—Arthur Janov[6]

Over time, all this holding, clinging, condemning, and judging hardens around our grief like barnacles on a ship. When we hold onto our feelings, they don't go away on their own. When we don't express them, when we don't allow ourselves to fully experience our own grief, sadness, and disappointment, they are prevented from falling away naturally. Instead, they are preserved intact, going into cold storage in our minds, where they can exert an invisible but potent effect on our lives. When we avoid confronting these feelings, we prevent their emotional energy from being discharged. To deny their existence is merely to hold them back, preventing ourselves from releasing them and letting them go. Like cars in gridlock, these emotions won't dissipate on their own; they have nowhere else to go. These emotions have a single destination, our consciousness, and will not turn off that road until they arrive, no matter how long it takes. So they wait, piling up, building an obstruction. And their emotional energy piles up too. Prevented from dissipating naturally, these unacknowledged feelings are forced to accumulate silently and invisibly within us, becoming evermore solid and formidable, growing dense roots deep into our psyches, burrowing their toxic tentacles into our attitudes and behaviors.

> Because of your stubbornness and your unrepentant heart, you are storing up wrath against yourself.
> —Romans 2:5

This grief, in effect, builds a logjam within us that cuts us off from an authentic experience of our own beings. So long as that wall remains in place, we are cut off from any truly authentic sense of feeling fully human, cut off, to at least some degree, from our own present, from our own normal moment-to-moment feelings and emotions. With the wall in place, we don't feel fully "here." This logjam also cuts us off from the past as well; inside that wall, all the traumas, feelings, and emotional reactions that we never allowed ourselves to fully release and experience in the past remain, still in their original condition, still waiting to be released so we can finally consciously experience them.

And of course this inner heaviness, this thick accumulation of unexperienced bitterness, unfelt grief, and unintegrated heartache, this looming unpaid emotional debt we owe ourselves, has become the epitome of all we fear most, causing us to resist it all the more, causing a self-repetitive cycle of avoidance begetting avoidance. Nathaniel Branden says, "Here is the basic pattern: First, we avoid what we need to look at because we do not want to feel pain. Then our avoidance produces further problems for us, which we also do not want to look at because they evoke pain. Then the new avoidance produces additional problems we do not care to examine—and so on. Layer of avoidance is piled on layer of avoidance, disowned pain on disowned pain. This is the condition of most adults."[7]

By the time we are adults, most of us have gone through years of bitterness and frustration, often never letting ourselves fully experience, express, and thereby release this grief, never realizing that this avoidance allows grief to accumulate into something far worse, into a sort of sediment that hardens around our hearts, eventually becoming as hard as a rock. Like clogged veins, this psychological sediment severely restricts communication between head and heart, conscious and unconscious. All these thick layers of disowned feelings, all this lifetime of armoring around our hearts, exhausts us, draining our energy, draining the resources that we're supposed to be using for coping with the "here and now."

There is eventually so much of our beings, consciousness, and resources trapped inside this wall that our potential for growth and healthy evolution is effectively stymied (which would explain why people keep getting caught in the same destructive behavior patterns lifetime after lifetime, according to PLR research). We can't go forward when so much of our beings is still frozen in backward glances:

All these little pieces, each stuck in its own frozen moment of past grief, do not remain silent. They find a voice. By the grace of God, they find a way to make their presence known to us as the urge to judge and condemn ourselves and others. But all this voice is doing is calling out for healing and forgiveness, as loudly as it can, in the only way it has available. With this recognition, we can finally begin the process of letting go of the judgment that hardened over the years around our grief.

A Baptism of Repentance for the Healing of Division

> It is tears that help dissolve the boundaries of the unconscious.
>
> —Arthur Janov[8]

The first step in letting go of all this pain, grief, and judgment, is to face up to our present reality, acknowledging the grief and pain within us, and trying our best to see it for what it is. When we finally summon the courage to approach our grief, we discover it has formed a dense wall, a dark unexplored barrier between heart and mind. We start to comprehend that this wall never completely prevented communication between the conscious and unconscious; simply, like a guard to a castle, this wall insisted that *it* be dealt with first. Like Glenn Close's character in the movie *Fatal Attraction*, the wall is there with its hands on its hips, saying, "I won't be *ignored*."

When we give up trying to do the impossible, when we stop using all our energy vainly trying to ignore this wall, when we gird ourselves with faith and courage and look into the blackness of our grief and confront it on its own terms, we realize how often we have distrusted what we feel in life, and discover the convoluted patterns of our unfinished grief. All the loss, all the injuries, all the disappointments of a lifetime (of many lifetimes?) lay there, encrusted in that wall of stony grief, holding us back from our own lives, locking us out of our own hearts.

> The pain-body, which is the dark shadow cast by the ego, is actually afraid of the light of your consciousness. It is afraid of being found out. Its survival depends on your

unconscious identification with it, as well as your unconscious fear of facing the pain that lives in you. But if you don't
face it, if you don't bring the light of your consciousness into
the pain, you will be forced to relive it again and again.
—Eckhart Tolle[9]

Standing at the base of this wall, we look up at its imposing heights, and
understand that our unreleased grief is immense. We start to grasp that we've
been desperately trying to elude the pain of our daily grief, fears, anger, our
daily sense of isolation, all the grief of a lifetime. We see that every iota of disowned grief is still there. To release this unexpressed grief, we must fully
breathe in and experience all our disappointments and unshed tears, accepting all the lost moments we never allowed ourselves to experience. As the
Greeks observed so long ago, the only way that seems to work is to be true to
ourselves, to experience all of our selves, including all of our authentic feelings. Tremendous energy is trapped inside the emotional logjam, and when
it is released, that grief flows in a magnificent torrent.

Yet nothing could be easier than releasing this stored-up pain into our
awareness. All we have to do is stop holding it back. Holding it all inside is
the hard part, not releasing it. Once it is released, we discover the true agony
was being separated from our authentic selves. Remarkably, this painful confrontation with the one thing we fear most opens a path to heavenly joy.

By illuminating the darkness of all our forgotten moments of helplessness
and hopelessness, fully immersing ourselves[10] in them so that they can finally
be experienced, released, and discarded, the armor around our hearts begins
to melt. Paradoxically, we find that being immersed in our pain is the only
thing that will empower us to move beyond it. Acknowledging and experiencing the truth of our pain is the only thing that will set us free from it.

The same thing that makes us sick, pain, makes us well.
The difference is only a matter of integration. No integration
means illness; integration means health.
—Arthur Janov[11]

That which you have will save you if you bring it forth
from yourselves. That which you do not have within you
[that which you remain unconscious of] will kill you if you do
not have it within you.
—The Gospel of Thomas 70

Of course, this is not a popular path. Confronting pain has never been popular, and probably never will be. Most psychological and spiritual practices today reflect humanity's reluctance to confront its pain and self-alienation, reinforcing people's defenses. Much of what passes for psychological care today has abandoned any therapeutic attempt to get to the *psychological* root of problems, but remains satisfied if symptoms can simply be controlled, whitewashed over with medication.

Similarly, many religious and spiritual approaches are equally disinclined to confront and resolve their followers' pain and grief, but instead depend on being able to control and repress the contents and activities of the unconscious.

This is nothing new; if the infamous "negative confession" in the Egyptian Book of the Dead tells us anything, it is that we humans have long preferred the easy route—trying to control, manipulate, and reprogram the unconscious instead of courageously and guilelessly facing up to it on its own terms. While the original purpose and meaning behind this confession seems to have been to promote authentic integrity, it seems to have become corrupted in Egyptian usage as the centuries wore on, eventually becoming a blatant attempt to circumvent one's guilt. Ancient Egypt, it seems, thought that even after one's death, if priests recited the right words over the corpse, they might still be able to hypnotically reprogram the dead person's unconscious. By convincing him to believe in his own innocence, it was apparently hoped that a person just might be able to escape punishment when his heart was weighed at the afterdeath judgment:

> I have caused no man to suffer. I have allowed no man to go hungry. I have made no man weep. I have slain no man. I have not given the order for any man to be slain. I have not caused pain to the multitude. I have not filched the offerings in the temples. I have not purloined the cakes of the gods. . . . I have not cheated in measuring of grain. I have not filched land or added thereto. I have not encroached upon the fields of others. I have not added to the weight of the balance. I have not cheated with the pointer of the scales. I have not taken away the milk from the mouths of the babes. I have not driven away the beasts from their pastures. . . . I am pure. I am pure. I am pure. I am pure.
>
> —Egyptian Book of the Dead, Chapter CXXV

Although the Egyptian people fervently believed in the effectiveness of these prayers 3,000 years ago, today one can easily paraphrase Shakespeare, "Thou dost protest too much, methinks"; their excessive assertions of innocence seem to emphasize their own doubt. Still, human nature hasn't changed since then; Egypt's "negative confession" seems to have a lot in common with all the "self-esteem affirmations" en vogue today. Even now, many hope to manually override the moral judgments of their unconscious souls, denying, rejecting, and repressing what exists there naturally, trying to install other, more pleasant (if less honest) thoughts in their place.

This practice is at odds with more than a hundred years of psychotherapeutic practice and study, which can be summed up in a single phrase: "what we can feel we can heal." Our challenge is clear, we need to be honest with ourselves, acknowledging and accepting our pain, breathing in all the years of grief we hide from ourselves, all the sorrows we tell ourselves aren't there. No substitute will work; no denial of inner reality will bring us the peace we crave. We need to get past our posturing, our fear and shame and unrequited loves. The only way to break down this wall is to confront it head-on; the only way to get past the pain is to dive boldly through the middle of it.

> Let each one of us dig down after the root of evil which is within one, and let one pluck it out of one's heart from the root. It will be plucked out if we recognize it. But if we are ignorant of it, it takes root in us and reproduces its fruit in our heart. It masters us. We are its slaves. It takes us captive, to make us do what we do not want, and what we do want we do not do. It is powerful because we have not recognized it. While it exists it is active. Ignorance is the mother of all evil.
>
> —The Gospel of Philip 83:19–32

Going through it, we find ourselves past it, in the merciful and comforting expanse of the heart, the only place that has room for all this pain. The mind is unable to handle this pain, and shrinks from it; this is what produced the wall in the first place. But in the heart, beyond our fear-encrusted defenses, lies the very thing that will heal us. By trusting in our hearts and breathing in our pain, experiencing it fully and immediately, we can finally feel everything we were supposed to feel, and at last heal everything inside.

> Those who know their pain and their grief most intimately often seem to be the lightest, the most care-free, the most healed of the people we meet.
>
> —Steven Levine[12]

It requires tremendous courage, trust, and faith to confront grief on its own terms. But we can do this. We can let our hearts open wide enough to embrace all this disowned pain. With faith, we can drag the terrifying shadows into the healing light of our awareness, the light they so desperately long for, so that there is finally nothing separating our head and heart. Without a wall between them, the two halves are made one. Thus, our inner pain, which we have always avoided, is paradoxically the very thing that can end our suffering and make us whole. As Jung said, "The answer obviously consists in getting rid of the separation between conscious and unconscious."[13]

No Pain, No Gain

> There is no birth of consciousness without pain.
>
> —Carl Jung[14]

The inner wall, Isaiah insisted, was built of sin. But why would it be a "sin" to deny one's feelings? Were "the Lord's rejected instructions" in Isaiah 30:9–14 the voice of the unconscious? After all, as Isaiah says, the dividing barriers in our psyches *were* erected by rejecting a voice, the voice of our unconscious. The voice of the soul, of the unconscious, of all the feelings and insights it sends to our conscious awareness, are, Isaiah seems to suggest, nothing less than messages from the Divine. When we repress or reject them, we reject the Voice of God Himself, a Voice that was *always* meant to be heard within our mind. Why would God wish to sometimes inject unpleasant messages, feelings, and insights into our mind? Why would a spiritual path cause us pain? Some, like Arthur Schopenhauer, say that our spiritual evolution, the growth of our conscious awareness, depends on it. "The capacity for feeling pain increases with knowledge. . . . A degree which is the higher the more intelligent the man is."[15]

This would have made perfect sense to the ancient Greeks. Gaining wisdom, knowledge, and enlightenment, they thought, is like wrestling fire from the gods: A person is going to get burnt in the process. The Gnostic Christians would have agreed: Jesus said in the Gospel of Thomas (82), "He who is near Me is near the fire, and he who is far from Me is far from the Kingdom."

Still, once we have confronted our inner demons and have been baptized in our own disowned pain, once this psychological blood-bath has washed us clean[16] of all that accumulated sediment, what is there to keep it from building up all over again? One must regularly perform inner housekeeping, regularly examining the heart and soul to see if any new experiences, feelings, or reactions have been unacknowledged or repressed. But this is an easy task, and not nearly as difficult as confronting the whole wall. Once the sediment of the wall has been washed away, one merely needs to perform relatively effortless soul-searches after that: "A person who has had a bath needs only to wash his feet; his whole body is clean" (John 13:10).

One might even expect this process to occur automatically, for someone who is in touch with his feelings would be less likely to behave immorally in the first place. With the wall down, one would again be aware of his sense of right and wrong, and would not find it easy to ignore the nagging directives of his soul. No longer allowing his behavior to be out of sync with his feelings and beliefs, he would have less to repress in the first place.

Finding the Third Soul: Resurrection of the Authentic Self

> What are post-Primal patients like? . . . It seems they are more homogenous. . . . I think the major difference is their value system. They value their time, the preciousness of life, beauty, the environment, and the sanctity of living things. By and large they know what they want and how to get it. They do not stay in situations or relationships that are bad for their mental health. They appear more alive now that the deadness has been lifted from their faces.
>
> —Arthur Janov[17]

Once the wall is down, one's mental system functions better. No longer shrinking from our own lives and our own selves, we are once again comfortable being ourselves, experiencing "life as it is" with all its natural feelings.

And now, perhaps, we see why NDE-ers return from their paranormal journeys with minds that work so much better. Their life review was essentially a form of psychological therapy, a process that normally takes years, all occurring in a timeless instant. They were able to transform all their inner pain into tears, crying their walls away. NDE-ers and Janov's Primal Therapy patients seem to get the same results from their journeys. In both cases, a significant change in brain function occurs, as a result of reliving and refeeling experiences, the relationship between the right and left hemispheres changes.

In Primal Therapy, patients spend several months reliving the past, releasing all their unshed tears. The same thing seems to take place in the NDE, except the process occurs in the blink of an eye during the life review. But fast or slow, the end result seems to be much the same: Subjects emerge from these self-discovery journeys with a healthier mind, more balanced and interactive brain hemispheres, and better attitudes, feeling more peace, love, and joy, feeling more free and spontaneous, feeling more "in the here and now." They no longer have huge chunks of their beings trapped in backwards glances. They are "all there." They have "made the two one." They are whole.

However, this raises a question. If the life review in NDEs works like Primal Therapy, then why doesn't the life review that occurs when someone dies perform the same function? We see abundant evidence that such a unification does not always occur after death. Those in the realm of bewildered spirits display unmistakable evidence of continued division, as do ghosts and poltergeists. For some reason, the life review that occurs after true death does not seem to always heal a person's inner division the way the life review does in an NDE. But why not? Why does the life review in NDEs succeed while the post-death life review fails?

Obviously, it is not the life review itself that achieves the transformation, but the fact that one returns to conscious awareness afterwards. The life review is originally experienced exclusively by the unconscious, it almost always occurs during the light stage. So these unconscious memories never have a chance to be reintegrated into the conscious mind, and no healing would result. The release of these blocked emotions into the conscious mind makes all the difference. The fact that the NDE-er returns to life after the Memory Review, carrying these reclaimed gifts back to consciousness, seems to enable these repressed memories to be reintegrated into the psyche, restoring wholeness.

Directions, Anyone? In Search of a Yoga That Works

Unfortunately, most of us will never have an NDE, and Primal Therapists are rare and expensive. So how are we supposed to find, confront, and dismantle *our* inner walls, so we too might reintegrate our halves and thereby prevent ourselves from fracturing at death?

This same question, it seems, was once the central preoccupation of many religions. Buddhism, Hinduism, Zoroastrianism, Judaism, Christianity, Egypt—mankind's ancient traditions agreed on one point: an eternally blissful, heavenly afterlife is *not* guaranteed. On the contrary, this was the most desirable and elusive of all goals. When Buddha reached enlightenment, he is said to have triumphantly cried out, *"I have reached the immortal!"* Achieving this ultimate goal was what these religions were about, but the way was narrow, and only a few ever actually achieved it. These traditions associated the acquisition of the blissful afterlife with inner work, with unification of the alienated parts of one's inner self.

Many Eastern traditions call this goal "nonduality," and the way to get there is called "the nondual path." Hinduism has distinguished many different paths to this inner union, calling them yoga, a word which, appropriately enough, means "union." Early Christianity seems to have had an equally simple directive: *"make the two one"* (Ephesians 2: 14, Gospel of Thomas 22). This ultimate spiritual goal has been described and pointed to by mystics of every tradition. It has been called "deification," "entering the Kingdom of God," "sanctification," "enlightenment," "satori," "samadhi," and "the marriage of soul and spirit." But by any name, it is nondual and undivided, and is always reached the same way, by "making the two one." In this ultimate state, all apparent oppositions are said to be extinguished; subject and object, form and function, before and after, emptiness and superabundance, life and death, being and nonbeing, I and Thou, Atman and Brahman, conscious and unconscious, soul and spirit, are all *one.*

Today, the paths people take to forge or discover this unity go by another name: inner work. One can't walk into a bookstore nowadays without finding a dozen just-published books on inner work, describing various paths to self-integration. These exercises are no longer recognized as religion; now they're called psychology. The shelves are crammed with works promising to help us integrate our intellects and emotions, our masculine and feminine sides, our heads and hearts, our left and right brains. All these books agree on the same fundamental point: we have split ourselves into pieces, and the only way we will ever find the peace, happiness, and fulfillment we seek is by restoring our original wholeness.

There seems to be an endless variety of ways people try to achieve this goal. If we want, we can attend programs at The Monroe Institute in Virginia which promise to restore our "original mind" by using a special technology to synchronize the left and right hemispheres of our brains. Or we can spend hours floating in one of John Lilly's "sensory isolation" tanks, which some say produces mental integration. Or if we want to be exotic, we can seek out a shaman, who will travel spiritually into the other world to find and help us reintegrate our lost pieces of our own souls. Everywhere we turn, we hear the same point being made in a thousand different ways, all saying that we lack integration, we've become self-alienated, split into pieces that no longer have much to do with each other. And, according to expert after expert in field after field, our happiness, health, and success, both on earth and in the great beyond, depend on reintegrating those pieces.

The Faster Yoga: Zen

The inner marriage of the conscious and unconscious is rare. When it occurs, it usually has been forged slowly, over the course of a person's lifetime. It is often said to be acquired through prayer, meditation, mindfulness, and soul-searching, through an unflinching devotion to personal integrity, through a commitment to moral transparency and being the same on the outside as on the inside. However, the tradition that the third soul *already* secretly exists inside us suggests that we might be able to sidestep this whole agonizing process, because, if the third soul exists already, then the whole division is an illusion. If so, then realizing the already-existing reality of this inner unity could theoretically occur in a single instantaneous jolt of recognition, as Zen Buddhism has long maintained (and some NDE-ers seem to demonstrate).

The Slower Yoga: Inner Work

Even if the division is an illusion, it's an illusion *we* chose, *we* created, and *we* continue to sustain every day. We have poured endless amounts of effort, determination, and will into keeping this inner wall up. Even if we do finally decide that we want this wall to disappear, it's going to stay where it is until someone dismantles it. And unless someone else volunteers to take on that dirty job for us,[18] our walls will remain standing until we dismantle them ourselves, or until they collapse under their own weight. Unfortunately, it will probably take as much conscious effort to remove each brick as it took unconscious effort to put up;[19] the wall separating the conscious and unconscious, even if illusory, is an illusion we built very solidly.[20]

Each brick in the wall is formed out of our own feelings and reactions and our willful rejection of them; paradoxically, each brick, containing left-brain will and right-brain emotion, actually reflects the wholeness it pretends to destroy. Why don't those bricks disappear? Because *we won't let them.*

Because they are part of us, part of our history, part of who we are and how we felt and what we chose to do about it. To expect them to disappear on their own, would be to deny the reality and worth of the feelings and choices that brought these bricks into existence in the first place. It would be to deny the reality of the self who originally had those feelings and chose to turn away from them. It makes sense that Zen Buddhism, which denies the existence of that self, is the only tradition that claims that a fast yoga is even possible.

Many feel that these approaches, these yogas and psychologies and exotic new age experiences, make things more complicated than they need be. The true spiritual path, they maintain, is simple: Live by all the light and knowledge that you have. Unfortunately, this is a tall order to fill when one's soul is unconscious, when all the light and knowledge that we have is tucked away in a big dark hole in the back of the mind. "To thine own self be true" goes the saying, but so long as we have a dark unexplored unconscious, this is the hardest thing to do. So long as half of a person's mind is unconscious, and huge chunks of our beings are hidden from our view, we cannot honestly say we know ourselves. How then are we supposed to be true to ourselves?

Unfortunately, many spiritual and psychological paths don't directly address the matter of the wall at all. Most ignore it; some even reinforce it. Many approaches try to overpower the wall one way or another, temporarily pushing it out of the way so the conscious and unconscious can interact more naturally for a few precious moments. Many such methods seem to work, especially during the brief time this effort is being applied. For short periods, as during prayer, or meditation, or Monroe Institute work, or in flotation tanks, or when hypnotized, or while on intoxicants or hallucinogens, it does seem as if one's mind operates at a higher, more healthy, more honest, more sensitive, more spiritual, more integral, more productive level.

But all too often, as soon as one relaxes the effort and stops trying to force the issue, one finds that the inner wall has slammed right back in place again, once more blocking communication between the two halves of the mind. Still, like water trickling over a dam, any long-term, consistently applied approach that helps the conscious and unconscious to interact will eventually dissolve the wall, allowing the feelings and memories trapped there to be unfrozen, reexperienced and reintegrated, leaving the person more healthy, human, and whole.

But once the wall *is* down, this interactivity occurs spontaneously and without effort; a more natural state of the mind seems to have been permanently restored. We can observe this mental integrity in NDE-ers, as well as in those rare few who have completed Primal Therapy and similar psychological and spiritual disciplines. Only directly confronting, experiencing, and integrating our own pain, it seems, actually cures what ails us. In comparison, all other spiritual disciplines are for wimps.

Seeking Full Integration: Reuniting with Our Own Past-Life Selves

Who and what we are now was invented in the past. The details of our present lives, selves, attitudes, conscious and unconscious behaviors were established in the past. If reincarnation is true, then everyone now living owes the substance and form of their selves to the distant past, and if they don't know their past, if they don't know what lies within their unconscious, then they don't know the basic facts of who they are or where they have come from.

Such people don't know why they do what they do or feel what they feel or like what they like or act how they act. If a person doesn't know his history, he doesn't know anything. He is a leaf that doesn't know it is part of a tree. If people do in fact have many more-or-less independently functioning past-life selves floating around inside the unconscious, then we are a patchwork of many people. But so long as all those past-life selves remain trapped in their own afterlife dreams, we remain divided, strangers to ourselves.

It may be possible to reintegrate unconscious souls of a past life into a person's present-day mind, reconnecting them one by one. In fact, there are a number of people today who claim to have done that. For example, from the time he was a small child, William Barnes (author of *I Built the Titanic*) had strange memories of another life that ended in a traumatic death. "At the age of four, I drew a ship with four smokestacks and told my parents: 'This was my ship, but she died.' I insisted my mother call me 'Tommie' and spoke of two brothers, a sister, aunts and uncles, none of whom my parents knew."[21]

Even before he approached a PLR therapist, Barnes was certain he'd died on the *Titanic*. But regression therapy awoke the past-life memories of Thomas Andrews, the man who oversaw the construction of that ill-fated vessel. Barnes now claims, after years of regressions, that the memories and mind of Andrews have been almost completely reintegrated into his conscious awareness, that the two men are now, for all practical intents and purposes, one being:

The physical vessel of Thomas Andrews is deceased, however many but not all of the memories remain of that lifetime. The memories of his struggles, his determination to do what was right, and his self-imposed guilt for what happened to *Titanic* remain with me. There are also many aspects of his personality that remain with me . . . Andrews's perspectives on life, his reactions to the world around him and some basic characteristics of his personality have always been a part of me. . . . Much of Tommie Andrews still resides in my heart of hearts. I realize now that my therapist's intention was not to integrate Thomas Andrews's personality into my life, but to help me reconcile myself to the fact that the integration already existed. Previously I was unable to differentiate my memories in "real time." . . . Although the regressions unleashed even more memories of my past-life as *Titanic*'s builder, they also helped me see on many different levels of consciousness, how and where (chronologically) those memories resided in my psyche. That new perspective saved my sanity and provided me with the tools I needed to reconcile my present life with my past life.

—William Barnes[22]

But there is a logistical problem with using PLR to restore our repressed past memories: it seems to take quite a bit of time to integrate even one past life into one's waking awareness. The memories come slowly and sporadically, even after the door between the two selves has been opened. Even after years of regression sessions, supplemented by meditation, great gaps can still remain in one's memories of a past life. If people have many past lives (as most authorities maintain), it would take more time to collect up and reintegrate one's past than one's present life has time for.

This is disturbing. It seems that if one does not succeed in reintegrating the total of past life memories before one dies, one would still be dying in a state of partial division, and so, in the next incarnation, one would have to start all over again. Even many Tibetan lamas, who are supposed to be among the holiest and most integrated of humans, often have little or no memory of their past lives, not even the most recent life. Even John the Baptist did not recall having been Elijah. So, seeking to reintegrate our past lives one by one via regression techniques ultimately seems to be a tool with limited uses, since one would not have enough time to reconnect with all one's past life selves in a single lifetime. The same limitation would probably apply to shamanic soul retrieval.

Missing Anything, Osiris?

But what if one *could* avoid dividing at death? If so, one would theoretically be able to reincarnate again and again without ever losing memory. One would have an "eternal name," a permanent and cohesive awareness of one's identity and history throughout the millennia. However, as great as that sounds, one would lose something in the process, the ability to generate new selves with different personalities and characteristics.

The ancient Egyptians understood this, and realized that purging all of one's pain was necessary before this eternal name could be acquired. The reader will perhaps recall that in Egyptian legend, Osiris was divided into pieces at his death, and then was restored to eternal life in the netherworld when those pieces were reunited. But when he was put back together, one piece was missing, his privates.

For ages, scholars have wondered what symbolic meaning this curious detail might carry. Genitals are of course associated with reproduction, and without any genitals, Osiris would seem to have purchased his eternal life at the cost of losing his ability to sire offspring. Now at first glance, this analysis doesn't make sense, because being dead and bodiless rules out that option. But perhaps not.

The binary soul doctrine suggests a cogent explanation for this mystery, suggesting that when we die, our unconscious soul becomes trapped in the netherworld while the conscious spirit goes on to reincarnate again. Of course, if the memory-bearing soul split off and was discarded between one incarnation and the next, the two incarnations would not remember or recognize each other as being the same person. They would seem alien to and distant from each other. Yet, since they were both produced by the same spirit, they might be viewed as related but not identical, rather like different generations of the same blood line. Thus, if we reincarnate without memory, it is rather like producing "offspring" of ourselves.

But if memory could be perfectly retained from life to life, then when a person reincarnates it would not seem as if a genuinely new and different and unfamiliar member of a new generation had been born. Instead, that new incarnation would seem far more closely related to the previous self, more equal and familiar, more like a brother-brother relationship than a father-son relationship. Thus, by avoiding the afterdeath division, one would lose the ability to produce reincarnational offspring. As far as reincarnating new offspring was concerned, one indeed would become as barren and fruitless as Adam and Eve, Abraham and Sarah,

Isaac and Rebekah, and Jacob and Rachel originally were, as incapable of producing new offspring as Osiris would have been without his genitals.

The ancient legends of the Jews and Egyptians associated the idea of barrenness with spiritual perfection. As bizarre and inexplicable as these themes seem at first glance, they make sense if one interprets them from a reincarnationist perspective. The Gnostics were apparently thinking along the same lines, insisting that spiritual perfection would cost a person the ability to beget offspring: "The heavenly man has many more sons than the earthly man. If the sons of Adam are many, although they die, how much more the sons of the perfect man, they who do not die but are always begotten. The father makes a son, and the son does not have the power to make a son. For he who has been begotten has not the power to beget, but the son gets brothers for himself, not sons" (The Gospel of Philip 58:17–26).

However, one's privates are not only for reproduction. The human body also uses them for waste disposal. In fact, one of the most perplexing mysteries to young children is why the same physical organ is used for such different purposes. However, this arrangement makes all the sense in the world from the perspective of the binary soul doctrine. So long as unprocessed psychic waste material still had not been eliminated, so long as a wall of repressed grief and pain still stood between the conscious and unconscious, so long as we remained divided, we would continue to "reproduce" new and unfamiliar selves when we reincarnated. But once the wall was eliminated and all of its unpleasantness was processed and released, then we would no longer have that ability to generate unfamiliar new selves via reincarnation. Spiritually, waste disposal and reproduction would seem to be intimately connected, and, it seems, our Creator decided to reflect that fact in how He designed the body. Obviously, He has a sense of humor.

What Goes in Must Come Out

These are rebellious people, deceitful children, children unwilling to listen to the Lord's instruction. Therefore, this is what the Holy One of Israel says: "Because you have rejected this message, relied on oppression and depended on deceit, this sin will become for you like a high wall, cracked and bulging, that collapses suddenly, in an instant."
—Isaiah 30:9–14

Unfortunately, if this wall inside us is not knocked down while we are alive, if we die while we're still in a state of self-alienation from our authentic feelings, death by itself may not fix anything. As we've seen, research into NDEs, PLRs, and other afterlife phenomena suggests that this inner division does not instantly become healed simply because we exit the physical body. "As a man thinketh, so he is," the ancients insisted.

Exactly as we conduct our lives, it seems, so will our deaths be. If one is full of illusion in life, his death will be full of illusion as well. If one has enlightenment in life, he will still have enlightenment in death. But if we have lived our lives in a state of self-alienated inner division, this will be our state in death. Enlightenment, it seems, must occur *before* death arrives; otherwise it will be too late.

> People who say they will die first and then arise are mistaken. If they do not first receive resurrection while they are alive, once they have died they will receive nothing.
> —Gospel of Philip 73:1–7f

Unfortunately, what we never let ourselves feel will *never* heal on its own, and every day that passes sees more and more of us slipping unhealed over death's threshold. What happens to those who die like this? What happens to all of us who aren't lucky enough to have NDEs, who aren't brave or rich enough to have Primal Therapy, who never dismantle their inner walls?

There may still be hope. Even those of us who, lifetime after lifetime, never summon the courage to confront this darkness on our own will probably not remain in a state of self-division forever. Why? Because, even if it does reincarnate again and again, the human mind is still a natural system, and a large measure of comfort can be found in that fact.

Science has taught us that all natural systems are self-regulating, tending to automatically compensate for imbalances, restoring balance and health on their own if they can. And because of this natural tendency, the wall in the psyche seems certain to fall in each of us sooner or later; since the wall produces an imbalance in the system, allowing one half to repress the other, we can be sure that this dividing barrier will eventually be overcome by the natural self-regulating mechanisms of the mind. It seems inevitable, the wall, "cracked and bulging" *will* fall sooner or later.

Our only choice is whether we want to tear it down safely now while we have the chance, dismantling it piece by piece so no one gets hurt, or whether we will continue to ignore its increasingly dilapidated and leaky condition, and run the risk of getting caught by surprise when it finally does come crashing down altogether.

13

The Old Path to the Third Soul: The One World Religion of the Pyramid Builders

The identical thing that we now call Christian religion existed among the ancients, and has not been lacking from the beginning of the human race until the coming of Christ in the flesh, from which moment on the true religion, which already existed, began to be called Christian.

—*Saint Augustine[1]*

In chapter 1, we saw that the binary soul doctrine is found in the traditions of Hawaii, Alaska, North America, South America, Australia, Egypt, India, Greece, Persia, China, and so on. Many additional examples could be cited, but one needn't examine every blade of grass to see which way the wind is blowing. There only seem to be two possible explanations for the uniformity of this belief around the world: either all these peoples arrived at the same conclusion independently, or they all inherited this belief from the same source.

The second explanation seems the more likely of the two, because the binary soul doctrine begins with a premise (that the human psyche has two parts) which our current, supposedly sophisticated, level of civilization has only recently (re-)discovered to be true. In fact, most of us today are still struggling to come to grips with this revelation. The average person still balks at neuropsychology's counterintuitive discovery that two independent minds coexist within the psyche. Therefore, it seems extremely unlikely that each of those early peoples could have independently gone through the advanced cultural processes of recognizing and accepting this truth as a given, and then proceeding from there. Far more likely is the proposition that a single culture once did most of the hard inner work that led to this realization, and then shared their insights with a number of less advanced cultures.

The evidence suggests, then, that an advanced culture once existed that disseminated its knowledge and belief systems across the globe. What is this if not an evidential arrow pointing in the direction of something like the legendary Atlantis? We cannot know for sure if the culture that originally disseminated the binary soul doctrine around the world was really Atlantis, but we have followed the evidence—the world-wide presence of the BSD—to its logical conclusion, which is that such a world-dominating culture probably did exist at some point in mankind's deep past, a culture which was able to spread its ideas fully around the world.

Some have argued that the main feature of Atlantis, the symbol of its culture, as it were, was the pyramid. And, just as the binary soul doctrine once covered the globe, so too did the practice of pyramid-building. Today, even though the ravages of time have reduced many once-proud pyramids to little more than piles of rubble, dozens of these stately buildings remain standing all over the planet.

In the Americas, pyramids still stand in Mexico, Belize, Guatemala, Peru, and Bolivia, and unconfirmed reports place still others in Brazil. The pyramid-building civilization of ancient Mesoamerica, today's archaeologists are discovering, was not only extensive, but also far older than once thought. A city of pyramids at Caral in Peru has recently been dated to 2,627 B.C., making it as old as the pyramids of the Nile. Many of the mysterious Indian mounds in North America seem to have originally been pyramids as well. Thousands of these artificially constructed hills have been found from Florida to lower Canada and from the Atlantic coast to the Mississippi Valley. One of the largest of these sites, Cahokia Mounds in Collinsville, Illinois, has a number of stepped pyramids, including Monks Mound, a huge sixteen-acre earthen pyramid with an interior of solid stone. Similar pyramidal mounds can be seen in Ocmulgee, Georgia; Moundsville, Alabama; Marietta, Ohio; and Emerald Mound, Mississippi. A stone pyramid has been reported beneath the waters of Wisconsin's Rock Lake so often it has become a local legend, although substantiation of these reports has proved elusive. However, the Rock Lake structure is made more believable by the presence of two truncated earthen pyramids three miles away, at Wisconsin's famous Indian site of Aztalan. Still other stone pyramids were reported in another underwater archaeological find off the coast of Cuba in 2001, but these reports also remain unconfirmed at the time of this book's printing.

Pyramids exist in Europe and Africa. Many can be visited in the ancient Sudanese city of Meroe, and over a dozen more may be seen in Greece, although many of these are in advanced states of decomposition. The Academy of Athens has dated their pyramid of Hellinikon to about 2720 B.C., predating the oldest Egyptian pyramid by at least 100 years. Six more European pyramids can be found near Guimar, a town on the eastern shore of Tenerife in Spain's Canary Islands.

Asia is no stranger to these monuments either: Ancient pyramids can be found in China, Japan, Korea, and Cambodia. A number of pyramids stand in a remote area near the Chinese city of Xian. While exact numbers are still in question, some estimate that as many as ninety pyramids dot the landscape there. Much like the pyramidal mounds found in North America, these structures are also made of clay and earth rather than stone. In appearance, however, the Chinese pyramids are more similar to those found in Mesoamerica.

On the Japanese island of Honsu, five miniature pyramids are strung along a ridge of Mount Kasagi about 100 meters apart. Called trignons by the Japanese, these ancient, precisely sculpted monoliths are about seven feet tall and twelve feet at the base, and, cut from a single block of stone, look for all the world like the missing capstones for the Egyptian pyramids. As this book goes to press, yet another underwater archaeological report is being investigated: In 1998 an ancient city containing one or more large pyramids was discovered 75 feet beneath the surface off the coast of Okinawa.

Korea has a number of pyramids. A seven-tiered, stone-stepped pyramid, thought to date sometime before 42 A.D., stands on the east slope of Mt. Wangsan. One of the best pyramids in South Korea is located at Soktapri, Andong, in the northern valley of Mt. Hakka. Another stepped pyramid is located in Seoul, and still another can be found near Taegu.

If legend is to be believed, India used to have a great number of pyramids. Most of them, folk tradition declares, were destroyed by Muslim invaders, but some still exist. For example, a group of three pyramids, collectively called the shore temples, can be found on the seashore of the village of Mahabalipuram. Two of these are dedicated to Siva, and the third, sandwiched between them, is dedicated to Vishnu. Similar pyramidal temples can also be found in Cambodia's Angkor (Angkor Wat and Angkor Thom) and in Java (Baphuon and Borobudur). One recently opened complex in Cambodia is Koh Ker, located in barren hill country fifty-three miles northeast of Angkor. At the western end of the structure is a hundred-foot-high square stone stepped pyramid with seven tiers.

Long ago, even more pyramids stood in Asia. The famous ziggurats of the Mesopotamians were monumental stepped pyramids, similar in appearance to the pyramids of Mesoamerica. Practically all the great cities of Mesopotamia had their own ziggurats, built with a core of mud brick and an exterior covered with baked brick. Approximately twenty-five ziggurats are known, scattered among Sumer, Babylonia, and Assyria.

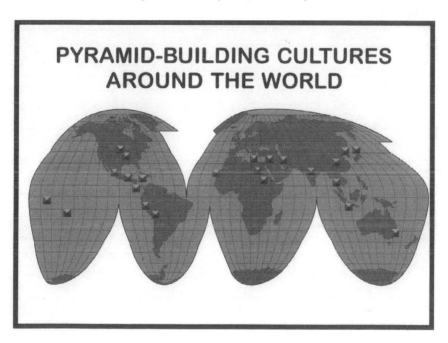

Pyramids were also once native to Australia, Tahiti, and Western Samoa. The town of Gympie in Queensland was once the unlikely site of a pyramid complex. The first Europeans to come into the area learned of them from the now extinct people known as the Dhamuri. Although most of these ancient pyramids have since been destroyed, photos and sketches of them remain from the first white man to come into the area. Meanwhile, the lone survivor stands on private land with a strict no-trespassing policy. Hundreds of miles to the east, another pyramid, the thirty-six-foot-tall Pulemelei Mound, stands on the island of Savai'i in Western Samoa. And even farther to the east, Tahiti also apparently once had a pyramid. Captain Cook reported that the Marae of Mahaiatea had a stepped pyramid with a base of 259 by 85 feet. Unfortunately, however, all that remains today is a pile of stones.

These ancient religious monuments were once found in Egypt, Mexico, Italy, Greece, Cyprus, Spain's Canary Islands, Ethiopia, India, Iraq, China, Thailand, Japan, Guatemala, Bolivia, Peru, Ecuador, Java, Samoa, Tahiti, and many other places. The idea that these cultures all independently decided to build the same colossal monuments stretches one's credulity, leading many to suspect that this idea, like the BSD, was originally a cultural hand-me-down from a single earlier source civilization. It is unlikely that different cultures would have independently decided to erect such similar monuments.

The vast majority of pyramids on the planet have four triangular sides and a square base. If pyramid-building was a random choice, then where are all the pyramids with three-sided bases and five-sided bases? It would have been just as easy to build a pyramid with a triangular or pentagonal base as it was to build them with square bases. And while a very small number of pyramids do have circular bases and rectangular bases, why do the vast majority come with square bases?

Something other than the simple laws of physics convinced all these different cultures to use this same shape. One can only conclude that this shape *meant* something to them, representing some idea or ideal that, whether they knew it or not, they all held in common. And from the size of the enormous pyramids still standing in Egypt, Mexico, and China, from the still-inconceivable burden it must have been for each of these ancient civilizations to build these mountainous structures, it is obvious that this commonly held idea, whatever it was, must have been supremely esteemed in each of these lands.

To conclude that cultures around the globe were thinking and acting along the same lines, taking on the same projects and dedicating themselves to the same ideals, is to conclude that a single, world-spanning culture once existed. The four-faced pyramid was indeed the most prominent symbol of such a culture. But what did this symbol mean?

Evidence exists that these pyramids *were* associated with similar ideas in different cultures. Virtually all pyramid cultures saw these monuments as having some sort of religious meaning, and a great many of these cultures also practiced mummification. Howard Reid comments: "We can say with confidence that people were mummifying their dead in Eastern Europe and North Africa, throughout Asia Minor, right across the Central Asian steppes, all around the Taklamakan desert and probably as far as the Gansu corridor."[2]

The list of mummy-making lands includes South America. In fact, like ancient Egypt, the Inca culture of South America had an entire industry that revolved around death and mummy-making, and there are remarkable parallels between the specific mummification techniques of the two lands. Egypt and the pre-Columbian cultures of the Americas both viewed their pyramids as "immortality machines." Not only did both peoples build gargantuan pyramids and mummify their dead; they both believed that their funerary ceremonies transformed the souls of the dead into immortal gods, beings who would live in the heavens forever. And, just as Egypt's most important funerary ritual was called "the opening of the mouth," the most important funerary ritual of ancient Mexico was called *p'achi,* which means, in part, "to open the mouth."[3]

Just as ancient Egypt believed that the hearts of the damned were swallowed in the underworld by a horrible monster called the Eater of the Dead, one of the levels of ancient Mexico's underworld was called *Teocoyolcualloya,* "place where beasts devour hearts." And, as ancient Egypt believed in a group of nine supreme beings called the *Ennead,* so ancient Mexico believed in a system of nine all-powerful gods.[4]

And, of course, the Egyptians of Africa, the Incas of Peru, and the Toltecs of Mexico all subscribed to the binary soul doctrine.

These uncanny parallels strongly suggest that these civilizations were closely related, possibly even springing from the same parent culture. Not only did the custom of building huge pyramidal religious monuments spread to cultures on opposite sides of the planet, but identical theological beliefs and practices apparently made the trip as well. On both sides of the planet, the pyramid was specifically associated with afterlife beliefs, which, in both cases, revolved around the binary soul doctrine. It seems reasonable to conclude that the pyramid and the binary soul doctrine must have been closely related in the original parent culture as well.

Was the pyramid once the *symbol* of the binary soul doctrine, in the same way that the cross is now the symbol of Christianity?

Symbols express or embody a concept, ideal, or abstract idea. Since both the ancient binary soul doctrine and the pyramid-as-monument seem to have originated in a prehistoric world-spanning civilization, it is reasonable to wonder if they are related. And the pyramid would be a perfect symbol for the binary soul doctrine, neatly explaining why the ancients chose a four-faced pyramid over any other design.

Human beings love symbols. We have a visual symbol for everything, and cultures at every stage of development seem to share this proclivity. It's a good bet that if there was a world-wide religion ages ago, it would have had a symbol as well. It's also a good bet that if there once was a world-spanning belief system on the planet, its most prominent symbol would still be familiar to us today, even if its doctrines no longer were.

The question is, if the binary soul doctrine *had* been the dominant belief of some ancient world-spanning civilization, how might this doctrine have been represented with a single symbol? Let's suppose that this symbol would have been a perfect representation of the doctrine it stood for, reflecting the three tenets of the binary soul doctrine:

1. Humans have two parts to their soul.

2. If people don't unite those parts in life, they divide in death, destroying identity and selfhood. To preserve one's self-aware identity after death, one must "make the two one," uniting these two parts into a single unit so that one's identity, memory, and subjective sense of self are preserved.

3. If these two parts are united, they become greater than the sum of their parts. This union produces a new dimension to the self, with new qualities. The union unveils new life, growth, freedom, potentials. The person is then more than human, in life and after death.

Let's start with the first point, that people have two parts to the souls. Let's represent that as two lines, side by side. For point two, let's make those two lines "one": transform them into a single character by crossing them at the center. This makes a new single mark, a cross, where before there had been two separate marks.[5] Point three, this union of the two parts creates a new quality. Here let's have a *third* line originating from the point of union of the two lines, coming out at a right angle to the cross. Imagine a wooden cross lying on the ground, and a beam of energy rising straight up from the center point. Now our symbol, which had been two-dimensional, is three-dimensional, suggesting that the union of the two parts generates new qualities not found in either of the two parts of the soul.

Our symbol, at this stage, would look a bit like someone had taken a piece from a child's set of toy jacks and cut one of the jack's six tongs off. It also looks like an old-fashioned X-shaped Christmas tree stand holding up a tree trunk with no branches. This doesn't seem to be a familiar symbol at all, until we consider the three-dimensional space defined by that symbol. *Connect all the lines and fill in the space, and a perfect four-faced pyramid appears.*

The pyramid, it seems, is a just cross that grew out from its center. Looking down at the pyramid from above it reveals the same cross we started with. The four-faced pyramid is a two-dimensional Christian cross that expanded into the third dimension. By crossing the lines, by simply uniting the two parts, this pyramidal symbol suggests one is transformed from a two-dimensional thing into a more impressive three-dimensional being. And the highest point of this symbol is *still* the point where the original two lines meet, for that union is the key to the growth that follows. The point of union, this symbol seems to say, is what causes the growth.

The pyramid is a *perfect* symbol for the binary soul doctrine! It says the same thing. It carries the same message. It *embodies* that message, the message of the old path, the path to eternal life.

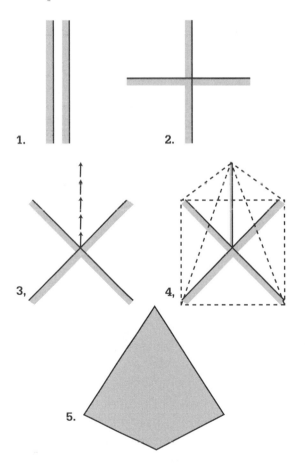

14

The Toltec Teachings: Living Voice of the Old Path

The indigenous Toltec people of Mexico . . . knew that we are double beings. They knew about the double nature of the world. That is why they call the world Omeyocan, or "the place of duality." That is why they give a name for each side of the world, and for each side of the duality we are: they named the rational side *tonal*, and our mysterious side *nagual*, the side of the silent knowledge. . . . Those ancient Toltecs were aware of our dual nature and envisioned the integration of the two sides of our being as the goal of human existence.

—*Victor Sanchez*[1]

The pyramid religion built titanic monuments to itself in Mexico, Egypt, and China, and spread its seed, the binary soul doctrine, into virtually every inhabited corner of the globe. As we saw in chapter 1, dozens of cultures around the world have retained traces of that ancient world religion. But in almost all cases, mere fragments of that once great faith are all that remain.

Some cultures remembered the problem but not the solution, while others remembered the solution but not the problem. Originally, the pyramid religion realized that the most important goal in life was to "make the two one," striving towards greater wholeness, unity, and integrity. This solution was in response to a perceived problem, based on an understanding that if one's soul and spirit were not sufficiently unified in life, they would divide at death. But in time, some of these cultures seem to have forgotten why they were seeking unity. They kept on trying to fix the problem without comprehending what was supposed to be broken in the first place.

Today, we can still see this dynamic in the cultural residues of the BSD. Many religions still urge us to seek integrity (morality), wholeness (holiness), and nonduality (the nondual), but most no longer associate this quest with any permanent problem that might develop in the afterlife if we fail. Many religions still realize, albeit dimly, that unity is the solution we seek, but they have forgotten the original problem that this solution was meant to solve.

Nonetheless, if unity is the solution, then division and duality must be the problem; if unity is what we are running to, then division must be what we are running from. Even Christianity seems to have once realized this, though it has long since betrayed and abandoned that pivotal insight. The Gospel of Thomas, a scripture many scholars believe was written mere decades after Jesus' death, was lost for nearly 2,000 years, not being rediscovered until the 1940s. When it was found again, the world found itself reading a startlingly different version of the familiar saying found in Matthew 6:24 and Luke 16:13, a pregnant new passage which strongly suggests that "making the two one" and overcoming duality originally played a major role in Christ's earliest teachings: "Jesus said, 'A person cannot mount two horses or bend two bows. And a slave cannot serve two masters, otherwise that slave will honor the one and offend the other'" (The Gospel of Thomas 47).

In fact, the theme of overcoming duality and division and "making the two one" occurs fourteen times in Thomas's gospel.[2] Unfortunately, this theme did not survive the passing of time in the Christian religion; and in much the same way, most of the other modern remnants of the ancient binary soul doctrine (the other traditions listed in chapter 1) have failed to retain anything more than fragments of its original theology.

What was that original theology? The pyramid religion seems to have contained three pieces of information: a definition of the threat facing humanity, a definition of the solution to that threat, and, most importantly, a set of clear and specific directions and injunctions to guide a person to achieve that solution—a yoga. Of these three pieces, the most extensive data was in the yoga, and so, of the three, the yoga would have been at the greatest risk of being compromised or lost as the years passed by.

And indeed, this does seem to be the case; a number of traditions have preserved the BSD report of the problem and/or its solution, but almost no cultures preserved any useful instructions on how to implement that solution. And without that, all the descendants of the BSD were impotent. Having lost the knowledge of how to *save* souls from death, many religions eventually settled for *controlling* them while they were alive.

Knowing that we must "make the two one" is not enough. We must also know *how*. Unfortunately, this precious knowledge, this yoga, was the most fragile part of the BSD. Even when we look to the exalted strongholds of the pyramid religions, Egypt, China, and Mexico, it seems that the corrosive sands of history erased that crucial detail, leaving us with the unnerving knowledge that this problem exists, tantalizing us with the knowledge that humanity once believed it had a solution, but denying us details about that solution. And so today, when we try to wrap our minds around the religious writings of ancient Egypt, the Christian Gnostics, and other cultures, we find their instructions and rituals completely opaque and meaningless. Still, all may not be lost.

A Surviving Remnant

In the latter days of the twentieth century, a long-forgotten religion began to reemerge from the shadows where it had been hiding since the earliest days of the European occupation of the New World. First reintroduced to us by Carlos Castaneda, the beliefs of Mexico's Toltecs have all the signs of being a genuinely ancient religious tradition. It is as rich, complex, and organized as any from the Old World, displaying the depth, beauty, and sophistication normally associated with millennia of cultural development. And not only does it seem to be one of the rare surviving exponents of the binary soul doctrine, it may have preserved the most complete record of that system's practices to help a person "make the two one."

The reemergence of the Toltec faith is a fantastic and completely unexpected stroke of luck. For centuries, it had looked as if the knowledge of both primary cultural centers of the ancient pyramid builders, Egypt and Mexico, had been all but erased from humanity's memory. We knew they had once been there, but we didn't know much else about them at all. Whatever wisdom ancient Egypt might have preserved from the earliest days of the pyramid culture was lost when its world-renowned libraries were burned to the ground by zealous Christians. After that, no one understood much about Egypt's beliefs until scholars figured out how to read Egyptian hieroglyphics in 1799.

And when the Christian world conquered Mexico in the sixteenth century, the same thing happened; virtually all their books were destroyed, along with most of their leaders, priests, and scholars. To this day, we *still* can't read a great deal of the writing left behind by the Mesoamerican civilizations. But now, Toltec culture has surprised us all, peeking its head out from around a corner like a little child who senses it is finally safe to come out again.

The history of Mexico's great Toltec empire is very sketchy, with few facts being certain. Although Spanish priests and scribes attempted to piece together the history of the Toltecs as it was handed down to them by the Aztecs, the information was confusing at best. Coming to power as the mysterious Mayan civilization was fading, the early history of the Toltecs is obscure. However, they are thought to owe many of their cultural attributes to the Mayans, who in turn are thought to have inherited theirs from the even more mysterious Olmecs, whose civilization is thought to date back at least to 1200 B.C. A number of customs, beliefs, and traditions established by the Olmecs persisted over the centuries, including their calendars, the ritual ball game, monumental architecture including pyramids and plazas, jaguar deities, jade carving, hematite mirrors, and monumental stelae and thrones.

The first thing we notice about the reawakening Toltec tradition is that, like many other religious traditions, this ancient Mexican faith held the attainment of eternal life as its ultimate goal. The average human, according to these teachings, does not automatically survive death intact, but usually finds his conscious awareness ripped away shortly after departing the dying body.

The Death-Defiers of Ancient Mexico

The power that governs the destiny of all living beings is called the Eagle, not because it is an eagle or has anything to do with an eagle, but because it appears to the seer as an immeasurable jet-black eagle, standing erect as an eagle stands, its height reaching to infinity. . . . The Eagle devours the awareness of all the creatures that, alive on earth a moment before and now dead, have floated to the Eagle's beak, like a ceaseless swarm of fireflies, to meet their owner, their reason for having had life. The Eagle disentangles these tiny flames, lays them flat, as a tanner stretches out a hide, and then consumes them; for awareness is the Eagle's food. . . . The Eagle, although it is not moved by the circumstances of any living thing, has granted a gift to each of

these beings. In its own way and right, any one of them, if it
so desires, has the power to keep the flame of awareness,
the power to disobey the summons to die and be consumed.
. . . The Eagle has granted that gift in order to perpetuate
awareness.

—Carlos Castaneda[3]

Much as Ecclesiastes 12 held that after death, "the spirit returns to God
who gave it," the Toltecs believed that one's conscious spirit is ripped away at
death, becoming reabsorbed into the godhead. But unlike many popular
interpretations of Ecclesiastes 12, the Toltecs saw this reabsorption as a terrible fate that ought to be avoided if possible. The Toltecs taught how to
avoid this afterlife fate, and in that respect, the Toltecs are on the same page
with other religious approaches. However, the Toltec path to that goal is startlingly different. Much like Hinduism and Buddhism, those on this path
acquire psychic abilities, many of which involve out-of-body experiences.

The Toltec teachings may have something in common with those of
Swedenborg, who wrote that a worldwide religion had once existed in the
centuries following the great flood, but that it eventually became corrupted.
Telling what may well be a related story, Toltec tradition declares that their
religion originally centered on the pyramids, but in time the followers of that
religion became corrupted and evil. In time, a revolution turned the Toltecs
away from corrupting practices, but it was at that time that their religious
practices turned away from the pyramids.

With his first book, *The Teachings of Don Juan,* Carlos Castaneda reintroduced Mexico's ancient religious tradition to the West, writing of his apprenticeship with a native Mexican shaman named don Juan Matus. Castaneda
eventually wrote twelve books about this obscure Mesoamerican tradition, in
which he experienced supernatural occurrences as fabulous as any in the
Bible. It was brave of him to include such extraordinary events in his books,
but it cost him many readers. Many were willing to entertain the possibility
that an advanced Mexican spirituality once existed, but few were willing to
grant credence to reports of flying or shapeshifting into crows or other animals. And even though Castaneda's books were consistently best-sellers, he
remained very controversial, with much of the world writing him off as a
charlatan whose only noteworthy skill was an ability to tell tall tales.[4]

However, in the years since, a number of other self-proclaimed Toltec
apprentices have come forth to substantiate Castaneda's bizarre claims. The
Toltec religion seems to have survived the millennia by using these kinds of

intimate one-on-one, teacher-to-apprentice relationships to transmit its teachings, rather than the more impersonal educational institutions the world is used to today. In the Toltec tradition, we are told, each master would collect a small number of students and personally transmit his wisdom to them, a process that would demand years of extreme dedication from both the teacher and his students. And those students who successfully passed the final test would in turn collect and teach their own small set of students.

In this way, the teachings were handed down from generation to generation without ever being widely noticed. Castaneda, however, tried to change all that, bringing this extraordinary cultural artifact into public view with his books. Unfortunately, the modern world was, for the most part, not ready to accept Castaneda's amazing but unsubstantiated claims.

However, in recent years other authors have come forward to provide independent substantiation of Castaneda's claims. In *A Toltec Path*, for example, Ken Eagle Feather[5] presents us with the very thing Castaneda's readers have sought for years, a simple, well-organized, and comprehensive overview of the Toltec teachings, providing Castaneda's readers with substantiating testimony from *another* member of don Juan's small band of apprentices. Eagle Feather says: "I first met don Juan while walking down Speedway Boulevard, a main avenue in Tucson. . . . Don Juan charged me with writing two books that would elaborate on Castaneda's material. . . . Two compatriots of Castaneda who have also published accounts of their interaction with don Juan are Florinda Donner, in *Being-in-Dreaming*, and Taisha Abelar, in *The Sorcerer's Crossing*."[6]

The Toltec religion, Eagle Feather, Donner, and Abelar maintain, revolved around a single goal: surviving death. The majority of people, according to Toltec thought, do not pass through the doors of death with their autonomous consciousness intact. Instead, upon departing the body, their awareness is "eaten" by the Eagle, the Toltec world's frightening and impersonal version of God. Surprisingly, many early Christians also believed that the souls of the unenlightened dead would be "eaten" in the next world: "Look for a place for yourselves within Repose, lest you become a corpse and be eaten" (The Gospel of Thomas 60). "God is a man-eater. For this reason men are sacrificed to Him" (The Gospel of Philip 63:1–3).

This Toltec concept of the majority of the souls of the dead being eaten by a supernatural being, while a few escape, sneaking past the Eagle to retain their autonomous identity and volition, seems eerily similar to an Egyptian idea. In ancient Egypt, those souls who were weighed on the scales of judgment and found wanting would be immediately eaten by the god Ammit, while those who survived this test would retain their wholeness and volition, becoming "like unto gods" in the next world.

The Toltec Rapture

> Don Juan says that team leaders carry the additional task of lighting up their entire energy bodies. Once they do, he says, the rest of the team entrains to the Fire from Within, and will "all be gone in an instant."
>
> —Ken Eagle Feather[7]

The Toltecs referred to this goal of surviving death with their awareness intact as acquiring "freedom," because the path to this goal not only made it possible for subjects to survive death, but gave them the ability to shift their conscious awareness from our normal, earthly dimension to an endless number of other real dimensions. The goal was to become capable of making such a shift whenever one wished, during life and after.

Mastering the necessary lessons on the path towards this goal also resulted in the student acquiring the ability to achieve OBEs (traveling in the "Dreaming Body") at will, and other supernatural talents. In the final moment of acquiring "freedom," Toltec masters would burn with the "Fire from Within," and literally disappear bodily from the world without so much as a puff of smoke. Toltec tradition maintains that entire civilizations have disappeared en masse in this way in the past, reminding one of the mysterious disappearance of the Anasazi and of Christianity's expectations of Rapture. Just as Christianity expects Christ to return one day to instantaneously transport His many followers to heaven, so too Toltecs believe that an accomplished master, or "*Nagual*," can take many others with him when he finally departs from this world via the Fire from Within.

The Toltec Yoga

The Toltec path toward this goal was based on the BSD idea that people are nonintegrated, out of balance, two-part beings, which is fully in keeping with Freud's view that our minds are malfunctioning, and with the Biblical view that the "Fall from Grace" in Eden left humanity in a state of "brokenness." As Castaneda said, "The two sides of a human being are totally separate, and it takes great discipline and determination to break the seal and go from one side to the other."[8]

Toltec tradition sometimes describes human beings as having two souls, and other times as having three, as so many other binary soul doctrine religions do. Castaneda called these the "three attentions." Toltec tradition describes the first two souls much as modern science describes the characteristics of the right and left hemispheres of the brain. The first attention (also called the "right-side awareness" or the *tonal),* is our normal everyday awareness. Like the conscious spirit, the *tonal* is associated with reason, rationality, common sense, verbal communication, will, and intent. The second attention (also called the "left-side awareness," or the *nagual),* is a mysterious, unfamiliar, and largely unused portion of the psyche more relevant to religious and supernatural matters.

Like the unconscious soul, the *nagual* is associated with silent knowledge, nonverbal behavior, nonanalytical reason, dreams, the vast unknown, and, at times, a debilitating weakness. And like the third soul, the third attention is only acquired when the first two attentions are successfully integrated (which only occurs, the Toltecs maintain, when the Fire from Within is ignited). Like other versions of the BSD, "making the two one" is the final goal of the Toltec faith: the marriage of the *tonal* and *nagual* into a unity. The entire Toltec path can be summed up as that—a quest for integration. And so, complete personal responsibility and being true to one's self are highly cherished ideals in the Toltec tradition.[9]

We are all divided, Toltecs believe, and this state of divided nonintegration will spell our doom at death. This division can be seen visually. By exercising and strengthening a person's *nagual* side, Toltec practitioners have found that it is possible to *see* in a new way, perceiving reality through the *nagual* half of one's mind. And when observing a living person in this way, Toltecs seers claim that all people appear to have a "gap" in their beings. This gap seems to be a reflection of the division between one's halves; if one integrates the halves, closing the "gap," then one will never die, the Toltecs say.

This is more easily said than done. The differentiation of the two parts must be completed before any integration can be successful. Only after the *tonal* and *nagual* sides are each separately recognized, distinguished, exercised, strengthened, and fully developed, can one begin to integrate both sides. The living Toltec tradition still offers extensive teachings for each side; in fact, the majority of the Toltec teachings involve specific exercises to strengthen each side before they are finally integrated. The lessons for the right side involve "stalking" (Castaneda's term) or "tracking" (Eagle Feather's term), requiring feats of exceptionally clear perception and analysis, while the lessons for the left side involve "dreaming," i.e., acting and observing during OBEs.

But even after the two sides have each been separately strengthened, there is still one task left. There is still a dividing barrier between them, a wall-like membrane that must be removed before integration can be achieved.

Recapitulation: The Toltec Baptism

They . . . could not break the seal, the membrane that separates their two sides.

—Carlos Castaneda[10]

To break through that membrane, the Toltecs used a procedure called "recapitulation." Integration of one's two sides was not possible until this recapitulation was accomplished and the wall was down; and since one's eternal life depended on that integration, recapitulation was accorded great importance in Toltec practice. This recapitulation is a practical procedure to confront, re-experience, and tear down the wall of grief described here in chapter 12. Eagle Feather says:

The recapitulation is an exercise to recall, review, release, and recharge energy. It rids you of assumptions and preconceptions. It frees locked energy and restores balance. . . . It is the most effective tool Toltecs use. . . . The idea is that all of your experiences have been stored inside your energy fields. As though they are energy cysts produced by stagnant conditional fields, they block the flow of energy, especially those resulting from trauma. They also keep awareness focused within their range of perception, and so prevent transformative shifts of consciousness.

—Ken Eagle Feather[11]

In a typical recapitulation, which might require months or years of effort, a person will try to recall all the events of one's life, reliving and releasing all the repressed emotions and psychological energy trapped in those past memories. In perhaps the most common method of recapitulation, the subject designs, builds, and enters a wooden box, and then uses certain time-tested breathing techniques to enter a slightly altered state of consciousness. According to Toltec tradition, this allows the unconscious, or *nagual* side of the mind, to exhume long-forgotten memories in startling detail, returning them to conscious awareness where they are vividly replayed, reconsidered, and if all goes well, released.

Castaneda briefly described this procedure in his book *The Eagle's Gift*, and a number of later Toltec apprentices and practitioners, including Ken Eagle Feather, Victor Sanchez, and others, have since expounded upon the technique. Together, they present the modern world with a millennia-old method of self-healing that seems to have a tremendous advantage over most conventional psychoanalytical approaches, perhaps because it begins with the premise that we are indeed two-part creatures, and then engages both of those parts in the journey back to wholeness.

The end result is usually great peace and lightness of being, as one finds that the psychological baggage one had been so used to carrying around is no longer there. Even some old-school Catholics once recognized the obvious connection between this cathartic practice and the Biblical injunction calling for a "baptism of repentance for the forgiveness of sins." Victor Sanchez notes: "There are the roots of the practice of recapitulation to be found among the Toltecs of the past as well as other ancient indigenous groups. *Tlacentlalia* is a word in Nahuatl (the language of the Toltec, Aztec, and many other indigenous groups in Mexico) that was translated by Alonso de Molina, a sixteenth-century Catholic friar, as 'gathering together the sins, bringing them to memory.'"[12]

My purpose here is not to present a detailed exploration of this practice, but only to inform the reader that the Toltec religion claims to possess an effective tool to help people tear down the wall that keeps the two halves of the self so separated.[13] Don Juan Matus said, "Seers who deliberately attain total awareness are a sight to behold. That is the moment when they burn from within. The Fire from Within consumes them. And in full awareness, they . . . glide into eternity."[14]

How did Toltecs trigger their "Fire from Within" integration once both sides were prepared and all the obstacles were finally removed? From all the different books by Toltec practitioners, it seems they had a variety of ways to accomplish this final integration. One was to intentionally create a momentary *increase* in the rift between the two parts, which is particularly interesting since NDEs seem to do the same thing and in many cases achieve similar results. Toltec apprentices report that it is difficult to simultaneously "occupy" both sides, viewing two different perspectives.[15]

Integration itself does not seem to be difficult to achieve once all the prerequisite preparations are complete. And when both sides of the subject's awareness *are* integrated, all the reports declare, the apprentice becomes a "person of knowledge" able to perform astounding feats of supernatural skill and awareness, and, it is thought, even to survive death with consciousness intact. That part of the story, of course, is basically the same as we find in many other versions of the binary soul doctrine. The unique feature of the reemerging Toltec faith is that it may still possess the pyramid religion's long-lost *yoga*, the all-important secret knowledge needed to actually "make the two one."

15

Forging a New Path to Immortality: Christ's Mission to Save the Human Race

For this reason faith came, it did away with the division.
—The Gospel of Truth 34:29

As good as it was, unfortunately the old path was not enough to solve humanity's problem. While it was effective on the level of the individual, the old path was a miserable failure on the level of the collective. It worked wonderfully when people tried it, but it was a path few ever started down, and fewer still completed. And even though generation after generation also produced healers who valiantly struggled to beat back humanity's ever-increasing division with various types of soul retrieval or soul-rescue techniques (whether shamanic, OBE, psychological, or ghostly), there have ultimately been too few of these spiritual warriors to make any meaningful impact on the pathology affecting our species. OBE pioneer Robert Monroe recognized this dilemma, as also does ghost rescuer Robert H. Coddington, who admitted: "We consider rescue of unaware souls a beneficent objective unto itself, even though aiding them, one individual at a time, may be like draining a lake one drop at a time."[1]

Alas, we may win a few minor battles now and then, but the real war seems all but completely lost. For every individual these soul retrieval specialists help, millions more slip by untouched, lost, and trapped in a merciless downward spiral of unconscious self-destruction. So, instead of getting closer to conquering the pathology that has gripped our species, humanity has kept inching inexorably closer to seeing *it* finally conquer *us*. Day after day, lifetime after lifetime, we slice off more and more fragments of ourselves, endlessly indulging in insane acts of self-betrayal that violate our integrity and endanger our health and safety, ignorantly drop-kicking shards of our being into the garbage dump we call the unconscious.

Everything has a price, so we probably shouldn't be surprised that we now find ourselves standing together at the ultimate precipice, wondering if our divisions will now finally be the end of us. There seems to be every reason to assume they might. When cells don't integrate with the rest of the system in a biological organism, it is called cancer. Left to their own devices, such pathologies inevitably destroy the whole organism. As Luke (11:17) warns, "Any kingdom divided against itself will be ruined, and a house divided against itself will fall."

At one time, the old path was believed to hold great promise. All the world once embraced it, believing it to be the answer to humanity's problems. People everywhere built huge monuments to it, but in the end it failed us. Despite the entire old path, despite all the binary soul religions, shamans, soul retrieval specialists, psychologists, and ghost-hunters, humanity is still imprisoned inside this pathology. Yes, from time to time a scattered few have been able to escape via the old path; but the vast majority of the Earth's tired, insecure, misinformed, and perpetually distracted population have never even tried to climb out of the trap on their own.

And that could very easily have been the end of the story.

Humanity needed help. Like an infant that had wandered into dangers it didn't understand and had no chance of coping with, humanity needed to be rescued. We had attacked the problem the best way we knew how, and had come up embarrassingly short. Despite a unified worldwide commitment to the old path, we failed in the end. Humanity came away from that sociological experiment as pathologically divided as ever, leaving nothing left to be done but humbly admit our inadequacy and hope for a miracle. We needed a savior.

The Ultimate Soul Retrieval

In *The Division of Consciousness*, I suggested that Jesus Christ not only mastered the old path (Ephesians 2:14), but figured out how to do something

**Christian art also says
"Make the two one"**

Jesus is credited by Ephesians 2:14 with having "made the two one," the same goal emphasized again and again in the Gospel of Thomas and other gnostic works, a goal that would have been extremely relevant and meaningful to the BSD-saturated cultures of the Mediterranean. For centuries afterwards, Christian art commonly displayed Christ making an obviously symbolic gesture—holding up two fingers held close together—as seen in this 6th century icon. Christian scholarship has long been divided on the original meaning of this gesture; some have maintained that it refers to Christ's double nature as God and man, while others have taught alternate explanations. But if this gesture dates from Christ Himself, perhaps it was not intended as a declaration of Christ's nature, but as a command to the viewer: *"To those who have eyes to see, here is the whole secret: make the two one!"*

new, taking the old path one step further than anyone had ever done before. His perfect integrity made it possible for Him to delay the activation of His "Fire from Within" transformation until after His physical death. Thus, when He finally underwent this transformation, He did it out of the body,[2] which released awesome, never-before-seen forces that catapulted His soul throughout space and time like the light of an exploding supernova, filling every nook and cranny of the universe with His presence. The Bible reports something similar: "He who descended is the very one who ascended higher than all the heavens, in order to fill the whole universe" (Ephesians 4:10).

One consequence of such an unprecedented maneuver was that Christ's unconscious soul became permanently conjoined to all other souls in the universe. He thus came to intimately and directly share in the psychological existence, experience, thoughts, feelings, and identity of every man, woman,

267

and child throughout history, something that presumably only God Himself had previously done, something that would indeed earn Jesus the title "Son of God." "On that day you will realize that I am in my Father, and you are in me, and I am in you" (John 14:20).

Such a forced universal mind-meld would have been just what the doctor ordered, providing a perfect solution for the problem plaguing humanity. Discovering our minds inside His own, Jesus would have found Himself in an unprecedented position of power, in the perfect position to single-handedly attack the whole pathology.

Our pain had become His pain. What we had collectively rejected, denied, ignored, and refused to experience consciously, He could embrace. He could now directly confront, and *therefore finally release*, all humanity's repressed pain and buried memories, everything we had stored up since the beginning of time (or at least since the beginning of the Division). "I remembered your tears and your mourning and your anguish; they are far behind us" (The Secret Book of James 10:9–10).

Jesus could finally release humanity from its ancient fear of this inner pain, a fear that had trapped and enslaved the whole species for millennia. He could finally *integrate* all the repressed pain and memories, finally fulfilling the evolutionary purpose to become integrated, integrating all the pain and memories by incorporating them all into *His own* conscious awareness. What we cowardly refused to integrate into ourselves, He bravely chose to integrate into Himself.

All this repressed material was essentially a debt we owed ourselves, a psychological debt that had grown so large it was threatening to destroy the whole human race. He paid this debt for us; or, as His followers put it 2000 years ago, He "paid for our sins." With trepidation, and with faith, but most of all with love for His fellow human beings, He used the Fire from Within to "take our sins upon Himself," just as the Christian Church has maintained for millennia.[3]

What few realize, however, is that even if He *did* pay our debts for us, that would still not actually *release* us from our indebtedness. There's no such thing as a free lunch, even for Christians. When one bank takes over another, assuming all its debts, the accounts of the first bank's debtors are not wiped clean, but transferred to the second bank. In the same way, when Jesus paid our debts for us, we did not simply become debt-free, but now, instead of merely owing ourselves, we now owed *Him*.

He now had leverage over us.

We never imagined that such a thing was even possible. We didn't realize that we had this vulnerability, because we had hidden these debts from our own view. To be unconscious of a debt is to be unconscious of a weakness and a vulnerability. But He knew they were there, and realized that if He could pay off these debts for us, He would be, in effect, taking over the whole human race.

And once He did, the only choice we had left would be whether to look at it as a friendly bail-out or a hostile takeover.

Of course, I can offer little proof for this hypothesis other than a handful of ancient scriptural passages from the Bible, from the Gospel of Thomas and from other sacred scriptures (which many scholars now suggest are actually older and more authentic than the canonical texts). However, Jesus' solution, as described in such scriptures, fits right in with the pathology described by modern psychology and the binary soul doctrine. The expansion of Jesus' perfectly integrated mind throughout the universe, melding in the process to all other human minds, would have provided a perfect and elegant solution to humanity's ancient spiritual dilemma. His perfect integrity would have become our own. "Jesus said, 'He who will drink from My mouth will become like Me. I myself will become he, and the things that are hidden will be revealed to him'" (The Gospel of Thomas 108). But instead of revisiting those arguments here, I will merely point the interested reader to my earlier work, *The Division of Consciousness*, which explores this hypothesis in some depth.

I *will* say here, however, that we all ought to hope mightily that this hypothesis *is* correct, for the old path is not enough. The old path, which required us to individually achieve personal perfection and complete integrity, the path that Judeo-Christian tradition calls "The Law of Moses," or "The Law," has plainly shown itself inadequate to our needs. Like communism, it *seems* like it would work if everyone followed it faithfully, but alas, that's the whole problem. We're not even faithful with ourselves, so how can we be expected to be faithful to anything else?

Christianity as the Old Path

> I am life. He who lives in me will never die.
>
> —Jesus Christ

If Jesus failed to meld His soul to ours, then humanity still remains locked inside the prison of soul-division, with no way out except for the old path, which humanity has already tested and found insufficient. On the other hand, if He *succeeded*, we may have been provided an alternate means of escape from that prison. By extension, Christianity may be unique among all other religions. The Church has, of course, always claimed that special status, but such claims have been met with doubt and derision by other faiths. The single largest stumbling block people of other faiths have with Christianity is the seemingly nonnegotiable and exclusivist passage *"I am the way and the truth and the life. No one comes to the Father except through me"* (John 14:6). *Is* Jesus the only way to eternal life?

Perhaps. If Jesus melded His soul to each of our own, then anyone who followed the old path, achieving union with their own soul, would at the same time be achieving union with Christ. The path to Jesus and the old path would then be one and the same thing. Conventional Christianity assumes that people are required to recognize Jesus by name and historical reputation, but the BSD suggests otherwise. If Jesus indeed is inside each of us, then the old path's goal—to become united with one's own true inner being—would be to become one with Jesus as well. If Jesus *is* inside us, then everyone following the old path of personal integrity, whether they call themselves Buddhists, Taoists, Hindus, Muslims, Jews, Toltecs, Jungians, Falun Gong, or whatever, *would be* being faithful to Jesus, even if they don't realize it. Some might do it without ever having even heard His name, and others might even while believing themselves to be His enemy.

Conventional Christianity, on the other hand, holds that if a person is over the age of reason and does not "know and accept Jesus," despite any other virtues he may have, will go to their doom regardless of any other considerations when he dies. Salvation in this scenario is essentially a matter of luck; a person has to be fortunate enough to be born in the right place and time. If one gets the right parents, education, and social environment, one will be likely to "accept Jesus" without even giving the matter much thought, a teaching which makes salvation dependent on sociological matters outside the individual's control. Similarly, millions around the world regularly engage in complex religious and theological debate with others, in the assumption that logic will allow them to figure out which faith is correct. Unfortunately, this again ties salvation to luck. Virtually all religions admit that people are confronted with a huge variety of religious options to choose from, but claim that only one of them will lead to salvation, all the rest to destruction. Is your salvation behind Door Number One, Door Number Two, or Door Number Three? If logic is the magic key, only the smartest would be able to figure out the correct answer; and since none of us control how much IQ we are born with, this scenario again makes salvation dependent more on our genetics than our spirituality.

The BSD, on the other hand, suggests that salvation is not dependent on which intellectual system one embraces, but on how true one is to oneself.

270

And in so doing, the binary soul doctrine puts a whole new twist on Christianity's prerequisite of "knowing and accepting Jesus." If the BSD is correct, then a person need not be lucky in the location of one's birth, the religion of one's parents, or the quality of one's IQ to receive salvation. The BSD suggests instead that this gift is available to all, and the price is paid by the heart, not the mind. Accepting Jesus would have nothing to do with acknowledging (or consenting to worship) a name or person or myth, and everything to do with honoring the input and insights and messages that rise up automatically from the depths of one's soul.

If Jesus is within each of us already, then whenever we seek to consciously honor and satisfy the needs and demands of our own souls, we would at the same time be "following Christ," whether we consciously realized it or not. Can anyone imagine a more beautiful system, or one more just or egalitarian? Simply by being true to ourselves, we automatically grow closer to Christ within. If the Word of God lives *a priori* inside the hearts and souls of all people as soon as they are born, then all have immediate access to it, and need not rely on circumstances for salvation. The source of the messages rising up from the soul, the BSD suggests, is far more noble, worthy, and divine than most people imagine. To seek a life of integrity, to be true to one's own self, would be to invite and allow Christ to take up residence in our hearts and souls, to live in and through us, in our actions and reactions. The only thing required of us would be a life of integrity, in which we listen to and honor the voice of wisdom and love that emerges unbidden from the depths of our psyches. All who unified their authentic selves would be unifying themselves with Jesus, living in Him as completely and profoundly as ever did any of the saints, prophets, or Apostles. The early Christians understood this well; Clement of Alexandria wrote "It is the greatest of all disciplines to know oneself; for when a man knows himself, he knows God."[4]

And those who were one with Him, Jesus promised, those who "lived in Him," would beat death. They would never lose consciousness of their own autonomous identities or personal histories. They would not fracture apart into pieces when their physical bodies died. *They would not die.* They would *never* die. This is a remarkable promise.

But perhaps even more remarkably, our research into the binary soul doctrine makes it clear that such a promise was actually nothing new. If being true to one's own inner self ends up being the same thing as being true to Jesus, then the Christian path *is* the old path. If so, and if that's all there is to the story, then nothing has really changed. And if nothing has changed, then Jesus Christ, and His church, would be irrelevant.

But this ancient promise, the promise of the worldwide pyramid religion, the promise of the old path, is but one of *two* immortality promises given by Jesus Christ:

> I am the resurrection and the life.
> He who believes in me will live, even though he dies;
> and whoever lives and believes in me will never die.
> —John 11:25–26

Prior to Jesus' life, only one such promise existed in all the religions of the world—the challenge of the old path. The only way to acquire eternal life was "making the two one." In different cultures this has been called entering the Kingdom of Heaven, enlightenment, finding Nirvana, living in the Tao, or simply living in God. However phrased, it was long thought the only path available, and required personal perfection and complete integrity. If a person was going to preserve his identity and memory and sense of self after leaving his body, he had to avoid the "second death"—he had to keep his mind from fracturing during the transition. Jesus' great gift to the human race seems to have been introducing an alternate option: faith. In the age Jesus lived in, every culture on earth would have seen the first part of the above promise as something new. It did not require any inner unity or personal perfection at all, but only something much easier to achieve: simple trust.

Christianity as a New Path

> I am resurrection. He who believes in me will live, even though he dies.
> —Jesus Christ

With the advent of Christ, a new hope was born—that even if one's soul and spirit *did* divide at death, that still wasn't necessarily the end of the story. Even after that, a person could still hope to have his divided parts united again. A person could hope to be reassembled. A person could hope to live again. Jesus taught *both* these hopes. There were now, He said, not one, but *two* paths to eternal life.

Today, conventional Christian teachings don't distinguish between these two claims any more than they distinguish between the soul and spirit. But they seem to have originally been two quite separate and distinct promises, one about resurrection, about rising up from the dead *after* one has died, and another quite different and far older promise about finding a *permanent* source of life, *never* dying at all. Both those who "believed" in Christ and those who "lived" in Christ would enjoy eternal life, Jesus promised, but how they would each come to receive that prize was very different.

Those who "lived" in Christ would *never* die: the soul and spirit would never split. They would *never* lose their memories or sense of personal identity after departing their earthly bodies. One who merely "believed" in Christ and didn't fully "live" in Him, though, would still die. That *self*, that identity, would still suffer the "second death" and cease to exist, at least for a while. But thanks to Christ, he would be resurrected again one day, reassembled, made whole again. The soul and spirit would split, but were guaranteed to be reunited eventually.

> I am the resurrection and the life.
> He who believes in me will live, even though he dies;
> and whoever lives and believes in me will never die.
> —John 11:25–26

> Whoever finds the interpretation of these words will not experience death.
> —The Gospel of Thomas 1

These two passages, the first from the Bible, and the second from the writings of the early Christian Gnostics, show themselves to be related, both indicating that Jesus' original message dared to include a claim that a person could actually avoid experiencing death altogether. But these two passages also show, by contrast, the dichotomy of doctrinal focus that eventually split the newborn Church into warring halves, Roman and Gnostic. Most of the New Testament revolves around the first option, faith; many of the works of Gnosticism, such as the Gospel of Thomas, the Gospel of Philip, and the Gospel of Truth, revolved around the second option, the old path. Almost as soon as it was born, the Church began cutting away pieces of itself; eventually the Roman half of the Church erased the Gnostic half right off the map.

Christian Theology's Missing Cornerstone

In recent years many elements of the Church have glossed over the concept of a coming universal resurrection as if embarrassed over such a seemingly absurd notion. This is but one casualty in the war within Christianity over the different ways death is portrayed in the scriptures. What happens when we die is a crucially important question for Christianity. After all, the conquering of death was the genesis of the whole movement. Yet, conventional Christian theology fails to account for many Biblical mysteries about death and the afterlife. For the greater part of 2,000 years, Christians have wondered why the next world is presented in so many different ways in the Bible. What, they ask, is the "Second Death" (Revelation 2:11)? What was "Baptism for the Dead" (1 Corinthians 15:29, see also appendix A)? Why is there an apparent reincarnational relationship between Elijah and John the Baptist (Matt. 11:14, 17:10–13, Mark 9:11–13, Luke 1:17)? What does the Bible mean when it states that the soul and spirit can divide from one another (Heb. 4:12)? And why does the Bible report that Jesus' actual mission was not merely to conquer death, but to "make the two one" (Eph. 2:14), eerily echoing the universal anthem of the binary soul doctrine?

The Bible, as it has come down to us today, seems to raise more of these questions than it answers, but the authors of the New Testament give the impression that it all made perfect sense to *them*. It is as if there is a fundamental piece to the picture that modern Christian theology isn't seeing, some key detail that was understood in the early church, but has been forgotten.

Like the rest of us, the Church exhibits the characteristics of being caught in a pathology that is tearing it apart. On the surface, the Church held together for nearly 1500 years, but with the Reformation, the apparent unity of Christianity began to fracture, a process that has accelerated ever since. There are now dozens of different Christian factions around the world, each with its own idea of what Christianity is about. And the more fractured Christianity gets, the weaker it gets. In fact, Christianity has fractured so thoroughly and deeply today that many around the world consider it an irrelevant, archaic, and dying perspective.

Why is Christianity fracturing so? This is the inevitable consequence of trying to base a system of thought on a fractured and incomplete model of life and death. Even many steadfast believers will admit that there seems to be a key point in Christian theology that the world isn't grasping—a crucial missing piece to the puzzle which, it is hoped, would finally make sense out of all the Bible's textual mysteries, showing *all* its statements about the afterlife to be logical, predictable, mutually consistent, and interrelated. The binary soul doctrine does that.

In the Old Testament, the fate of the dead is described in many seemingly contradictory ways. Thirty-two times, the soul is referred to as being able to die, but the spirit is presented as *never* dying, instead always returning to God after the person's death. Some passages seem to suggest that the dead cease to exist altogether after physical death, but others seem to present the dead as weakened, still-existing and partially functioning ghostly spirits.

The New Testament doesn't clear this up. There the dead are often said to be "sleeping," which is often taken to mean they are in some sort of stasis. But other passages suggest one's soul goes immediately to Heaven or Hell after death, where it continues to be active and aware. And a few passages suggest that the spirits of the dead sometimes return to life on earth by reincarnating. One theme, however, weaves in and around all these others—*all* the world's dead will be reawakened to physical life one day, at the universal resurrection.

These different ways of portraying the fate of the dead have caused great division within Christianity. Today some believe that after death the soul ceases to exist altogether until it is re-created by God during the universal resurrection. Others believe the soul continues to exist, but in a sleep-like dormancy, until it is reawakened for the resurrection; still others believe the dead remain active and aware at all times between their deaths and the resurrection. Curiously, this last group tends to believe that the dead experience not one, but two Judgments. People, they insist, are judged once immediately after dying, and sent either to Heaven or Hell as appropriate. But then at the resurrection they are plucked out of heaven or hell, re-judged, then sent back in again. Many subscribe to this last perspective, even though it seems to reduce what was once thought of as the supreme biblical hope—the universal resurrection of Judgment Day—to a pointless and redundant event.

The binary soul doctrine clears most of this up. If the unconscious was cut off from the conscious mind after death, it would find itself falling ever deeper into unconsciousness, where it would behave automatically and subjectively, unaware of anything external. It would have nothing to focus its attention on except whatever feelings and memories it contained within itself.

Being automatic in nature, it would review those memories and feelings again and again. Such a state seems to be described in the scriptures, in such phrases as "division of soul from spirit" (Heb. 4:12), "being cut off," "falling into the pit," "sleeping," and "treading the winepress." "Being cut off" suggests the separation of the unconscious from the conscious, while "falling into the pit" reflects the increasing depths of the unconscious experienced after this separation, and "sleeping" reflects a deeply unconscious state. "Treading the winepress" suggests what it might feel like to perpetually reprocess one's memories, squeezing out every drop of feeling and meaning from the life lived, churning through them again and again. And if one's conscious and unconscious split, rupturing the fabric of the person's very being, then in a very real sense that person would not exist anymore. A person indeed would, as some passages in the Bible declare, "return to dust" and be no more.

Christianity's Unique Attitude toward the Second Death

Many binary soul cultures, including Israel's close neighbor Egypt, believed that the second death was absolutely the worst thing that could happen to a person. Its victims were thought doomed beyond all hope; they would cease to exist, and would never exist again. This very same phrase— "the second death"—also appears in the Bible (Rev. 2:11), but there, we see something new, something found nowhere else in the ancient world: the suggestion that even the dreaded second death might not be an insurmountable defeat. The binary soul doctrine suggests why Christianity alone seems to have had no fear of it: Thanks to Jesus, even those who did suffer the second death could eventually be returned to life, in the great universal resurrection.

Reincarnation vs. Resurrection

The binary soul doctrine also explains how reincarnation fits into Christianity. The one place reincarnation does *seem* to make an appearance in the Bible—the John and Elijah connection—precisely fits the BSD pattern. John the Baptist is specifically identified as being Elijah (Matt. 11:14, 17:17), and is even declared to possess the very same spirit that had lived earlier as Elijah (Luke 1:17). Yet when he was asked, John *denied* being Elijah (John 1:21). This is precisely what would be expected if Elijah's unconscious soul, which stored all his memories, had been cut away from his conscious spirit before it reincarnated.

This troublesome, inconvenient relationship between Elijah and John has long been a thorn in the side of the Church. These passages *sound* like they are talking about reincarnation, and it is challenging to argue that they are not. Yet Christian theologians have been struggling to do that for nearly 2,000 years. Why? Because, without the BSD, it is even *more* challenging to integrate reincarnation into the rest of the Christian message. As things stand today, the Church is firmly convinced that if reincarnation is correct, then *everything* Christianity believes must be completely wrong. If people naturally rise from death by themselves through reincarnation, then what need have they for any concept of a universal resurrection, or for that matter, a savior who guarantees that resurrection? If we routinely come back to life again and again, the wind goes out of the sails of the Christian promise of eternal life. If we are already enjoying eternal life, one must ask "What did Jesus save us from?" Jesus' resurrection is the entire foundation and promise of the Church, but if reincarnation is real, then we *already* survive death, so there seems no need for Jesus' noble sacrifice.

Many calculate that public acceptance of reincarnation would kill Christianity as it currently stands. The Church believes that if reincarnation is proven correct, then Jesus' whole life is transformed into a sad joke, saving those who had no need of being saved. Unfortunately, with scientific evidence supportive of reincarnation piling up, the Church's stance is getting ever more tenuous. Many clerics holding high positions already doubt some of its most basic tenets, but, seeing themselves as stewards devoted to their vessels, they intend to go down with their ship.

Christianity is in a dire predicament, and is losing courage. Reincarnation research is ongoing in universities around the world, and thousands of people are experimenting with past-life regression. In recent years a number of researchers have published extensive reports of young children claiming to recall data from previous lives, and in a number of cases, this data has been substantiated.[5] The Church has painted itself into a corner in its retreat from reincarnation. Within a generation, the battle of reincarnation vs. the Church will be fought and over, and virtually everyone expects Christianity to lose.

It doesn't have to.

Today we stand at a critical threshold, at which the destiny of the Church will be decided forever: Either Christianity finds a way to embrace these new discoveries about reincarnation, or it will perish. Fortunately, the binary soul doctrine shows how reincarnation and resurrection can both be true—one half of us, the conscious spirit, reincarnates again and again, while the other half, the unconscious soul, does not arise again until it is resurrected. Christianity's entire dilemma, it turns out, is based on a single, reversible mistake: the assumption that the soul and spirit were one and the same thing.

Of course, this still leaves us asking: "What *did* Jesus save us from?" Amazingly, the answer seems to be the same as always. He saved our souls from death. Our *souls,* not our spirits. The spirit apparently never dies, but Jesus may indeed have found a way to save our souls from death, the soul which lives but one life and then is discarded into Heaven or Hell. Unable to prevent the second death from occurring in most people, Jesus' rescue efforts seem to have revolved primarily around finding a way to reverse it, getting all those discarded souls to come back to life one day.

The marriage of reincarnation and resurrection would change things on both sides of the fence. In the religions of the East where reincarnation is accepted, little spiritual urgency is felt. Unlike the anxiety that characterizes Western religions, people of the East often take comfort in their belief that if they don't address spiritual issues in the current life, there will always be more opportunities to do so on down the road. What's the hurry to awaken, if a number of lifetimes are available?

But while the East knew about reincarnation, the West knew about Judgment Day, and realized that time was limited, that there *is* such a thing as "too late." Traces of reincarnation still exist within the earliest teachings of Christianity, but this doctrine was not emphasized, eventually being jettisoned from the tradition altogether. Why? Perhaps because the West realized that the opportunities for future incarnations are *not* unlimited. There will be, according to Judeo-Christian tradition, a great finale to history during which all our past dead will rise again. Unlike the East, which teaches that fresh opportunities never end, the West was convinced that we get only so many chances to "get it right." If one is still procrastinating and the work is still unfinished when Judgment Day comes around, then it would be too late.

Day of the Dead

The binary soul doctrine suggests that we all have died, split, and reincarnated many times in the past. Lifetime after lifetime, it declares, people keep discarding their souls into the blackness of the unconscious before reincarnating. If so, the numbers of souls trapped in the unconscious would have kept increasing down through history, with nothing to be done about it. And that, the binary soul doctrine suggests, was Christ's mission—to free those captives and prisoners trapped in the pit of the unconscious. To save the dead.

> The LORD has sent me to bind up the brokenhearted, to proclaim freedom for the captives and release from darkness for the prisoners.
>
> —Isaiah 61:1

> The Son of Man came to seek and to save what was lost.
>
> —Luke 19:10

Of course, if we all have many past-life selves, this would change the meaning of the universal resurrection. If reincarnation is real, then the only way our lost dead could possibly return to life is by having the memories of our past selves reawaken in our minds. Admittedly, this is a very strange concept, but even more strange is the fact that it actually seems to be reflected in the scriptures, which describe a *great invasion* taking place during Judgment Day, an invasion which causes much of the world to go mad. An "ancient and enduring army" (Jer. 5:15), the "most ruthless of all nations" (Ezekiel 28:7), will invade the world, the Bible says. What army would be more ancient, enduring, or ruthless than an army of the reawakened dead invading the minds of the living?[6]

Jesus' Role

I *am* the resurrection.

—Jesus Christ

Was this universal resurrection inevitable or did Jesus personally bring it about? Would the resurrection occur if Jesus had never even been born? We don't know. Perhaps His actions directly caused the coming resurrection, or perhaps it was already on its way and all He did was make it possible for us to survive the event when it does arrive. The answer depends on whether or not the Division is an illusion.

If the Division *is* an illusion, then the underlying unity of the soul and spirit has always existed. If so, then the apparent division between them was only temporary, and eventually they would have reunited on their own without any assistance. Since the psyche is a natural system, it will automatically try to compensate and adjust for any imbalances. Like a gyroscope, it can be counted on to eventually find its own center again without any outside help. And when that balance is restored, what had been separated will be reconnected.

Eventually the wall between the two separated parts would have collapsed on its own, allowing the repressed contents of the primordial unconscious to flood into the conscious. In this scenario, the most Jesus could have done would have been to make it possible for us to *survive* this traumatic reunion, helping us integrate all our past-life memories, feelings, and selves into some kind of structured and cohesive order. In other words, perhaps all He ultimately did was ensure that this coming reunion would be an *integration* instead of a melting pot.

It wouldn't have to be. Even if it was inevitable that our divided parts had to reunite one day, that doesn't mean they would necessarily have to integrate. Instead, they could melt together, regressing to their predifferentiated state, in the process, causing all the differentiated parts to lose their separate qualities. Instead of ending up integrated and functional (like the highly organized ones and zeros of a computer program), all the memories, thoughts, identities, and experiences of humanity could be meaninglessly shuffled together like a deck of cards, losing all the meaning in the data. The coming psychological reunion, in other words, posed the ultimate danger that it could result in chaos, melting and dissolving memory and identity, the foundational elements of the human ego. And indeed, repeated references to melting, the melting of people *and* the melting of the foundational elements of the world, *are* scattered among the Bible's prophecies of Judgment Day:

> As they gather silver, brass, iron, lead, and tin into the midst of the furnace to blow fire upon it and melt it, so will I gather you in my anger and fury, and I will leave you there and melt you.
> —Ezekiel 22:20

> The day of the Lord will come as a thief in the night, in . . . the elements shall melt with fervent heat, the earth and the works in it shall be burned up. . . . all these things shall be dissolved.
> —2 Peter 3:11

The idea that all the psychological material humanity has stored up since the beginning of time could one day come flooding back into our conscious awareness at once is unspeakably horrendous, and begins to explain why the coming of this Judgment Day was portrayed so dreadfully in the Bible. Caught in the middle of such a chaotic inner flood of images, memories, and past-life selves, the average frail human psyche wouldn't stand a chance, being completely disintegrated under the torrent. Everyone whose sense of self depended upon maintaining his own inner lies would perish when the dividing wall in the psyche finally came crashing down. Interestingly, from the perspective of the BSD the Old Testament is also replete with warnings of such an event during Judgment Day:

> This is what the Sovereign LORD says: In my wrath I will unleash a violent wind, and in my anger hailstones and torrents of rain will fall with destructive fury. I will tear down the wall you have covered with whitewash and will level it to the ground so that its foundation will be laid bare. When it falls, you will be destroyed in it; and you will know that I am the LORD.
>
> —Ezekiel 13:13–14

On the other hand, if the Division is real, then there might never be a universal resurrection. If our parts have genuinely been completely divided, there would be no reason to expect them to reunite on their own. Thus, creating such a reason might have been Jesus' primary motivation. By using His death as a tool to absorb all our past memories into Himself, He might have primed the pump for the eventual coming of Judgment Day, for the eventual release of humanity's past-life memories and repressed soul-pain into our full conscious awareness. In this scenario, Christ's return brings a baptism of psychological fire: "I have cast fire upon the world, and look, I'm guarding it until it blazes" (The Gospel of Thomas 10). "He will baptize you with fire" (Matthew 3:11).

Do we know for sure whether this universal resurrection is going to occur? Is there any reason to take this warning seriously other than old religious scriptures? That again depends on whether the Division is real or an illusion. If the Division *is* an illusion, the living system of the human psyche is really still whole, and the two parts are still securely connected. If this is the case, then any apparent division between them is but a temporary illusion that is certain to disappear one day, which would make the eventual reunification of the two parts (i.e., the resurrection) an inevitability, regardless of any other considerations.

On the other hand, if the Division is real, there is no solid evidence (besides the scriptures) that the divided parts will ever reunite. And considering how awful such a reunification would be to experience firsthand, many might hope the divided parts *never* reunite . . . if not for the fact that this would also guarantee that the human race would never know true immortality. I don't know which of these two dreadful options we should prefer, but that decision may be out of our hands anyway. Jesus may have already chosen *for* us, choosing life. Even with all its pain and horror, He has reportedly chosen life, both for Himself and for us. At any rate, one thing is certain: The ultimate success of any coming resurrection would depend on Jesus having first completed His job of processing and integrating all of humanity's memories into His own personal consciousness.

And a job that size would probably take some time, even for someone like Him.

16

The Third Day: Consummation

Don't you know that you yourselves are God's temple?
—I Corinthians 3:16

[There is] a veil at the entrance to the tabernacle [of the temple].
—Exodus 40:5

Jesus, who went before us, has entered [within the veil of the temple] on our behalf.
—Hebrews 6:19–20

I am . . . in you.
—John 14:20

Jesus [said], "Destroy this temple, and I will raise it again in three days."
—John 2:19

On the third day he will be raised to life.
—Matthew 17:23

> With the Lord a day is like a thousand years, and a thousand years like a day.
>
> —2 Peter 3:8

> On the third day a wedding took place.
>
> —John 2:1

> On that day you will realize that I am . . . in you.
>
> —John 14:20

> I will appear in the cloud [behind the veil of the temple].
>
> —Leviticus 16:1

> The veil of the temple was rent in twain . . . and . . . the graves were opened; and . . . many . . . saints which slept arose and came out.
>
> —Matthew 27:51

These passages show the Bible repeating the same story I have told in my two books, reaffirming with very few passages that:

- We are constitutionally divided. (Our minds are temples of God, and each of our temples contain a partition dividing it into two sections.)

- Jesus entered into the hidden, divided-off sections of the temples long ago, and now lives and works inside each of us.

- Three "days" after his death, He will return, allowing us to plainly see Him standing there inside our minds, appearing in the cloudy, hard-to-see place "behind the veil" of each of our temples. This will coincide with or involve a special marriage, probably between Him and us.

- The dividing veil behind the halves of our minds will be ripped down, causing our dead to rise up as well.

And if the passage of 2 Peter 3:8 ("With the Lord a day is like a thousand years, and a thousand years like a day") is any indication, then the third "day" since Christ's death starts soon, on or around April 3, 2033 A.D.

The Third Day Since Christ's Death Starts on April 3, 2033 A.D.

The First Day: 33 A.D.–1033 A.D.
The Second Day: 1033 A.D.–2033 A.D.
The Third Day: 2033 A.D.–3033 A.D.

Conclusion

A New Vision of Life and Death

Then I saw a new heaven and a new earth,
for the first heaven and the first earth had passed away.
—Revelation 21:1

Is this binary soul doctrine truly the secret of death? Could this strange notion, once extolled throughout the entire world, have been a prehistoric first principle from which our modern-day religions eventually evolved? Is it indeed religion's missing link, a precious heirloom that might finally allow the estranged families of Hinduism, Buddhism, Judaism, Christianity, and Islam to reunite in a rich rediscovery of their common bloodline? Perhaps so. Many people today certainly *feel* that the BSD has the ring of truth. And why not? Founded upon the neuropsychological findings of modern science, it offers intellectually honest and reasonable explanations for virtually all reported afterlife phenomena, sketching a truly seminal model of life and death that includes and transcends those that came before it. The BSD has impressive credentials as well, with every major civilization on earth having testified to its authenticity. It is backed by a mountain of evidence from a multitude of sources. I have tried to present a fairly broad and deep survey of the facts, but the full weight of the data supporting this hypothesis is so overwhelming that no one book could ever report more than just a fraction of all the relevant material.

It is my great hope that this discovery will play the role of a healing revelation, providing a common ground for people of many different faiths and backgrounds. Imagine the whole world uniting in a common belief system that actually made sense, a universal creed based in the very traditions, phenomena, and science they *already* believe in. The BSD, we must remind ourselves, does *not* ask the whole world to abandon their previous beliefs and embrace some strange new idea. On the contrary, the BSD gives us all reason to even more enthusiastically celebrate our current traditions, but at the same time, *for the first time*, we can now take a fresh new look at the seemingly foreign beliefs of all the other peoples of the earth. And when we do, we are amazed, because we can now see that all the other nations of the earth have really been believing the same thing we have all along! The BSD simply points out the hidden connections between what we already knew to be true, and what others knew to be true. The BSD adds nothing new; all the pieces to the puzzle have always been near at hand. It simply assembled them into a single picture.

All belief systems are attempts to explain the unknown. Each presents a model of reality that tries to give some sense of meaning to life. The world can seem a huge and terrifying place, with frightful turns of fate; it is human nature to seek to become aware of a larger overlying order that might make sense of these things. We find it comforting to believe we understand the nature of such a larger order; much of the anxiety life has to offer is lessened by such beliefs.

Until now, however, our faiths have offered only partial explanations of the nature of death; not one has even attempted to demonstrate that the whole truth of the matter has been found. The Western tradition does not explain, for example, the variety of fates people are incarnated into, just as the Eastern tradition does not explain why people must forget their past lives, or, for that matter, what those fractured-off slivers of the psyche are doing during subsequent incarnations. The Western does not explain the data coming out of past-life regression research; nor does the Eastern explain the findings emerging from near-death experience research. Neither explains the behavior of ghosts. Neither attempts to explain how the binary nature of the human psyche would affect the transition from life to death. Neither explains the enormous variety of religious traditions throughout the world, nor the underlying pattern of division beneath them. Neither explains how the dead might rise again. Neither explains what the binary soul doctrine explains.

Neither rests on anything resembling a scientific foundation. The BSD's greatest advantage is that it is based on already-established scientific knowledge.

Modern science has, over the last century, recognized, identified, and qualified the conscious and unconscious halves of the human psyche, discovering these two minds coexisting within the left and right hemispheres of the human brain. These are already well-known components of living people, not opinion, conjecture, or in any way theoretical.

The BSD asks a very simple, obvious, logical question: "based on what we already know about these components of the human psyche, if they still continued to exist after death, what would they experience then, and would they function?" And the innate characteristics of these two mental components correspond perfectly to the reports about death and the afterlife that we find being repeated in past and present cultures all over the globe.

I did not invent this binary soul doctrine. At most, I rediscovered it. When I review my research, reflecting that this same discovery has been made in the past, and forgotten, by the Egyptians, the Persians, the Greeks, the Chinese, the Hawaiians, the Jews, and innumerable other tribes in Europe, Asia, Africa, and North and South America, I realize how fragile this discovery is, and how easy it would be to lose it again.

Even now, a century after Freud and Jung stunned the world with scientific proof that our psyches are differentiated into two parts, most people act as if this discovery never occurred. Many still doubt that the unconscious soul even exists, after 100 years of consistent and unimpeachable scientific evidence.

The binary soul doctrine declares that the purpose, mission, and meaning of human life is to be found in making these two "one." Yet, for humanity as a whole to achieve such an integration, we must first be collectively convinced that the unconscious actually exists. No progress can be made at all until that first step is taken. Unfortunately, discoveries made by authorities alone do not do the trick. Such discoveries have occurred again and again, only to be forgotten or ignored. For Man to go forward along this path, the existence of the soul must be shown to him, must be made real to him, in a way that he cannot possibly deny or ignore ever again.

And that, I suspect, may be what Judgment Day is meant to achieve.[1]

Evidence

> When a true theory appears, it will be its own evidence.
> Its test is that it will explain all evidence.
> —Ralph Waldo Emerson

When I began this search, I don't think I had any particular precon-
ceived notions, except a belief in the ability of sincere seekers to eventually
find answers to their questions. I believed that if I looked for an answer I
would find it, and I believed that since there must have been many other sincere seekers in humanity's past, those answers must have been discovered
before, repeatedly.

So I started searching through humanity's various teachings and reports,
always assuming that any report that people had found reason to perpetuate
for any length of time probably had "something to it." Despite the apparent
difference between the various traditions, despite all the superficial appearances which, at first glance, did not seem to have anything in common, I
held firm in my conviction that these traditions had all been originated and
perpetuated by honest and sincere seekers. And so, I reasoned, they somehow must all belong to the same overall reality. Somehow, I was convinced,
the different reports had *all* succeeded in reporting accurate information
about life after death.

When only one piece of evidence supports a theory, that theory is still
unproven. But when the whole set of evidence still supports that theory, that
theory should be considered proven. Such is the case with the BSD. As we
saw in chapters 1 through 7, all the data, all the eyewitness testimony and all
the circumstantial evidence, points in the same direction.

Outside of the BSD, the peculiar and anomalous details of afterlife
reports remain completely mysterious and inexplicable. Within the BSD par-
adigm, they make sense and can even be anticipated. The theory explains
the afterlife data being currently reported, it explains the ancient existence
of similar beliefs, and it is in complete accord with the most modern scientific findings on the nature of the human psyche.

Implications

Well then, if the BSD is true, so what?

If it is, then today's most popular teaching about death and the afterlife,
that "death is just a doorway, and nothing to be afraid of," is a gross misrep-
resentation. Quite the contrary, if such a division *can* occur, then at death we
are in danger of having our most fundamental and intimate *self* violently
ripped apart. In effect, the "I" that each of us had known all through life
would no longer exist at all.

If you think that's bad, this is worse: If the BSD is true, then death
becomes a serious matter again, and so, by extension, does the whole issue

of personal integrity. For millennia in virtually every culture, death was a matter of the most serious concern in which the most horrendous fate could await. But, in stark contrast to virtually the whole of human tradition, today's new age view is that death is nothing to be afraid of, and one's moral character is entirely irrelevant to what happens after you die. But if the BSD is true, we suddenly understand why the earliest Christians went to astounding extremes to avoid violating their inner sense of right and wrong on even the smallest and most insignificant issues. They clearly saw their afterdeath fate precariously balancing on their own personal integrity during life, and this fact also testifies to the validity of the BSD. The binary soul doctrine supports the traditional mandates of soul care—what a Christian calls salvation—while pointing out the incompleteness of the new age description of the afterlife states. The BSD affords us the ability to see beyond centuries of debris and errors and wrong turns in Christian theology. It allows us to understand, at least partially, the original message of that tradition, and the urgency of its efforts to achieve "salvation" and "eternal life." These goals have seemed foolish anachronisms for the last twenty-five years, since the dawn of modern afterlife research. With life after death seemingly proven by so many different branches of research, the urgent efforts of early Christianity to save souls has recently seemed foolish and unnecessary. But once we recognize that an afterdeath soul-division is possible, those ancient concerns again seem worthy of our attention.

If you think that's bad, this is even worse: If the BSD is true, most of us have probably already gone through life after life, making no progress, repeatedly working like dogs, getting nowhere, dying, dividing in two, and starting from scratch all over again.

And if you think that's bad, this is worse still: If the BSD is true, we have nothing to look forward to but more of the same, doomed to remain stuck in this cycle, doomed to reincarnate and lose our past selves again and again forever, *unless* one of the following two things is true:

1. Jesus Christ really did single-handedly reverse the whole Division, and we will one day see the reintegration of all the separated souls and spirits of all mankind since the beginning, in a psychologically cataclysmic event once called "Judgment Day," or

2. Each of us, through extreme and dedicated effort, individually reintegrates on our own, reacquiring all our own past life selves in the process.

Unfortunately, the second option seems more of a long shot than the first. Everyone who is reading this is a member of a species that has existed for at least 40,000 years. If reincarnation is true (and the evidence seems to be pointing more and more firmly in that direction), then it would seem that most if not all of us living today have not, even in all that time, managed to achieve integration on our own. And 40,000 years of consistent failure leaves little room for hope that we will *ever* get our acts together on our own. Despite all the variations of the Old Path that still exist in the world, from Buddhism to Hinduism, Judaism to Huna, Islam to Gnostic Christianity, the law of inertia suggests that the vast majority of us will just keep on reincarnating, dividing, and forgetting, reincarnating, dividing, and forgetting, *forever* . . . or until some outside force acts upon us.

Lamentations

Many don't like the BSD simply because it seems new and unfamiliar, but it has been around a lot longer than any of our contemporary models of death. Others complain that the BSD makes it seem that we cease to exist at death, and, unfortunately, that *would* seem to be one valid way of looking at it. It all depends on what part one identifies with. If we identify with the conscious spirit that eternally reincarnates, we could truthfully say that one never dies, never ceases to exist. And many religions *have* said this. If we identify instead with the unconscious soul that becomes trapped in a dream world after death, we could say that the afterlife is eternal and unchanging, that man is destined to die but once, and then face judgment. And many religions have said this as well. But, if we identify with the *product* of the union of the soul and spirit, then, if those two parts disengage at the end of a lifetime, we could say that one has truly ceased to exist, in much the same way that a car ceases to exist when its parts are dismantled and shipped to various different places. And many religions have said this as well.

But the whole story is not shown in any of these scenarios, *if* the Judgment Day event reunites all the unconscious souls and conscious spirits that have separated down through history, then all will eventually be restored. But until that day, the dead are *not* quite what they were when alive, any way we look at it.

Many point out that the soul-division predicted by the BSD seems inconsistent with a number of afterlife reports in which the dead seem to still have all their earthly mental faculties intact. And yes, the BSD does indicate that everyone who has not yet achieved complete soul-spirit integration, all who have not yet reached "enlightenment," will suffer the soul-division between lives. But the BSD does not indicate that this division always occurs as soon as one departs the dying body; on the contrary, the full division might not occur until just before the next incarnation.

Others, bristling against childhood memories of Sunday sermons on fire and brimstone, feel very strongly that any and all suggestions that death might bring an unfortunate afterlife fate should never be taught. But, given all the NDE-ers' reports about the existence of the hellish realm of bewildered spirits,[2] and given all the OBE-ers' and ghosthunters' reports of encountering mindless, zombie-like souls of the dead trapped in their own dreams, memories, and nightmares, it seems that humanity's ancient concerns about hellish afterlife experiences are not without merit.

Another thing many resist is the idea that there is only one Truth. The novelist Douglas Adams parodied this attitude in his novel *Life, the Universe, and Everything*, describing a future in which the world's philosophers come together to protest the construction of a supercomputer that was supposed to finally and decisively answer all the ultimate questions. It was more important, those nearsighted philosophers argued, for everyone to be able to have their own opinions on these matters than for the actual truth to ever become known. Many today feel this way, insisting that since we all have different views, they should all be viewed as being equal, and all views should be equally respected. Unfortunately, this attitude is simply wrong; all views and all interpretations are *not* equal. Some are better and some are worse. For example, to interpret *The Grapes of Wrath* as being a story about an elephant that could fly would be a poor interpretation. What makes one interpretation superior to another is that the superior one will make more reasonable sense of all the data than will the inferior.

Another complaint that has been leveled against the BSD is that it just seems too cruel; God would never be so merciless as to allow us to suffer such a division, or allow us all to be trapped forever in such a self-destructive cycle. All I can offer in response to such complaints is that the study of history leaves this author very hesitant to make *any* assumptions about what God is and is not willing to allow us to experience. Given what we have seen Him allow to be experienced on *this* side of death's door, what assumptions can we make about what He might allow anywhere else? Still, perhaps such objections are correct after all. Perhaps God *did* love us so much He made sure we wouldn't remain trapped forever in such a cycle. The BSD does not, in and of itself, actually *prove* that Jesus Christ defeated the whole Division and saved us all from an eternity of cyclical self-destruction; but it certainly gives us ample reason to *hope* He did.

Probably the most common criticism of the BSD, of course, is that much of the evidence supporting it comes from afterlife phenomena—from the paranormal. There is still a sizable portion of the modern world that rejects any data that falls into that category. However, the fact that so many people are reporting the same phenomena, and *have* been, all throughout history, is a sociological fact worth noting. Whenever any sizable subset of the human race reports having similar experiences, those experiences deserve to be recognized as legitimate aspects of the human experience. To ignore, deny, and reject thousands upon thousands of consistent reports coming from every culture in every time period in history is inexcusable, even if those reports do address so-called "paranormal" phenomena. The fact that such large numbers of consistent reports are flooding in, and that similar reports have been recorded in ages long past, testifies that these phenomena are not truly abnormal at all.

We have none of us ever touched a star, yet no one denies that they exist. For that matter, most of us have never even visited Wyoming, yet, because the reports about Wyoming are many and consistent, we do not doubt that Wyoming exists. So then, when reports about afterlife phenomena are also many, and, from the perspective of the BSD, also consistent, why would we still doubt that they reflect genuine realities as well?

If, when confronted with all this evidence, we do still entertain such doubts, perhaps it is simply because mankind has spent ages feeding and nurturing one of its most favorite ideas—that mysteries such as this will never be solved. I believe this is nothing more than an erroneous belief, an empty myth. But even if it is, it will still blind us as long as we continue to embrace it.

> Argue for your limitations, and sure enough, they're yours.
>
> —Richard Bach[3]

The idea that some things are just not meant for us to ever know or understand is a well-worn position. Many once assumed that Man was never meant to cross the ocean, or travel faster than a running horse, or harness electricity, or fly, or reach towards the moon, planets, and stars. Yet we eventually did do all these things, and today most of us can't even imagine having never done so. Death is the ultimate fear, the ultimate mystery, the ultimate enemy of the human race. Anything that helps humanity conquer this fear is to be cherished. In any case, one thing's for sure—we're definitely not going to do it by assuming we can't. To shut oneself off from the possibility of discovering Ultimate Truths is to do nothing but ensure that such truths will never be found. To put limitations on the truths we are willing to recognize only limits the truths we do recognize, not the existence or validity of the truths themselves. When the Wright Brothers successfully flew their first airplane, even though many people came from near and far to watch and bear witness to this amazing feat, for a long time the local newspaper editor stubbornly refused to make the short journey into the nearby countryside to verify the story and report it officially to the world. Why? Because he "knew" that such flight was impossible, and so assumed without checking that the stories were bunk. In the same way, mankind has believed for centuries that the mysteries of the afterlife were categorically outside the realm of human understanding.

This book, I hope, will inspire many to question that assumption.

Jubilations

The BSD performs a priceless service; by revealing an underlying scientific foundation for so many of humanity's different reports and traditions about the afterlife, it makes it possible for us to again believe in life after death. By no longer being forced to assume that if one set of reports was correct, another equally substantiated set of different reports had to be wrong, the BSD grants them all a new level of credibility. The BSD stands as evidence that neither the Eastern nor Western teachings were wrong in their fundamental views about life after death, bridging the two viewpoints by revealing their common origins in the dynamics of the human psyche.

It also acts as a bridge to integrate and reconcile science and religion, showing the original scientific basis of many of our present belief systems. And in its promise that all our past lives are not really lost, but might be recovered one day, it is tremendously reassuring, suggesting that one day we might not only see eternal life stretching out in front of us, but stretching out behind us as well.

But in tying our moral, emotional, intellectual, and psychological integrity in this world to our afterlife in the next, it is the supreme challenge. As challenging as it is, however, this is by far the greatest gift the BSD holds for humanity. What we need in *this* world, after all, is more loving, kind, considerate, and tolerant human relations. No one questions this. The only question is how we achieve it. Obviously, a more loving and kinder world cannot be legislated, and so it must arise from within. It can only come from within each individual person, and that will only happen when people stop reject-ing the input from their own souls, when they finally stop refusing to listen to, and follow the advice of, their own inner "small still voices," when they stop dividing themselves from within, pushing away the input from the unconscious, destroying their own integrity.

The BSD is the perfect key to achieving that goal. The most powerful human instinct is that of self-preservation. If it finally sinks into people's heads that their own self-preservation depends on their own moral, emo-tional, intellectual, and psychological integrity, we will then see the majority of our species start trying to behave with true integrity.

The BSD, I believe, is the key to achieving true civilization on our planet. It may be our only hope. We try to pretend we are civilized now, of course, but it is getting more and more obvious that something is wrong with our current approach. The first step in integrity is to open our eyes, simply acknowledging what already *is*, right here and right now. And when we open our eyes, we see that our current experiment at civilization seems to be rac-ing to self-destruct in a dozen different ways all at the same time, with the only question being which will do us in first.

Will it be atomic, chemical, or biological warfare, or global warming or overpopulation or drugs or sexual diseases or just plain insanity? Will we just keep ignoring all the signs of sickness around us, and *inside* us, until each and every one of us is massively self-medicating and self-distracting every sin-gle hour of the day? Will we continue to deny global warming even as the ice shelves disintegrate and sea levels rise?

Will we, as consumers and investors, continue to give our money and support to businesses that ravage the land and exploit the psychological weaknesses of our neighbors, further deteriorating the already-unhealthy state of our planet and our society? Will we continue to simultaneously ignore and exploit the poor until their festering despair and bitterness com-pletely disrupts our lives? Will terrorism become such a integral component of our culture that we stop sending our kids to school, or going out to stores, parks, and theaters? Will more of our own friends and neighbors go berserk, gunning down their fellow students, coworkers, and/or family members, until all public places are fitted with metal detectors and armed guards?

Will obscenities like the O. J. Simpson trial, the 2000 U.S. presidential election, and the Catholic church's pedophilia scandal become so common they end up destroying all hope in truth and justice, careening us into anar-chy? Will we continue to lie to teachers, students, employees, employers, investors, insurance companies, friends, neighbors, loved ones, the IRS, and *ourselves*, even when we know that lying itself is what is ultimately responsible for destroying our minds, our bodies, our marriages, our families, our communities, our industries, our nations, and our world?

We already know the answers: without a dramatic change in our attitudes, without a really huge, world-shaking transformation in our collective opinion on the relative importance of integrity, none of these disturbing sociological phenomena are going to swerve from their present course. We humans need a reason to believe in integrity again, a reason to collectively conclude that there is *nothing* relative about the importance of integrity. We need a reason to elevate personal integrity above all other values, above math and science, above sports, above profits.

The binary soul doctrine is that reason. It doesn't simply give us a reason to believe in life after death again, it gives us a reason to believe in *integrity during life* again. It gives us a collective reason to listen to the voice of our own consciences, a reason for each of us to try to really do the very best we can do, and be the very best we can be. It gives us a reason to wholeheartedly embrace our ideals again.

This one issue—integrity—is the missing piece to the puzzle that is our world. It is the lost sheep that must be reacquired at all costs, without which all the remaining sheep are not even worth protecting. Nothing else can substitute for our wholeness, or hide its absence. And today, the writing is on the wall for all to see: without integrity, our experiment at civilization is doomed to self-destruct in short order.

But *with* it, all our highest and best potentials become likelihoods.

Amazingly, the secret of death is also the secret of life.

Appendix A
What Was Baptism for the Dead?

Let the dead bury their own dead.

—Jesus Christ

As near as we can tell, the earliest form of Christian theology revolved around the idea of salvation of the dead. It was perhaps *the* major theme. We know that Jesus' post-death descent into the netherworld was thought to have somehow helped to achieve this result. We also know that a widely accepted branch of early Christianity practiced something called "baptism for the dead" (I Cor. 15:29). And while we no longer know what this "baptism for the dead" ritual was about, its a safe bet it was related to "salvation of the dead."

We know from the Gnostic scriptures discovered in Egypt in the 1940s that some elements of that early Christian church taught its followers to "raise their own dead" by "looking within" and "knocking on themselves." For example:

> Then, if one has knowledge [gnosis], he receives what are his own and draws them to himself . . . consuming . . . death by life. . . . Raise up those who wish to rise, and awaken those who sleep.
>
> —The Gospel of Truth 21:11–15; 25:15–19; 33:6–8

> Light the light within you. Do not extinguish it. Raise your dead who have died, for they have lived and died for you. Give them life. They shall live again. Knock upon yourself as upon a door, and walk upon yourself as upon a straight road.
>
> —The Teachings of Silvanius 107:14–33

The concepts in these passages, of "awakening one's own" and "consuming death by life" by "raising up those who sleep," of "raising your own dead" by "lighting the light within you" and "knocking on yourself" suggest a close relationship to early Christian theology's focus on saving the dead. But these obscure passages, as well as the mysterious Biblical passage that labels the salvation of the dead with the intriguing phrase "baptism for the dead," seem to assume that Jesus' efforts in the netherworld were not completely sufficient by themselves. Instead, they suggest that, in addition to Jesus' accomplishments, something more is also required by the living before the dead can truly be "saved." The living must also successfully accomplish a task, and only *then* will the dead be completely "saved."

What was this task? What was "baptism for the dead"? Conventional Christianity doesn't know.

As we've seen, there is a great deal about Jesus' model of life and death that Christianity doesn't comprehend. This doesn't prevent us from celebrating His teachings, but it may cause us to unwittingly prostitute them. Jesus' teachings are never celebrated more than they are at funerals, when all His comforting promises about salvation and eternal life are dusted off and run up the flagpole so everyone can salute them, hoping this will help them feel a little better about the death of their loved ones.

But Jesus' purpose was not to merely console us in the face of death, but to *conquer* death, and to help us do the same thing. The difference between what *He* thought He was teaching us and what the world decided He was teaching us is illustrated by something He said about life and death that will never be quoted at any funeral: "Let the dead bury their own dead." This seemingly insensitive passage is a thorn in the sides of funeral directors, but our collective discomfort and reluctance to embrace this passage should not be taken as a sign to turn away from His words, but to consider them more closely.

Why would Jesus say this? It is as if He was suggesting that *the living should not bury their dead*, but this meaning has been overlooked for 2,000 years. The passage carries the unsettling implication that those who do bury their dead will then become dead by doing so, and by extension, it also suggests that either the living who do not bury their dead will not die, and/or that the living who exhume their dead will not die.

Which did He mean? Perhaps both, but in any case, I do not believe He was referring to the physical corpses of the dead, but to *the dead themselves*. As can be seen in the Gnostic passages quoted earlier, a living tradition and practice in early Christianity was based on this goal of exhuming the dead, raising their *souls* back to life! I am convinced that those Gnostic passages are directly related to His canonical comment about the dead burying their dead, and also to the mysterious practice of "baptism for the dead."

Did Jesus teach (as the Gnostics maintained) that it is the duty and obligation of the living to exhume their own *dead past-life selves*, by looking within, by knocking on oneself and receiving what is one's own—just as the Gnostic scriptures demand, just as PLR pioneers are doing today?

Perhaps He did. Was this the ancient Christian practice called "baptism for the dead"? Perhaps it was. What do we know about that practice? Not much, but we can be sure what it *wasn't*. They might have tried to raise their past-life selves via some sort of PLR, and baptize them while those past-life selves were momentarily conscious again. However, such a practice would most assuredly *not* be "baptism *for* the dead," but rather "baptism *of* the dead." But that's just semantics.

At any rate, such a process would not work, because if the past-life self was allowed to rise up to full consciousness, again becoming the same person it had been in previous life, that reawakened self would be no more inclined to get baptized now than he had been when he was originally alive.

No, it would seem that the Biblical phrase points in the right direction. The current incarnation, the self alive today, would have to *also* be conscious, standing in as a substitute or representative for the dead person so he could use his own will to speak for, and make choices for, that past-life self. In order to baptize a past-life self, today's present self would have to commune together with that past-life self, the two joining consciously together in the same mind enough to communicate and interact with one another, thus allowing the baptism of the present self, the choices of the present lifetime, to flow directly into the past-life self.

Thus, it seems that the Gnostic Christians believed that if the living had received baptism, they could transfer it to all their other past-life selves as well, saving their whole beings from one end of history to the other:

> The dead shall arise! . . . The thought of those who are
> saved shall not perish. . . . Does not that which is yours exist

with you? Yet while you are in this world, what is it that you lack? This is what you have been making every effort to learn. . . . Nothing saves us from this world. But the all which we are—we are saved. We have received salvation from end to end. Let us think in this way! Let us comprehend in this way!

—The Treatise on the Resurrection 46:7–47:31

Those early Christians felt that the salvation they received from Christ was like yeast: if it was successfully inserted into their being at any point, during any of their incarnations, it would eventually spread throughout their being, saving all their past-life souls:

He told them still another parable: "The kingdom of heaven is like yeast that a woman took and mixed into a large amount of flour until it worked all through the dough."

—Matthew 13:33

Appendix B

Integrity and the Nondual

Integrating the conscious and the unconscious means far more than merely dredging a certain amount of backlogged unconscious messages up to our conscious awareness. That would just be the first step, clearing away the logjam of unprocessed material in the unconscious. The full goal would seem to be much more ambitious—to create a perfectly integrated and unified psyche in which unlimited interaction continuously occurs between the conscious and unconscious.

In all us less-than-enlightened folks, this does not happen. Instead, the two halves of the psyche take turns at the helm: during the day, the conscious mind is in charge, and then at night the unconscious takes over. But in the highly integrated psyches of humanity's spiritual success stories, this familiar rhythm seems to be changed. "Holy Men" of today and yesterday tell us the same thing—they require less sleep. Why? Perhaps because they are simultaneously operating both sides of the psyche more of the time, and so have less need for the compensation of sleep. All natural systems, such as the mind, tend towards a state of balance. When one side goes to an extreme, the other side responds with a compensating movement in the opposite direction. Perhaps the only reason we sleep and dream at night is because the unconscious is not allowed to adequately function while we are awake, and so the system compensates by giving the unconscious equal time at night. But if the wall were down, allowing the two halves of the mind to always function in tandem, so that neither was operating at the expense of the other, then this compensation would no longer be required, and the person would find he or she needed less sleep. Just as the "spiritually accomplished" have been reporting for millennia.

With the wall down, future messages from the unconscious soul would be far less likely to be rejected or denied or refused, no matter how challenging they might be to our conscious egos. With such an efficiently functioning system, messages from the unconscious soul would no longer get automatically rejected, and so, future backlogs or logjams would be less likely to build up. We would not be divided any more; our inner beings would be whole and unfractured and uncompromised; in short, we would have structural integrity. Because of this, it seems, we would be far more inclined to behave with moral integrity.

Moral integrity or structural integrity? Why does language use this same word to point to these two apparently different meanings? The word "integrity," of course, is related to words such as integer, integral, and integrated, all of which point to a similar underlying concept—the idea of a pure undivided unity. When we speak of a piece of wood, or a piece of iron, the word "integrity" brings to mind a solid wholeness with no defects, splits, holes, or weaknesses. But when one speaks of the integrity of a person, why then do we think immediately of the perfection of moral qualities, and not of constitutional unity as we do with physical materials? Obviously, this is because we had forgotten about the binary quality of the human soul (even though language itself had *not*).

Our sense of morality rests in the unconscious. When we do something that deep down inside we feel was wrong, the unconscious always tries to tell us this (as in the universal cliché "I just knew in my heart that it was the right [or wrong] thing to do"). But in all us less-than-enlightened folks, the moral sense shares its home with all the repressed material we also force down into the unconscious over the course of our many lives, and this material, once there, functions automatically, compelling us to do various things largely without being aware of it, or at least without being aware of why we are doing it. So long as the contents of the unconscious remain unknown and hidden, the moral sense that resides there must compete with these automatic behavior patterns, and often fails.

The conscious mind is dominant, and the stronger of the two, and can repress the messages from the unconscious (except for a little bit that always manages to leak through), and often does. The more the voice of the unconscious is repressed in order to avoid its moral judgments, the more a person also finds that he or she becomes cut off from his own feelings and emotions. This is why it is a classic cultural image that the most evil people in the world seem to feel no emotions, for in the process of turning off the voice of their own morality, they had to block the voice of the entire unconscious, and so became cut off from their own feelings as well.

However, once the constitutional integrity of the psyche is restored, once all the repressed material in the unconscious is cleared away, we would be less inclined to ignore the voice of our unconscious soul. Not only would we be less willing to push its messages away, we would actually be inclined to actively *seek out* those messages and listen to them more closely. Now, while those messages would often be moral in nature, it would not necessarily be our conscious intent to be moral *per se,* so much as it would be our intent simply to honor and appreciate and integrate the messages of the soul into our conscious awareness, whatever those messages happened to be. Basically, we would be less willing to lie to ourselves about how we felt and about what we felt was right and what we felt was wrong. And from that would come moral behavior. This process might not transform us immediately into moral people, but it would make us less inclined to lie to ourselves, and from that, in time, would come moral behavior.

Integrity is "integral" to spirituality itself. A person who does not possess the first could only pretend (or deceive himself) that he had the second. Radio's "Dr. Laura" is one voice speaking this message, insisting that true spirituality requires the most perfect and unflinching self-honesty, responsibility, and integrity. The concept that these two things, spirituality and integrity, are related—no, not merely related, but that they totally depend on one another—often seems to be utterly lacking from today's new age thought. The ancient binary soul doctrine, however, explains why integrity has always been traditionally taught to be a prerequisite for spirituality, why, in fact, pure integrity actually *constitutes* spirituality.

In Search of . . . the Nondual

Perhaps nonduality *is* the answer; after all, teacher after teacher seems to have pointed in that same direction. But if so, then what precisely is the question? What is the problem that must be overcome? Wouldn't it be duality— experiencing reality, life, and even *oneself* as dual, as divided, as two divided and alienated parts instead of one perfectly united and integrated whole?

Paradoxically, the very same Eastern philosophies that hold nonduality up as the ultimate goal tend to dismiss the entire right-brain unconscious human soul, with all of its subjective feelings, moral attitudes, and personal memories, as completely irrelevant. In fact, to attain the ultimate goal, many Eastern philosophies maintain that one's subjective half needs to be entirely discarded, blaming it for preventing us from experiencing nonduality in the first place. Of course, many others take the exact opposite approach, insisting that we can simply say, "It is right because it *feels* right," and ignore, deny, and reject the intellectual half of one's being, even when the objective self is saying, "No, it is wrong. It doesn't make sense."

But if we can only honor our feelings by rejecting the voice of the intellect, or if we can only honor our objective intellectual selves by rejecting our subjective feeling selves, isn't this, either way, still only honoring half of our Maker and half of ourselves? When we are not acting from our full selves, but only from selected bits and pieces, then we are not being fully *who we are*, and so will inevitably fail to reach our highest potential and greatest good.

Still, most people seem to assume that it's easier to reject one side in favor of the other. For example, men have historically favored allowing the objective conscious mind fuller expression, while relegating the expression of the subjective unconscious to a back burner, while women did the exact opposite. Isn't this the opposite of nondualism? How can we hope to achieve nonduality if we are splitting ourselves apart to do it? How can we know ourselves if we are rejecting half of ourselves? Aren't we acting rather like the split-brain patient who had one hand trying to button up his shirt while the other hand was trying to unbutton it? Division is the problem, not the solution.

To reject the soul, the BSD suggests, is the original problem. The unconscious soul is subjective, feminine, emotional, intuitive, artistic, caring, nurturing, loving. And these are precisely the qualities that humanity has repressed, to its own detriment, for thousands of years. To say that the rejection of the soul is necessary for salvation is to authorize and encourage the continued rejection and repression and denial of all the values the soul provides. To approve the rejection of the feminine soul is to give unwitting approval to the continued repression of women by men, to approve the domination of the strong over the weak in all avenues of society and civilization. It is to reject art in favor of science, to reject faith in favor of reason. The unconscious soul is where our feelings reside, where they come from. Our feelings are what make us human, what allow us to care and feel for each other. No salvation that leaves this out is worthy of the name.

In the final analysis, any approach to solving humanity's problems, whether individual or collective, must come from and satisfy both the head and the heart, both our male and our female, both our right and left brains.

Sooner or later, all attempted solutions that don't satisfy both halves of the equation will be abandoned as ineffective and unworkable. This is a lesson that our religious leaders, as well as our politicians, should have figured out a long time ago. Humanity has tried for millennia to place male above female, science above faith, logic above feeling, Republicans over Democrats, law and order above right and wrong, justice over love, and it never works.[1] Having tried this partisan, divisive, fractured approach for millennia, we as a species should be about ready by now to admit that it just doesn't work. Society as a whole, as well as its individuals, have all just been stunted and crippled by this naive approach.

The simple truth is, human beings are *not* more right-brain than left-brain, not more head than heart, not more intellect than emotion, and not vice-versa. Whenever we find ourselves in a dilemma and willfully choose to honor one side by rejecting, denying, and ignoring the needs of the other side, we betray half of ourselves, dividing both our selves and our world in two. The only successful solution would seem to be to integrate them together, balancing them as Taoism teaches, "making the two one" as early Christian doctrine taught, achieving *true* "nonduality."

Appendix C

How Can *Belief* Save Anything?

Christianity does something virtually no other religion ever did, making one's salvation dependent on belief rather than on hard-won accomplishments, on faith instead of works. Jesus promised "He who believes in me will live, even though he dies," and since then, all other religions have been doubtfully wondering how mere belief is supposed to change anything.

I addressed this question in part in *The Division of Consciousness*, but like so much else, there seems to be two distinct elements to the answer. That earlier book only explored one of them: how trust in Jesus Christ might save one from the worst moment of the Judgment Day scenario—the Baptism by Fire—when all the repressed soul-pain accumulated down through history is finally shotgunned into humanity's conscious minds.[1] But I didn't examine how belief might also be able to save one *prior* to that event, how it could prevent one's soul from suffering alone in hellish dreams during the period after death but before Judgment Day.

The answer, again, would seem to revolve around Jesus' great accomplishment, melding His soul to our own. Via such a connection, we would no longer be cut off from other people after death, for Jesus' soul, and through Him, all others' as well, would then exist *inside* our own. Following our after-death soul-division, the experience of our unconscious souls would still revolve exclusively around their own inner contents. However, Jesus' accomplishment *changed* those contents.

307

The scriptures suggest that this inner connection to Jesus is conditional; we must activate it before the connection will be functional. How to do this, those texts declare, could not be more simple; we simply need to seek Him: "All who call on the name of the Lord will be saved." However, in the mentally crippled afterlife of the separated soul, such an act would be more challenging than it sounds, as we would be unable to rationally figure out that this is the correct response to the situation. Our faith would have to be so ingrained in us that this sort of response was already part of our automatic habitual behavior. Whatever we do by habit during life, our unconscious souls will continue to automatically do after they have separated from their conscious spirits. Thus, the teachings of the Church, which put all its hopes in peoples' faith in Jesus, would not be mistaken at all, but dead-on accurate. Conditioning the populace to have such faith in Jesus that individuals pray earnestly to Him in response to all life's challenges would be exactly their ticket to escaping the isolation and insanity of the soul's divided afterlife. Even though one's soul would still be separated from one's own spirit, it would still be connected to Jesus' soul, and through Him, immeasurably more. Thus, the picture of the faithful soul's divided afterlife changes from an intellectually crippled mind churning alone through its incriminating memories, dreams, and hallucinations (hell), to a mind that, while still functionally limited, now finds itself enveloped within a loving community of others happily dreaming in unison (heaven).

And so now, finally, at the very end of the book, we find what the NDE community has been looking for since the very first pages. The binary soul doctrine has now *perfectly* reproduced the heaven and hell of NDEs.[2] While chapter 3 did examine numerous parallels between NDEs and the BSD, one crucial detail was left unaddressed until now. While many of the denizens of hell, according to NDE reports, indeed do seem to be caught up in a private one-person nightmare just as the BSD predicted, the occupants of heaven seem to consistently enjoy the community of others. *They* do not dream alone.[3] And without considering Jesus' contribution to the situation, such community was inconsistent with the experience predicted by the BSD. But once Jesus' accomplishment is factored into the equation, the reports coming from the NDE community make sense down to the last detail.

What does this mean? If NDE-ers' reports of community in heaven are to be believed, then *the BSD can only be true if Jesus' accomplishment is as well.*

Endnotes

Introduction

1. A view substantiated by a historic series of carefully controlled double-blind scientific experiments recently carried out by the University of Arizona's Human Energy Systems Laboratory, as described in Gary E. Schwartz's 2002 book, *The Afterlife Experiments.*

Chapter 1

1. Four of these—the *sekhem*, or "image"; the *khaibit*, or "shadow"; the *ren*, or "name"; and the *ab*, or "heart"—were all closely related to the *ka*, and seem to have perhaps simply been aspects, characteristics, or features of the *ka*.

2. Budge, *Osiris and the Egyptian Resurrection*, 68.

3. Intriguingly, the exact same word, *ka*, is also the ancient Hindu name for the highest of all gods. This Hindu word *ka* translates as "who," another word which, like the Egyptian *ka*, also revolves around the question of personal identity.

4. Wheeler, *Walk Like an Egyptian*, 37.

5. The actual Egyptian title of this work is *Per Em Hru*, which, according to Ramona Louise Wheeler, author of *Walk Like an Egyptian*, is more properly translated "Instructions on How to Emerge Awake."

6. In ancient Mexico, where the world's other great pyramids were built, their funerary ceremonies also included a ritual called the "Opening of the Mouth," which is thought to have also been intended to ensure a positive afterlife for the deceased.

7. For more on the Toltec version of the binary soul doctrine (BSD), see chapter 14.

8. Chopra, *How To Know God*, 276.

9. Long, *The Secret Science Behind Miracles*, 81.

10. Long, *Growing Into Light*, 40.

11. Judaic Mysticism also holds that the soul has an all-important meeting with a female figure shortly after death, the *Shekhinah*.

12. For more on the five soul-elements in modern Judaism, see Morse, *Searching for Eternity.*

13. For two in-depth discussions on the presence of the binary soul doctrine in the original theology of the Christian church, see my 1997 book *The Division of Consciousness* and Poliakov, *Whereunto Shall I Liken This Generation?*

14. Percival, *The Seven Ecumenical Councils of the Undivided Church.*

15. 11th Canon, 4th Ecumenical Council.

16. Some of these lost gospels may date all the way back to the first century. Indeed, scholarly opinion has it that the Gospel of Thomas may even be older than some of the Biblical gospels; the Jesus Seminar, for example, dated it to 50–60 A.D. All we know for sure, though, is that it was written sometime between the mid 1st and 2nd centuries.

17. Jean-Yves Leloup, *The Gospel of Mary Magdalene*, 31.

18. This occurred only a few brief years after the church found itself operating under the "benevolent" supervision of the state. When the Roman Emperor Constantine converted to Christianity, he began giving the church orders, which, being grateful simply for no longer being the official enemy of the state, the church followed without too much resistance. Constantine's involvement with the church came just after he consolidated his power within the Roman Empire. And in much the same way that he overcame his political opposition to emerge as the single authority of an undivided Empire, so too he wished to overcome the apparent divisions within the church. But the result of his meddling, critics have maintained, was the complete jettisoning of an authentic wing of Jesus' teachings, which had existed from the very earliest days the gospel was preached.

19. Huston Smith, in "Huston Smith: The Psychology of Religious Experience," a 1998 episode of the TV series *Thinking Allowed* with Jeffrey Mishlove.

20. Meggitt, "Walbiri Religion," *The Encyclopedia of Religion.*

21. Budge, The Egyptian Book of the Dead, 266–269.

Chapter 2

1. Schiffer, *Of Two Minds,* 79–85.

2. Ibid., 45.

3. Ibid., 84–85.

4. The mind has thus far only been shown to be *affected* by brain function. Just because a radio gets broken doesn't mean the station stopped broadcasting.

Chapter 3

1. As quoted by Kenneth Ring in *Lessons from the Light*, 52.

2. Such as ketamine abuse or oxygen deprivation.

3. Ring, *Mindsight*, 23.

4. As "slugged out" in the Summer 2000 issue of *The Journal of Near-Death Studies.*

5. As quoted by Kenneth Ring in *Lessons from the Light*, 109.

6. Fenimore, *Beyond the Darkness*, 91–92.

7. As quoted by Barbara Rommer in *Blessing in Disguise*, 53.

8. As quoted by Peter Fenwick in *The Truth in the Light*, 178.

9. According to a study by Peter Fenwick and David Lorimer of 350 NDE-ers living in the U.K., as described in *The Truth in the Light*, Fenwick, 69.

10. As quoted by Peter Fenwick in *The Truth in the Light*, 52–53.

11. As quoted by Jean Ritchie in *Death's Door*, 81–82.

12. NDE-er Avon Pailthorpe, as quoted by Peter Fenwick in *The Truth in the Light*, 48.

13. Arthur Janov, *The New Primal Scream*, 53.

14. *My Descent into Death*, 15.

15. As quoted by Peter Fenwick in *The Truth in the Light,* 74.

16. NDE-er quoted by Raymond Moody in *Life After Life,* 54.

17. In the same way, people blind since birth who receive sight find that even though they are now receiving the visual data, it doesn't make any sense to them.

18. Quoted by Melvin Morse in *Transformed by the Light,* 142.

19. These terms are often a source of confusion. The terms conscious mind and unconscious mind, coined by the psychoanalytical pioneers in the early 1900s, are quite misleading. Both halves of the psyche actually possess equal but opposite quantities of consciousness, merely quite different qualities of same. The unconscious is actually anything but. However, the conscious mind cannot see into the unconscious, and it was that myopic conscious mind that gave the unconscious the misleading name it still carriers today.

20. As quoted by Peter Fenwick in *The Truth in the Light,* 108.

21. An apt phrase originally coined by Dr. Moody in *Reflections on Life After Life.*

22. As quoted by Barbara Rommer in *Blessing in Disguise,* 28.

23. As quoted by Peter Fenwick in *The Truth in the Light,* 85.

24. As quoted by Barbara Rommer in *Blessing in Disguise,* 174.

25. As quoted by Barbara Rommer in *Blessing in Disguise,* 157–158.

26. Storm, *My Descent into Death,* 18.

27. Margot Grey, *Return From Death,* 58.

28. Lundahl, *The Eternal Journey,* 263.

29. Ornstein, *The Right Brain,* 93.

30. Fenwick, *The Truth in the Light,* 220.

31. As quoted by Melvin Morse in *Transformed by the Light,* 149.

32. As quoted by Peter Fenwick in *The Truth in the Light,* 60.

33. Fenwick, *The Truth in the Light,* 116.

34. In *Life at Death: A Scientific Exploration of the Near-Death Experience,* 183.

35. In Moody's *Reflections on Life After Life,* 10.

36. As quoted by Barbara Rommer in *Blessing in Disguise,* 149.

37. Rawlings, *Beyond Death's Door,* 4–5 .

38. Branden, *The Art of Living Consciously,* 36.

39. Grey, *Return from Death,* 53.

40. As quoted by Barbara Rommer in *Blessing in Disguise,* 149.

41. As quoted by Barbara Rommer in *Blessing in Disguise,* 158.

42. Long, *The Secret Science behind Miracles,* 272.

43. As quoted by Melvin Morse in *Transformed by the Light,* 252–253.

44. Moody, *Reflections on Life After Life,* 18–21.

45. Ingerman, *Soul Retrieval,* 115.

46. Fenimore, *Beyond the Darkness,* 95.

47. Atwater, *Beyond the Light,* 36–37.

48. Fenwick, *The Truth in the Light,* 189.

49. As quoted by Maurice Rawlings in *Beyond Death's Door,* 87.

50. As quoted by Barbara Rommer in *Blessing in Disguise,* 78–79.

51. Storm, *My Descent into Death,* 20–21.

52. Ibid., 25.

53. As quoted by Barbara Rommer in *Blessing in Disguise,* 42.

54. In Moody's *Reflections on Life After Life,* 38.

55. Ring, *Lessons from the Light,* 281.

56. David King, personal communication.

57. Actually, since those in the Realm of Bewildered Spirits seem, in some respects at least, to display stronger signs of soul-division than do those in the realm

of light, one would expect a *higher* percentage of soul-division cases occurring in hellish NDEs.

58. Quote taken from the unpublished case files of Barbara Rommer, with permission.

59. As quoted by P. M. H. Atwater in *Beyond the Light*, 11.

60. As quoted by Barbara Rommer in *Blessing in Disguise*, 136.

61. In Rommer's *Blessing in Disguise*, 152–153.

62. Atwater, *Beyond the Light*, 182 .

63. As quoted by Peter Fenwick in *The Truth in the Light*, 108.

64. As quoted by Kenneth Ring in *Lessons from the Light*, 52.

65. Janov, *The New Primal Scream*, 288.

66. Rawlings, *Beyond Death's Door*, 62–63.

67. As quoted by Melvin Morse in *Transformed by the Light*, 262.

68. Atwater, *Beyond the Light*, 163.

Chapter 4

1. Newton, *Destiny of Souls: New Case Studies of Life Between Lives*, 2.

2. Wilber, *A Brief History of Everything*, 155.

3. Jung, "The Structure and Dynamics of the Psyche," para. 383, 186.

4. Newton, *Destiny of Souls*, xi.

5. Janet Cunningham, personal communication.

6. Whitton and Fisher, *Life Between Life*, 189, 97, 122, 142, 35, 35, 98.

7. Ibid., 8, 26, 21, 28.

8. Weiss, *Many Lives, Many Masters*, 111.

9. Ibid., 39–40.

10. Fiore, *You Have Been Here Before*, 33, 119, 136, 236.

11. Steiger, *You Will Live Again*, 15.

12. Ibid., 50, 55.

13. Ibid., 59.

14. Ibid., 54.

15. As quoted by Brad Steiger in *Returning from the Light*, 98.

16. Woolger, *Other Lives, Other Selves*, 38.

17. Ibid., 298–299, 302, 294.

18. Janet Cunningham, personal communication.

19. Ring, *Lessons from the Light*, 152.

20. Moody, *Reflections on Life After Life*, 38.

21. Whitton and Fisher, *Life Between Life*, 28.

22. Whitton and Fisher, *Life Between Life*, 29.

23. Janet Cunningham, personal communication.

24. Janet Cunningham, personal communication.

25. Goldberg, *Peaceful Transition*, 7.

26. Whitton and Fisher, *Life Between Life*, 47.

27. Ibid., 75.

28. Janet Cunningham, *Journal of Regression Therapy*, December 1994.

29. Woolger, Roger J. "Death, Transition, and the Spirit Realms: Insights from Past-Life Therapy and Tibetan Buddhism," in Volume XIII, Number 1 (December 1999) of *The Journal of Regression Therapy*, Thelma B. Freedman, Editor.

30. Ibid.

Chapter 5

1. Newton, *Destiny of Souls: New Case Studies of Life Between Lives,* 62.
2. Guiley, *Harper's Encyclopedia of Mystical and Paranormal Experience,* 26–27.
3. Guggenheim and Guggenheim, *Hello from Heaven!*
4. Quoted by Bill and Judy Guggenheim in *Hello From Heaven!* 82.
5. Ibid., 19.
6. Guiley, *Encyclopedia of Ghosts and Spirits,* 14.
7. Ogden, *The Complete Idiot's Guide to Ghosts and Hauntings,* 191–192.
8. Myers was one of the original founders of the Society for Psychical Research in 1882.
9. Denning, *True Hauntings,* 82.
10. Coddington, *Earthbound,* 6, 18, 31, 48, 34, 227.
11. Denning, *True Hauntings,* 17.
12. Baker, *Ghosts and Spirits,* 155.
13. McHarg, *Research in Parapsychology,* 17–19.
14. Wilson, *Poltergeist,* 290.
15. McHarg, *Research in Parapsychology,* 289.
16. Wilson, *Poltergeist,* 99, 102.
17. Interestingly, in a number of possession cases (which are like poltergeists in many respects) the possessing spirit has seemed to lack any sense of personal identity, often calling itself "no one," "nobody," or "nothing." While possessing spirits often claim to be individuals, they almost never reveal any trace of real personal identity. Swedenborg's explanation for this is a lot like the binary soul doctrine; he taught that such possessing spirits had their personal memories taken from them at death, forcing them to rely on the memories and abilities of the people they are able to possess.
18. McHarg, *Research in Parapsychology,* 102, 151–152, 172, 290, 300, 357, 377–378.
19. Baker, *Ghosts and Spirits,* 137.
20. P. M. H. Atwater, *Beyond the Light,* 48.

Chapter 6

1. Ingerman, *Soul Retrieval,* 18–19.
2. Interestingly, many shamans also rely on a rhythmic beat to achieve the OBE state—drumming.
3. Robert Monroe, *Ultimate Journey,* 11, 6–7.
4. Ibid., 24, 11, 252, 12, 11, 88.
5. Ibid., 102–103.
6. Ibid., 254, 117–118.
7. Ibid., 152.
8. Ibid., 206.
9. DeMarco, *Muddy Tracks,* 58.
10. Monroe, *Ultimate Journey,* 253.
11. Which makes one wonder if all the world's NDE-ers today are potential shamans.
12. Ingerman, *Soul Retrieval,* 20.
13. Ibid., 72–73.
14. Ibid., 112.
15. Rosalind Heywood, *The Infinite Hive,* as quoted by Colin Wilson in *After Life: Survival of the Soul,* 43.
16. Celia Green, *Out-Of-Body Experiences,* as quoted by Colin Wilson in *After Life: Survival of the Soul,* 58.
17. Ibid.

18. G. N. M. Tyrell, *The Personality of Man*, as quoted by Colin Wilson in *After Life: Survival of the Soul*, 56.

19. Ibid.

20. Ibid., 57.

21. Robert Bruce, "Treatise on OBE and Astral Projection," part 7.4 of volume 2, 1994–1999.

22. Poetry was once a trusted sign of spiritual authenticity. Virtually all our established religions can trace their origins to inspired spiritual poetry. The prophets of the Old Testament uttered the Word of God as poetry, as also did the inspired seers and mystics of Greece, India, and Persia. In short, poetry was once seen as a badge of spiritual authenticity. And why not? Poetry, like perhaps nothing else, testifies that art and language—the two halves of the mind—are working in unison.

23. Robert Bruce, *Astral Dynamics*, 410, 376–77.

24. Ibid., 395, 418, 471, 472.

25. Ibid., 396.

26. Bruce, "Treatise on OBE and Astral Projection."

Chapter 7

1. Edgar Cayce, in a speech in Washington, D.C., February 3, 1935.

2. Emanuel Swedenborg, *Heaven and Its Wonders and Hell*.

3. Ibid., para. 499.

4. Ibid., para. 480.

5. Ibid., para. 508.

6. Ibid., para. 527.

7. Ibid., para. 464.

8. Ibid., para. 455.

9. Ibid., para. 479.

10. Ibid., para. 480.

11. Ibid., para. 363.

12. Ibid., para. 380.

13. Ibid., para. 506.

14. Ibid., para. 327.

15. Edgar Cayce reading 900–21 M 29, *The Complete Edgar Cayce Readings for Windows*. Virginia Beach: A.R.E. Press, 1995.

16. Edgar Cayce reading 5749–3, *The Complete Edgar Cayce Readings for Windows*. Virginia Beach: A.R.E. Press, 1995.

17. Edgar Cayce reading 294–15, *The Complete Edgar Cayce Readings for Windows*. Virginia Beach: A.R.E. Press, 1995.

18. Hugh Lynn Cayce, *No Death*, 52.

19. Bro, *Edgar Cayce on Religion and Psychic Experience*, 58.

20. Edgar Cayce reading 5756–4, *The Complete Edgar Cayce Readings for Windows*. Virginia Beach: A.R.E. Press, 1995.

21. Edgar Cayce reading 900–304, *The Complete Edgar Cayce Readings for Windows*. Virginia Beach: A.R.E. Press, 1995.

22. Edgar Cayce reading 900–16, *The Complete Edgar Cayce Readings for Windows*. Virginia Beach: A.R.E. Press, 1995.

23. Bro, *Edgar Cayce on Religion and Psychic Experience*, 52.

24. Ibid., 95.

25. Edgar Cayce reading 5756–4, *The Complete Edgar Cayce Readings for Windows*. Virginia Beach: A.R.E. Press, 1995.

26. Edgar Cayce reading 900–21 M 29, *The Complete Edgar Cayce Readings for Windows*. Virginia Beach: A.R.E. Press, 1995.

27. Cayce lecture in February 1934, as quoted by Hugh Lynn Cayce in *No Death*, 189.

28. Bro, *Edgar Cayce on Religion and Psychic Experience*, 34. And in this sentiment, Cayce echoed the thoughts of the early Christian Gnostics, who wrote "He who is ignorant until the end is a creature of oblivion, and he will vanish along with it" (The Gospel of Truth 21: 34–35).

29. Ibid., 261.

30. Steiner, *Theosophy*, 4.

31. Ibid., 55–56.

32. Ibid., 78.

33. Ibid., 100.

34. Ibid., 93–94.

35. Van Praagh, *Reaching to Heaven*, 46.

36. Ibid., 71, 92–93, 67.

37. Atteshlis, *The Esoteric Teachings*, 25.

38. Ibid., 34.

39. Atteshlis, *The Esoteric Teachings*, 114.

40. Markides, *The Magus of Strovolos*, 22.

41. Ibid., 109.

42. Atteshlis, *The Esoteric Teachings*, 44.

43. Ibid., 35.

44. Markides, *Fire in the Heart*, 258.

45. Atteshlis, *The Esoteric Teachings*, 143–144.

46. Markides, *Fire in the Heart*, 257–258.

47. Castaneda, *The Eagle's Gift*, 163–164.

48. This tradition is explored in greater depth later in this book, in chapter 14: The Toltec Teachings.

Chapter 8

1. Schiffer, *Of Two Minds*, 28–29.

2. Piattelli-Palmarini, *Inevitable Illusions*, 32–33.

3. P. M. H. Atwater, personal communication.

4. It would have been preferable, of course, if the evidence suggested that those in the realm of light were not divided at all, but that does not seem to be the case. Many aspects of their experience points to a division already at least partly underway. If the unconscious was isolated away from the conscious mind after death, it would lose the ability for objective, rational, independent thought, the ability for verbal communication skills, and the free will ability to make fresh new choices and decisions, but it would still retain its subjectivity, emotions, memory, receptiveness, responsiveness, and the ability to perceive forms, patterns, context, connectedness, and relationships. As we saw in chapter 3, these are precisely the defining qualities of the light stage of NDEs.

5. See, for example, Ian Stevenson's work.

6. See *The Division of Consciousness* to read an explanation of how the BSD predicts and explains the existence of the devil.

7. Wilber, *The Marriage of Sense and Soul*, 32–33.

8. As quoted by Carlos Castaneda in *The Fire from Within*, 52.

9. I explore this question in depth in *The Division of Consciousness*.

Chapter 9

1. And one that virtually no one seems to recognize as surprising or out of the ordinary. This nonchalance is almost as surprising as the illusion itself. We are apparently so used to living in a world saturated with pairs of equal opposites that the apparent equality of the sun and moon strikes us as perfectly natural and proper.

2. Unlike the sun, the moon's surface retains the recorded impressions of its history—every crater and rock formation tells a story. The sun's fiery surface, on the other hand, is eternally new, living exclusively in the present moment.

3. The perfect equality of their apparent sizes being proven beyond doubt by eclipses suggests to "all who have ears" that they were indeed meant for each other, a match made in heaven (excuse the pun).

4. It is often declared that everything is energy, and since energy is never lost, nothing can ever be truly lost. The problem with this argument is that everything is *not* merely energy. My computer, for example, is composed of matter/energy, but it also has another absolutely vital quality—form. If an atomic blast blew up my computer, all its mass would be perfectly converted to energy, and nothing of that mass would be lost, *if* all we were concerned with was just the substance (mass/energy) of the computer.

The substance of my computer can never really cease to exist. You can chop it to pieces, grind it to dust, or disintegrate it with a nuclear bomb, but its substance, its matter/energy, will never be lessened by the slightest iota. However, its form can be lost entirely. What does that mean? That all its data, all its information, is vulnerable. Without that information, the mass of the computer would be worthless. And that information is only found, not in the substance of the computer (mass/energy), but in the particular *form* that substance had been taking on the hard drive on my computer. In the same way, ancient Egypt saw the *ba*, or substance of a person, as being invulnerable, unharmed by death, but the *ka*, or form of a person, was desperately vulnerable. Thus, "all" is not merely energy alone, for that is but half the equation for "all." "All," then, is energy *and* form dancing together. One, the energy, is immortal and invulnerable, the other, the form, is not.

5. Emerson, *Compensation*.

6. Walsch, *Conversations with God, Book 1*, 23–25.

7. Wilber, *A Brief History of Everything*, 91, 254–255.

8. Williamson, *A Course in Miracles*, 209.

9. Ibid., 210.

10. Ibid., 206.

11. Ibid., 215.

12. Ibid., 347-348.

13. Wilber, *The Marriage of Soul and Spirit*, 52–53.

14. The idea that God is growing is challenging to accept from the traditional Western take on theology. On the one hand, God is supposed to be infinite and changeless, which suggests that growth is out of the question. But on the other hand, God is supposed to be alive, and everything that is alive is growing in one way or another. When growth stops, death begins.

Chapter 10

1. House of Commons, 12 April 1935, as quoted in "Finest Hour: Journal of the Churchill Center and International Churchill Societies," No. 101, Winter 1998–99, Washington, D.C.

2. Jesus said, "I am come that they might have life, and that they might have it more abundantly." See how this is relevant in chapter 15.

3. Which reminds one of Genesis 1:1–2: "In the beginning . . . the earth was void and without form, and darkness was upon the face of the deep."

4. Jung, "The Archetypes and the Collective Unconscious," in *The Collected Works of C. G. Jung.*

5. Lotteries are but one example.

6. Janov, *The New Primal Scream*, 271.

7. Wilber, *A Brief History of Everything*, 161.

8. From Lionel Trilling, "Sincerity and Authenticity," cited in Bloom, *Modern Critical Views: Sigmund Freud*, 99.

9. Janov, *The New Primal Scream*, 69.

10. Wilber, *A Brief History of Everything*, 108–109.

11. Ibid., 87–88.

12. Janov, *The New Primal Scream*, 318.

13. Dr. Sabine C. Herpetz, as quoted by Alan Mozes in "Psychopathic Criminals Lack Fear Factor, Emotion," Reuters Health: New York, Friday October 12.

14. Jung, "Civilization in Transition," in *The Collected Works of C. G. Jung.*

15. Ken Wilber, *A Brief History of Everything*, 22.

16. Reminding us of the Biblical promises that "God is not mocked" and "The Lord is a God of justice."

17. Janov, *The New Primal Scream*, 40.

18. Wilber, *A Brief History of Everything*, 154–155.

19. Janov, *The New Primal Scream*, 31.

20. Long, *Growing into Light*, 21.

Chapter 11

1. Commonly translated as "rib," the part that was taken away from Adam is more properly translated as "side," suggesting that a whole side of Adam, one whole half of his being, was removed from him to create Eve.

2. The text emphasizes that the elder child originally held the birthright until it was taken away from him, partly through deception and partly due to his own foolishness. Much the same thing could be said of the unconscious soul. As we will see in chapter 12, it may only be by turning away from the messages of our own unconscious souls that we bring division and exile upon ourselves at death.

3. Thus originating the legend of the Lost Tribes of Israel.

4. Interestingly, the Jewish prophets promised that the lost tribes would be found one day; not only would they return en masse to the land of Israel, but they would even be given rulership over the other kingdom when they did return. Even though these prophecies were in their own scriptures, however, the people of Judah laughed at such predictions, asking "How could a lost people who have been assimilated into the bloodlines of other cultures ever be recovered?" But if the binary soul doctrine is correct, then this prophecy could refer to the return of the lost and exiled past-life souls of mankind. If so, then what will be the kingdom they conquer when they return?

5. If the Jews, the "chosen people," were indeed chosen for this purpose, to reflect the spiritual condition of the human soul, then when the world sees the Palestinians and the Jews successfully resolve their differences and form a healthy union, we might reasonably expect the final reconciliation of the soul and spirit, i.e., Judgment Day, to soon follow.

6. Which is something that Isaac might not have done in his life at all prior to that moment. Asking God to let his wife get pregnant was the first time the Bible

record indicates that Isaac prayed to God since almost being offered up as a burnt sacrifice to that same God as a young child. It was probably no small matter to Isaac to now be forced to ask favors from that seemingly irrational and fearsome Being, and the Bible does not indicate how many years he waited before finally breaking down and asking for help from the God he feared, and, quite possibly, hated. But it must have been some number of years indeed, for Rebekah was labeled "barren" as if no question about the matter remained.

7. Stan Tenen, on the Meru Foundation website at http://www.meru.org.

8. As posted on an e-list, November 1999, and later published on the Meru Foundation website.

9. Later in this book, when we get to the chapter on pyramids (chapter 13) and the chapter on the "Fire from Within" (chapter 14), we will see even more meaning in this first word.

10. Chapters 5 through 10 deal with the story of Noah and the Flood, which almost seem to belong to a different book altogether. Then in chapter 11, the saga of all the divisions of Abraham and his descendants begins.

11. Stan Tenen, as posted on an e-list, May 2000.

Chapter 12

1. Since the Jewish scriptures also emphasize the concept of an eternal name, they too seem to have embraced this goal.

2. Which reminds this author of the computer programmer's motto—"Garbage in, garbage out."

3. Sigmund Freud, *New Introductory Lectures in Psychoanalysis*, as quoted in Seldes, *The Great Thoughts*, 148.

4. Levine and Levine, *The Grief Process: Meditations for Healing.*

5. Tolle, *The Power of Now*, 29–30.

6. Janov, *The New Primal Scream*, 6.

7. Branden, *The Six Pillars of Self-Esteem*, 114.

8. Janov, *The New Primal Scream*, 9.

9. Tolle, *The Power of Now*, 31.

10. This was the original meaning of the term "baptism."

11. Janov, *The New Primal Scream*, 281.

12. Levine and Levine, *The Grief Process: Meditations for Healing.*

13. Jung, "The Structure and Dynamics of the Psyche," in *The Collected Works of C. G. Jung.*

14. Jung, "The Development of Personality," in *The Collected Works of C. G. Jung.*

15. Arthur Schopenhauer, *The World as Will and Idea* (1819), as quoted in Seldes, *The Great Thoughts*, 372.

16. Does this offer new insights into the biblical concept of being "washed in the blood of the Lamb"?

17. Janov, 365.

18. Which may indeed have occurred—see chapter 15.

19. It's not hard to dismantle the wall once one decides to do it; all one need do is examine its bricks and experience their content, and the wall dissolves away on its own. The hard part is deciding to do this, working up the courage and resolve to face one's fear and confront this mental content on its own terms.

20. In the darker reaches of the psyche, it seems, we are *all* "Master Masons."

21. William Barnes, personal communication, 1999.

22. William Barnes, personal communication, July 23, 2000.

Chapter 13

1. St. Augustine, *Librum de vera religione*, chapter 10.
2. Reid, *In Search of the Immortals: Mummies, Death, and the Afterlife*, 60.
3. Hancock, *Fingerprints of the Gods*, 142–143.
4. Ibid., 142, 141.
5. Isn't this already a symbol we are familiar with, the visual symbol for Christ, Who indeed was supposed to have "made the two one" (Ephesians 2: 14–1)?

Chapter 14

1. Sanchez, *The Toltec Path of Recapitulation*, 23.
2. See the Gospel of Thomas 3, 11, 22, 47, 48, 49, 61, 61, 72, 89, 105, 106, and 114.
3. Castaneda, *The Eagle's Gift*, 172–173.
4. Even though their own Judeo–Christian tradition was saturated with similar reports.
5. A name given to him by don Juan.
6. Eagle Feather, *A Toltec Path*, 11–12.
7. Ibid., 244–245.
8. Castaneda, *The Eagle's Gift*, 228.
9. This is an ideal sorely lacking in many other new age teachings.
10. Castaneda, *The Eagle's Gift*, 230.
11. Eagle Feather, *A Toltec Path*, 169.
12. Sanchez, *The Toltec Path of Recapitulation*, 7. Sanchez runs intensive recapitulation workshops in Mexico.
13. I believe this is the same "barrier of resistance" Freud found between the conscious and the unconscious, as well as the wall in Isaiah 30 and the veil of the temple symbolized in Matthew 27:51.
14. Castaneda, *The Fire From Within*, 120.
15. Robert Bruce reported much the same thing.

Chapter 15

1. Coddington, *Earthbound*, 209.
2. Even the Egyptians who attempted to reunite the soul and spirit after death believed that the physical body was necessary for success; thus their obsession with mummification.
3. Concluding on their own that the old path wasn't enough, mystics around the world seem to have anticipated the need for just such a rescue effort. In China's *Tao Te Ching*, for example, we find "The highest goodness, water-like, does good to everything and goes unmurmuring to places men despise." (*Tao Te Ching* 8), and "World sovereignty can be committed to that man who loves all people as he loves himself." (*Tao Te Ching* 13).
4. Paedagogus III, 1.
5. See, for example, Ian Stevenson's work.
6. See *The Division of Consciousness* for more on this.

Conclusion

1. When will that event occur? When Christianity began, its members associated the birth of the Church with the dawn of the Age of Pisces, adopting the sign of the fish as their symbol (which actually seems quite appropriate, from the perspective of

the BSD, with Christ being viewed as that fish that was released to swim freely within the collective unconscious). And the prophecies of the Church pointed to the "End of the Age," or the beginning of the next age, which would be the Age of Aquarius, as being when this massive pouring-out of all the contents of the unconscious would occur. And what is the symbol of Aquarius? A man pouring out water from a container. What better symbol, secured through the distant ages, of the eventual pouring-out of all the memories, egos, and past-life souls that have been stored up within the collective unconscious for who-knows-how-many tens of thousands of years?

2. I've been using this term all through this book, a term originally coined by Raymond Moody. However, I would be amiss not to point out that, from the perspective of the BSD, it is a misleading term, as those who are inhabiting that realm would seem to actually be unconscious souls, not conscious spirits.

3. Bach, *Illusions*.

Appendix B

1. Or, in each of these cases, we've also tried vice-versa.

Appendix C

1. The horrors of that moment, I argued, could be avoided by making a simple choice, but one so illogical and seemingly lethal that it could only be done by someone with perfect faith.

2. Of course, many NDE-ers never intentionally called to Jesus after separating from their bodies, yet still had heavenly afterlife experiences. Indeed, many NDE-ers insist that one's avowed religious dogma has no relevance in NDEs. However, as we saw in chapter 15, "seeking Jesus" might not have as much to do with calling out "Lord, Lord," as it does with trying to be faithful to one's own integrity. The BSD suggests that all who had faith in the value of their own integrity and sought *it* during their lives would be credited with having faith in Jesus and seeking Him. And so, if one sincerely "sought Jesus" in this way during one's life, that behavior would be automatically replayed during the life review, ensuring one's communion with Jesus in the afterlife.

3. Indeed, when there's more than one person involved, the word "dreaming" may no longer be appropriate at all. This is even more true when one considers that at least one of the minds of the community of heaven—that of Jesus Christ—is *not* divided. He still possesses a fully functional conscious mind, which seems to be shared with all other souls there. Thus, just as the reports of NDE-ers reflect, those in heaven suffer a less pronounced loss of left-brain function compared to those in hell.

Bibliography

Adams, Douglas, *Life, the Universe, and Everything.* (New York: Harmony Books, 1982).

Atteshlis, Stylianos, *The Esoteric Practices.* (Nicosia, Cyprus: Herausgeber, 1994).

———, *The Esoteric Teachings.* (Nicosia, Cyprus: Herausgeber, 1992).

Atwater, P. M. H., *Beyond the Light.* (New York: Avon Books, 1994).

Saint Augustine, *Libra de Vera Religione.*

Bach, Richard, *Illusions.* (New York: Delacorte Press, 1977).

Baker, Alan, *Ghosts and Spirits.* (London: Orion Publishing, 1999).

Barnes, William, *Thomas Andrews, Voyage into History: Titanic Secrets Revealed thru the Eyes of her Builder.* (Gillette, NJ: Eden Books, 2000).

Bhattacharyya, Sibajiban, "Indian Philosophies," *Encyclopedia of Religion.* (New York: MacMillan, 1987).

Blakney, R. B., trans., *Tao Te Ching.* (New York: New American Library, 1983).

Bloom, Harold, ed., *Modern Critical Views: Sigmund Freud.* (New York: Chelsea house Publishers, 1985).

Boldman, Robert, *Sacred Life, Holy Death.* (Santa Fe, N.Mex.: Heartsfire Books, 1999).

Branden, Nathaniel, *The Art of Living Consciously.* (New York: Simon & Schuster, 1997).

———, *The Six Pillars of Self-Esteem.* (New York: Bantam Books, 1994).

Brandon, S. G. F., *The Judgment of the Dead.* (New York: Charles Scribner's Sons, 1967).

Bremmer, Jan, "Soul: Greek and Hellenistic Concepts," *Encyclopedia of Religion.* (New York: MacMillan, 1987).

Bro, Harmon H., *Edgar Cayce on Religion and Psychic Experience.* (New York: Warner Books, 1988).

Browne, Sylvia, *The Other Side and Back.* (New York: Dutton, 1999).

Bruce, Robert, *Astral Dynamics.* (Charlottesville, Va.: Hampton Roads, 1999).

———, "Treatise on OBE and Astral Projection." (Unpublished document, 1994–1999).

Buckley, Jorunn Jacobsen, "Mandaean Religion," *Encyclopedia of Religion.* (New York: MacMillan, 1987).

Budge, E. Wallis, trans., *The Egyptian Book of the Dead, Papyrus of Ani.* (New York: Dover, 1967).

————, *Osiris & the Egyptian Resurrection.* (New York: Dover, 1973).

Buscaglia, Leo, *Personhood.* (New York: Fawcett Books, 1986).

Castaneda, Carlos, *The Eagle's Gift.* (New York: Simon and Schuster, 1981).

————, *The Fire from Within.* (New York: Simon and Schuster, 1984).

Cayce, Hugh Lynn, and Edgar Cayce, *No Death.* (Virginia Beach, Va.: ARE Press.)

Chopra, Deepak, *How to Know God.* (New York: Harmony Books, 2000).

Churton, Tobias, *The Gnostics.* (New York: Barnes & Noble Books, 1987).

Clement of Alexandria, *Paedagogus.*

Coddington, Robert H., *Earthbound.* (New York: Kensington Publishing, 1997).

Crehan, Joseph, "Near Eastern Societies," in A. Toynbee and A. Koestler's (eds.), *Life After Death.* (New York: McGraw-Hill, 1976), 97–122.

Cunningham, Janet, *Journal of Regression Therapy.* (Riverside, Calif.: Association for Past-Life Research and Therapy, 1994).

Davies, Steven, "Soul: Ancient Near Eastern Concepts," *Encyclopedia of Religion.* (New York: MacMillan, 1987).

DeMarco, Frank, *Muddy Tracks.* (Charlottesville, Va.: Hampton Roads, 2001).

Denning, Hazel M., *True Hauntings.* (St. Paul, Mn: Llewellyn Publications, 1996).

Eagle Feather, Ken, *A Toltec Path.* (Charlottesville, Va.: Hampton Roads, 1995).

Effland, Richard, *"Death: what was it?"*
   http://www.mc.maricopa.edu/anthro/egypt/cultdeath.html

El Mahdy, Christine, *Mummies, Myth, and Magic.* (New York: Thames and Hudson, 1989).

Emerson, Ralph Waldo, *Compensation.* (N.p., 1841).

Evans-Wentz, W. Y., trans., *The Tibetan Book of the Dead.* (New York: Oxford University Press, 1960).

Fenimore, Angie, *Beyond the Darkness.* (New York: Bantam Books, 1995).

Fenwick, Peter and Elizabeth Fenwick, *The Truth in the Light.* (New York: Berkley Books, 1995).

Fiore, Edith, *You Have Been Here Before.* (New York: Ballantine Books, 1978).

Ford, Debbie, *The Dark Side of the Light Chasers.* (New York: Riverhead Books, 1998).

Freud, Sigmund, *New Introductory Lectures in Psychoanalysis.* (New York: Norton, 1965).

Gallop, George, Jr., and William Proctor, *Adventures in Immortality.* (New York, McGraw-Hill, 1982).

Gibson, Arvin S. "Religious Wars on Healthy Competition in the NDE Movement?" *The Journal of Near-Death Studies,* (New York: Human Sciences Press, Volume 18, Number 4, Summer 2000).

Gnoli, Gherardo, "Iranian Religions," *Encyclopedia of Religion.* (New York, MacMillan, 1987).

Goldberg, Bruce, *Peaceful Transition.* (St. Paul, Minn.: Llewellyn Publications, 1997).

Grey, Margot, *Return from Death.* (New York: Arkana, 1985).

Guggenheim, Bill and Judy Guggenheim, *Hello from Heaven!* (New York: Bantam Books, 1995).

Guiley, Rosemary Ellen, *The Encyclopedia of Ghosts and Spirits.* (New York: Facts on File, 1992).

————, *Harper's Encyclopedia of Mystical and Paranormal Experience.* (San Francisco: HarperSanFrancisco, 1991).

Hancock, Graham, *Fingerprints of the Gods.* (New York: Crown Books, 1995).

House of Commons, (British), 12 April 1935. As quoted in "Finest Hour: Journal of the Churchill Center and International Churchill Societies," Washington, D.C. 101, Winter 1998–99.

Ingerman, Sandra, *Soul Retrieval: Mending the Fragmented Self.* (San Francisco: HarperSanFrancisco. 1991).

International Bible Society, Holy Bible, New International Version. (New York: International Bible Society, 1978).

Janov, Arthur, *The New Primal Scream.* (Wilmington, Del.: Enterprise Publishers, 1991).

Jung, C. G., *The Collected Works of C. G. Jung.* Herbert Read et. al., eds. (New York: Pantheon Books, 1953).

Leloup, Jean-Yves, trans., *The Gospel of Mary Magdalene.* (Rochester, Vt.: Inner Traditions, 2002).

Levine, Stephen and Ondrea Levine, *The Grief Process.* (Boulder, Colo.: Sounds True Publications, 1999).

Lewis, James, *Encyclopedia of Afterlife Beliefs and Phenomena.* (Washington D.C.: Visible Ink, 1995).

Long, J. Bruce, "Underworld," *Encyclopedia of Religion.* (New York: MacMillan, 1987).

Long, Max Freedom, *The Huna Code in Religions.* (Marina del Rey, Calif.: DeVorss Publications, 1965).

———, *Introduction to Huna.* (Cottonwood, Ariz.: Esoteric Publications, 1975).

———, *The Secret Science Behind Miracles.* (Marina Del Rey, Calif.: DeVorss and Company, 1948).

———, *Growing into Light.* (Vista, Calif.: Huna Research Publications, 1955).

Lundahl, Craig R., and Harold A. Widdison, *The Eternal Journey.* (New York: Warner Books, 1997).

Markides, Kyriacos C., *The Magus of Strovolos.* (New York: Arkana, 1985).

———, *Fire in the Heart.* (New York: Arkana, 1990).

McHarg, J. F., *Research in Parapsychology.* (Metuchen, N.J.: Scarecrow Press, 1973).

Meggitt, M. J., "Walbiri Religion," *Encyclopedia of Religion.* (New York: MacMillan, 1987).

Monroe, Robert, *Ultimate Journey.* (New York: Doubleday, 1994).

Moody, Raymond A., Jr., *Coming Back.* (New York: Bantam Books, 1992).

———, *Life After Life.* (Covington, Ga.: Mockingbird Books, 1975).

———, *Reflections on Life After Life.* (New York: Bantam Books, 1977).

Morse, Don, *Searching for Eternity: a Scientist's Spiritual Journey to Overcome Death Anxiety.* (Memphis, Tenn.: Eagle Wing Books, 2000).

Morse, Melvin, with Paul Perry, *Transformed by the Light.* (New York: Villard Books, 1992).

Mozes, Alan. "Psychopathic Criminals Lack Fear Factor, Emotion," Reuters Health: New York, Friday October 12 (SOURCE: *Archives of General Psychiatry* 001;58:737-735).

Neumann, Erich, *The Origins and History of Consciousness.* (Princeton, N.J.: Princeton University Press, 1954).

Newton, Michael, *Destiny of Souls.* (St. Paul, Minn.: Llewellyn Publications, 2000).

———, *Journey of Souls.* (St. Paul, Minn.: Llewellyn Publications, 1999).

Novak, Peter, *The Division of Consciousness.* (Charlottesville, Va.: Hampton Roads, 1997).

Ogden, Tom, *The Complete Idiot's Guide to Ghosts and Hauntings.* (Indianapolis, Ind.: Macmillan USA, 1999).

Ornstein, Robert, *The Right Brain.* (New York: Harcourt Brace and Company, 1997).

Oxford Dictionary of Quotations, Rev. 4th Edition. (New York: Oxford University Press, 1996).

Percival, Henry R., ed., *The Seven Ecumenical Councils of the Undivided Church,* Vol XIV of *Nicene and Post Nicene Fathers,* 2nd series. (Edinburgh: T&T Clark; Grand Rapids, Mich.: Wm. B. Eerdmans, 1988).

Piattelli-Palmarini, Massimo, *Inevitable Illusions.* (New York: John Wiley and Sons, Inc., 1994).

Poljakov, Evgenij, *Whereunto Shall I Liken This Generation?* (St. Petersburg, Russia: Two Plus Three Ltd., 1993).

Rawlings, Maurice, *Beyond Death's Door.* (New York: Bantam Books, 1978).

Reid, Howard, *In Search of the Immortals.* (New York: St. Martin's, 2001).

Ries, Julian, "Immortality," *Encyclopedia of Religion.* (New York: MacMillan, 1987).

Ring, Kenneth, *Life at Death.* (New York: Coward, McCann, and Geoghegan, 1980).

———, and Sharon Cooper, *Mindsight.* (Palo Alto, Calif.: William James Center for Consciousness Studies, 1999).

———, and Evelyn Elsaesser Valarino, *Lessons from the Light.* (Portsmouth, N.H.: Moment Point Press, 2000).

———, "Religious Wars in the NDE Movement: Some Personal Reflections on Michael Sabom's *Light & Death.*" *The Journal of Near-Death Studies,* (New York: Human Sciences Press, Volume 18, Number 4, Summer 2000).

Rinpoche, Sogyal, *The Tibetan Book of Living and Dying.* (San Francisco, Calif.: HarperSanFrancisco, 1994).

Ritchie, Jean, *Death's Door.* (New York: Dell Publishing, 1994).

Riviere, Claude, "Soul: Concepts in Primitive Religions," *Encyclopedia of Religion.* (New York: MacMillan, 1987).

Robinson, James M., translator's director, *The Nag Hammadi Library in English.* (San Francisco, Calif.: Harper & Row, 1977).

Rommer, Barbara, *Blessing in Disguise.* (St. Paul, Minn.: Llewellyn Publications, 2000).

Ruskin, John, *Emotional Clearing.* (New York: Broadway Books, 2000).

Sabom, Michael. "Response to Kenneth Ring's 'Religious Wars in the NDE Movement: Some Personal Reflections on Michael Sabom's *Light & Death.*'" *The Journal of Near-Death Studies* (New York: Human Sciences Press, Volume 18, Number 4, Summer 2000).

Sanchez, Victor, *The Toltec Path of Recapitulation.* (Rochester, Vt.: Bear and Co., 2001).

Schiffer, Fredrick, *Of Two Minds: The Revolutionary Science of Dual-Brain Psychology.* (New York: Free Press, 1998).

Schwartz, Gary E., *The Afterlife Experiments* (New York: Pocket Books, 2002).

Seidel, Anna, "Afterlife: Chinese Concepts," *Encyclopedia of Religion.* (New York: MacMillan, 1987).

Seldes, George, *The Great Thoughts.* (New York: Ballantine Books, 1985).

Springer, Sally P., and Georg Deutsch, *Left Brain, Right Brain.* (New York: W. H. Freeman and Company, 1985).

Steiger, Brad, *Returning from the Light.* (New York: Penguin Books, 1996).

———, *You Will Live Again.* (Nevada City, Calif.: Blue Dolphin Press, 1996).

Steiner, Rudolf, *The Essential Steiner.* R. A. McDermott, ed. (San Francisco, Calif.: HarperSanFrancisco, 1984).

———, *Theosophy.* (New York: Anthroposophic Press, 1971).

Stevenson, Ian, *Twenty Cases Suggestive of Reincarnation.* (Charlottesville, Va.: University of Virginia Press, 1974).

Storm, Howard, *My Descent into Death.* (London: Clairview, 2000).

Stoyanov, Yuri, *The Other God: Dualist Religions from Antiquity to the Cathar Heresy.* (New Haven, Conn.: Yale University Press, 2000).

Strong, James, "Dictionary of the Hebrew Bible." *The New Strong's Exhaustive Concordance of the Bible.* (New York: Nelson Publishers, 1984).

Swedenborg, Emanuel, *Heaven and Its Wonders and Hell,* George F. Dole, trans. (West Chester, Pa.: Swedenborg Foundation, 2000).

Tenen, Stan, http://www.meru.org (1999).

Tober, Linda M., and F. Stanley Lusby, "Jewish Afterlife," *Encyclopedia of Religion*. (New York: MacMillan, 1987).

Tolle, Eckhart, *The Power of Now*. (Novato, Calif.: New World Library, 1999).

Van Baaren, T. P., "Afterlife: Geography of Death," *Encyclopedia of Religion*. (New York: MacMillan, 1987).

Van Nooten, Barend A., and Gary B. Hilland, trans., *Rig Veda*. (Cambridge, Mass: Harvard University Press, 1994).

Van Praagh, James, *Reaching to Heaven*. (New York: Dutton Books, 1999).

———, *Talking to Heaven*. (New York: Dutton Books, 1997).

Walsch, Neal Donald, *Conversations with God, Book 1*. (New York: G. P Putnam's Sons, 1995).

———, *Conversations with God, Book 3*. (Charlottesville, Va.: Hampton Roads, 1998).

Watterson, Barbara, *The Gods of Ancient Egypt*. (New York: Facts on File, 1984).

Weiss, Brian L., *Many Lives, Many Masters*. (New York: Fireside Books, 1988).

Wheeler, R. L., *Walk Like an Egyptian*. (New York: Allisone, 1999).

Whitton, Joel L. and Joe Fisher, *Life Between Life*. (New York: Warner Books, 1986).

Wilber, Ken, *A Brief History of Everything*. (Boston: Shambhala Publications, 1996).

———, *The Marriage of Sense and Soul*. (Boston: Shambhala Publications, 1999).

Williams, Kevin, "Near-death experiences and the afterlife."
http://www.neardeath.com (1999).

Williamson, Marianne, *A Course in Miracles* (Farmingdale, N.Y.: 1975).

Wilson, Colin, *After Life*. (St. Paul, Minn.: Llewellyn Publications, 2000).

———, *From Atlantis to the Sphinx*. (New York: Fromm International, 1996).

———, *Poltergeist*. (St. Paul, Minn.: Llewellyn Publications, 1993).

Woolger, Roger J., *Other Lives, Other Selves: A Jungian Psychotherapist Discovers Past Lives*. (New York: Bantam Publishing, 1987).

Zandee, Jan, *Death as an Enemy According to Ancient Egyptian Conceptions*. (New York: Arno Press, 1977).

Index

Hampton Roads Publishing Company

...for the evolving human spirit

Hampton Roads Publishing Company
publishes books on a variety of subjects,
including metaphysics, health,
visionary fiction, and other related topics.

For a copy of our latest catalog, call toll-free
(800) 766-8009, or send your name and address to:

Hampton Roads Publishing Company, Inc.
1125 Stoney Ridge Road
Charlottesville, VA 22902

e-mail: hrpc@hrpub.com
Website: www.hrpub.com